BABY BIRTH

ベビーバース

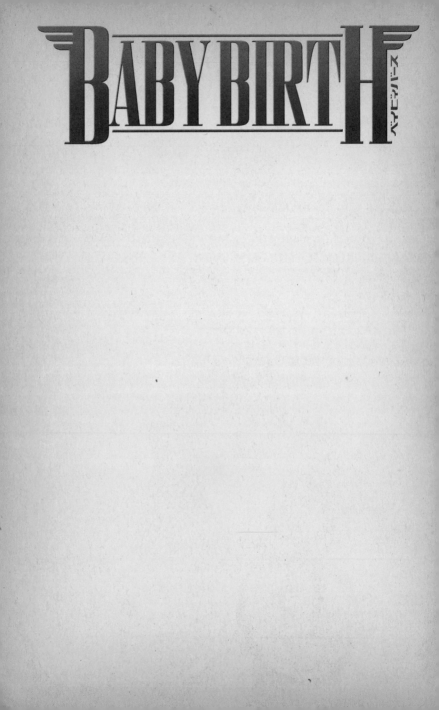

ALSO AVAILABLE FROM TOKYOPOP®

MANGA

For more information visit www.TOKYOPOP.com

*INDICATES 100% AUTHENTIC MANGA (RIGHT-TO-LEFT FORMAT)

CINE-MANGA™

NOVELS

TOKYOPOP KIDS

ART BOOKS

ANIME GUIDES

062703

BABY BIRTH

ベイビーバース

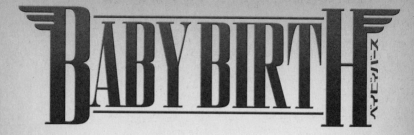

Volume 1

by
Sukehiro Tomita
&
Haruhiko Mikimoto

TOKYOPOP®

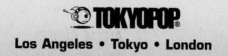

Los Angeles • Tokyo • London

Translator - Nan Rymer
English Adaptation - Jim Krueger
Associate Editor - Paul Morrissey
Copy Editors - Tim Beedle and Aaron Sparrow
Retouch and Lettering - Brian Bossin
Cover Layout - Raymond Makowski

Editors - Mark Paniccia & Rob Tokar
Managing Editor - Jill Freshney
Production Coordinator - Antonio DePietro
Production Manager - Jennifer Miller
Art Director - Matthew Alford
Editorial Director - Jeremy Ross
VP of Production - Ron Klamert
President & C.O.O. - John Parker
Publisher & C.E.O. - Stuart Levy

Email: editor@TOKYOPOP.com
Come visit us online at www.TOKYOPOP.com

A 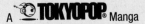 Manga

TOKYOPOP Inc.
5900 Wilshire Blvd. Suite 2000
Los Angeles, CA 90036

ISBN: 1-59182-372-2

First TOKYOPOP printing: September 2003

10 9 8 7 6 5 4 3 2 1

Printed in the USA

ACT.0 Prologue

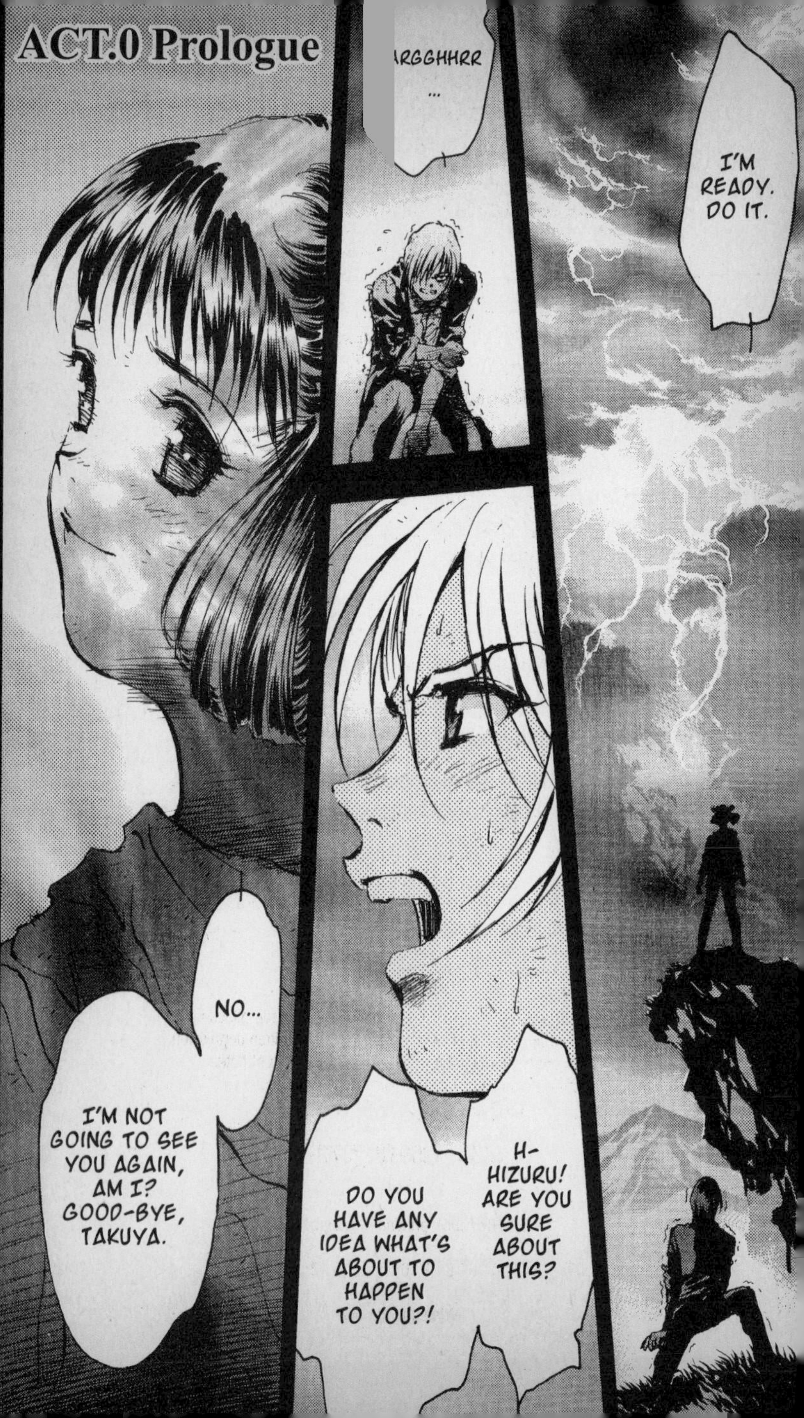
I'M READY. DO IT.
ARGGHHRR ...
H- HIZURU! ARE YOU SURE ABOUT THIS?
DO YOU HAVE ANY IDEA WHAT'S ABOUT TO HAPPEN TO YOU?!
NO...
I'M NOT GOING TO SEE YOU AGAIN, AM I? GOOD-BYE, TAKUYA.

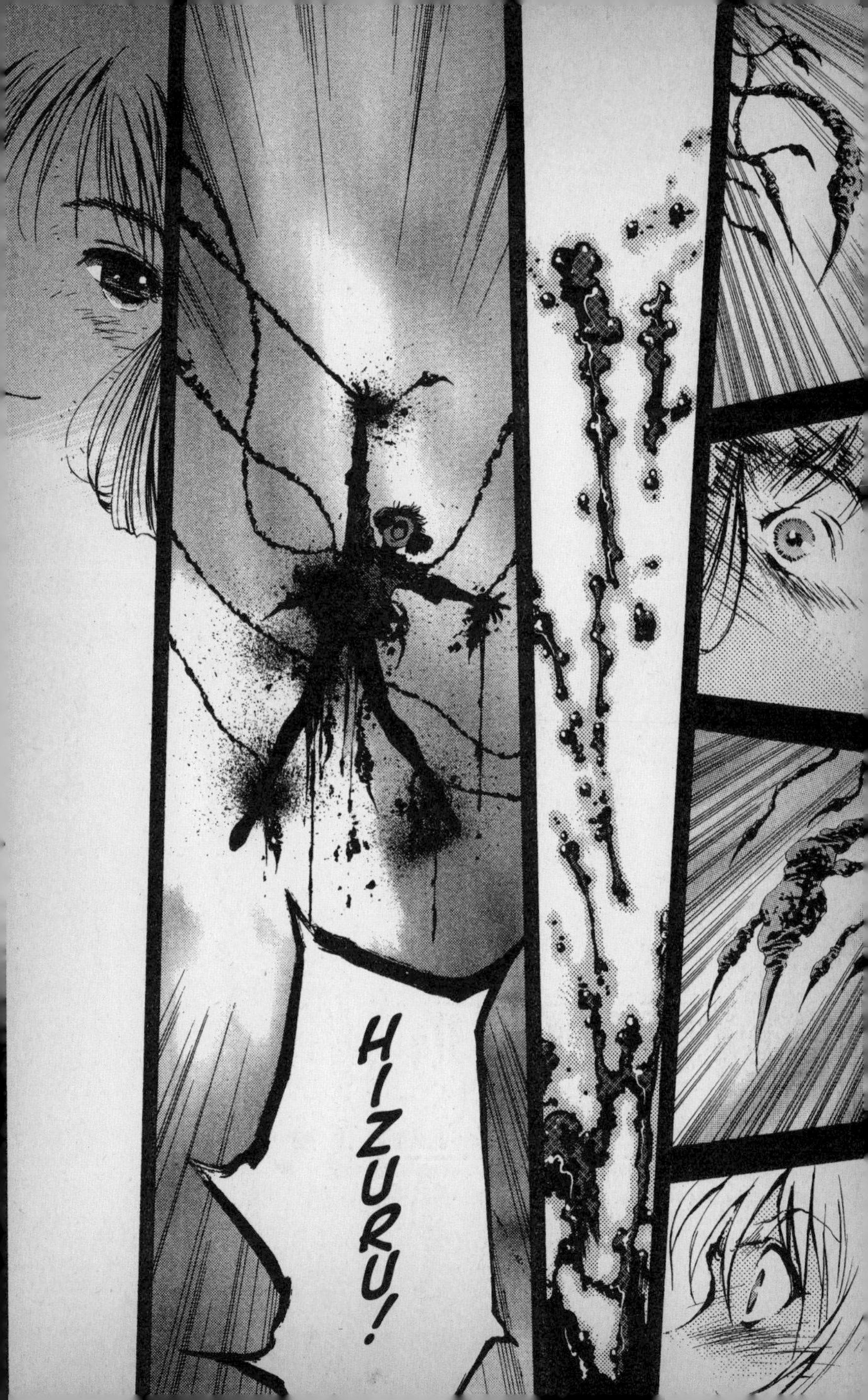
HIZURU!

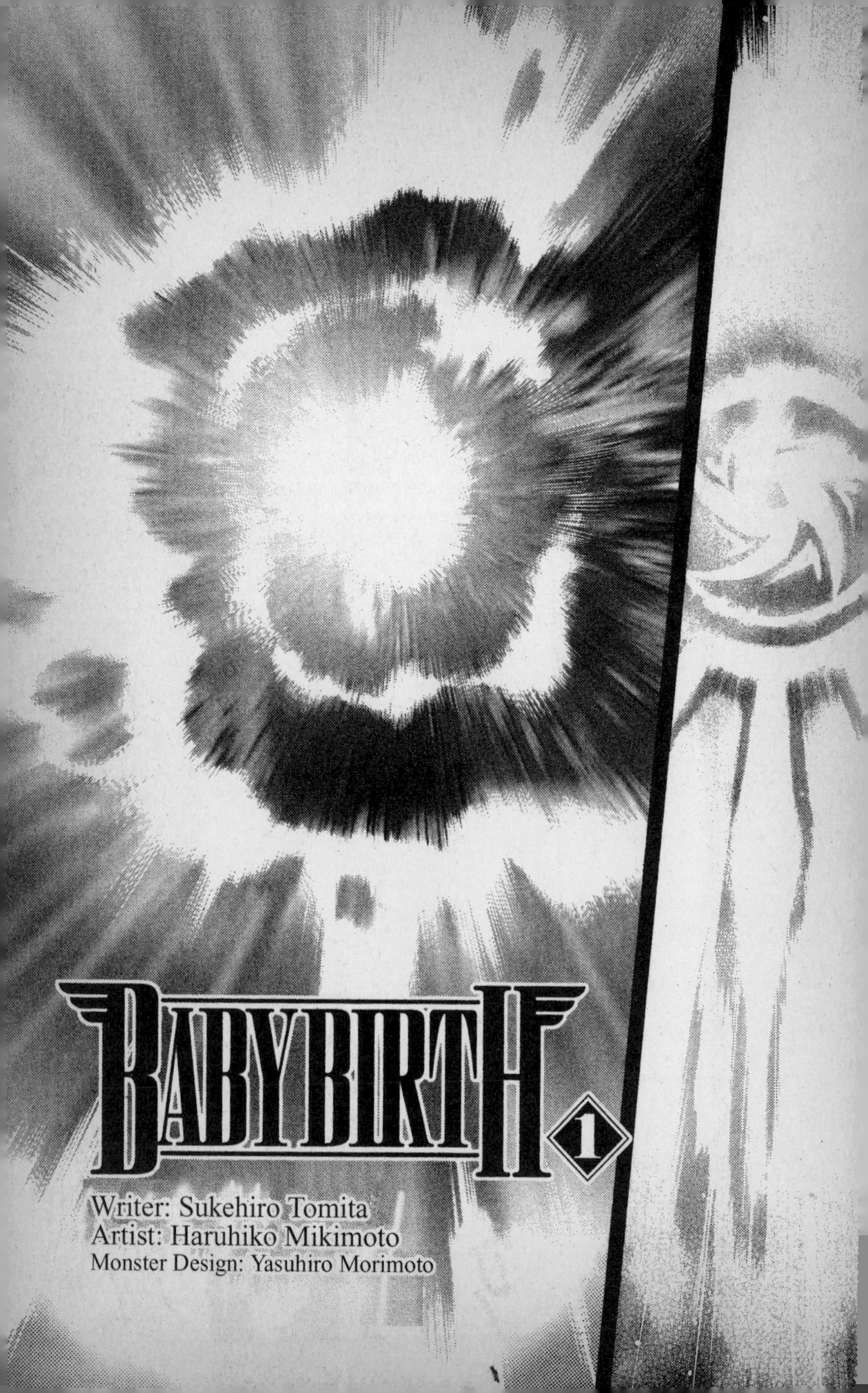
BABYBIRTH
1
Writer: Sukehiro Tomita
Artist: Haruhiko Mikimoto
Monster Design: Yasuhiro Morimoto

THANK YOU...

ACT. 1 A Chance Meeting

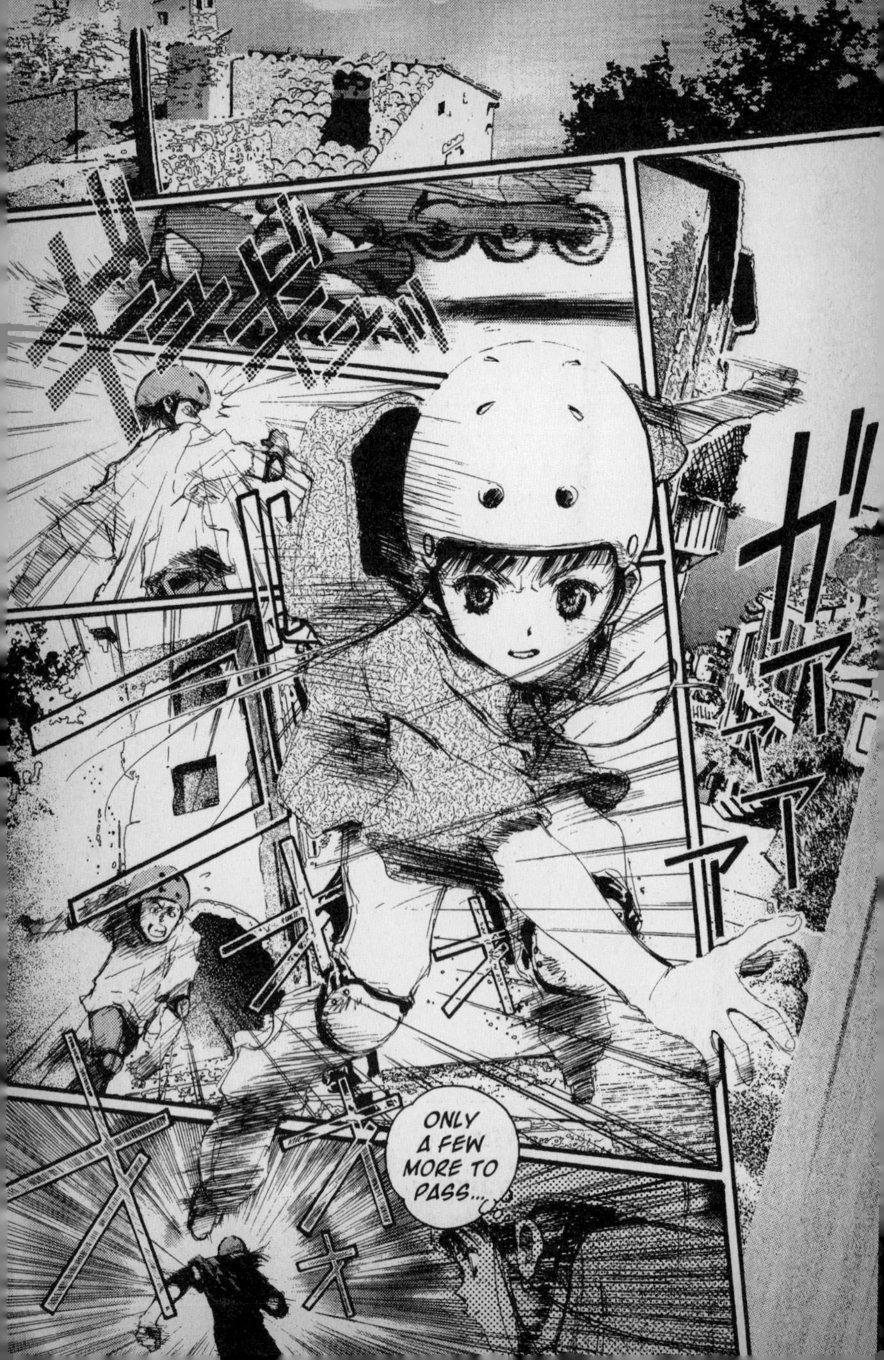
ONLY A FEW MORE TO PASS...

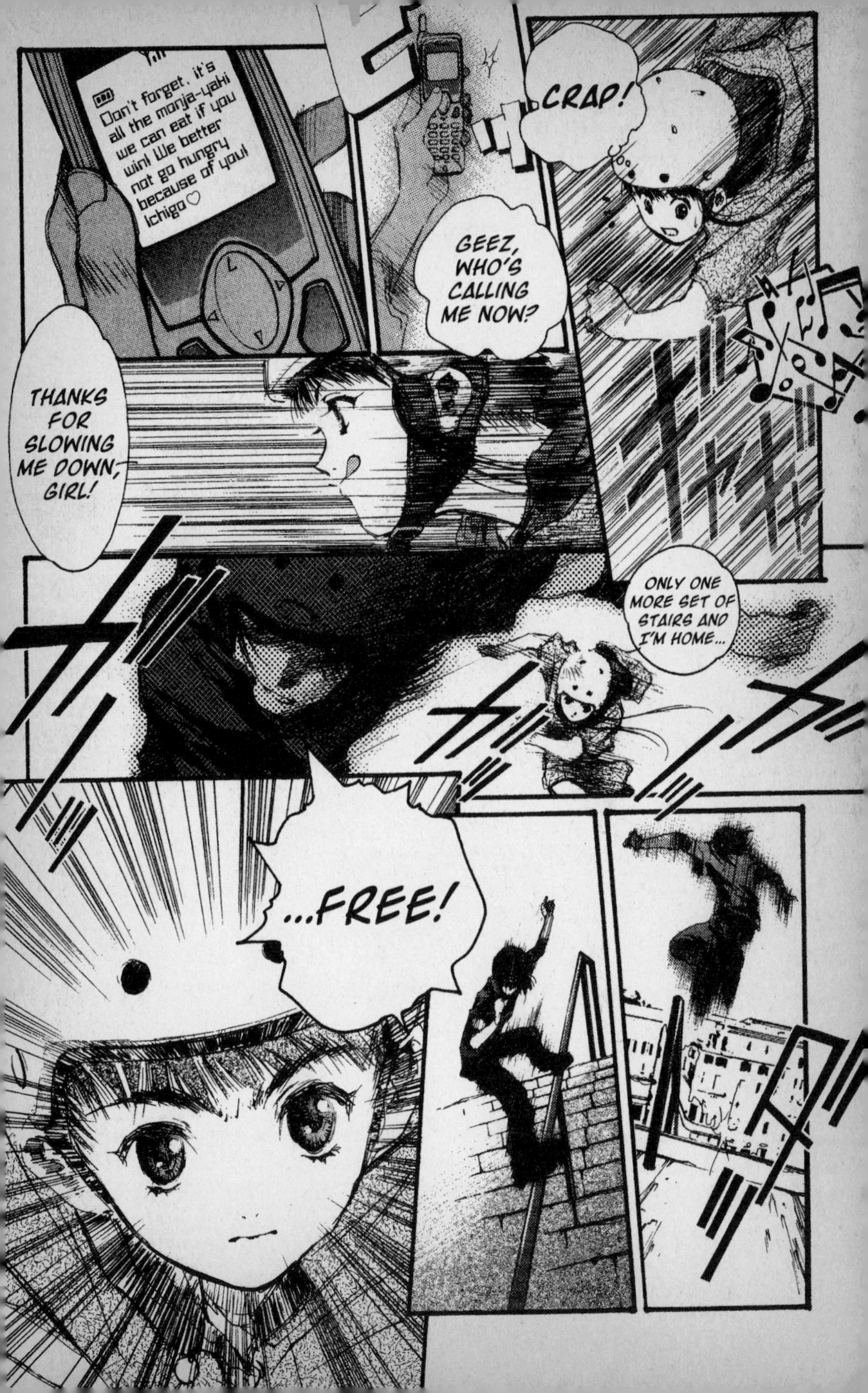
CRAP!
GEEZ, WHO'S CALLING ME NOW?
Don't forget, it's all the monja-yaki we can eat if you win! We better not go hungry because of you! Ichigo♡
THANKS FOR SLOWING ME DOWN, GIRL!
ONLY ONE MORE SET OF STAIRS AND I'M HOME...
...FREE!

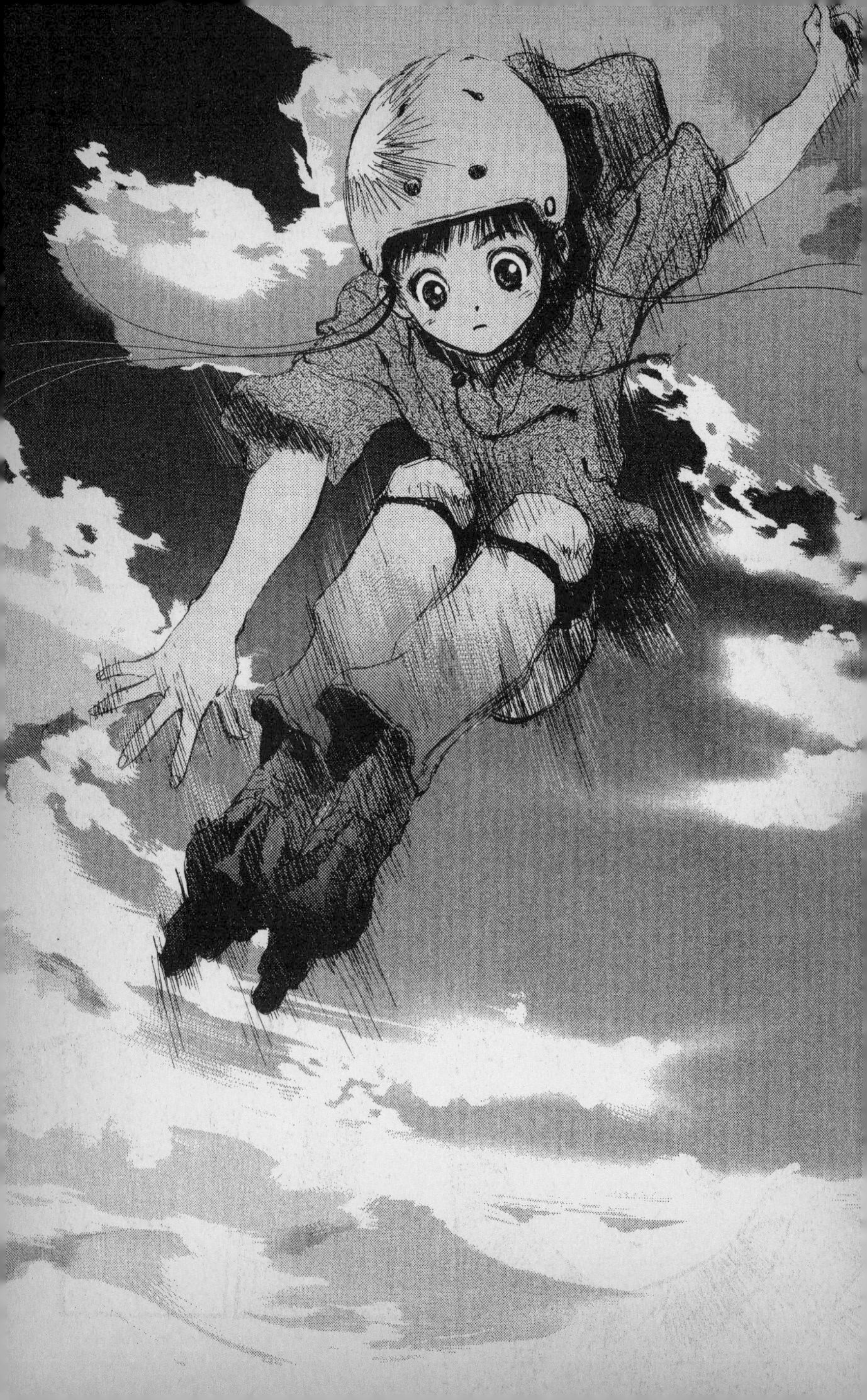

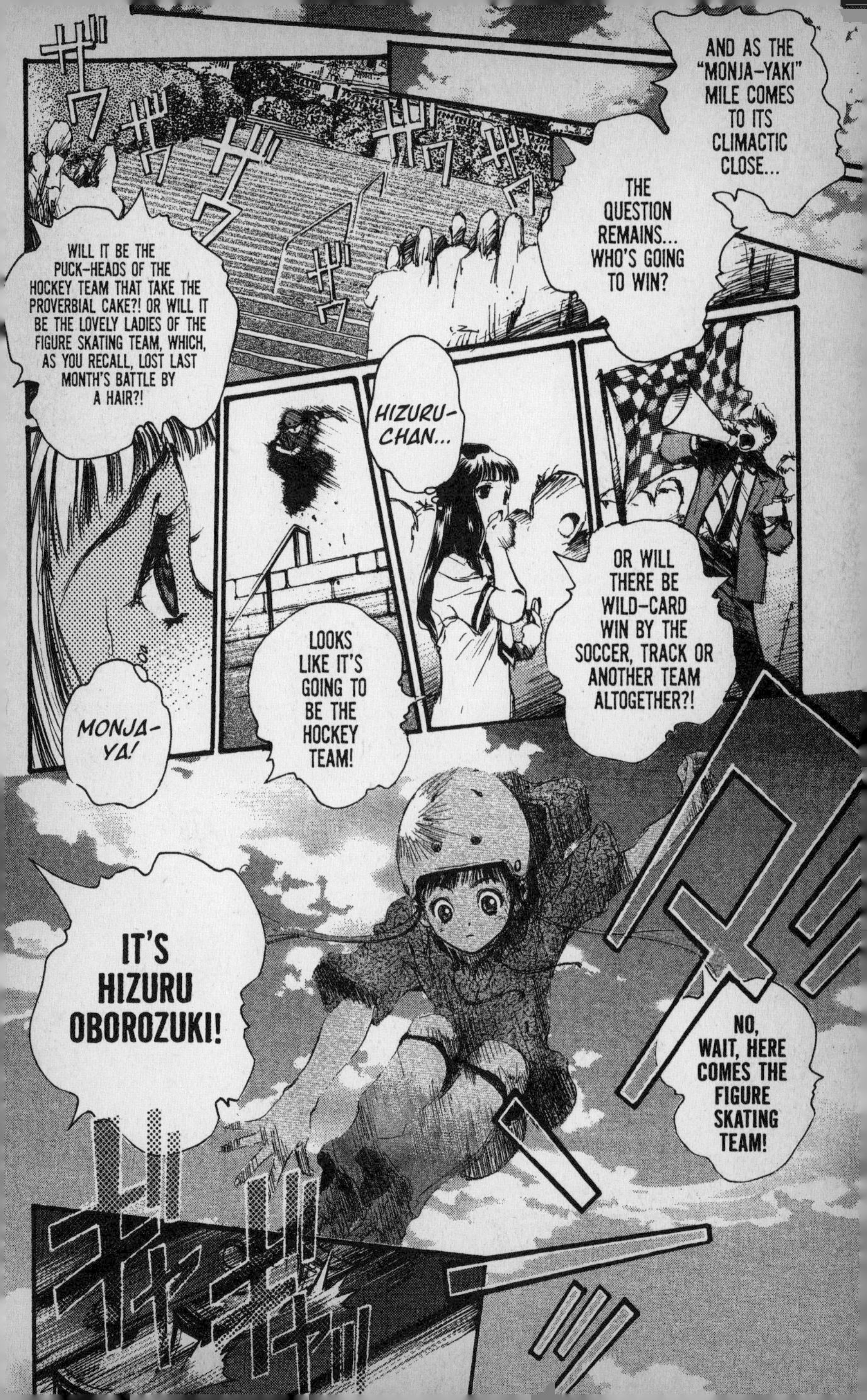
AND AS THE "MONJA-YAKI" MILE COMES TO ITS CLIMACTIC CLOSE...
THE QUESTION REMAINS... WHO'S GOING TO WIN?
WILL IT BE THE PUCK-HEADS OF THE HOCKEY TEAM THAT TAKE THE PROVERBIAL CAKE?! OR WILL IT BE THE LOVELY LADIES OF THE FIGURE SKATING TEAM, WHICH, AS YOU RECALL, LOST LAST MONTH'S BATTLE BY A HAIR?!
OR WILL THERE BE WILD-CARD WIN BY THE SOCCER, TRACK OR ANOTHER TEAM ALTOGETHER?!
HIZURU-CHAN...
LOOKS LIKE IT'S GOING TO BE THE HOCKEY TEAM!
MONJA-YA!
NO, WAIT, HERE COMES THE FIGURE SKATING TEAM!
IT'S HIZURU OBOROZUKI!

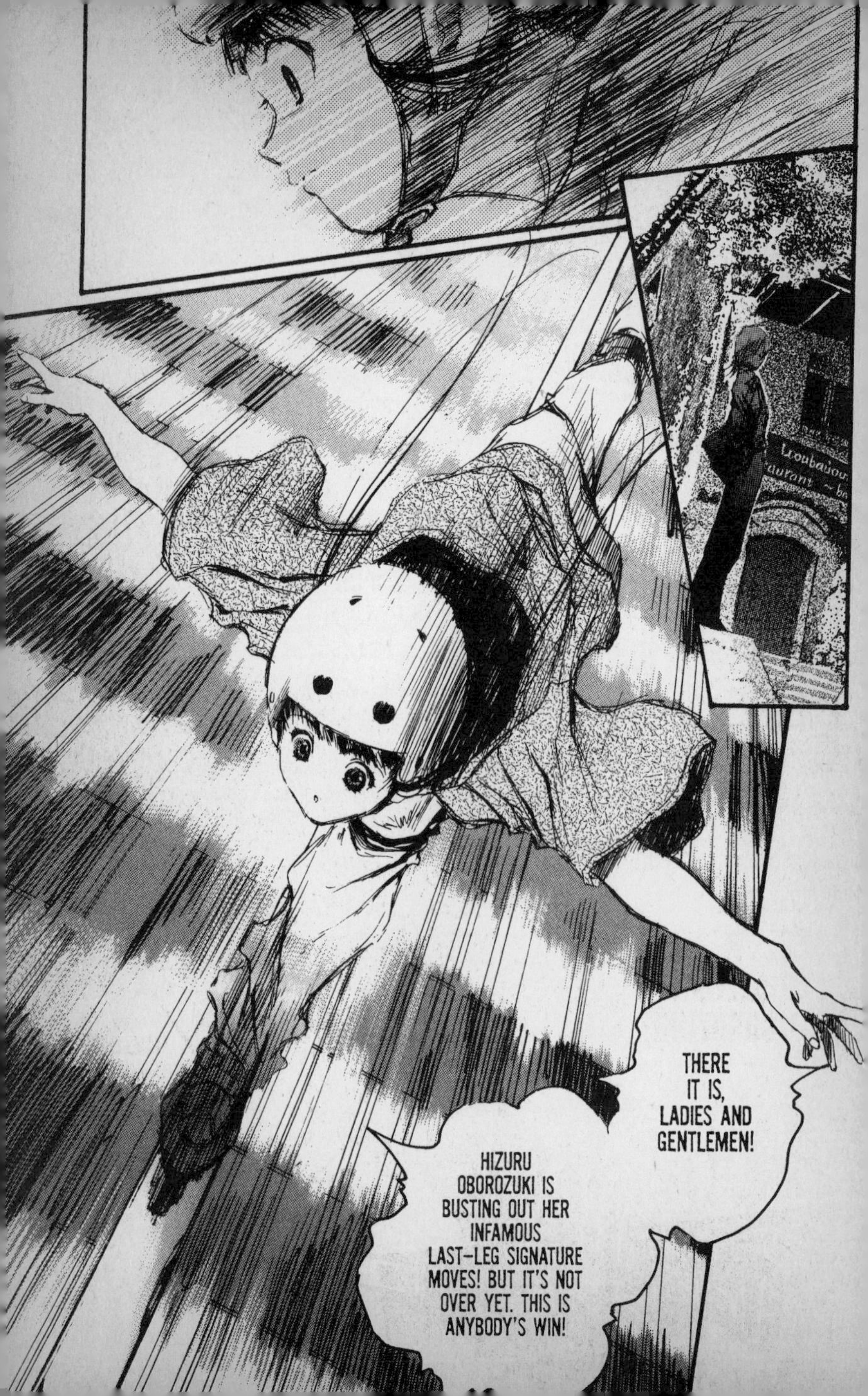
THERE IT IS, LADIES AND GENTLEMEN!
HIZURU OBOROZUKI IS BUSTING OUT HER INFAMOUS LAST-LEG SIGNATURE MOVES! BUT IT'S NOT OVER YET. THIS IS ANYBODY'S WIN!

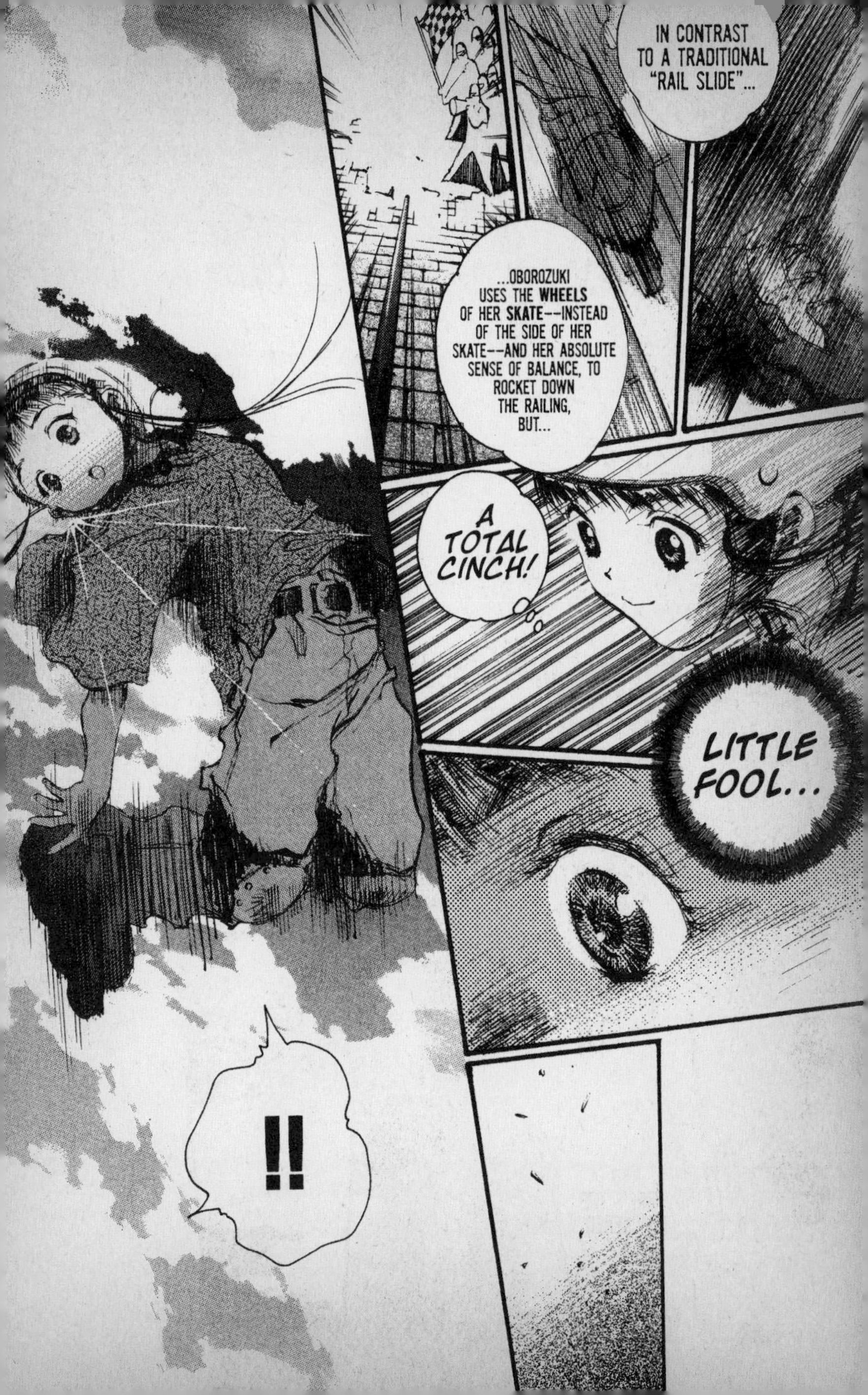
IN CONTRAST TO A TRADITIONAL "RAIL SLIDE"...
...OBOROZUKI USES THE WHEELS OF HER SKATE--INSTEAD OF THE SIDE OF HER SKATE--AND HER ABSOLUTE SENSE OF BALANCE, TO ROCKET DOWN THE RAILING, BUT...
A TOTAL CINCH!
LITTLE FOOL...
!!

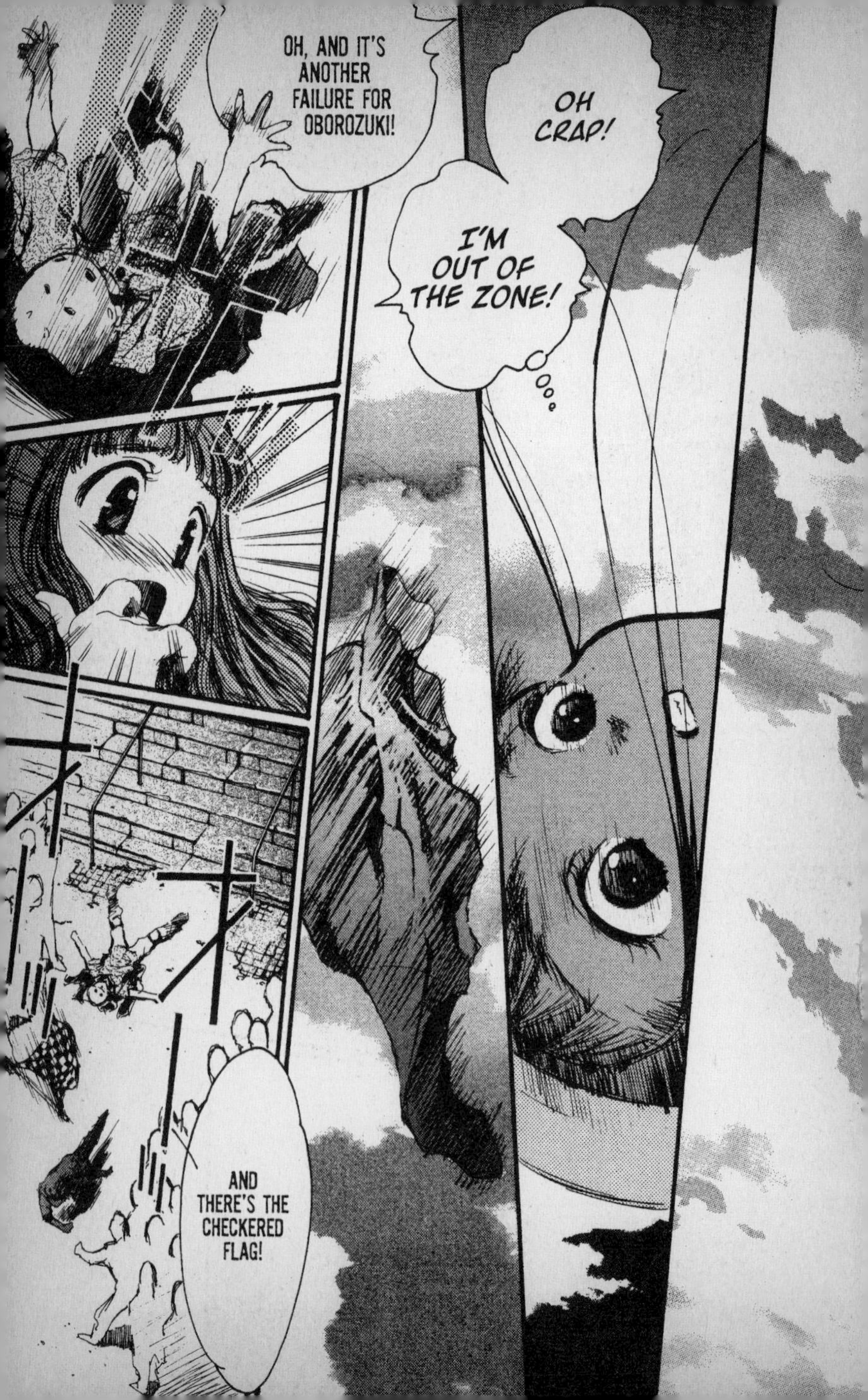
OH CRAP!
I'M OUT OF THE ZONE!
OH, AND IT'S ANOTHER FAILURE FOR OBOROZUKI!
AND THERE'S THE CHECKERED FLAG!

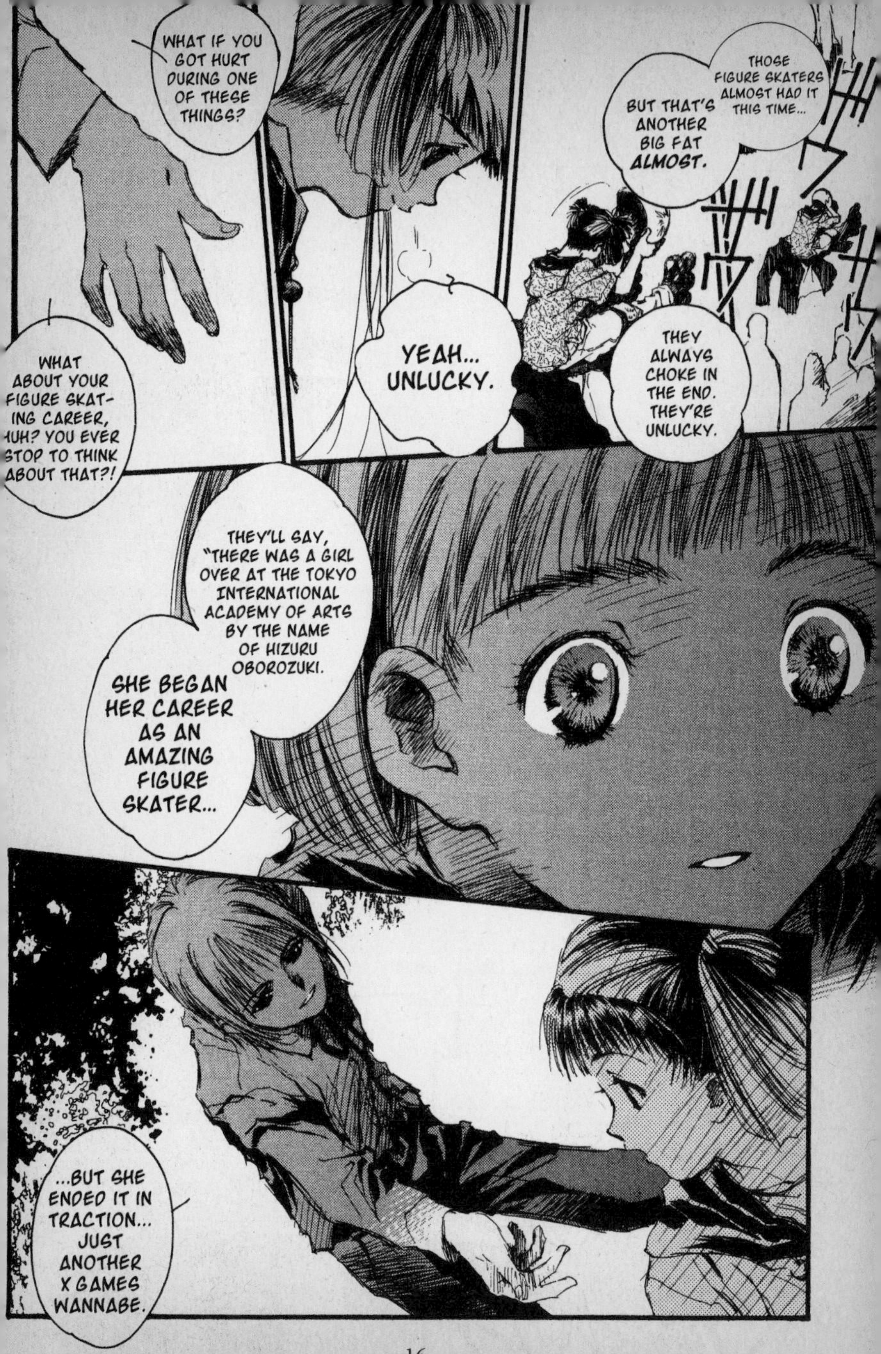
THOSE FIGURE SKATERS ALMOST HAD IT THIS TIME...
BUT THAT'S ANOTHER BIG FAT ALMOST.
THEY ALWAYS CHOKE IN THE END. THEY'RE UNLUCKY.
YEAH... UNLUCKY.
WHAT IF YOU GOT HURT DURING ONE OF THESE THINGS?
WHAT ABOUT YOUR FIGURE SKAT-ING CAREER, HUH? YOU EVER STOP TO THINK ABOUT THAT?!
THEY'LL SAY, "THERE WAS A GIRL OVER AT THE TOKYO INTERNATIONAL ACADEMY OF ARTS BY THE NAME OF HIZURU OBOROZUKI.
SHE BEGAN HER CAREER AS AN AMAZING FIGURE SKATER...
...BUT SHE ENDED IT IN TRACTION... JUST ANOTHER X GAMES WANNABE.

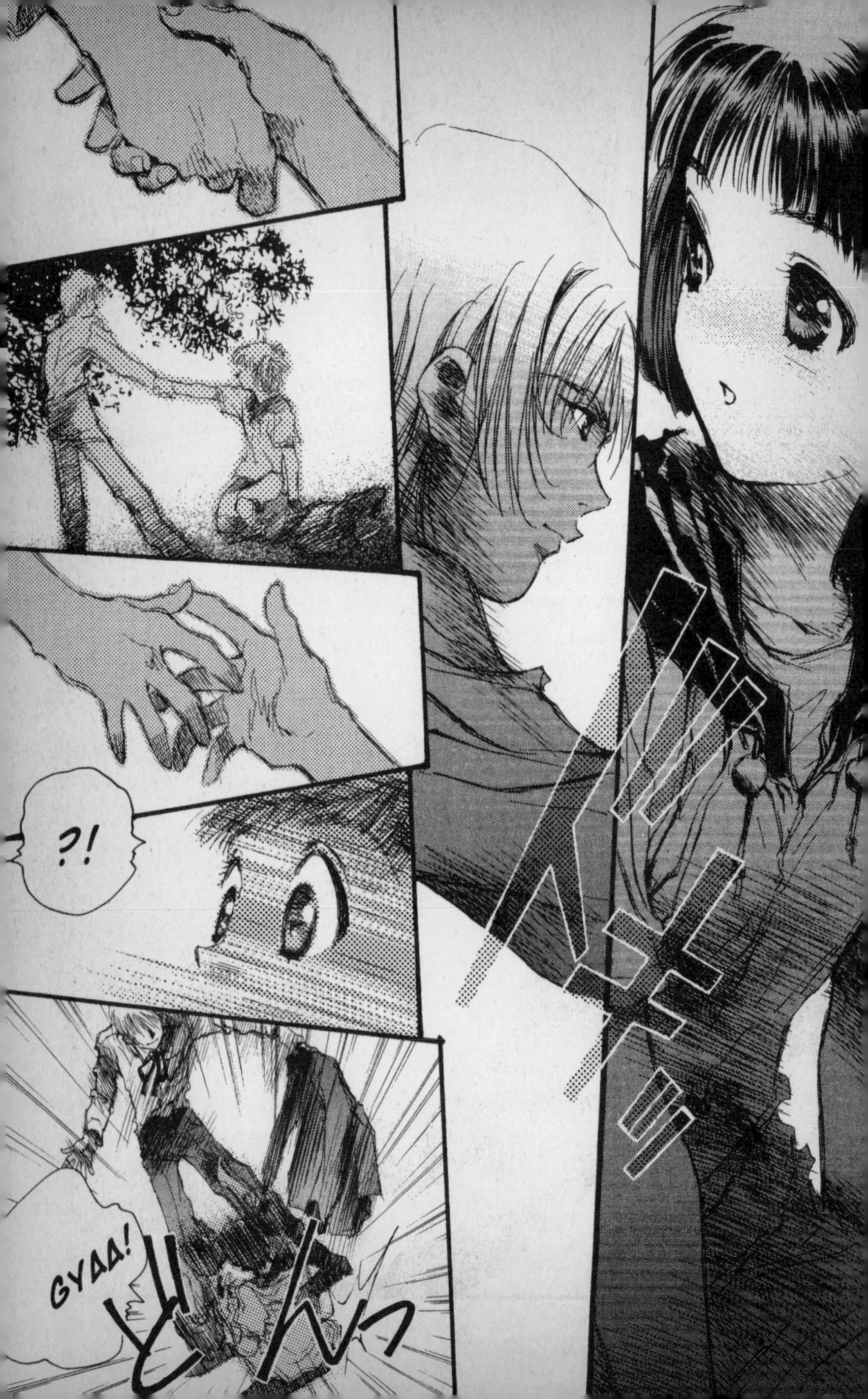
?!
GYAA!

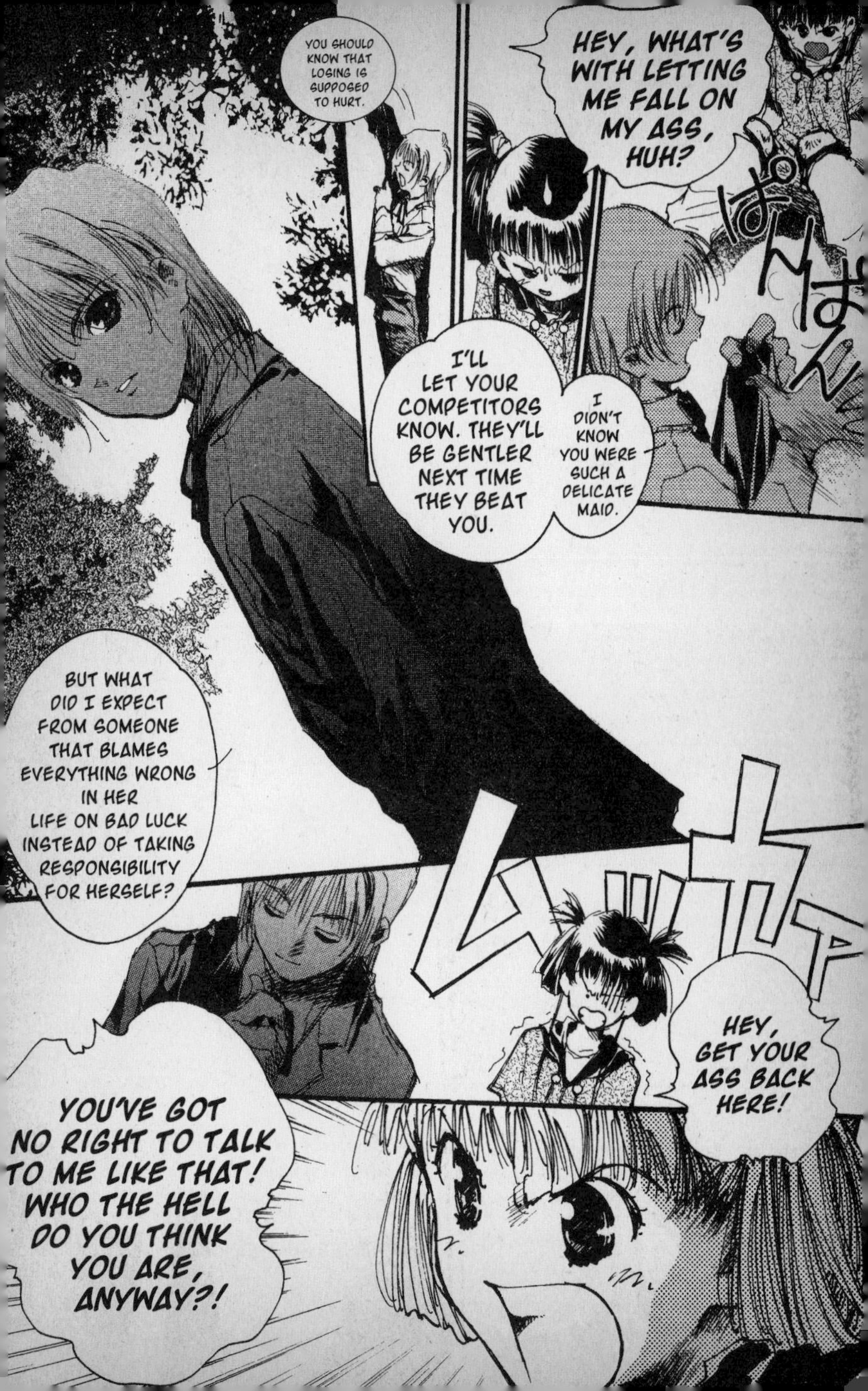
HEY, WHAT'S WITH LETTING ME FALL ON MY ASS, HUH?
I DIDN'T KNOW YOU WERE SUCH A DELICATE MAID.
I'LL LET YOUR COMPETITORS KNOW. THEY'LL BE GENTLER NEXT TIME THEY BEAT YOU.
YOU SHOULD KNOW THAT LOSING IS SUPPOSED TO HURT.
BUT WHAT DID I EXPECT FROM SOMEONE THAT BLAMES EVERYTHING WRONG IN HER LIFE ON BAD LUCK INSTEAD OF TAKING RESPONSIBILITY FOR HERSELF?
HEY, GET YOUR ASS BACK HERE!
YOU'VE GOT NO RIGHT TO TALK TO ME LIKE THAT! WHO THE HELL DO YOU THINK YOU ARE, ANYWAY?!

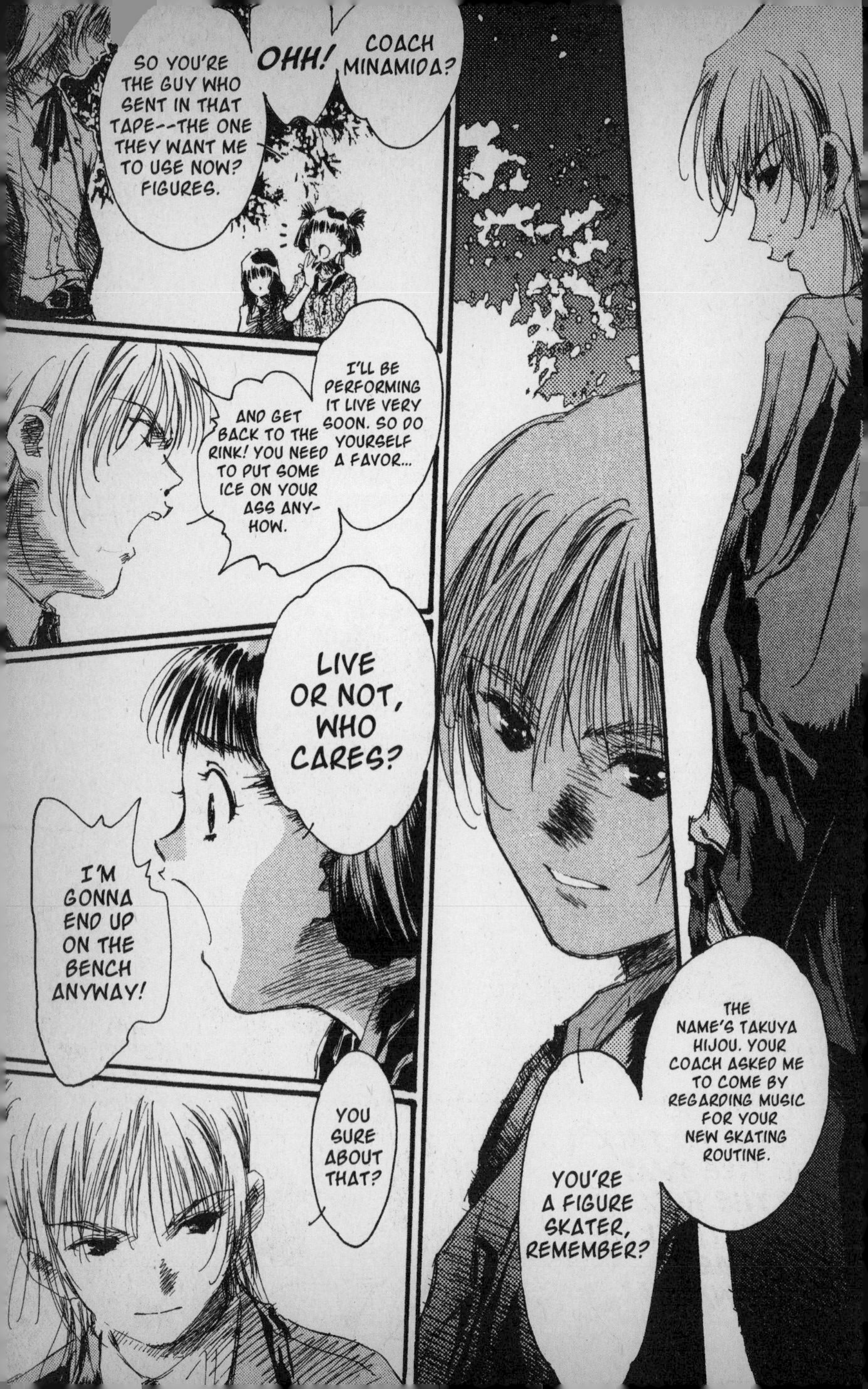
THE NAME'S TAKUYA HIJOU. YOUR COACH ASKED ME TO COME BY REGARDING MUSIC FOR YOUR NEW SKATING ROUTINE.
YOU'RE A FIGURE SKATER, REMEMBER?
COACH MINAMIDA?
OHH!
SO YOU'RE THE GUY WHO SENT IN THAT TAPE--THE ONE THEY WANT ME TO USE NOW? FIGURES.
I'LL BE PERFORMING IT LIVE VERY SOON. SO DO YOURSELF A FAVOR...
AND GET BACK TO THE RINK! YOU NEED TO PUT SOME ICE ON YOUR ASS ANY-HOW.
LIVE OR NOT, WHO CARES?
I'M GONNA END UP ON THE BENCH ANYWAY!
YOU SURE ABOUT THAT?

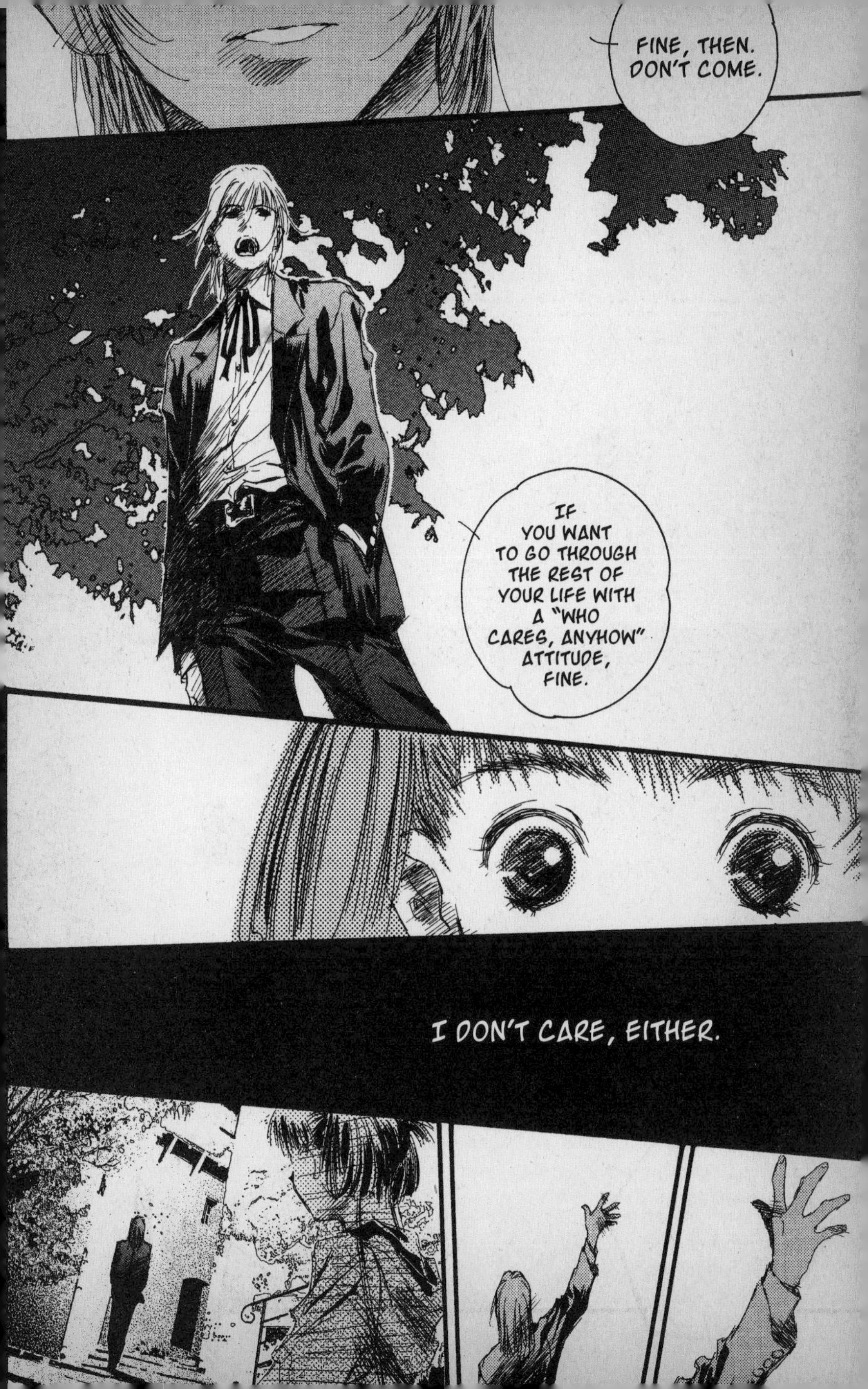
FINE, THEN. DON'T COME.
IF YOU WANT TO GO THROUGH THE REST OF YOUR LIFE WITH A "WHO CARES, ANYHOW" ATTITUDE, FINE.
I DON'T CARE, EITHER.

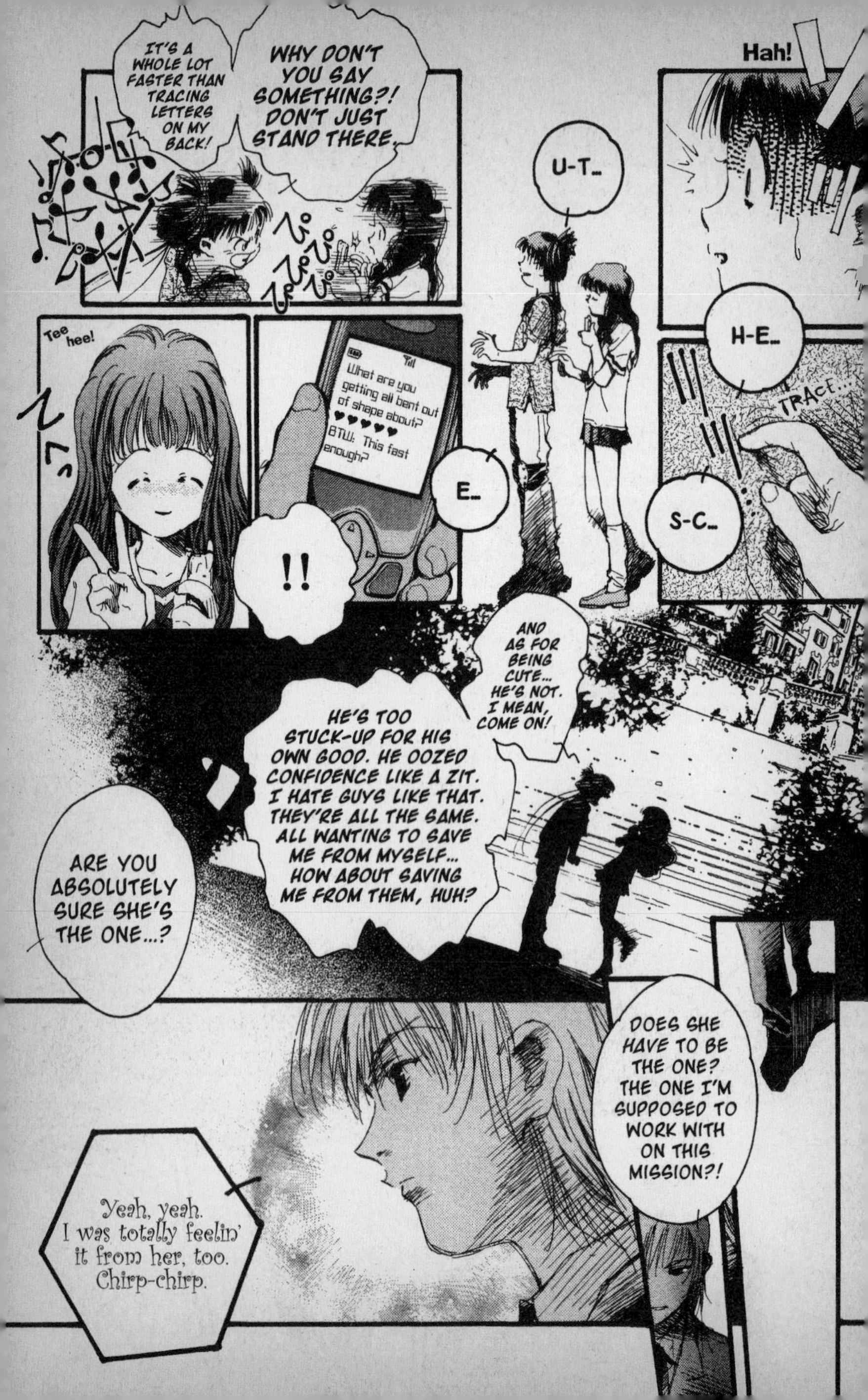
Hah!
H-E..
TRACE...
S-C..
U-T..
E..
WHY DON'T YOU SAY SOMETHING?! DON'T JUST STAND THERE.
IT'S A WHOLE LOT FASTER THAN TRACING LETTERS ON MY BACK!
!!
What are you getting all bent out of shape about? ♥♥♥♥♥ BTW: This fast enough?
Tee hee!
AND AS FOR BEING CUTE... HE'S NOT. I MEAN, COME ON!
HE'S TOO STUCK-UP FOR HIS OWN GOOD. HE OOZED CONFIDENCE LIKE A ZIT. I HATE GUYS LIKE THAT. THEY'RE ALL THE SAME. ALL WANTING TO SAVE ME FROM MYSELF... HOW ABOUT SAVING ME FROM THEM, HUH?
ARE YOU ABSOLUTELY SURE SHE'S THE ONE...?
DOES SHE HAVE TO BE THE ONE? THE ONE I'M SUPPOSED TO WORK WITH ON THIS MISSION?!
Yeah, yeah. I was totally feelin' it from her, too. Chirp-chirp.

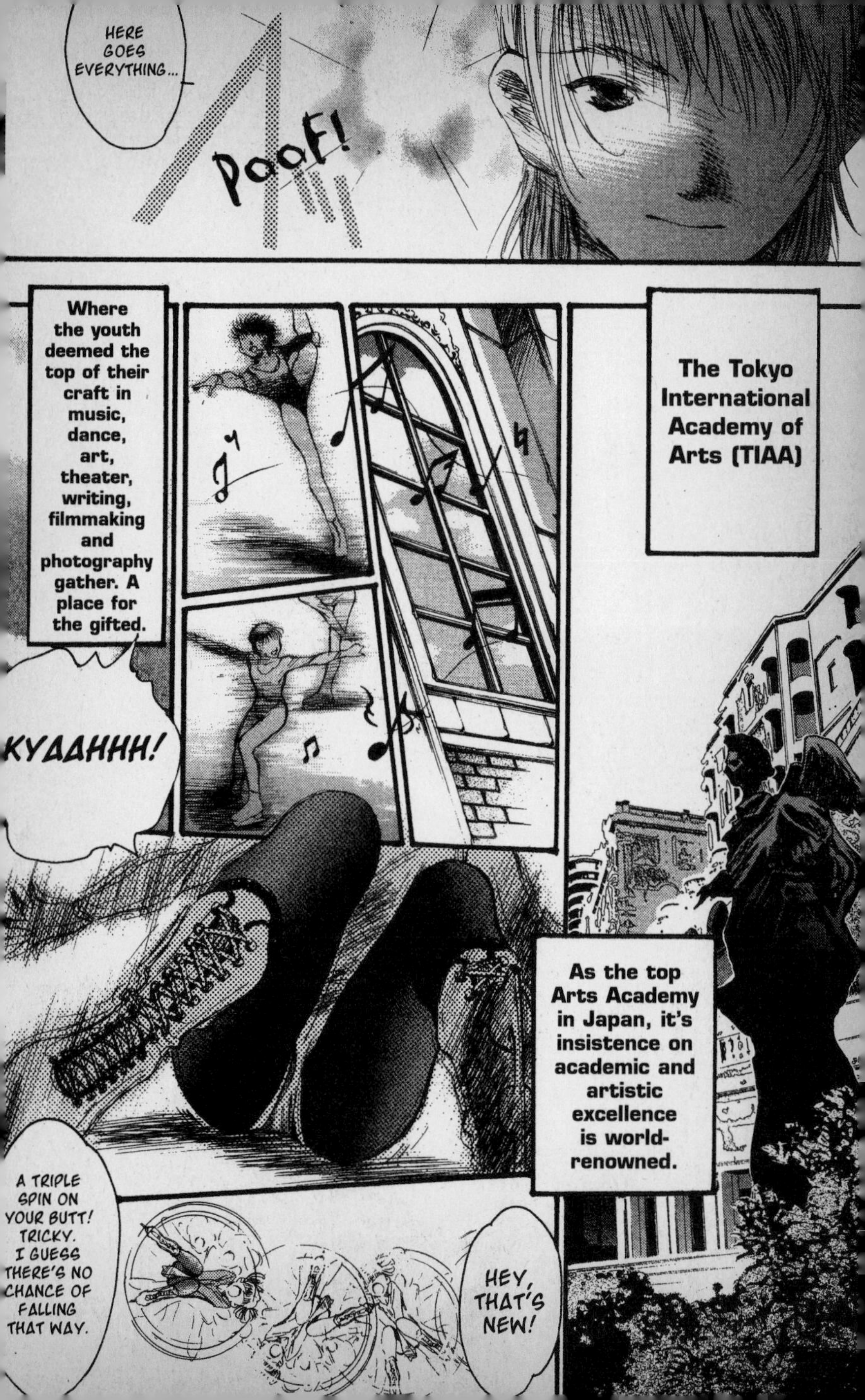
HERE GOES EVERYTHING...
POOF!
The Tokyo International Academy of Arts (TIAA)
Where the youth deemed the top of their craft in music, dance, art, theater, writing, filmmaking and photography gather. A place for the gifted.
KYAAHHH!
As the top Arts Academy in Japan, it's insistence on academic and artistic excellence is world-renowned.
HEY, THAT'S NEW!
A TRIPLE SPIN ON YOUR BUTT! TRICKY. I GUESS THERE'S NO CHANCE OF FALLING THAT WAY.

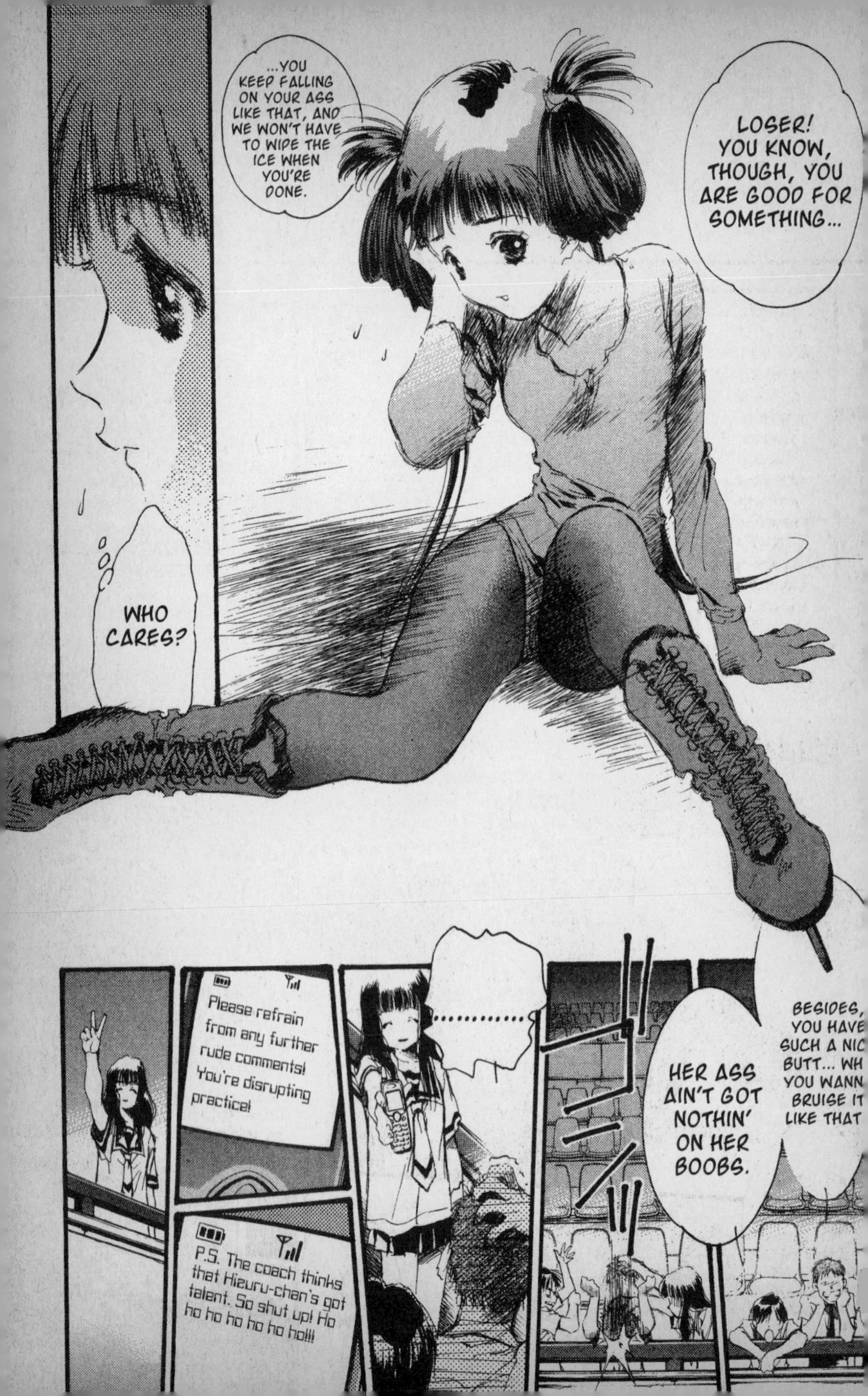
LOSER! YOU KNOW, THOUGH, YOU ARE GOOD FOR SOMETHING...
...YOU KEEP FALLING ON YOUR ASS LIKE THAT, AND WE WON'T HAVE TO WIPE THE ICE WHEN YOU'RE DONE.
WHO CARES?
BESIDES, YOU HAVE SUCH A NIC BUTT... WH YOU WANN BRUISE IT LIKE THAT
HER ASS AIN'T GOT NOTHIN' ON HER BOOBS.
....
Please refrain from any further rude comments! You're disrupting practice!
P.S. The coach thinks that Hieuru-chan's got talent. So shut up! Ho ho ho ho ho ho ho!!!

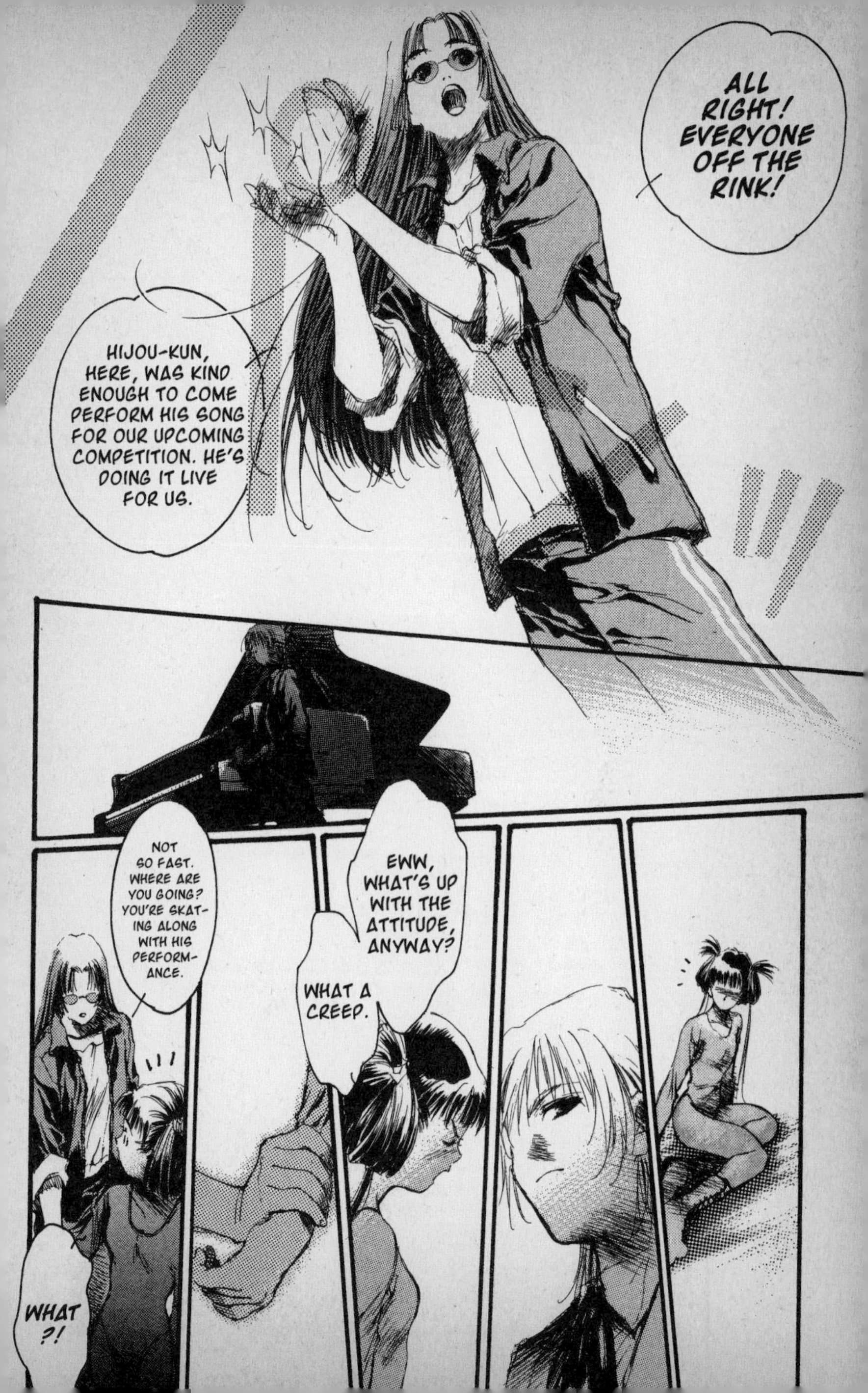

ALL RIGHT! EVERYONE OFF THE RINK!
HIJOU-KUN, HERE, WAS KIND ENOUGH TO COME PERFORM HIS SONG FOR OUR UPCOMING COMPETITION. HE'S DOING IT LIVE FOR US.
EWW, WHAT'S UP WITH THE ATTITUDE, ANYWAY?
WHAT A CREEP.
NOT SO FAST. WHERE ARE YOU GOING? YOU'RE SKAT-ING ALONG WITH HIS PERFORM-ANCE.
WHAT ?!

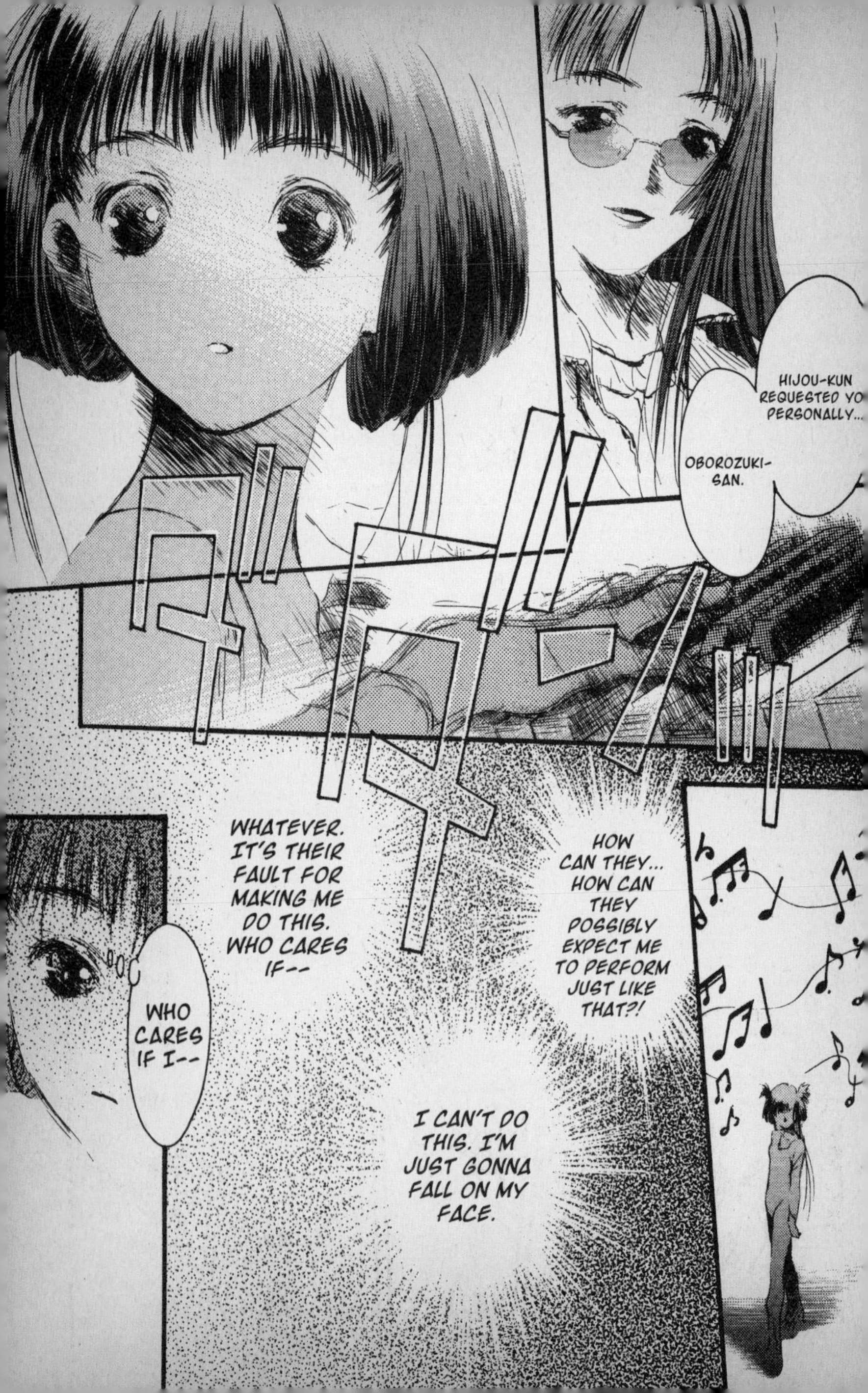
HIJOU-KUN REQUESTED YO PERSONALLY...
OBOROZUKI-SAN.
HOW CAN THEY... HOW CAN THEY POSSIBLY EXPECT ME TO PERFORM JUST LIKE THAT?!
WHATEVER. IT'S THEIR FAULT FOR MAKING ME DO THIS. WHO CARES IF--
I CAN'T DO THIS. I'M JUST GONNA FALL ON MY FACE.
WHO CARES IF I--

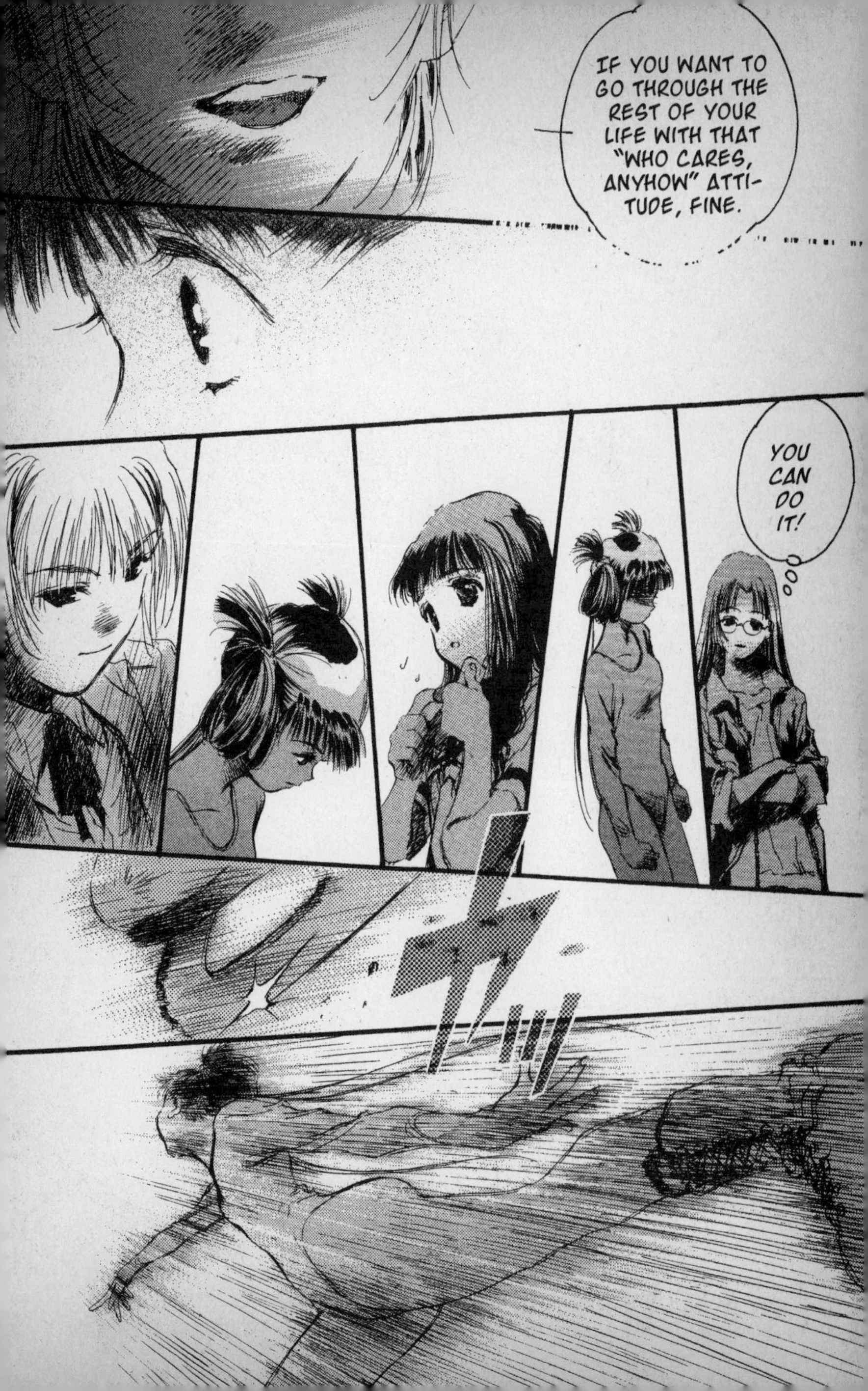
IF YOU WANT TO GO THROUGH THE REST OF YOUR LIFE WITH THAT "WHO CARES, ANYHOW" ATTI-TUDE, FINE.
YOU CAN DO IT!

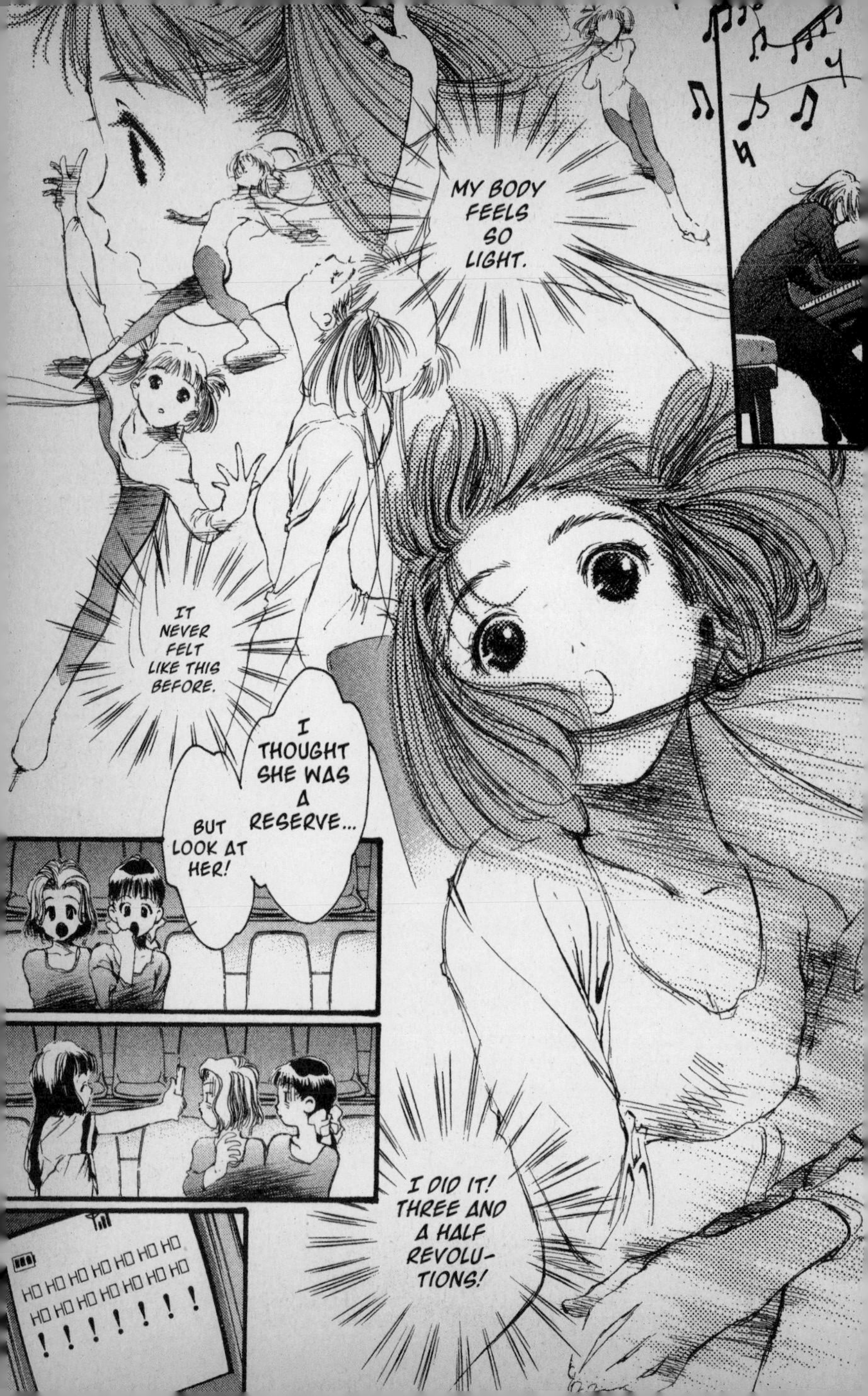
MY BODY FEELS SO LIGHT.
IT NEVER FELT LIKE THIS BEFORE.
I THOUGHT SHE WAS A RESERVE...
BUT LOOK AT HER!
I DID IT! THREE AND A HALF REVOLU-TIONS!
HO HO HO HO HO HO HO HO HO HO HO HO HO HO HO HO HO HO HO HO HO !!!!!!!!!

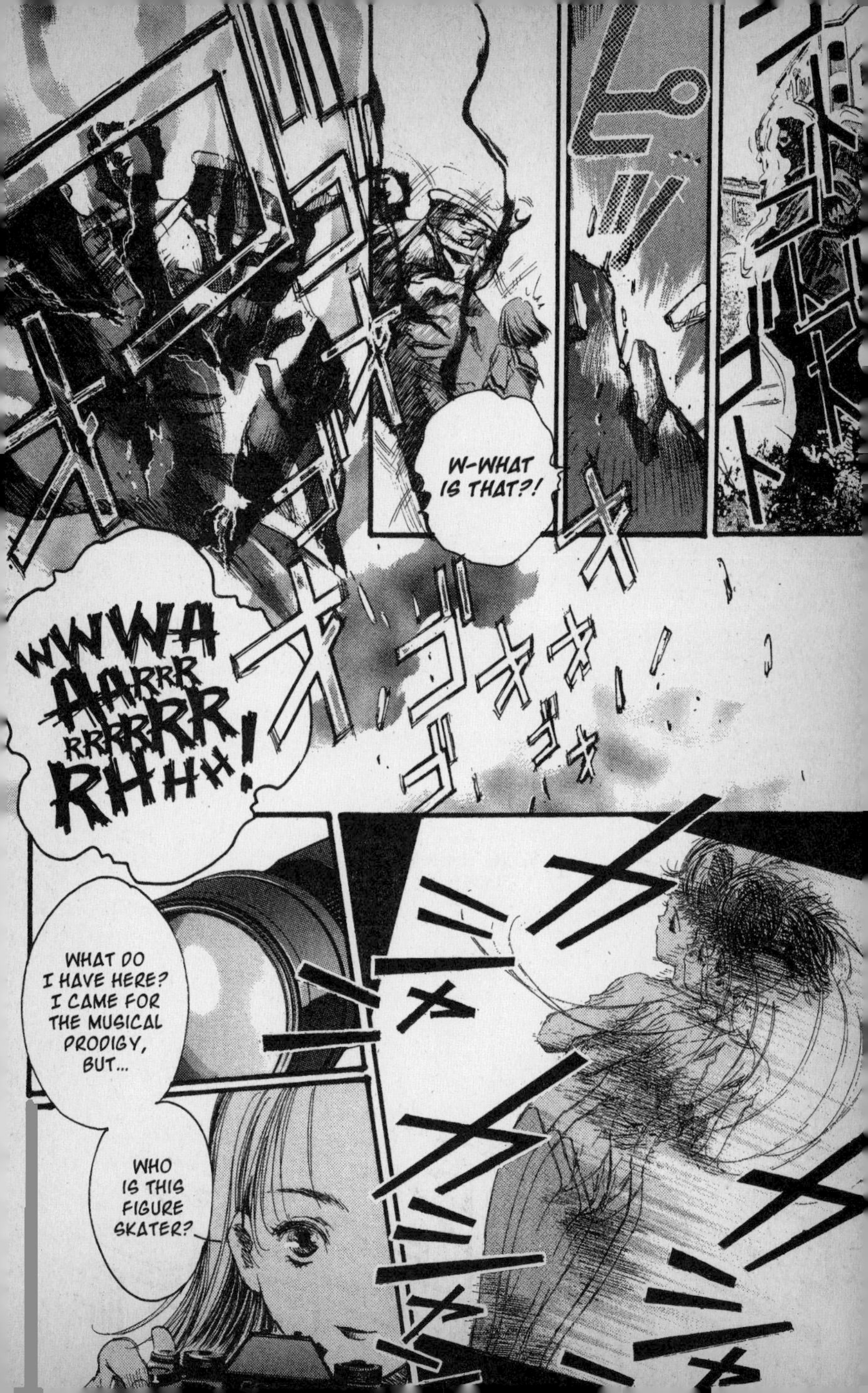
W-WHAT IS THAT?!
WWWAAARRRRRRRRRRRHHH!
WHAT DO I HAVE HERE? I CAME FOR THE MUSICAL PRODIGY, BUT...
WHO IS THIS FIGURE SKATER?

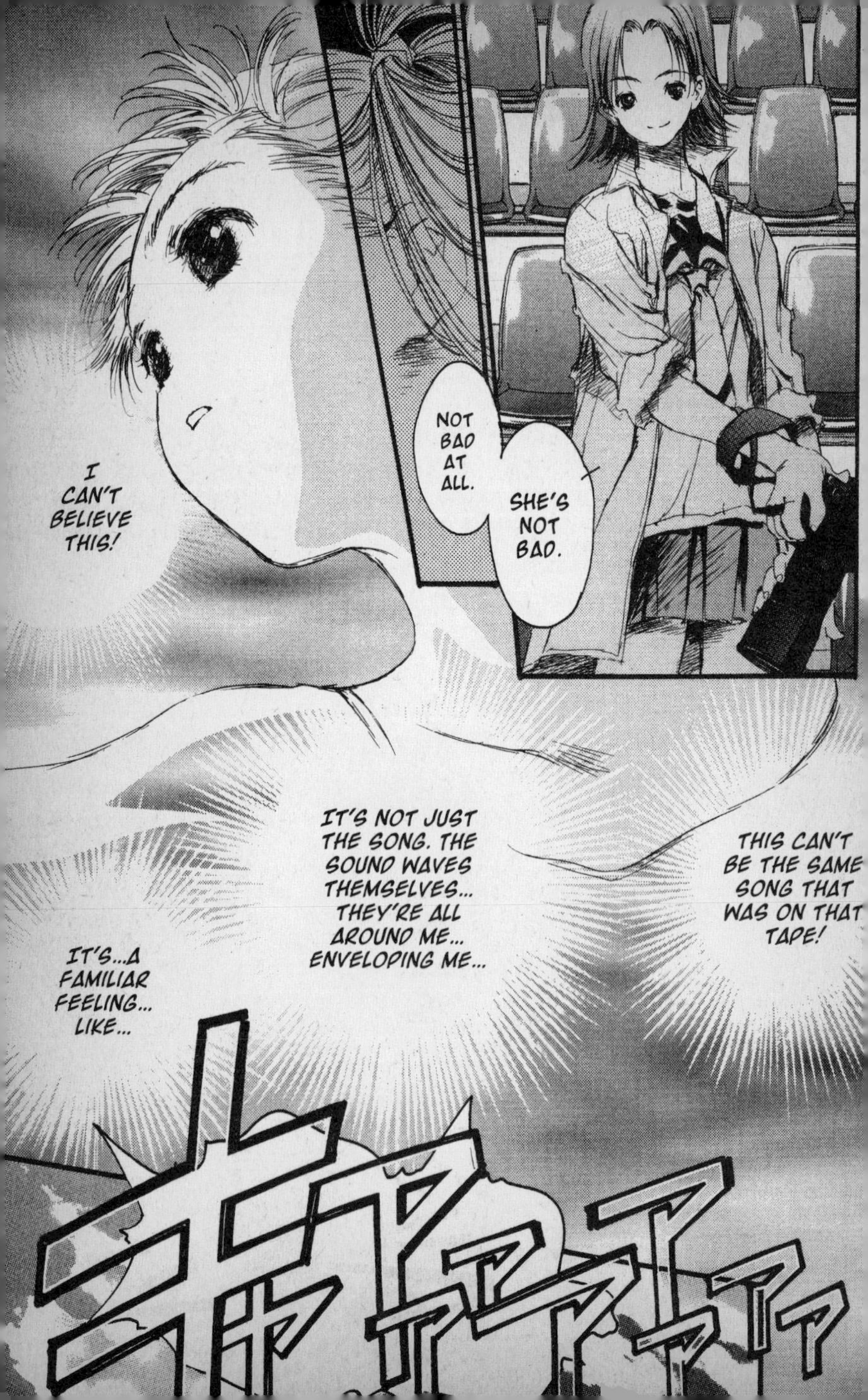
NOT BAD AT ALL.
SHE'S NOT BAD.
I CAN'T BELIEVE THIS!
THIS CAN'T BE THE SAME SONG THAT WAS ON THAT TAPE!
IT'S NOT JUST THE SONG. THE SOUND WAVES THEMSELVES... THEY'RE ALL AROUND ME... ENVELOPING ME...
IT'S...A FAMILIAR FEELING... LIKE...

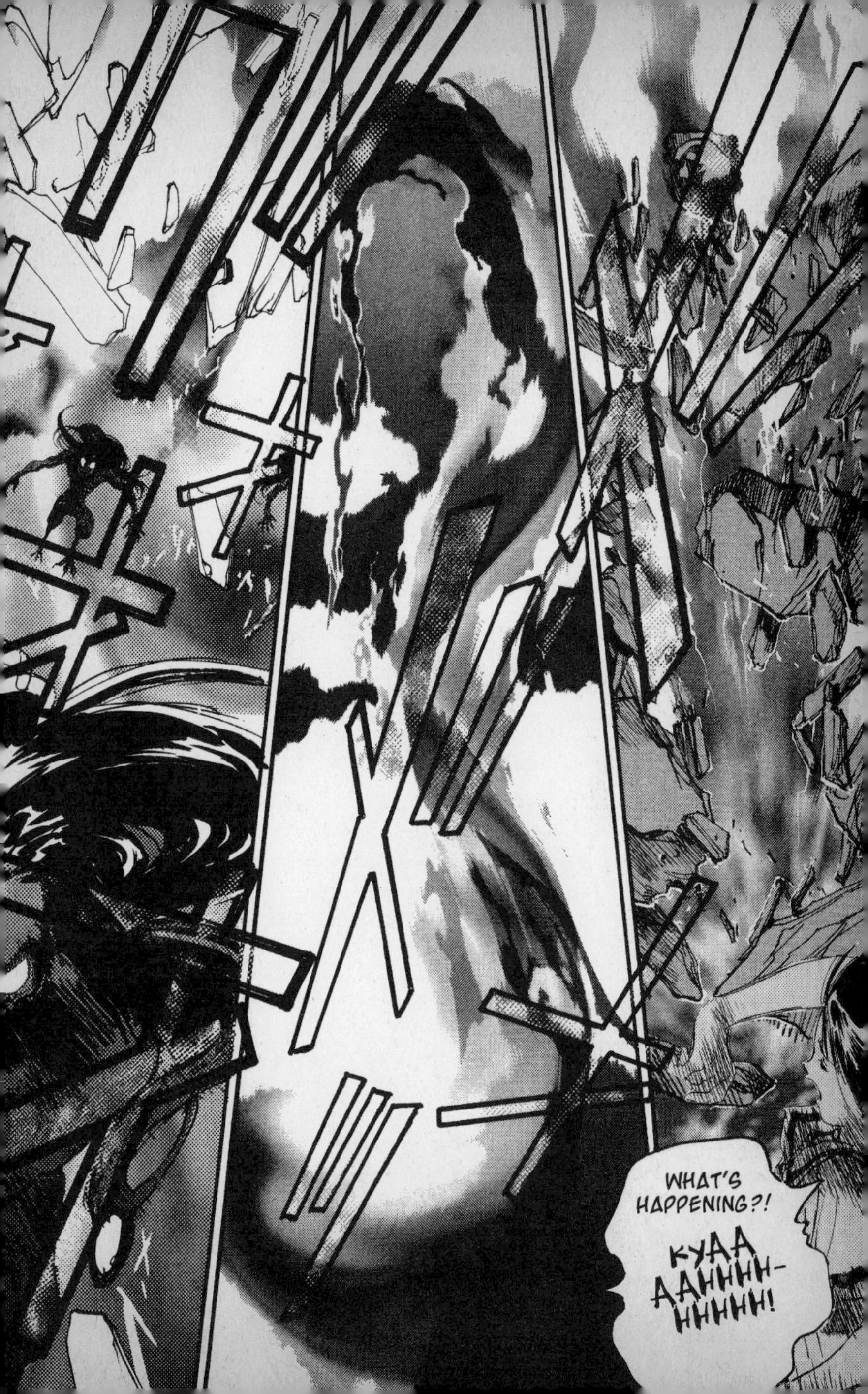
WHAT'S HAPPENING?!
KYAA AAHHHH-HHHHH!

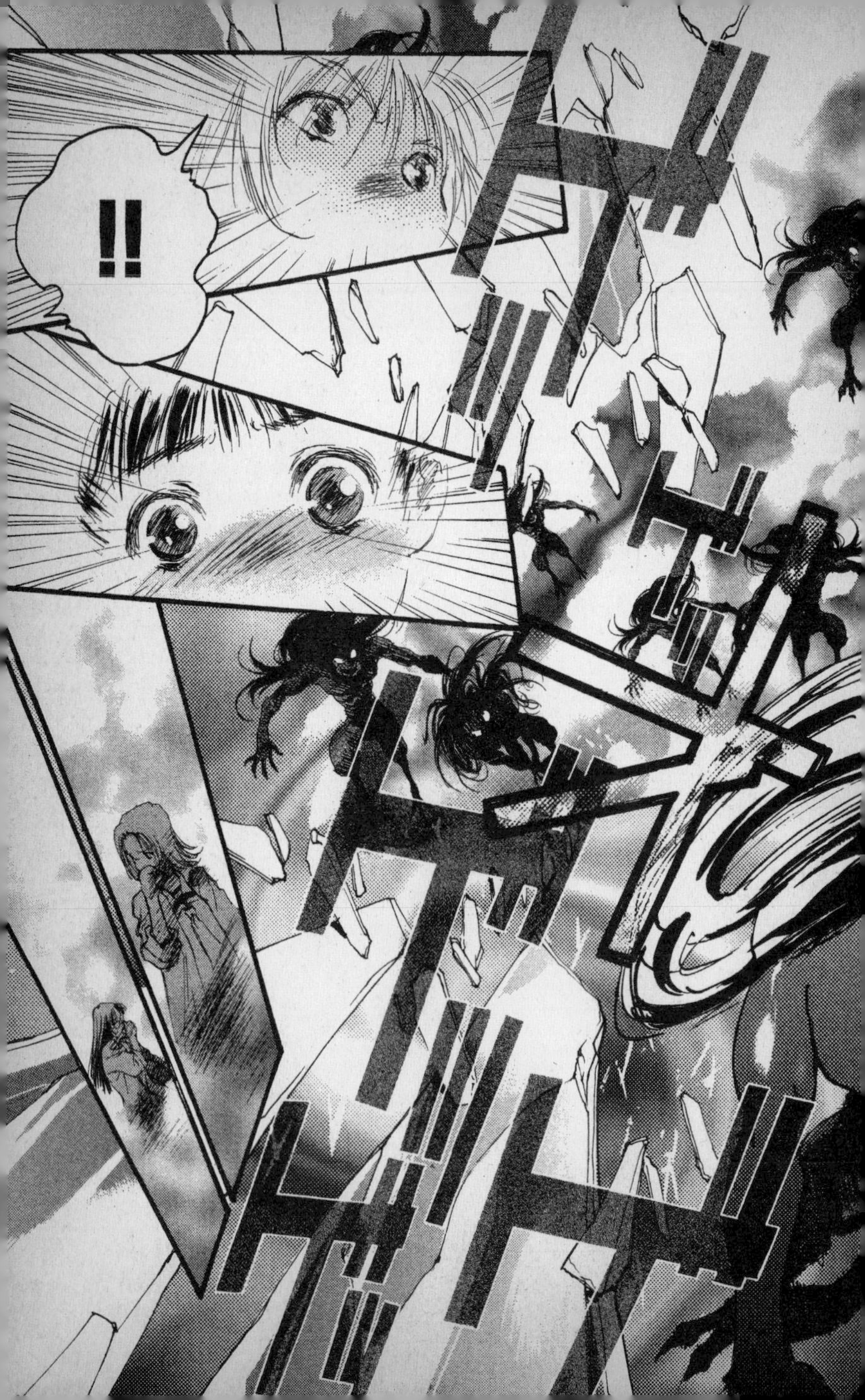
!!

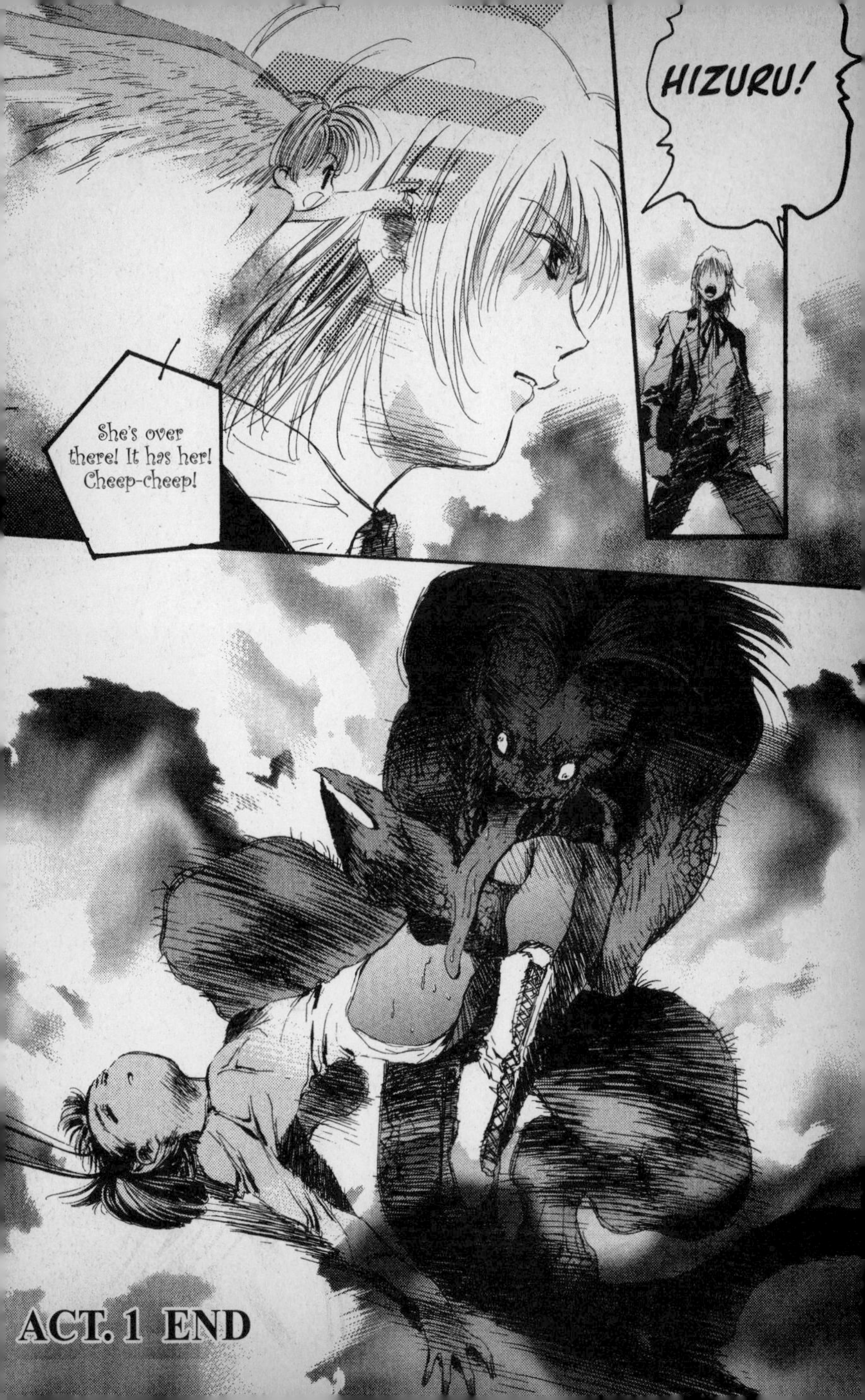
HIZURU!
She's over there! It has her! Cheep-cheep!
ACT. 1 END

ACT. 2 Resonance

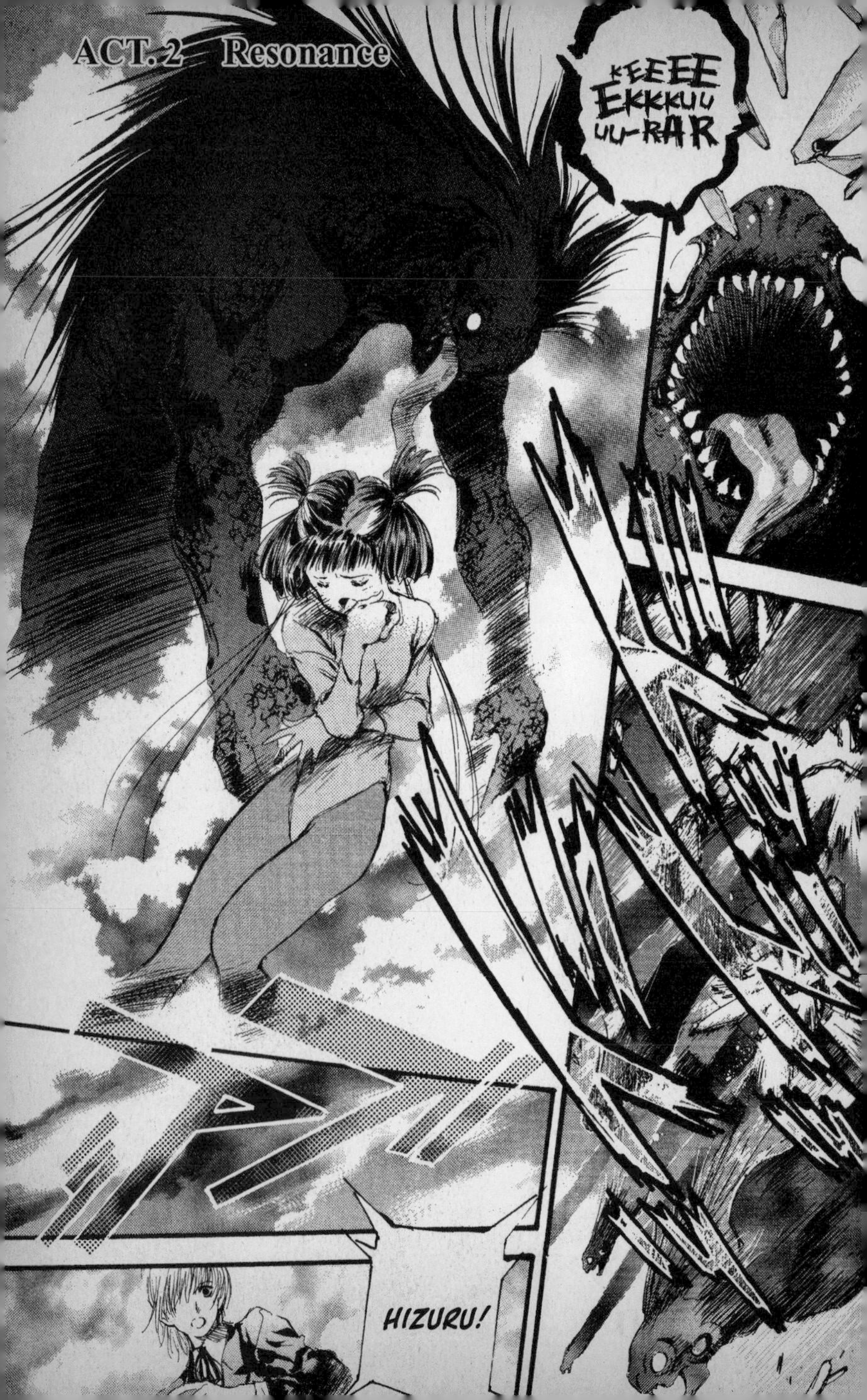
KEEEEEKKKUUUU-RAR
HIZURU!

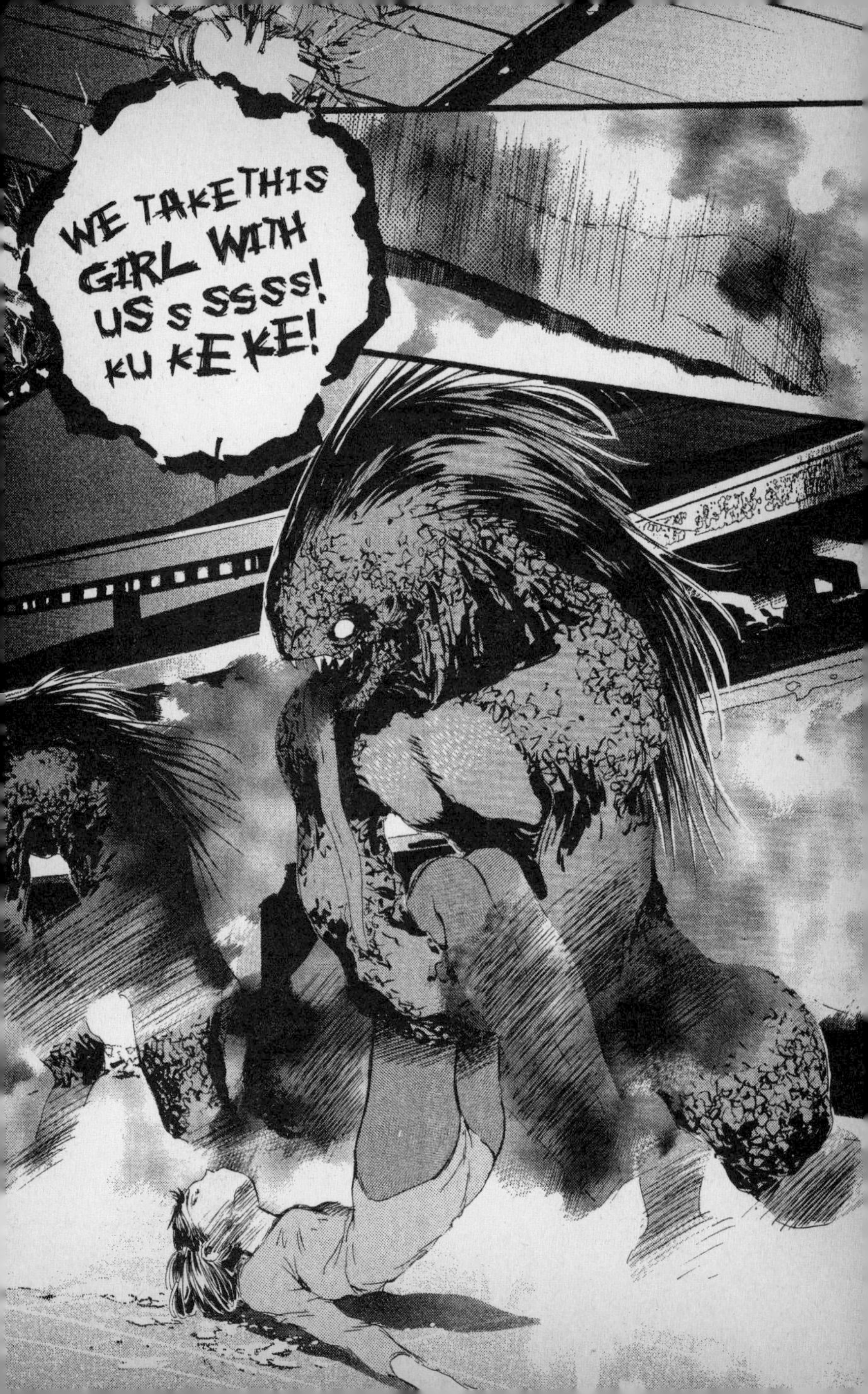
WE TAKE THIS GIRL WITH US s SSSSS! KU KEKE!

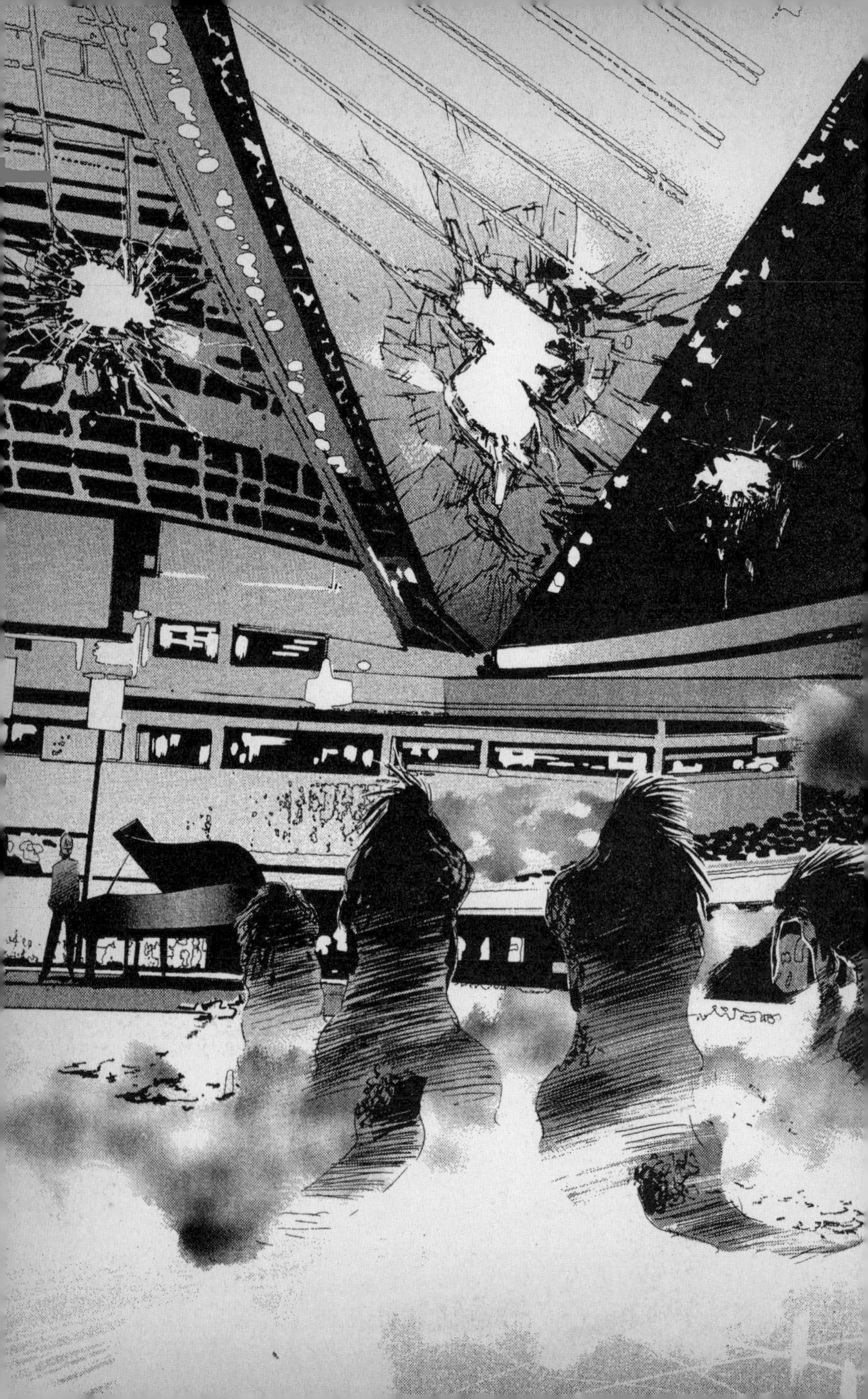

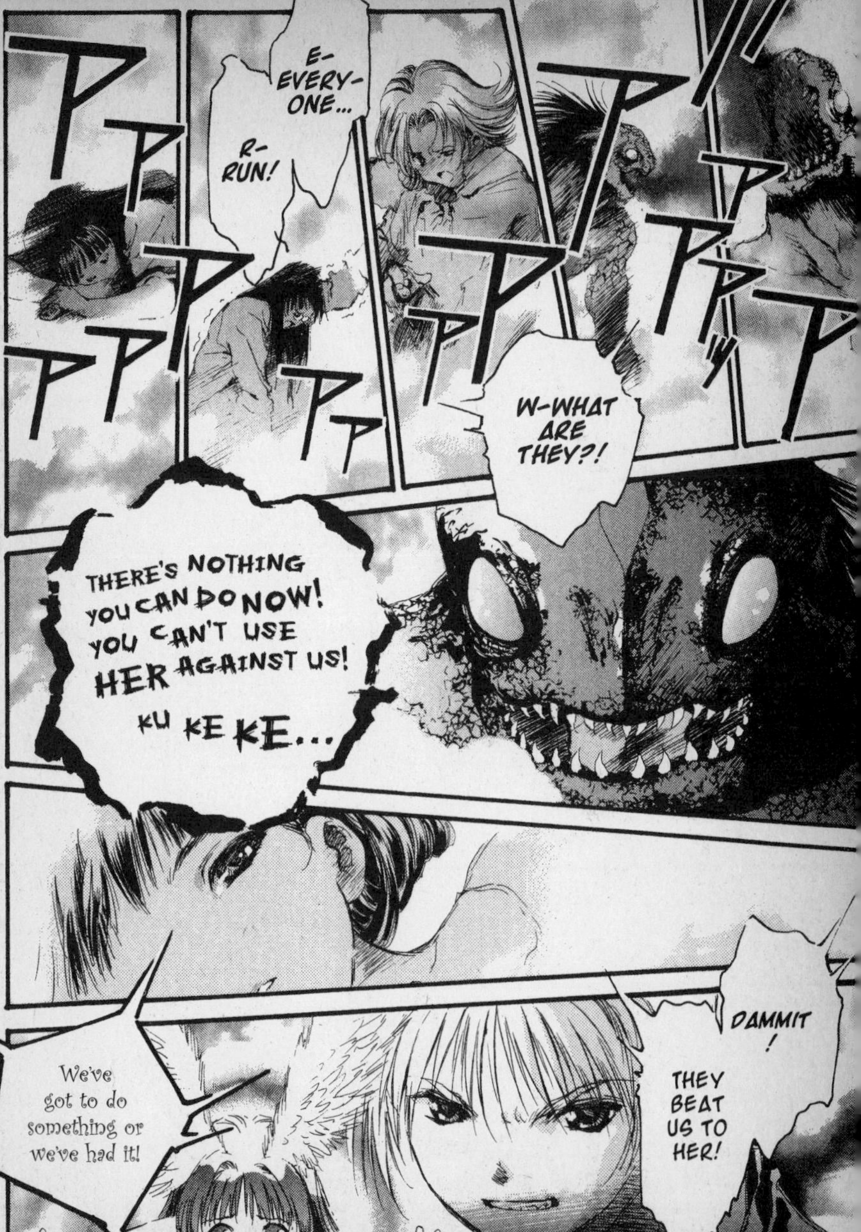
E-EVERY-ONE...
R-RUN!
W-WHAT ARE THEY?!
THERE'S NOTHING YOU CAN DO NOW! YOU CAN'T USE HER AGAINST US!
KU KE KE...
DAMMIT!
THEY BEAT US TO HER!
We've got to do something or we've had it!

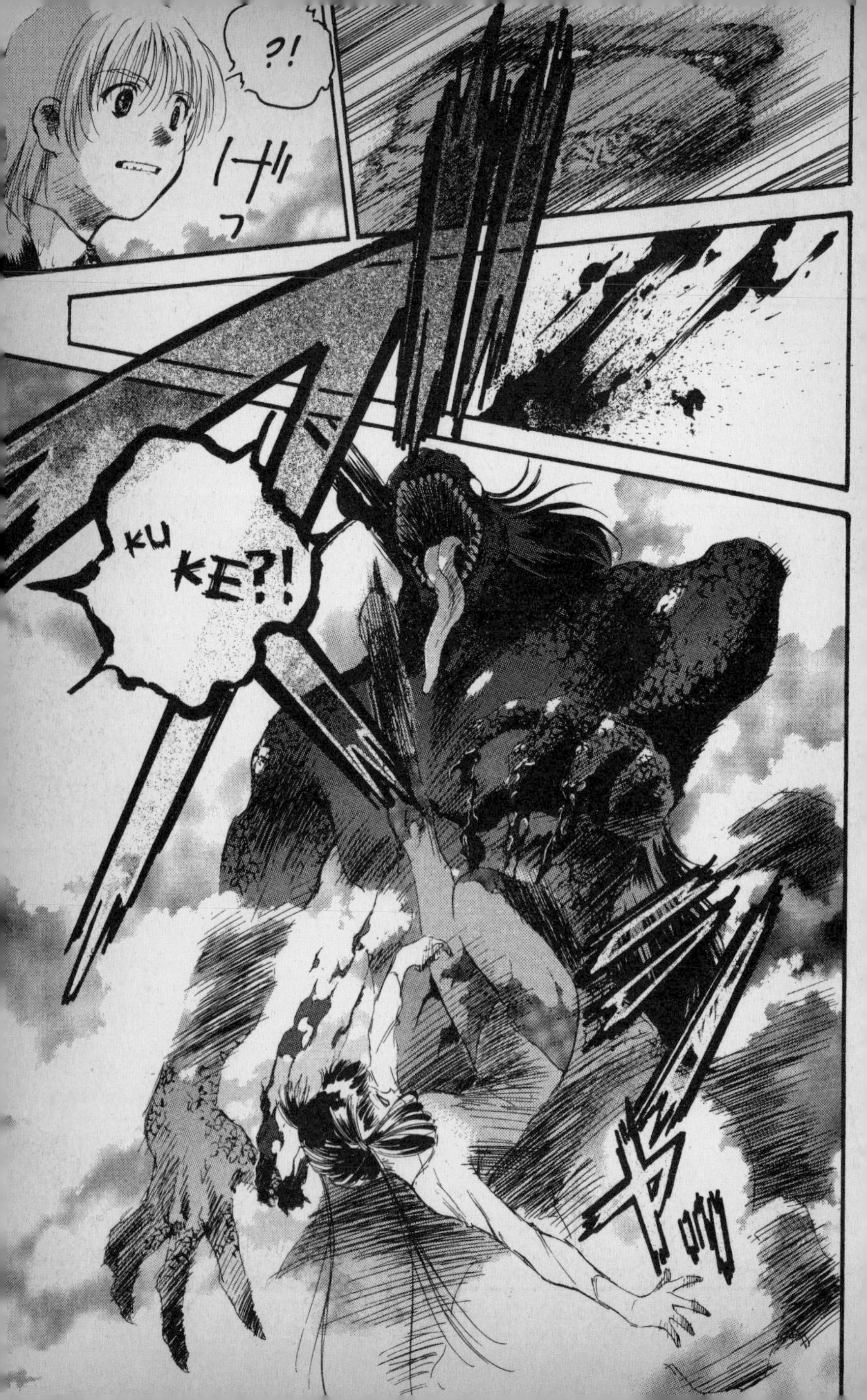
?!
げッ
KU KE?!

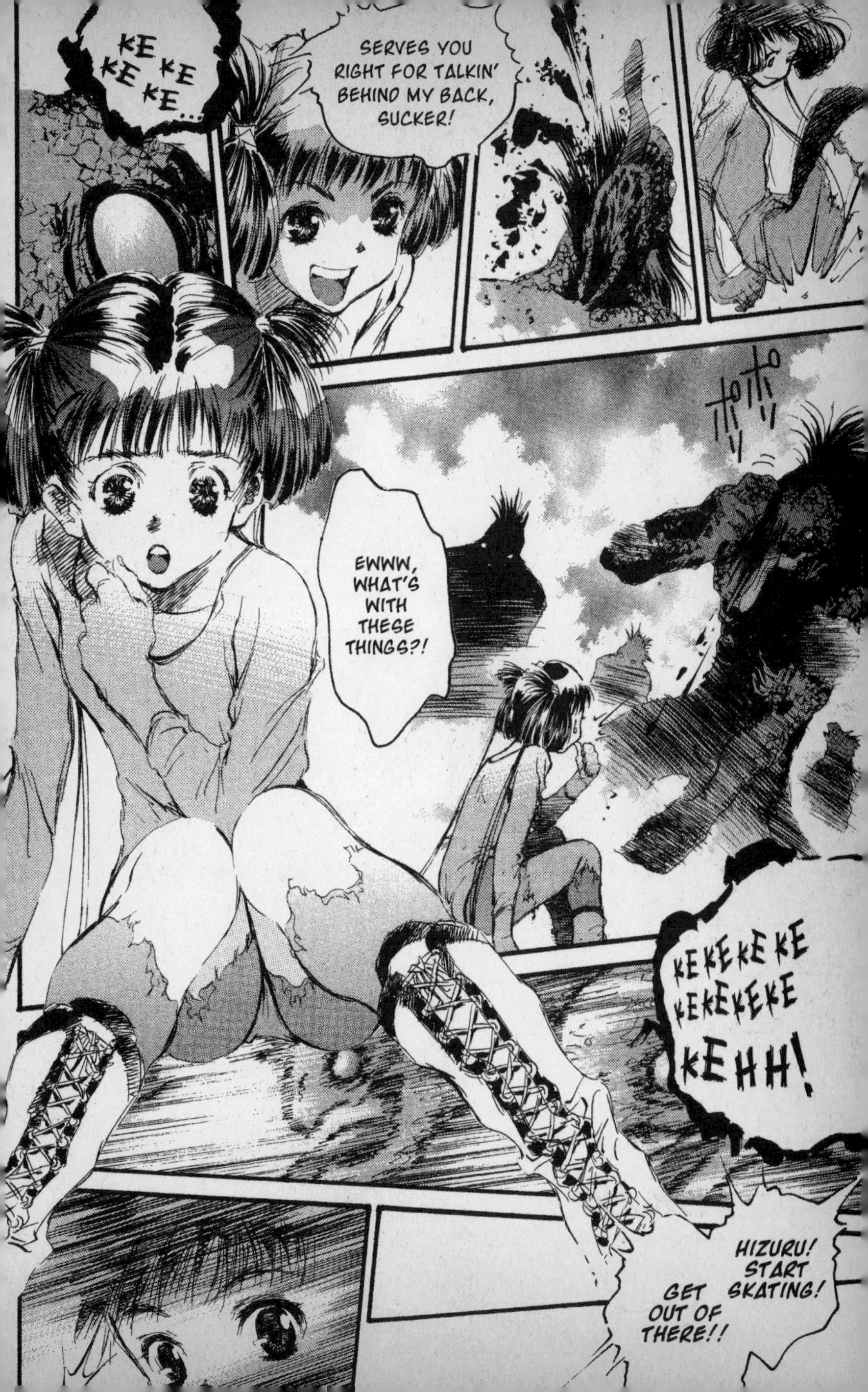
SERVES YOU RIGHT FOR TALKIN' BEHIND MY BACK, SUCKER!
KE KE KE KE KE...
EWWW, WHAT'S WITH THESE THINGS?!
KEKEKEKEKE KEKEKEKEKE KEHH!
HIZURU! START SKATING!
GET OUT OF THERE!!

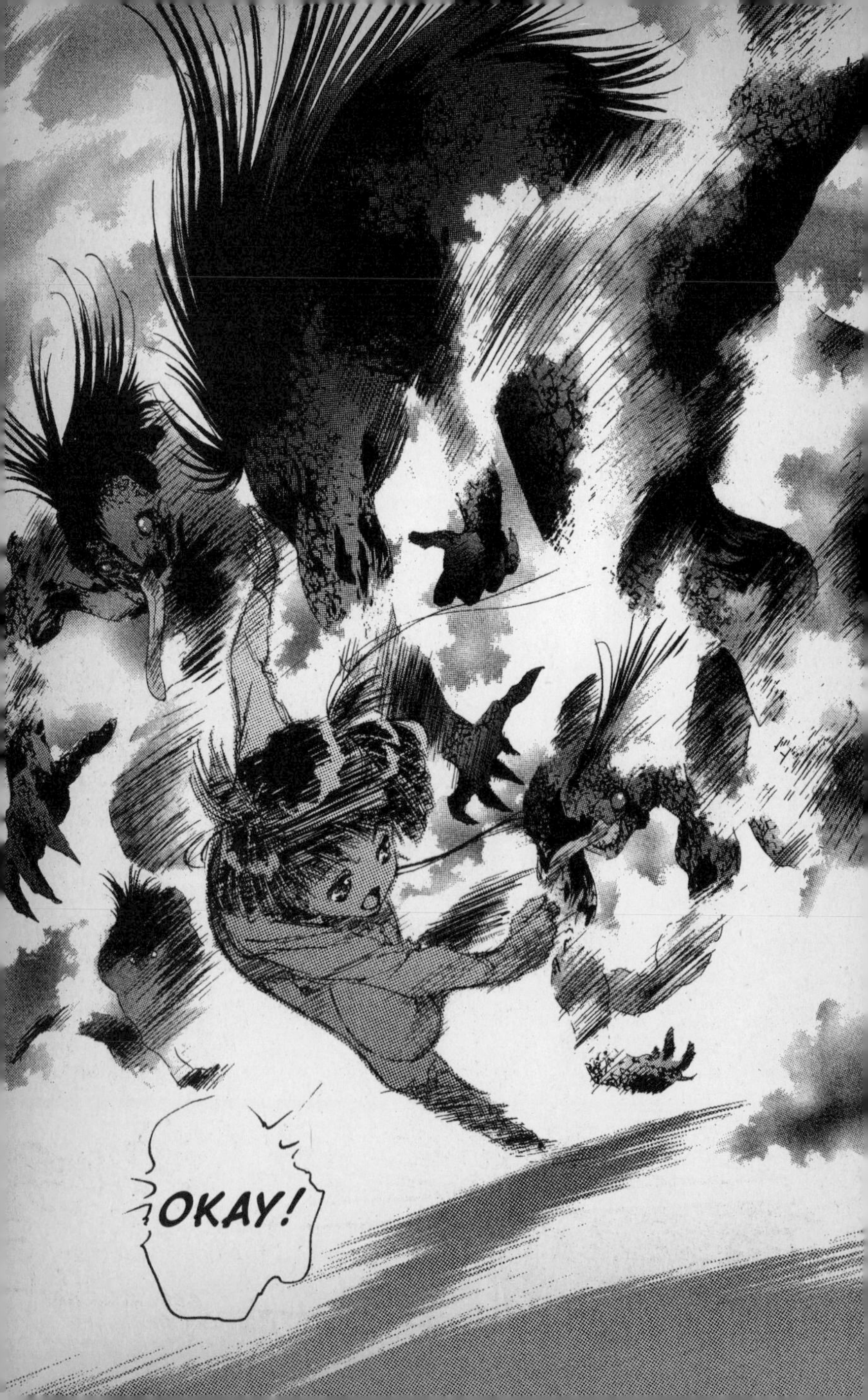
OKAY!

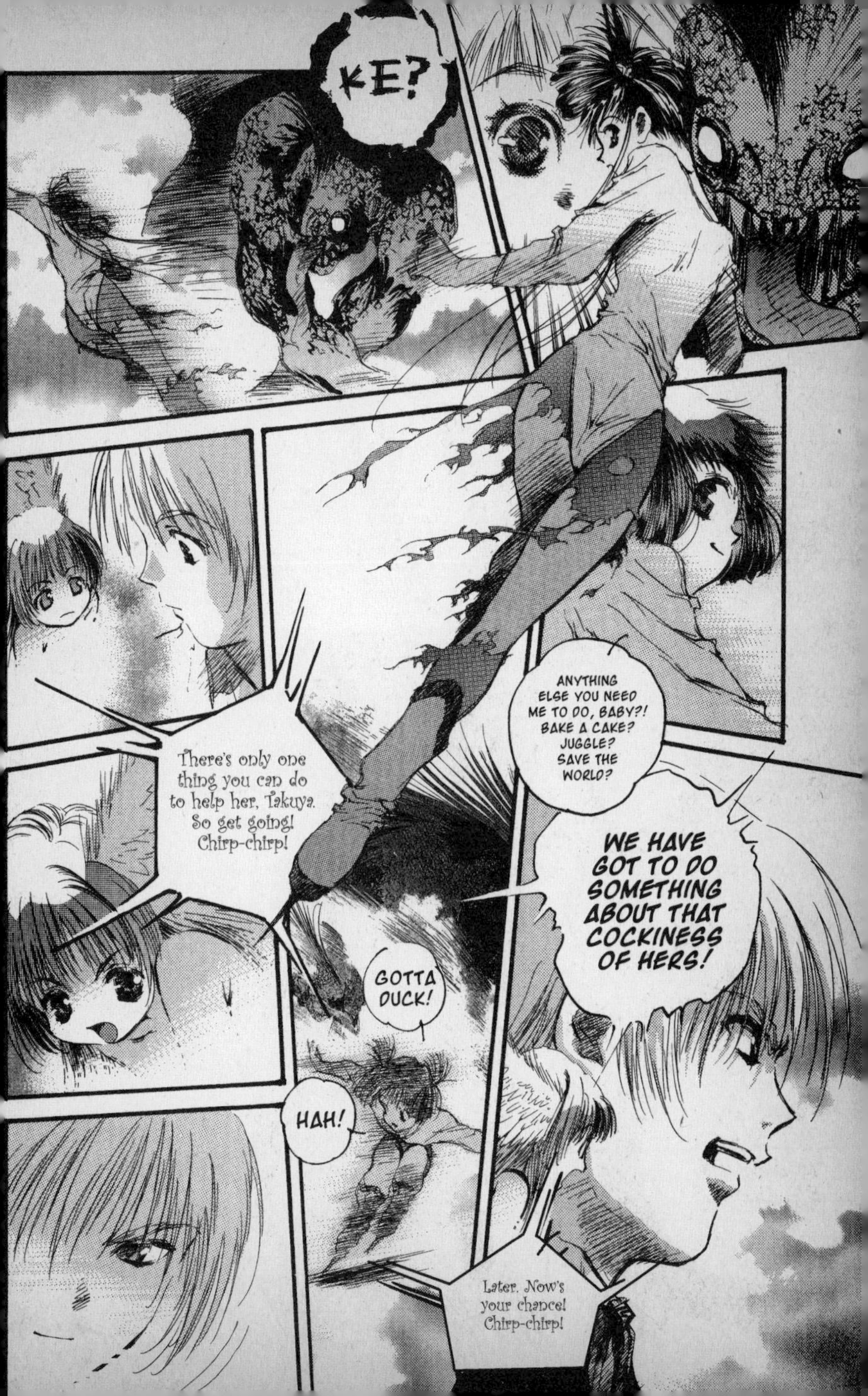
KE?
ANYTHING ELSE YOU NEED ME TO DO, BABY?! BAKE A CAKE? JUGGLE? SAVE THE WORLD?
There's only one thing you can do to help her, Takuya. So get going! Chirp-chirp!
WE HAVE GOT TO DO SOMETHING ABOUT THAT COCKINESS OF HERS!
GOTTA DUCK!
HAH!
Later. Now's your chance! Chirp-chirp!

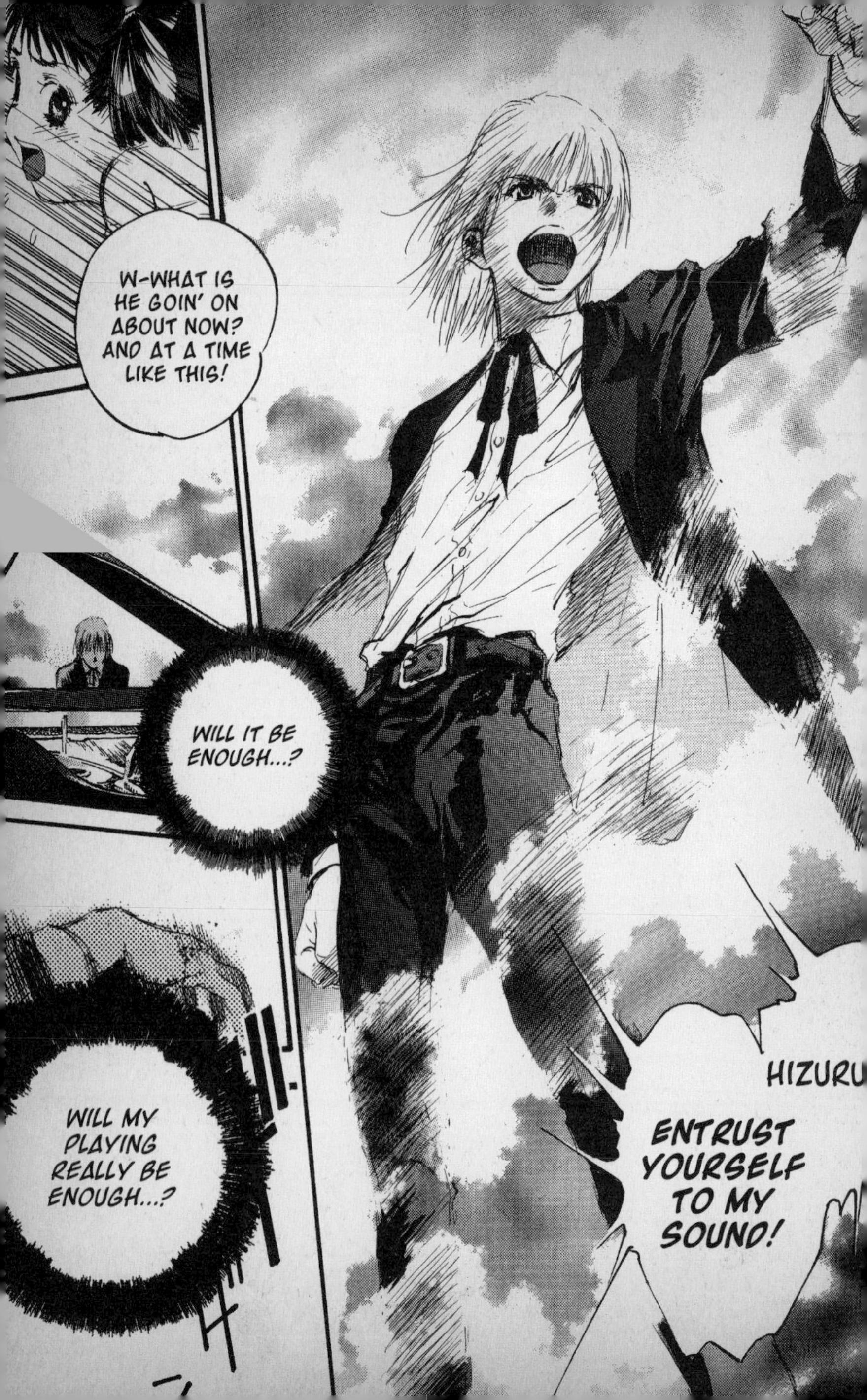
HIZURU
ENTRUST YOURSELF TO MY SOUND!
W-WHAT IS HE GOIN' ON ABOUT NOW? AND AT A TIME LIKE THIS!
WILL IT BE ENOUGH...?
WILL MY PLAYING REALLY BE ENOUGH...?

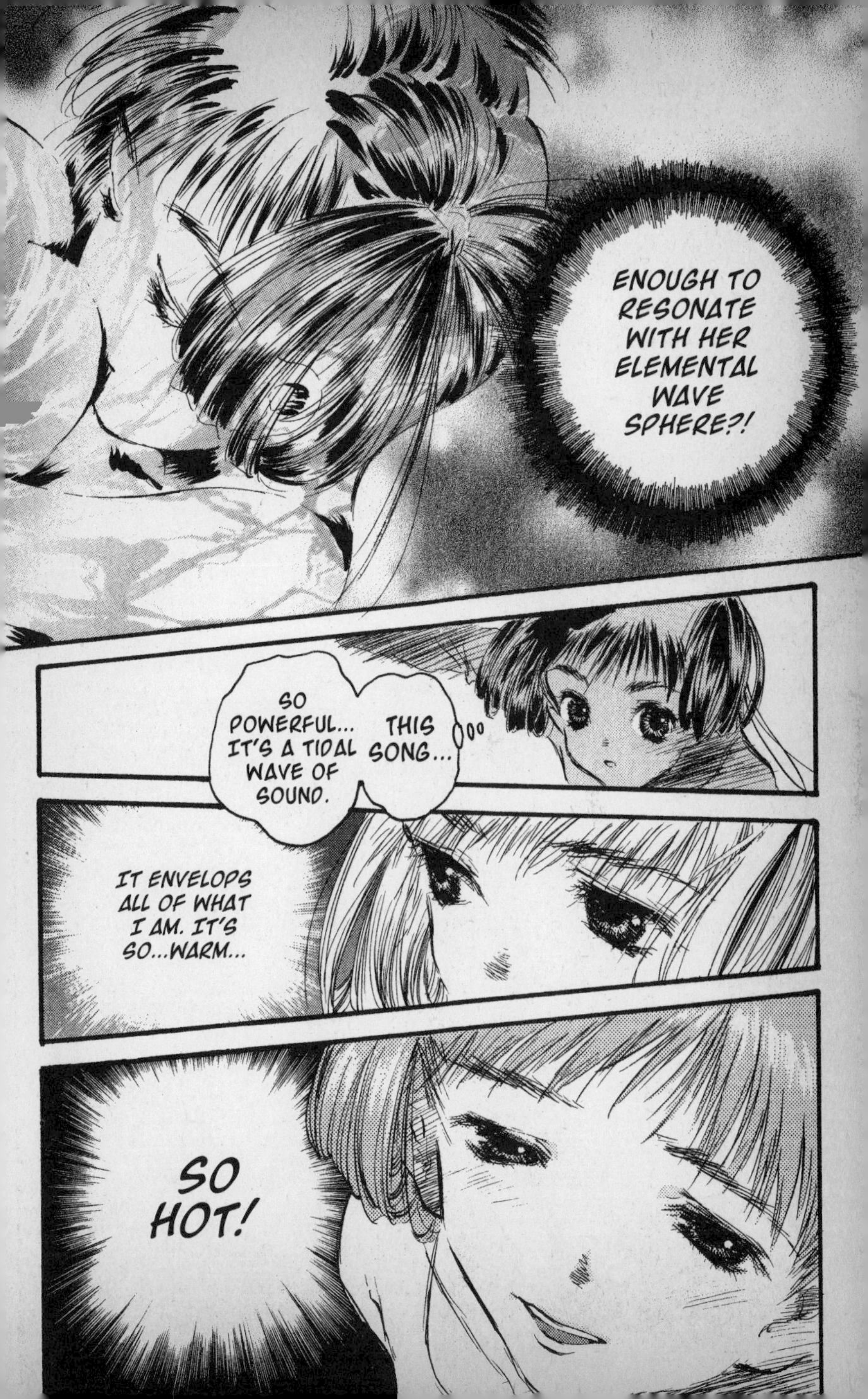
ENOUGH TO RESONATE WITH HER ELEMENTAL WAVE SPHERE?!
THIS SONG...
SO POWERFUL... IT'S A TIDAL WAVE OF SOUND.
IT ENVELOPS ALL OF WHAT I AM. IT'S SO...WARM...
SO HOT!

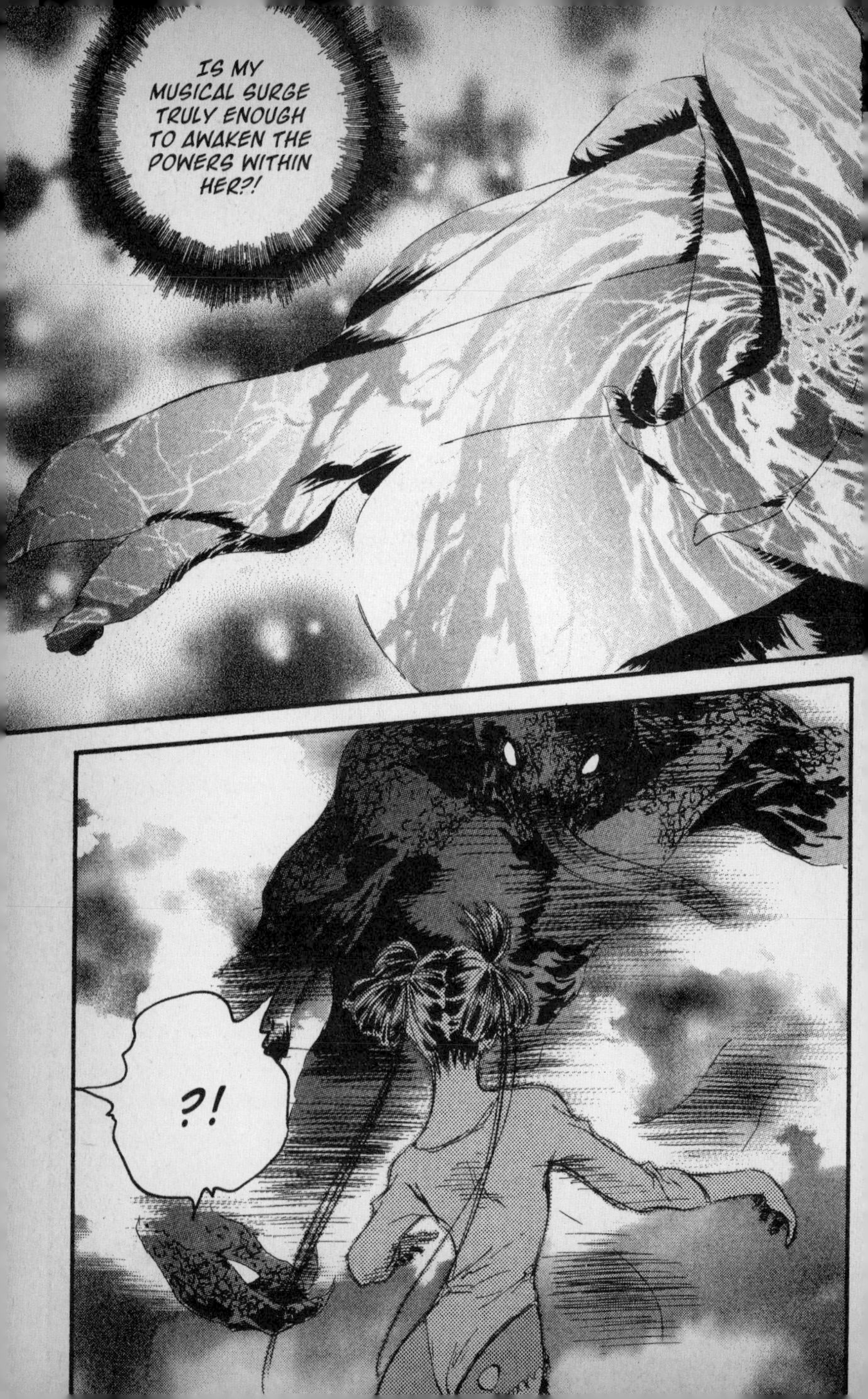
IS MY MUSICAL SURGE TRULY ENOUGH TO AWAKEN THE POWERS WITHIN HER?!
?!

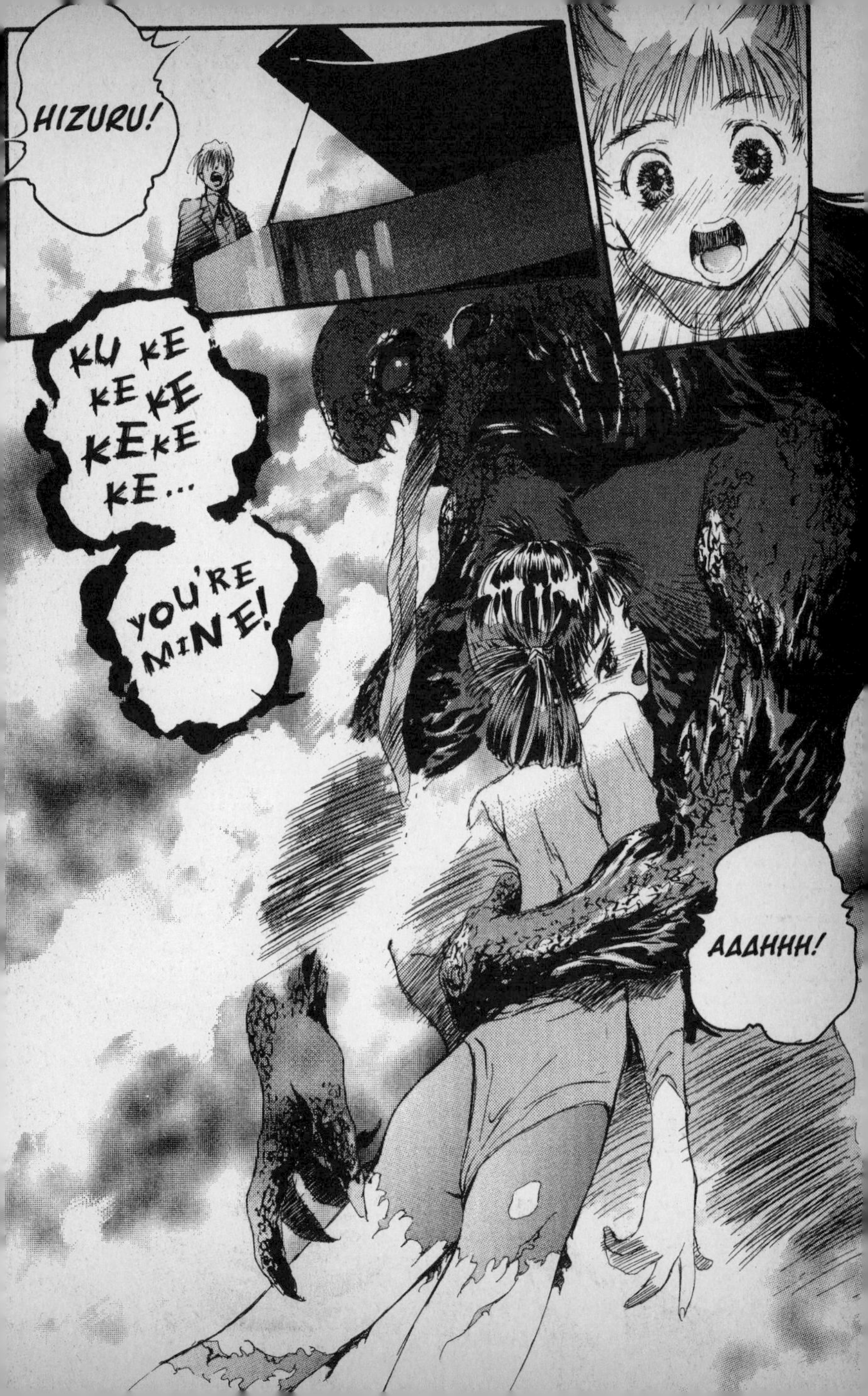
HIZURU!
KU KE KE KE KE KE KE...
YOU'RE MINE!
AAAHHH!

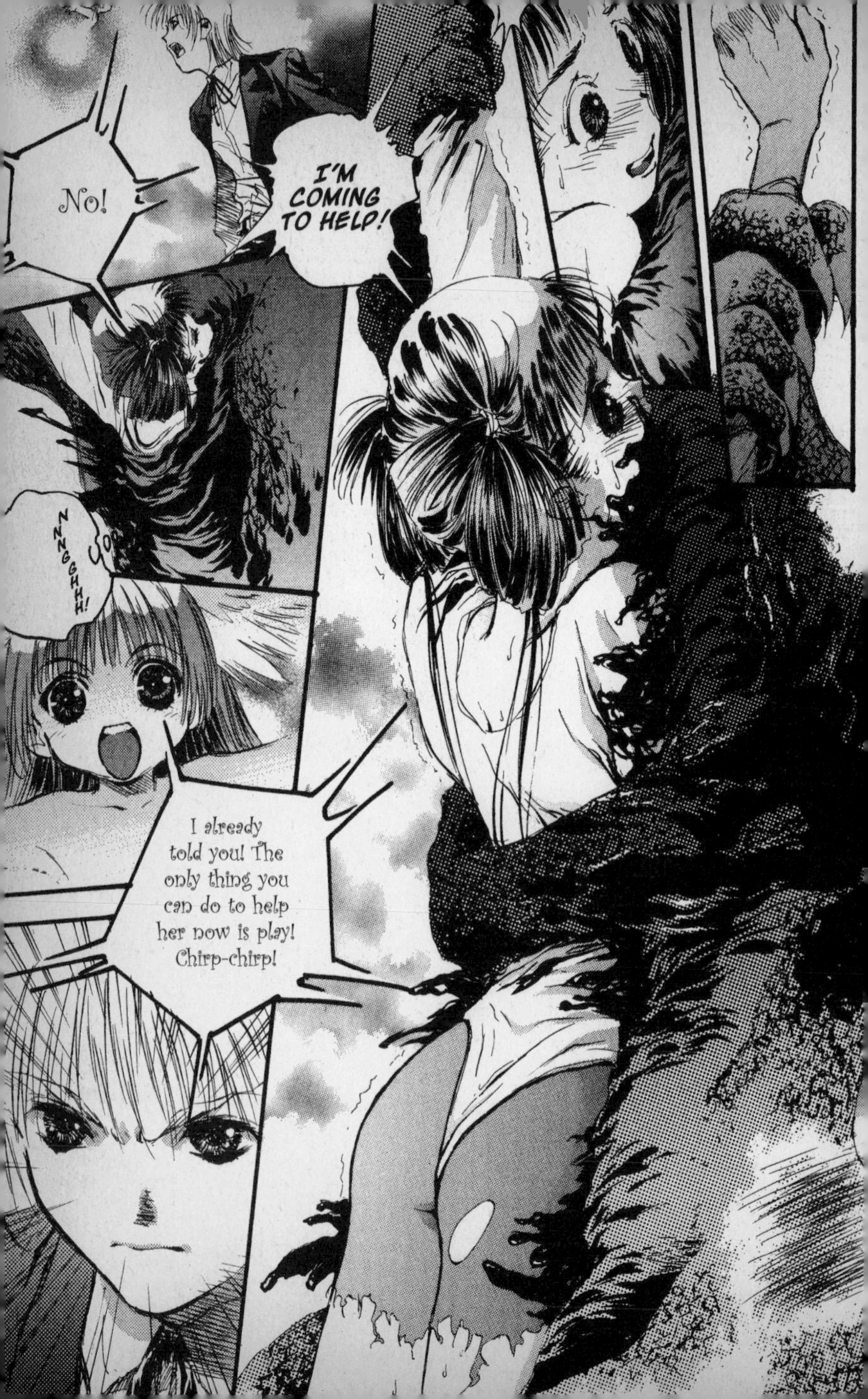
I'M COMING TO HELP!
No!
NNNGGHHH!
I already told you! The only thing you can do to help her now is play! Chirp-chirp!

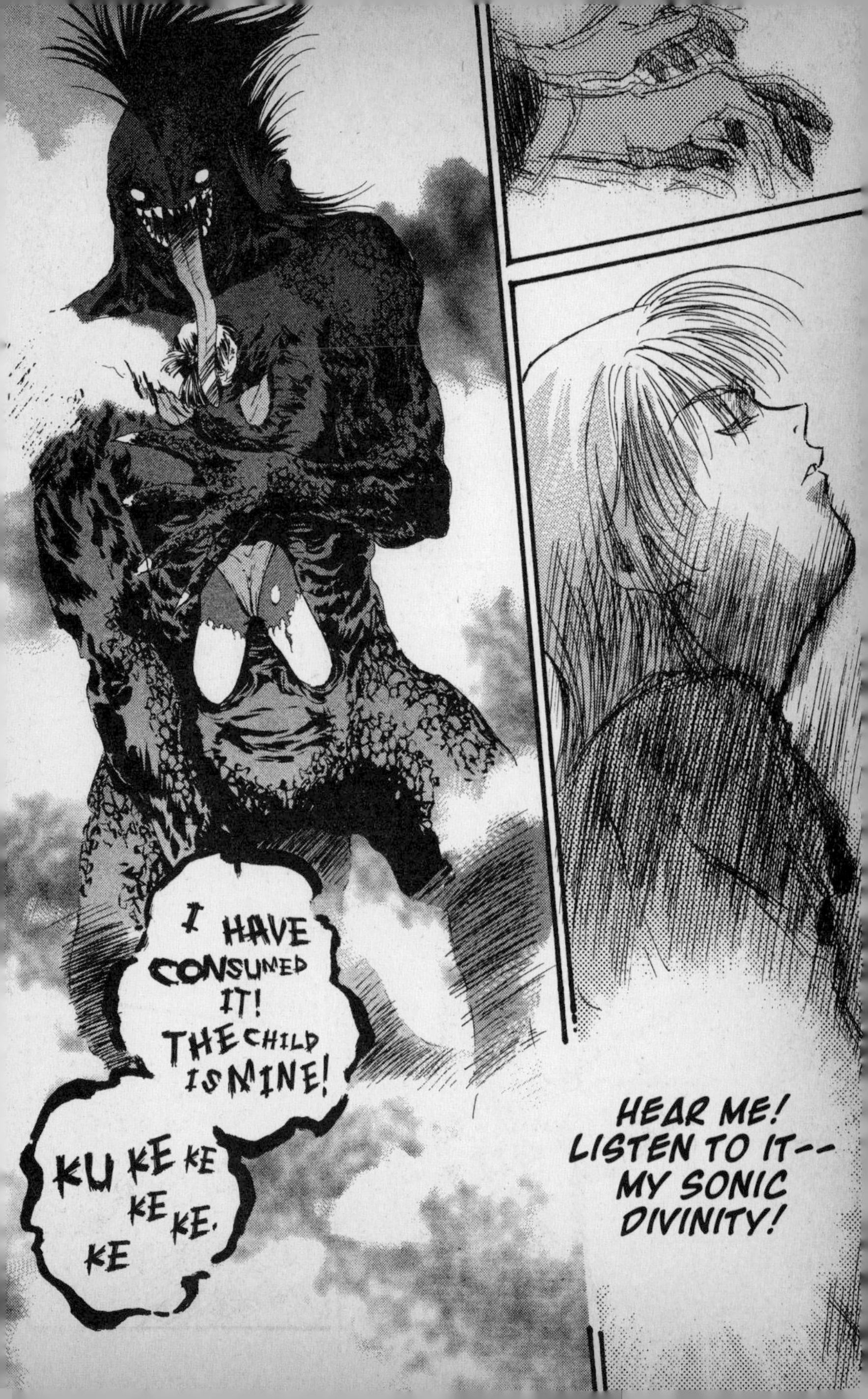
HEAR ME! LISTEN TO IT-- MY SONIC DIVINITY!
I HAVE CONSUMED IT! THE CHILD IS MINE!
KU KE KE KE KE. KE

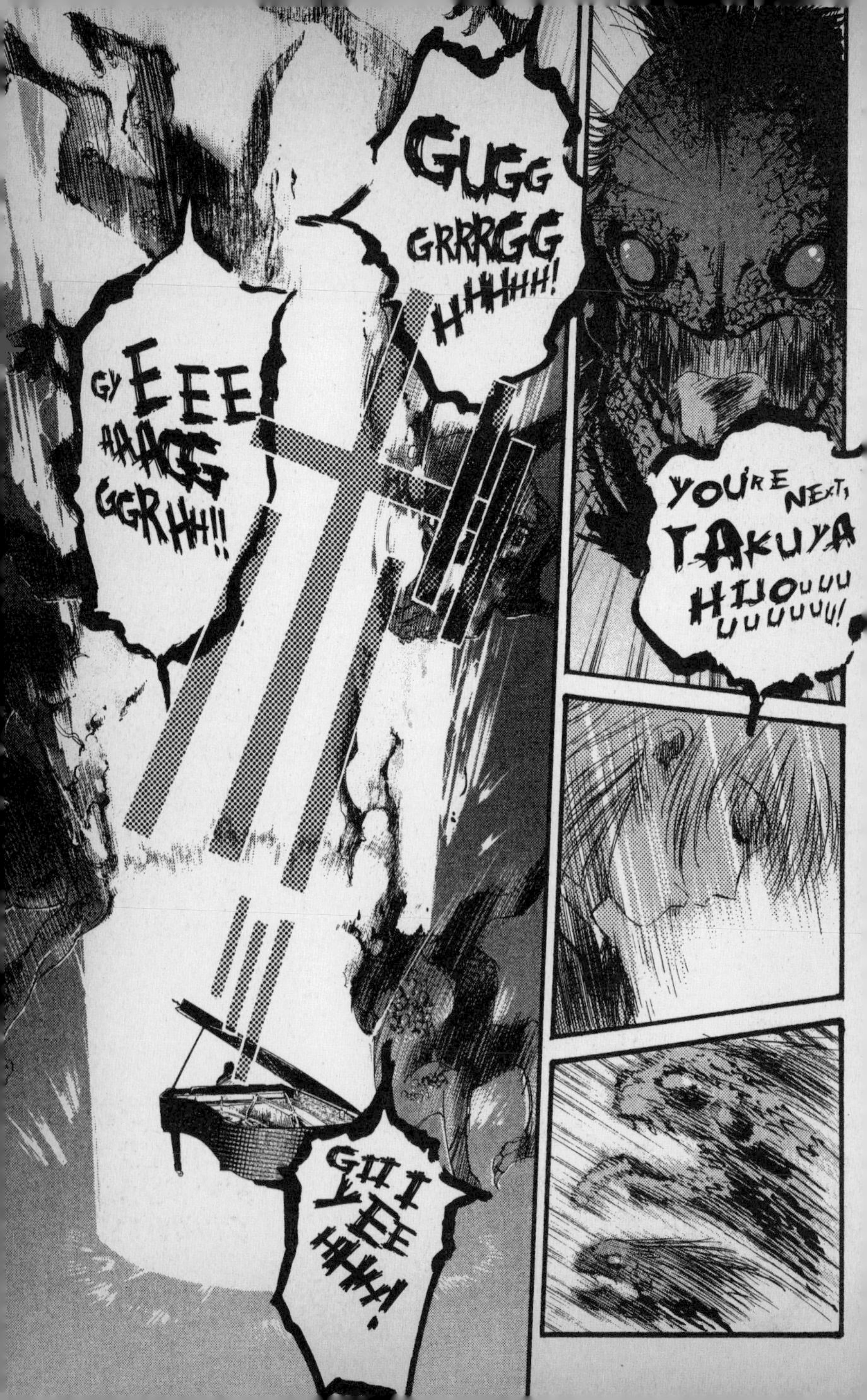
YOU'RE NEXT, TAKUYA HIJOUUUUUUUUU!
GUGG GRRRGG HHHHHH!
GYEEE AAAGG GGRHH!!
GUI YEE HHHH!

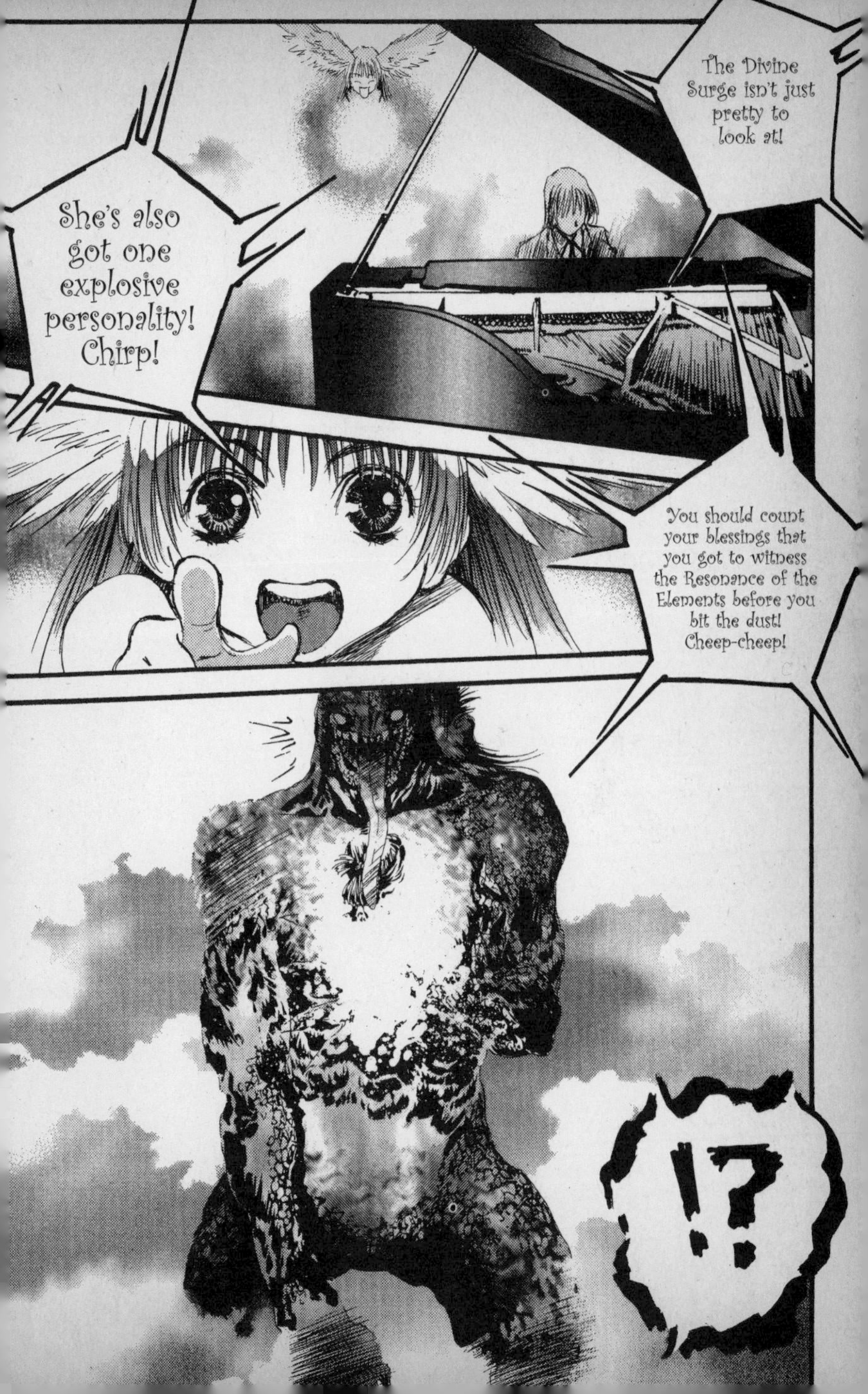
The Divine Surge isn't just pretty to look at!
She's also got one explosive personality! Chirp!
You should count your blessings that you got to witness the Resonance of the Elements before you bit the dust! Cheep-cheep!
!?

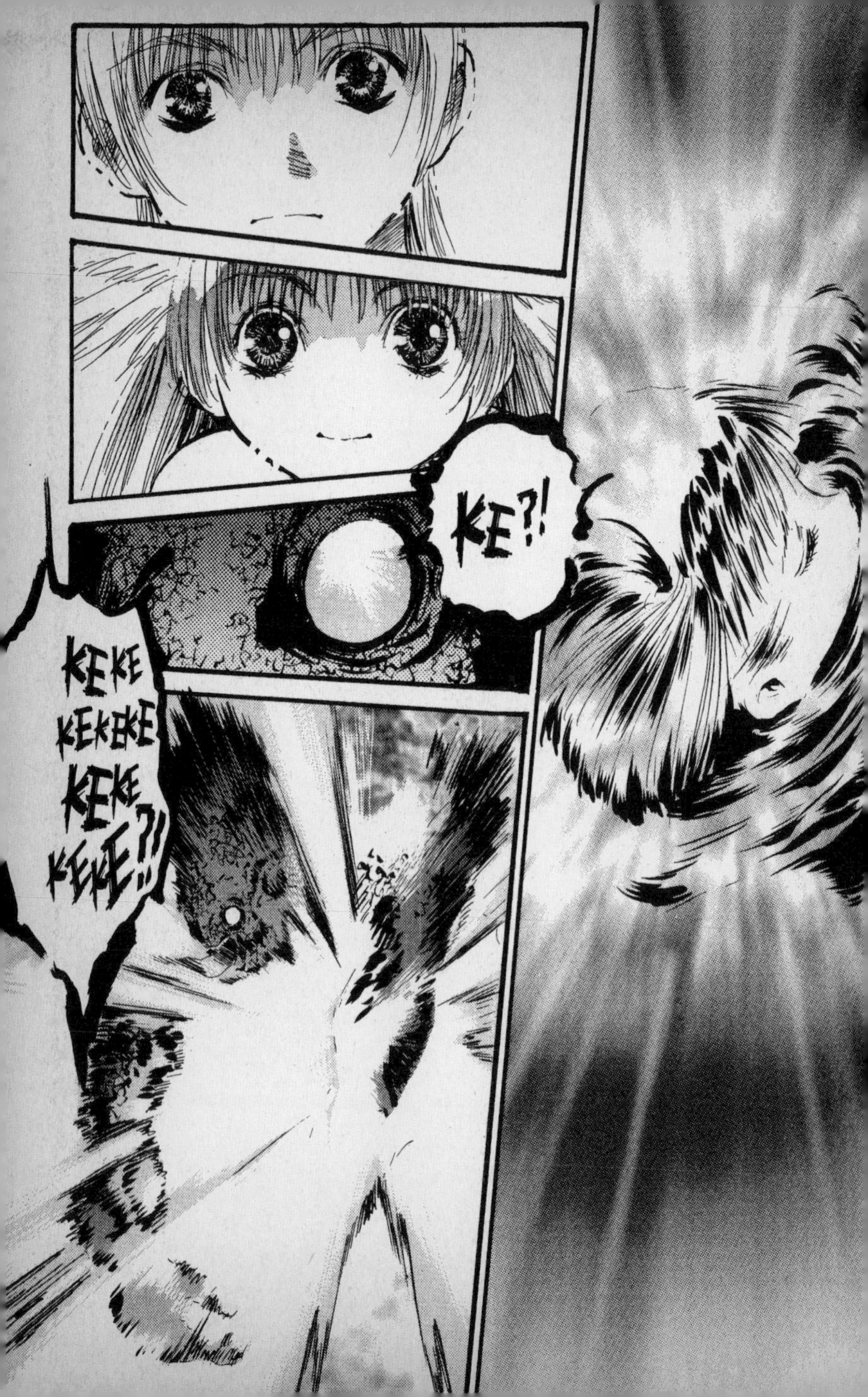
KE?!
KEKE KEKEKE KEKE KEKE?!!

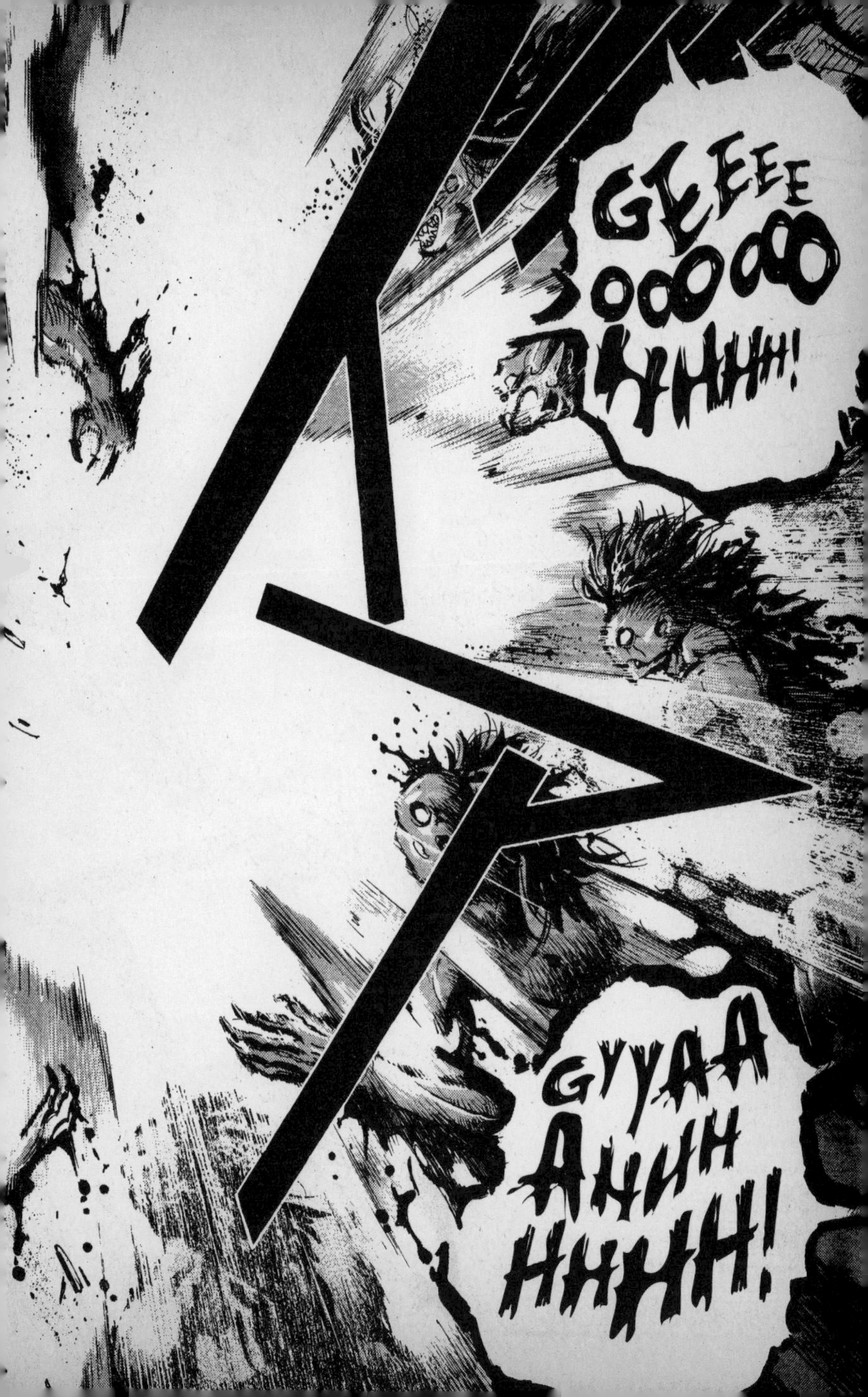
GEEEE
OOOOOO
AHHHH!
GIYAA
AHHH
HHHH!

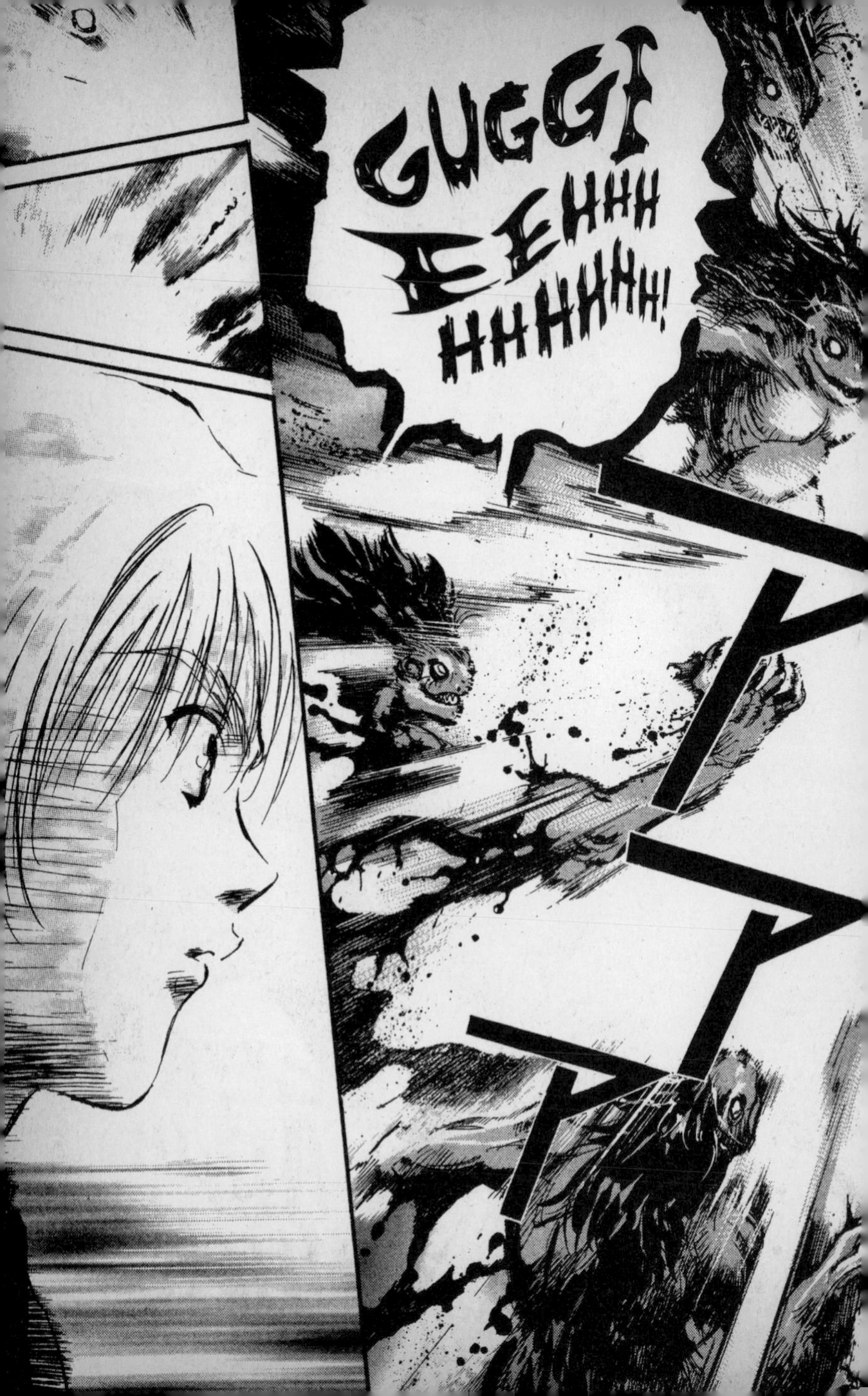
GUGGIEEHHHHHHHHH!

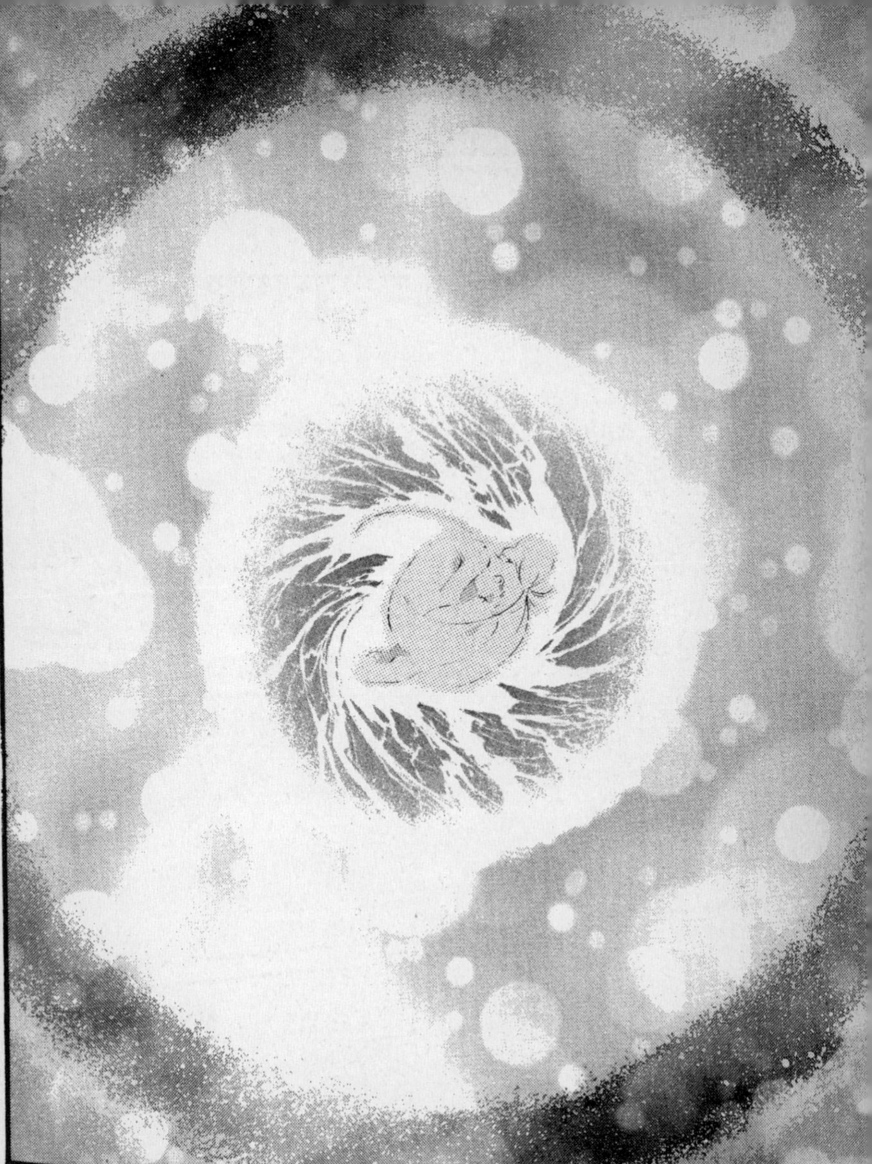
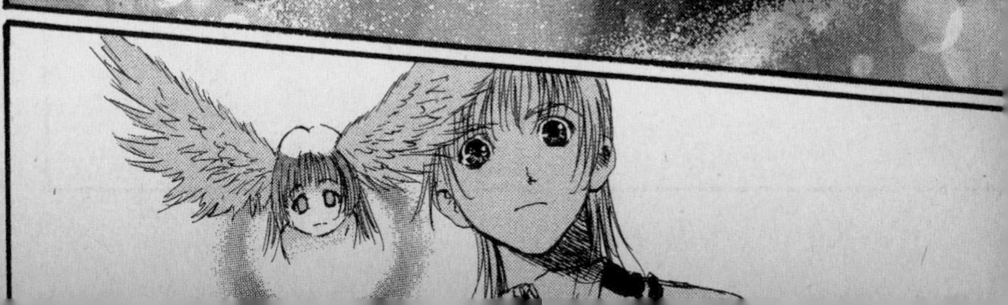

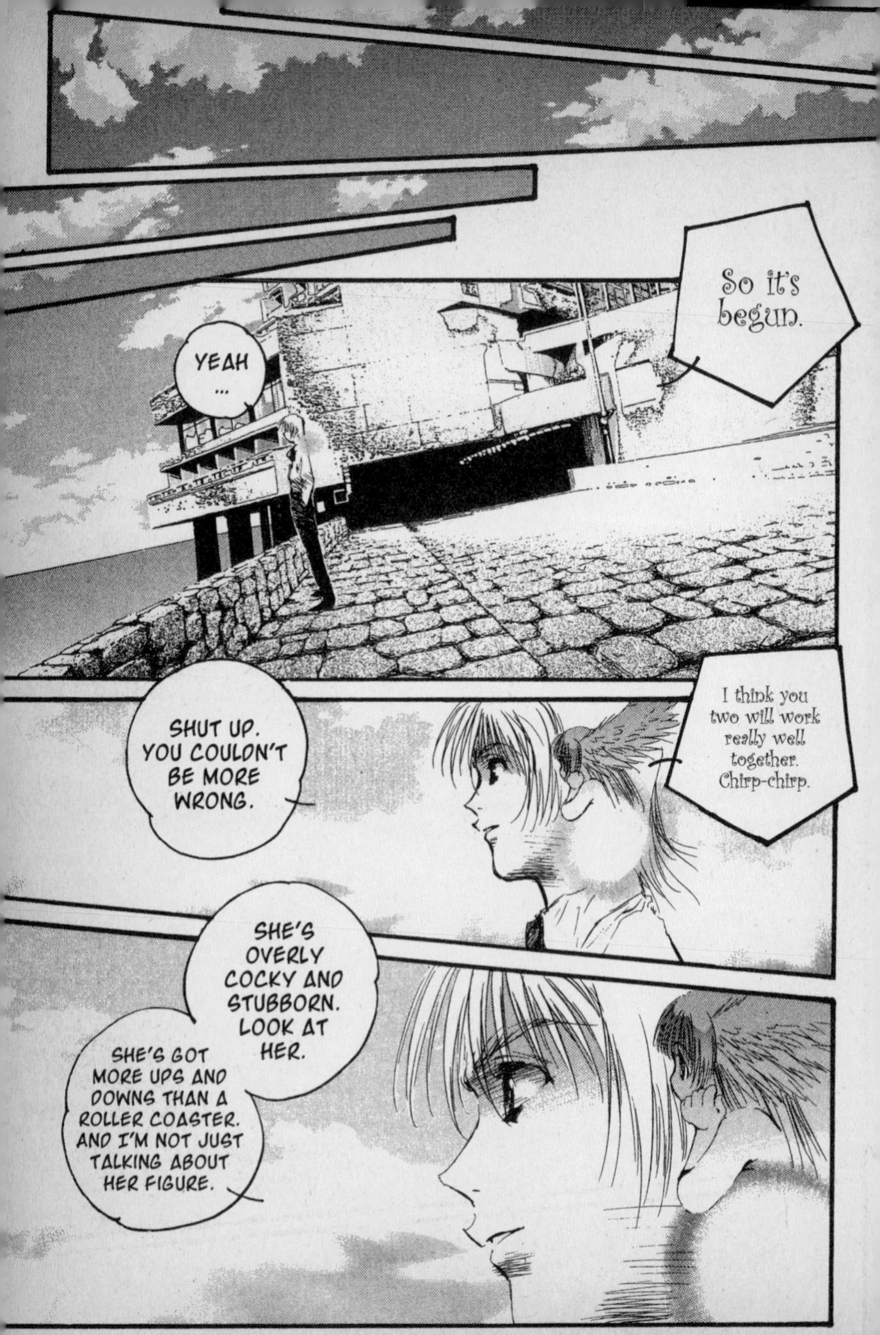
So it's begun.
YEAH ...
I think you two will work really well together. Chirp-chirp.
SHUT UP. YOU COULDN'T BE MORE WRONG.
SHE'S OVERLY COCKY AND STUBBORN. LOOK AT HER.
SHE'S GOT MORE UPS AND DOWNS THAN A ROLLER COASTER. AND I'M NOT JUST TALKING ABOUT HER FIGURE.

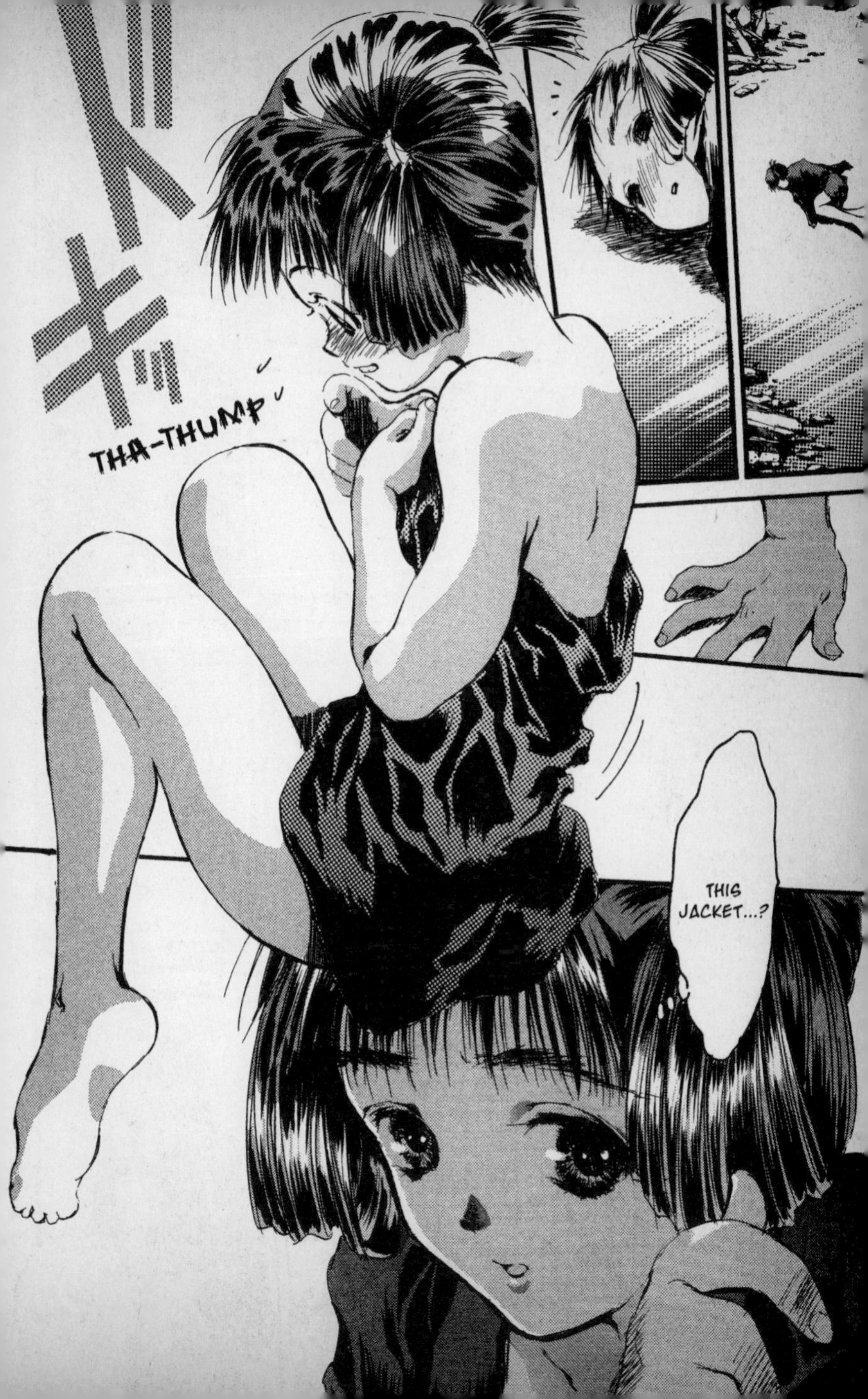
ドキッ
THA-THUMP
THIS JACKET...?

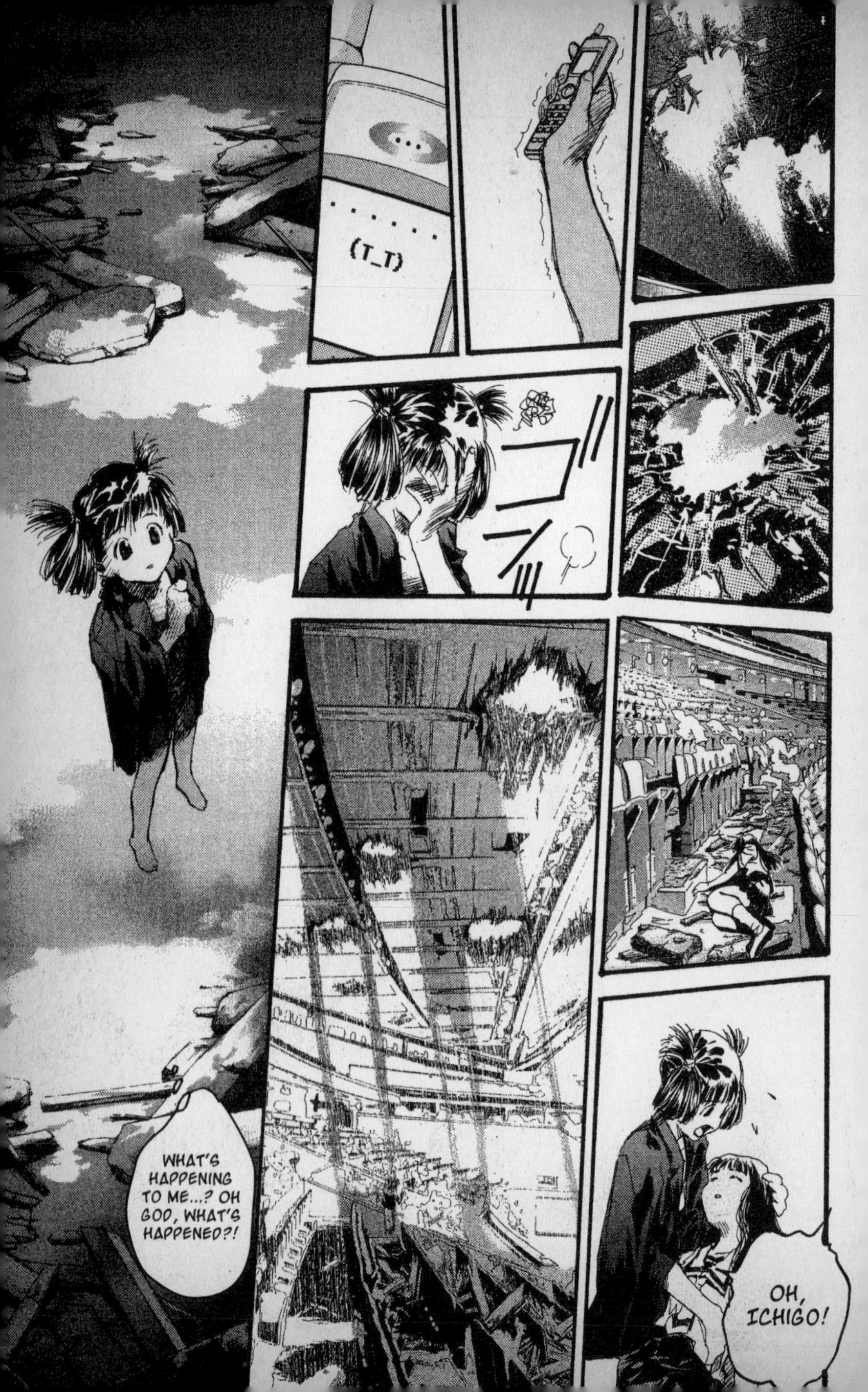
...
......
(T_T)
OH, ICHIGO!
WHAT'S HAPPENING TO ME...? OH GOD, WHAT'S HAPPENED?!

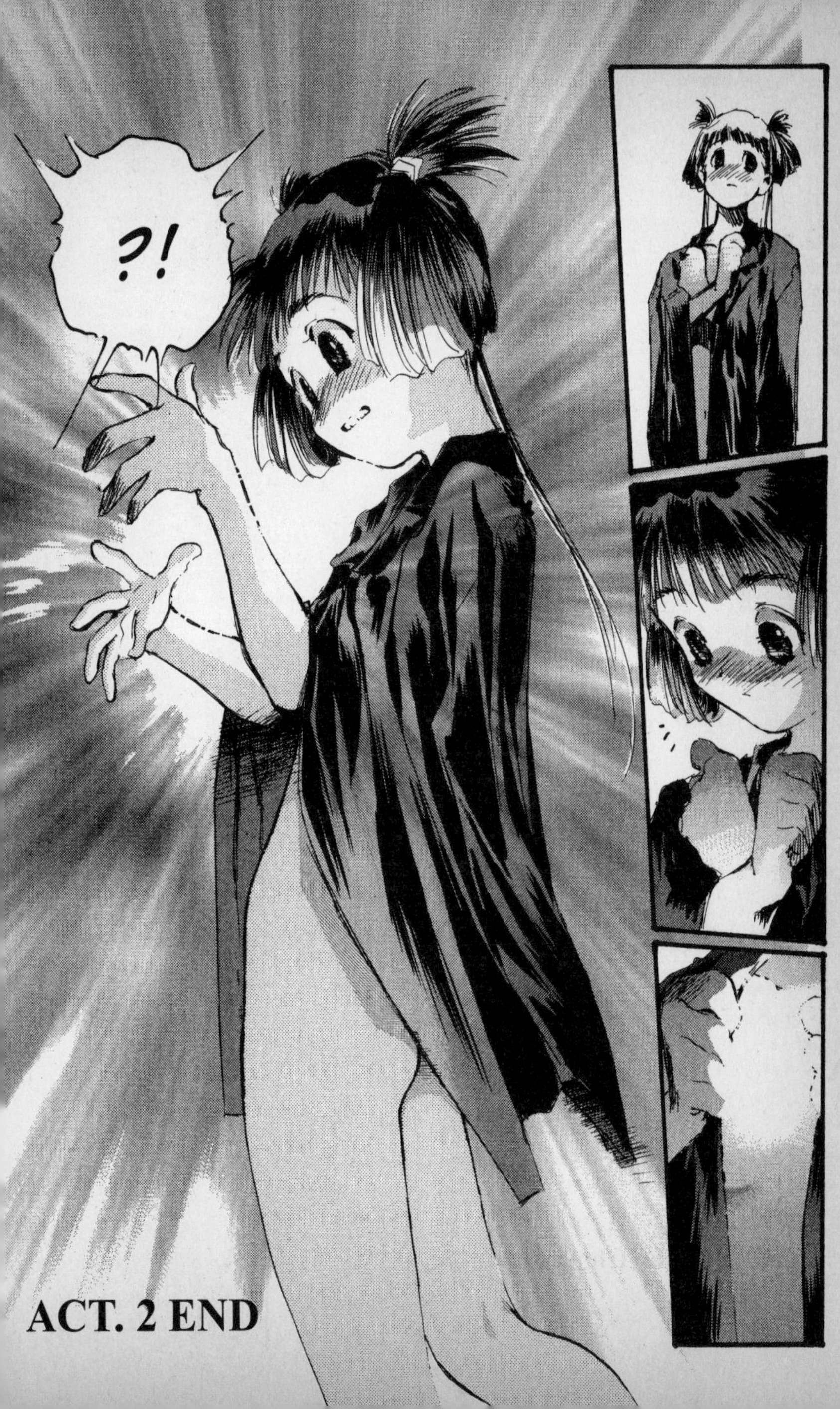
?!
ACT. 2 END

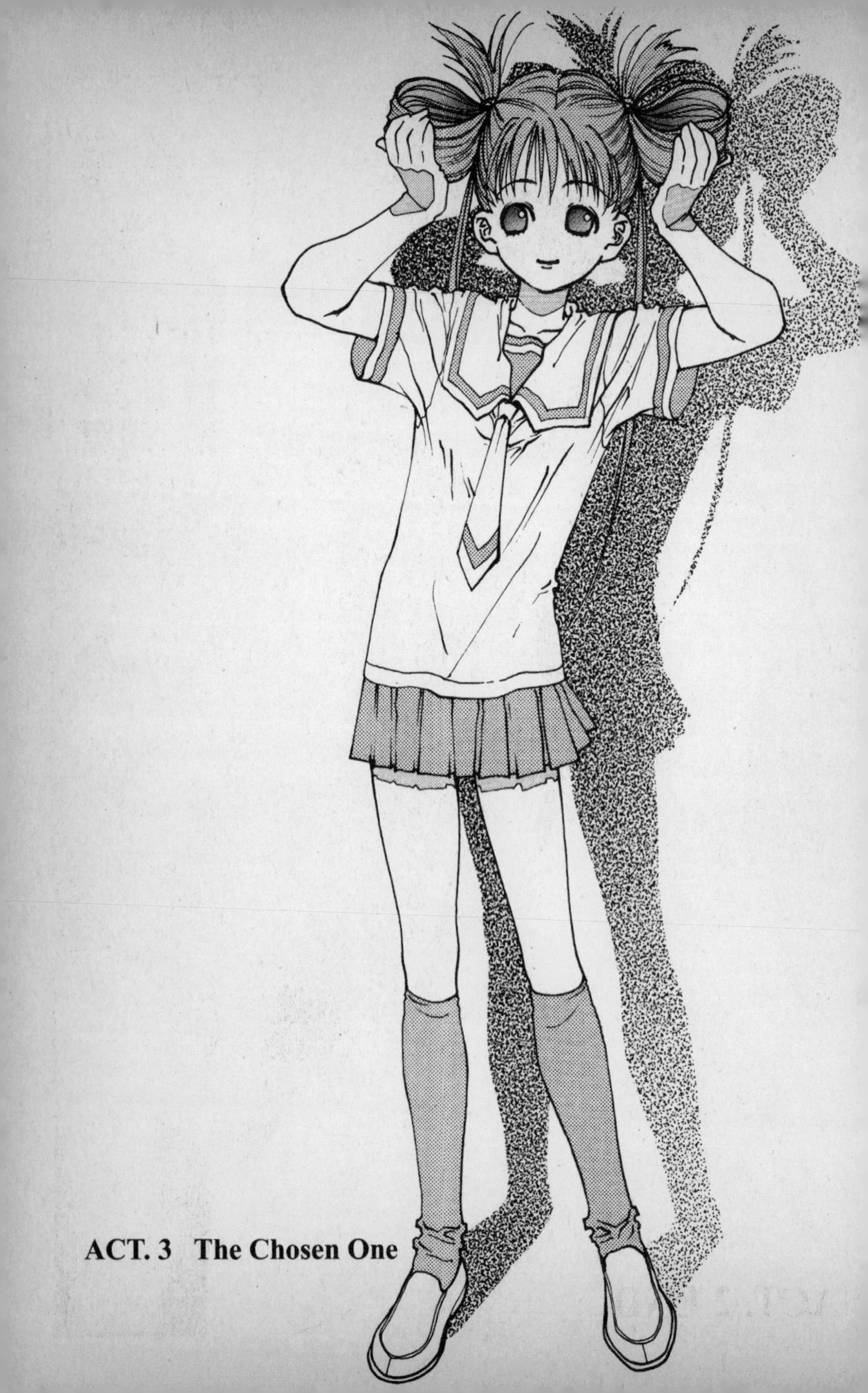

ACT. 3 The Chosen One

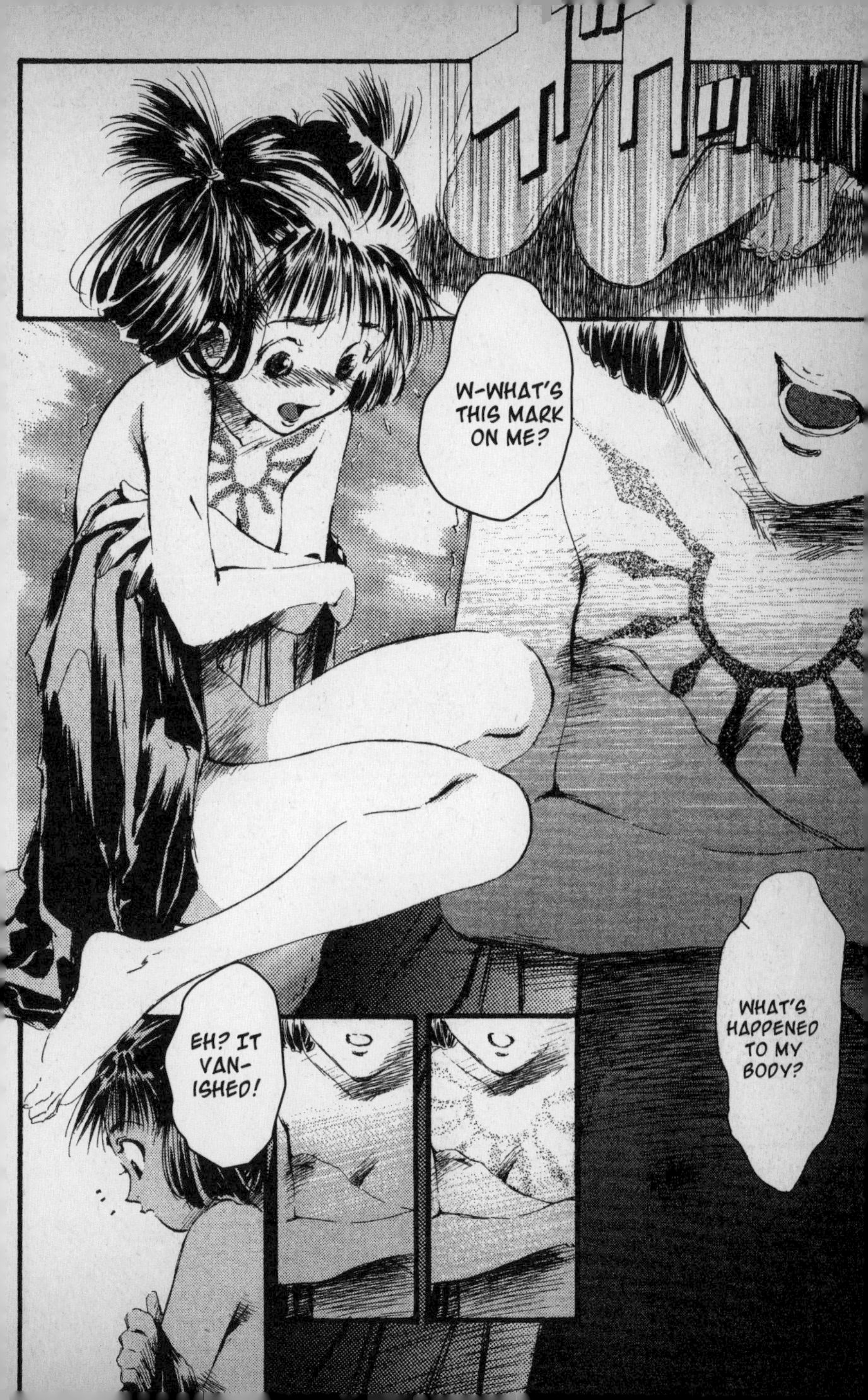
W-WHAT'S THIS MARK ON ME?
WHAT'S HAPPENED TO MY BODY?
EH? IT VAN-ISHED!

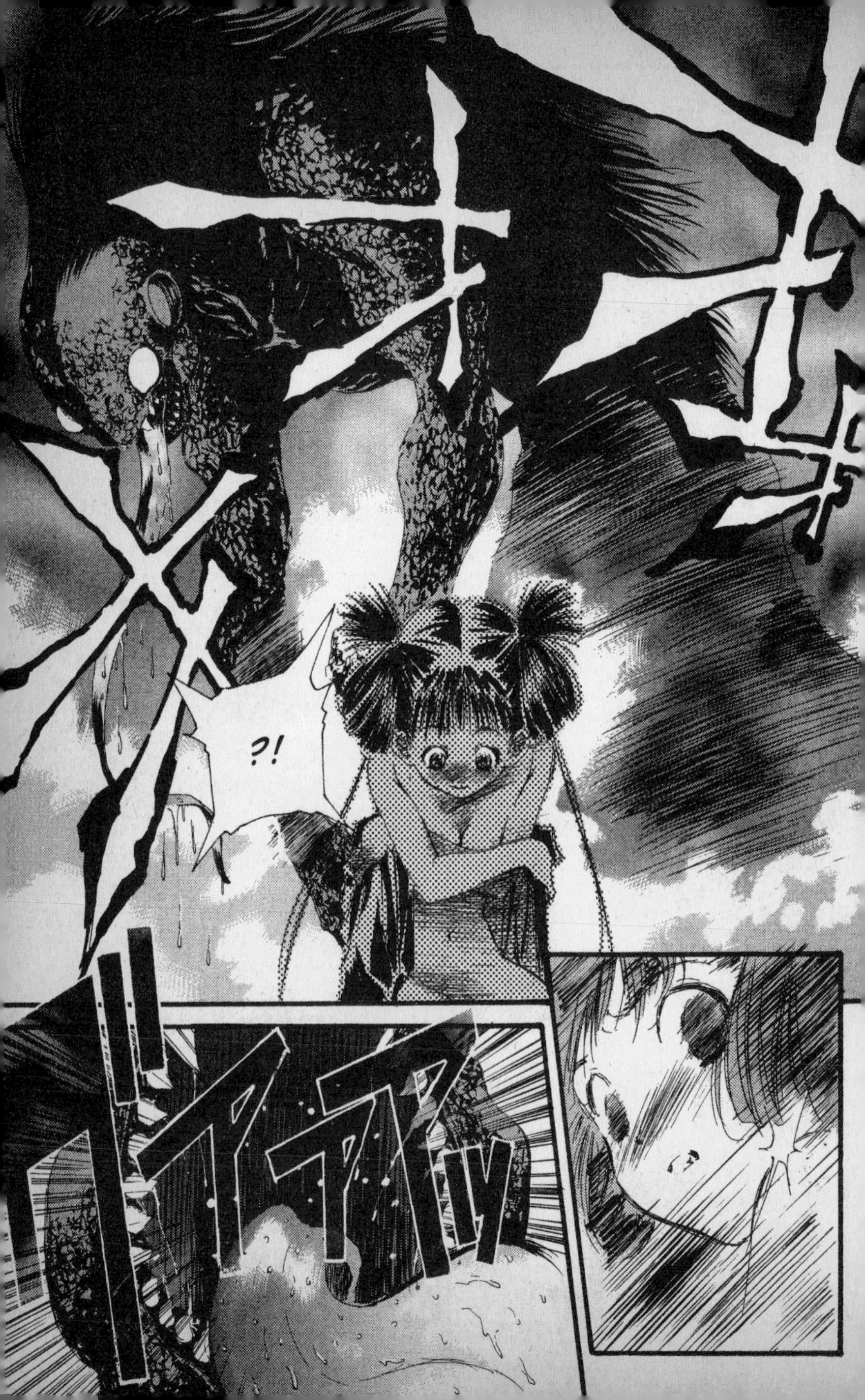
?!
ドアアアッ

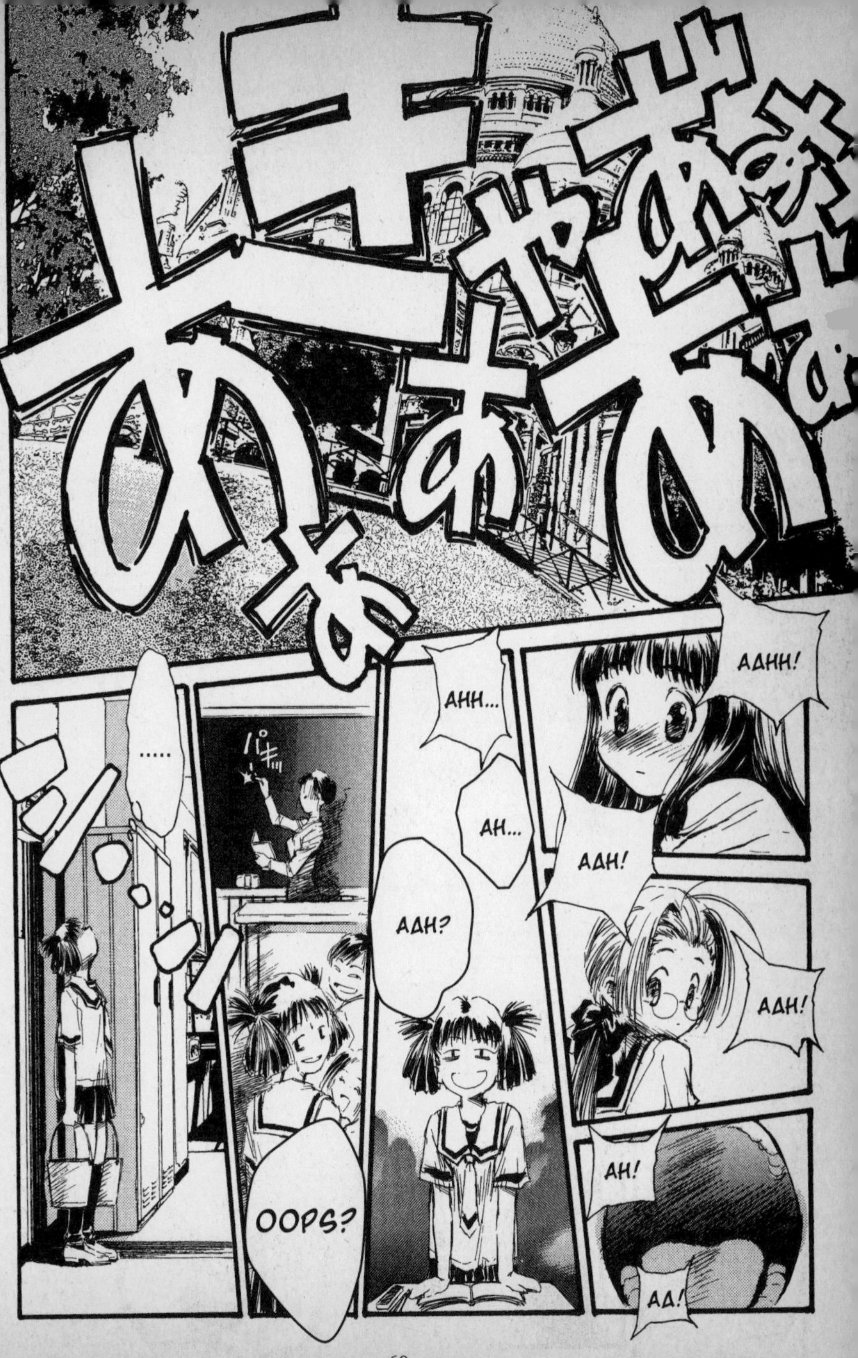
AAHH!
AAH!
AAH!
AH!
AA!
AHH...
AH...
AAH?
OOPS?
.....

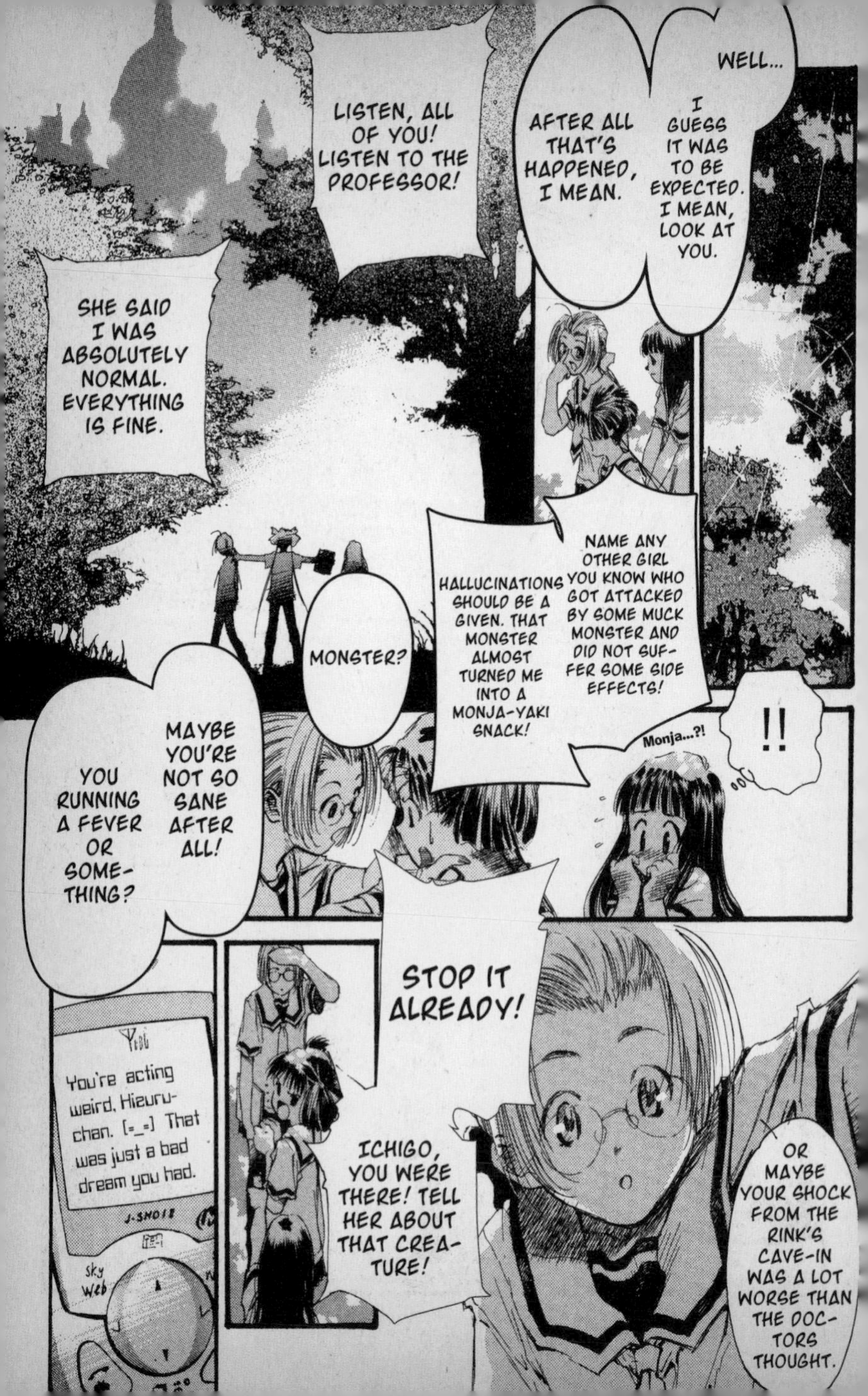
WELL...
I GUESS IT WAS TO BE EXPECTED. I MEAN, LOOK AT YOU.
AFTER ALL THAT'S HAPPENED, I MEAN.
LISTEN, ALL OF YOU! LISTEN TO THE PROFESSOR!
SHE SAID I WAS ABSOLUTELY NORMAL. EVERYTHING IS FINE.
NAME ANY OTHER GIRL YOU KNOW WHO GOT ATTACKED BY SOME MUCK MONSTER AND DID NOT SUF-FER SOME SIDE EFFECTS!
HALLUCINATIONS SHOULD BE A GIVEN. THAT MONSTER ALMOST TURNED ME INTO A MONJA-YAKI SNACK!
MONSTER?
!!
Monja...?!
MAYBE YOU'RE NOT SO SANE AFTER ALL!
YOU RUNNING A FEVER OR SOME-THING?
OR MAYBE YOUR SHOCK FROM THE RINK'S CAVE-IN WAS A LOT WORSE THAN THE DOC-TORS THOUGHT.
STOP IT ALREADY!
ICHIGO, YOU WERE THERE! TELL HER ABOUT THAT CREA-TURE!
You're acting weird, Hizuru-chan. [=_=] That was just a bad dream you had.
J-SH018
Sky Web

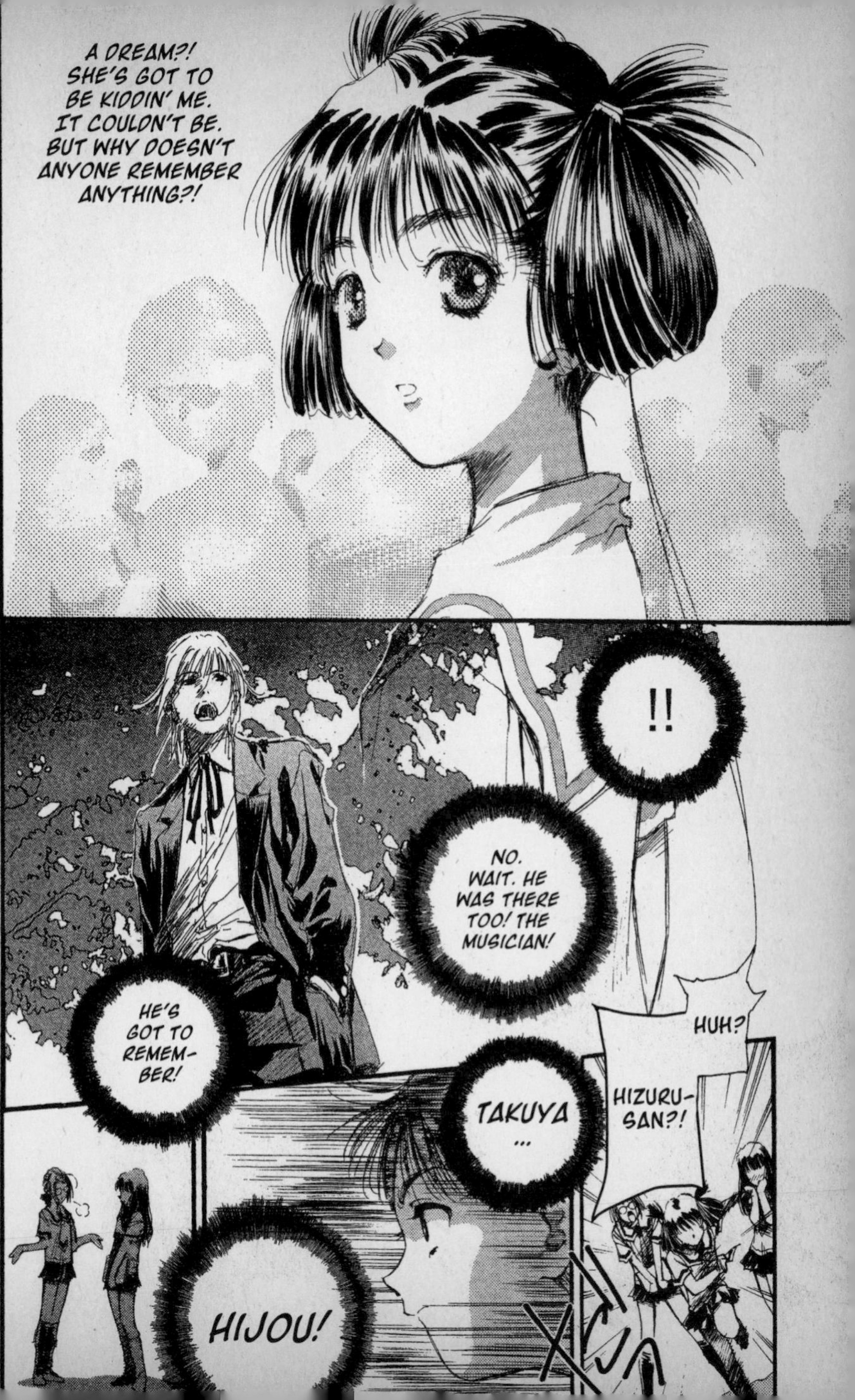
A DREAM?! SHE'S GOT TO BE KIDDIN' ME. IT COULDN'T BE. BUT WHY DOESN'T ANYONE REMEMBER ANYTHING?!
!!
NO. WAIT. HE WAS THERE TOO! THE MUSICIAN!
HE'S GOT TO REMEMBER!
HUH?
HIZURU-SAN?!
TAKUYA ...
HIJOU!

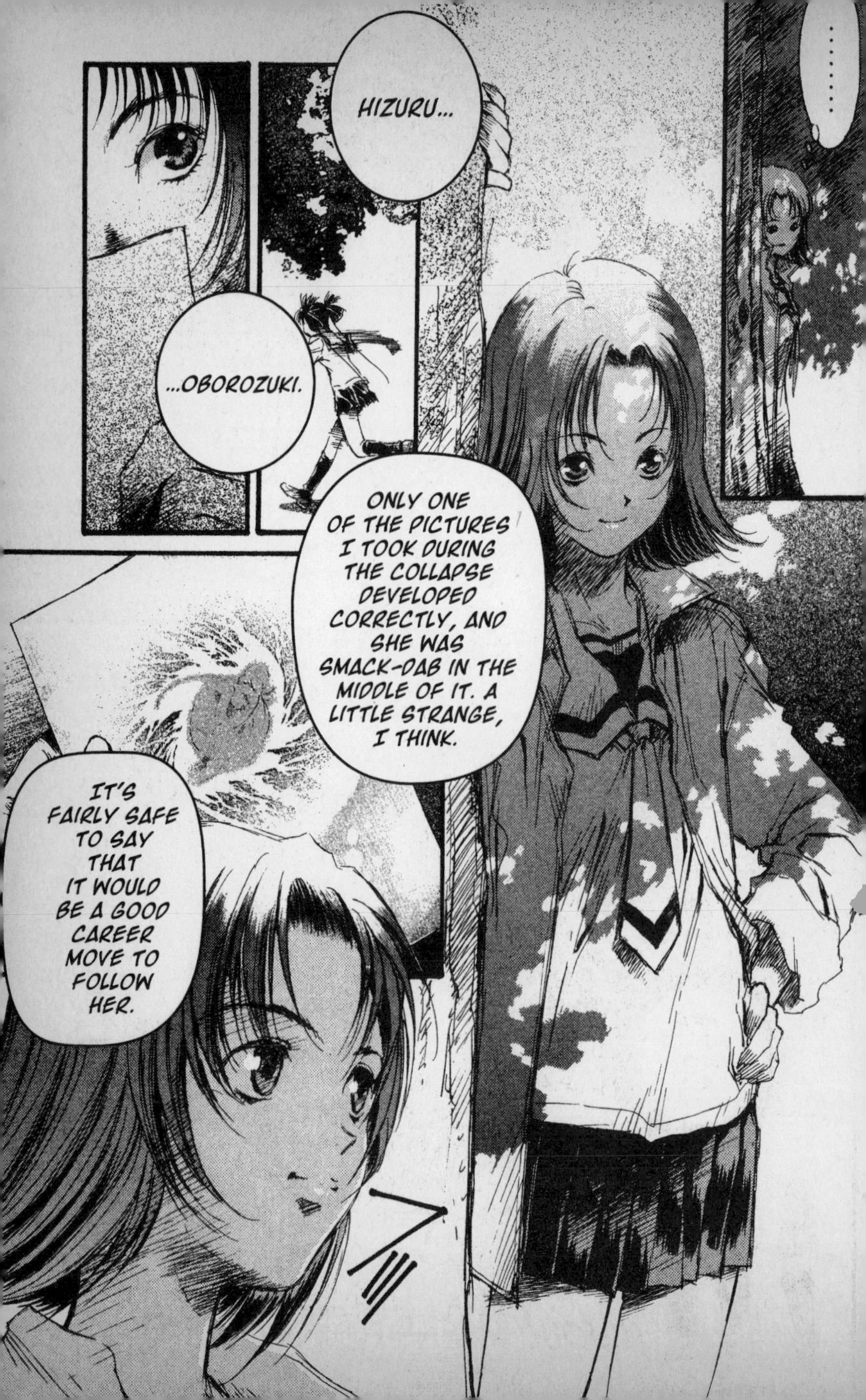
......
HIZURU...
...OBOROZUKI.
ONLY ONE OF THE PICTURES I TOOK DURING THE COLLAPSE DEVELOPED CORRECTLY, AND SHE WAS SMACK-DAB IN THE MIDDLE OF IT. A LITTLE STRANGE, I THINK.
IT'S FAIRLY SAFE TO SAY THAT IT WOULD BE A GOOD CAREER MOVE TO FOLLOW HER.

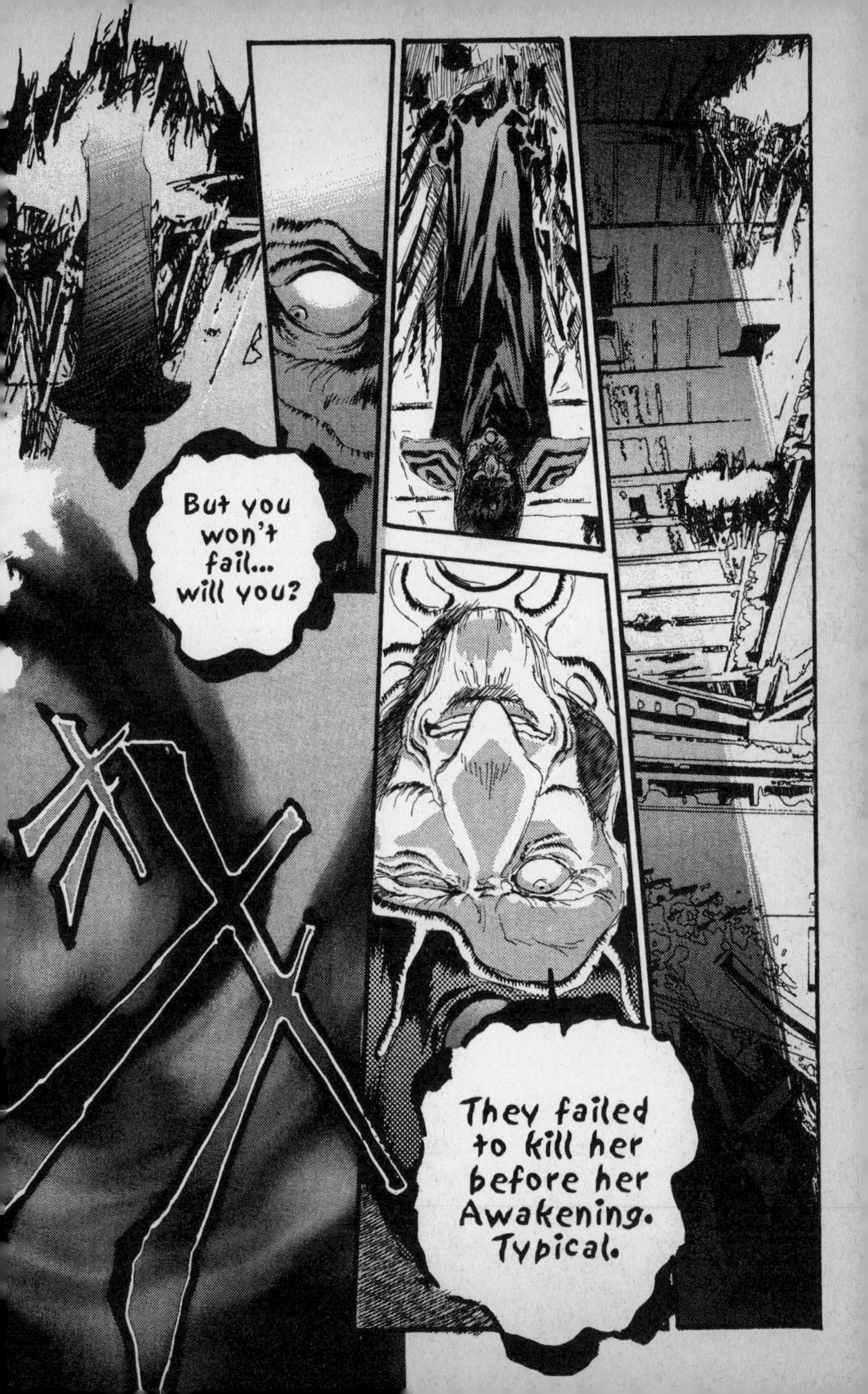
They failed to kill her before her Awakening. Typical.
But you won't fail... will you?

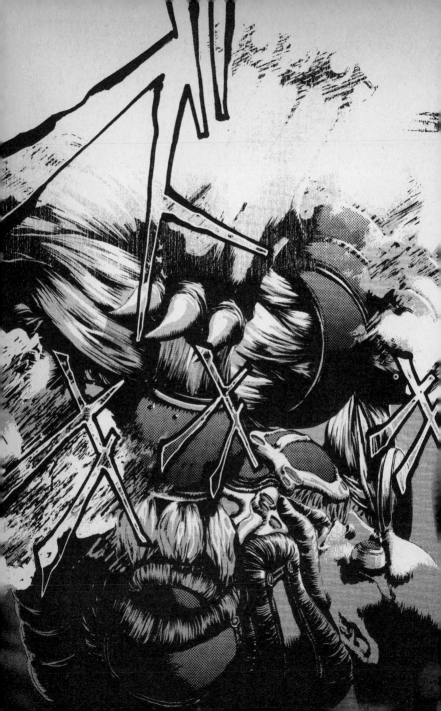

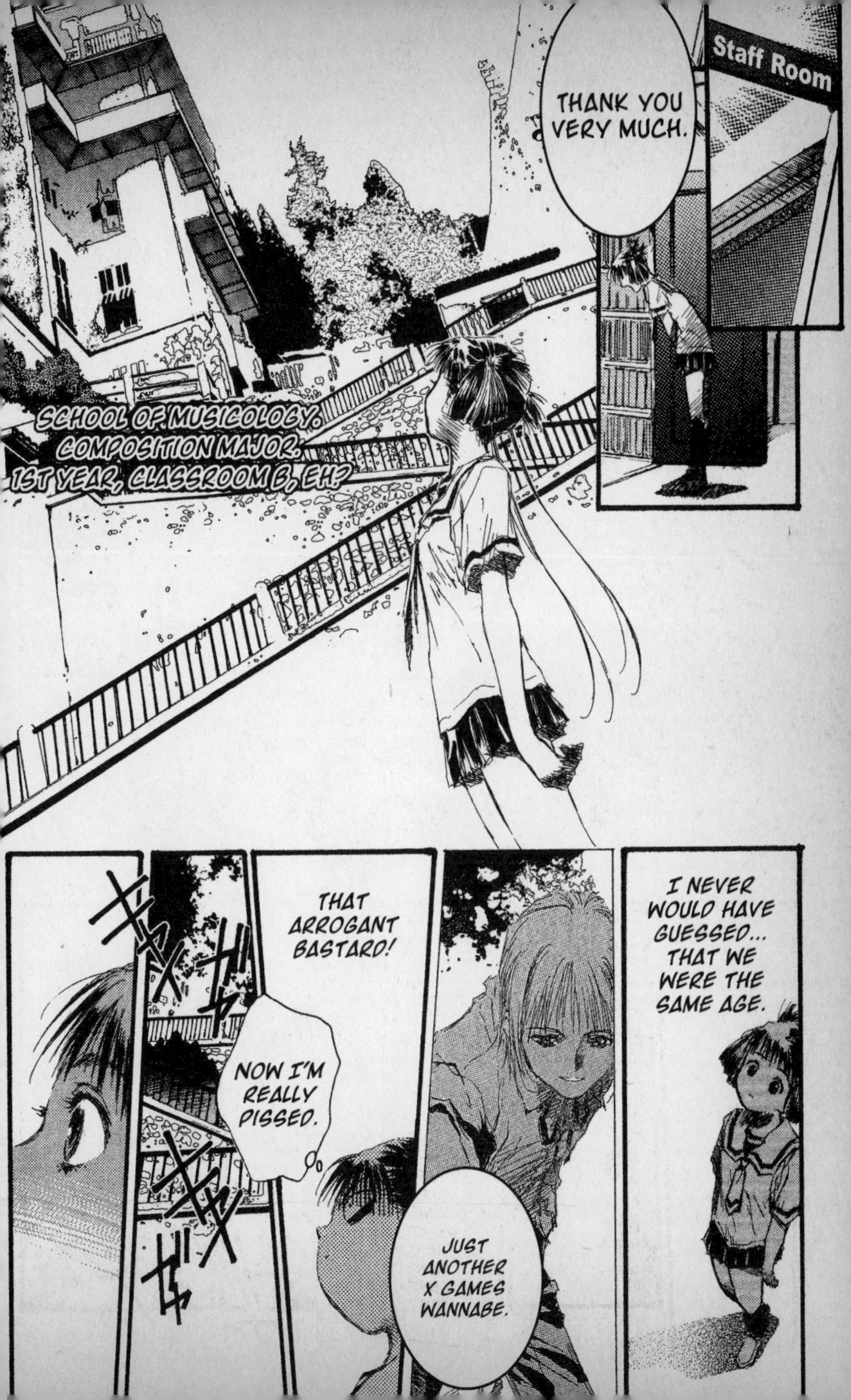
Staff Room
THANK YOU VERY MUCH.
SCHOOL OF MUSICOLOGY. COMPOSITION MAJOR. 1ST YEAR, CLASSROOM B, EH?
I NEVER WOULD HAVE GUESSED... THAT WE WERE THE SAME AGE.
JUST ANOTHER X GAMES WANNABE.
THAT ARROGANT BASTARD!
NOW I'M REALLY PISSED.

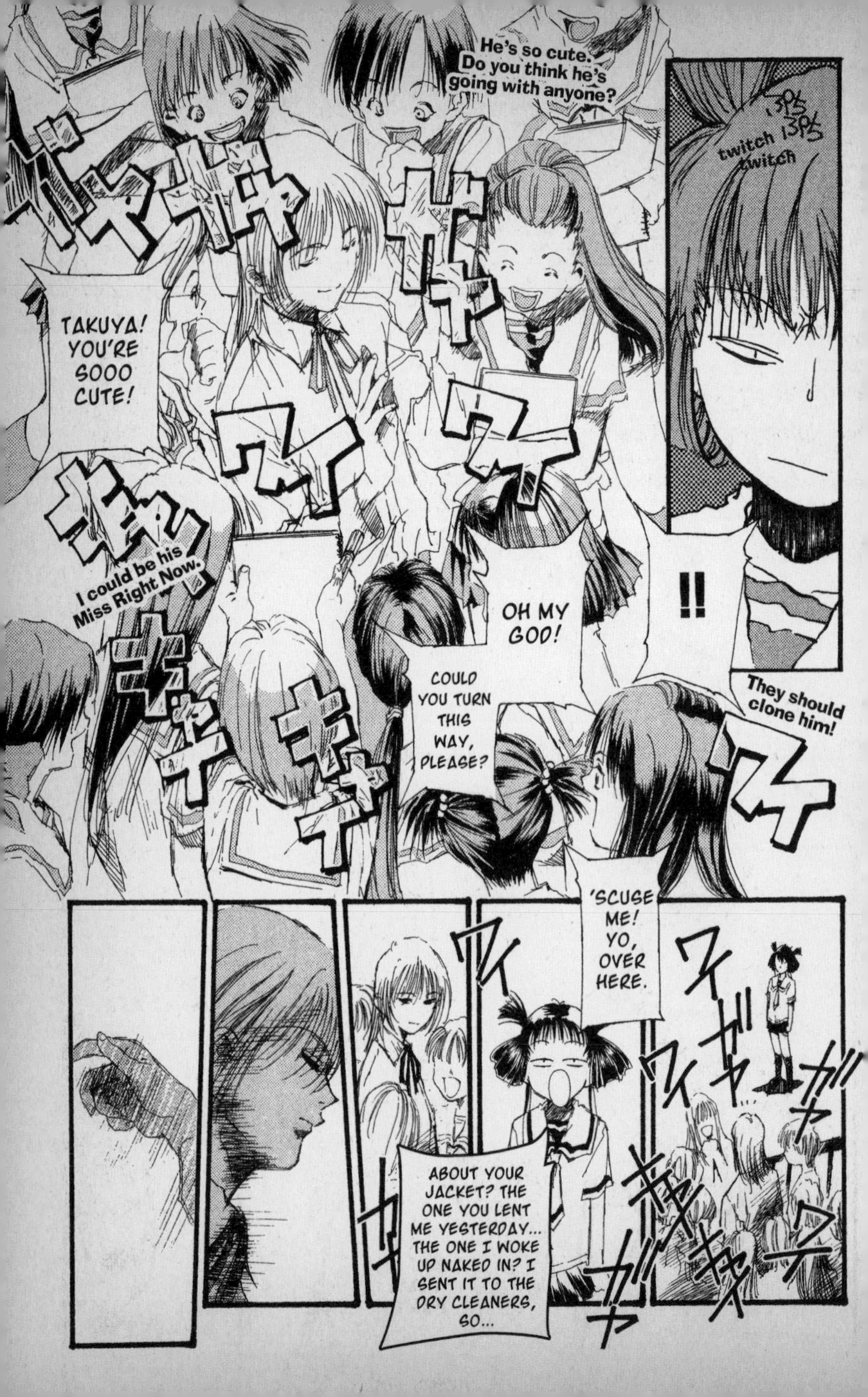
He's so cute. Do you think he's going with anyone?
twitch twitch
TAKUYA! YOU'RE SOOO CUTE!
!!
OH MY GOD!
I could be his Miss Right Now.
They should clone him!
COULD YOU TURN THIS WAY, PLEASE?
'SCUSE ME! YO, OVER HERE.
ABOUT YOUR JACKET? THE ONE YOU LENT ME YESTERDAY... THE ONE I WOKE UP NAKED IN? I SENT IT TO THE DRY CLEANERS, SO...

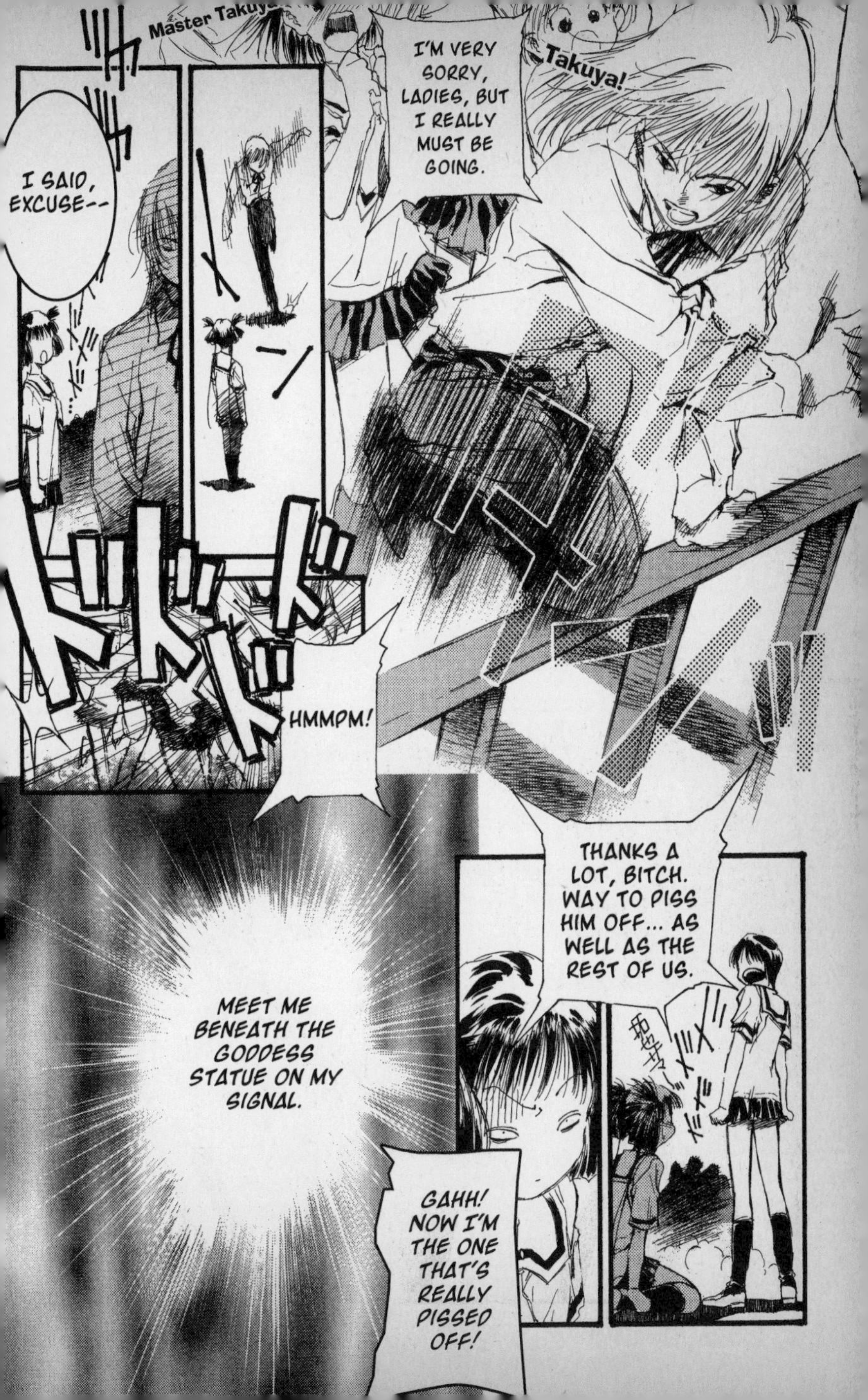
Takuya!
Master Takuya
I'M VERY SORRY, LADIES, BUT I REALLY MUST BE GOING.
I SAID, EXCUSE--
HMMPM!
THANKS A LOT, BITCH. WAY TO PISS HIM OFF... AS WELL AS THE REST OF US.
GAHH! NOW I'M THE ONE THAT'S REALLY PISSED OFF!
MEET ME BENEATH THE GODDESS STATUE ON MY SIGNAL.

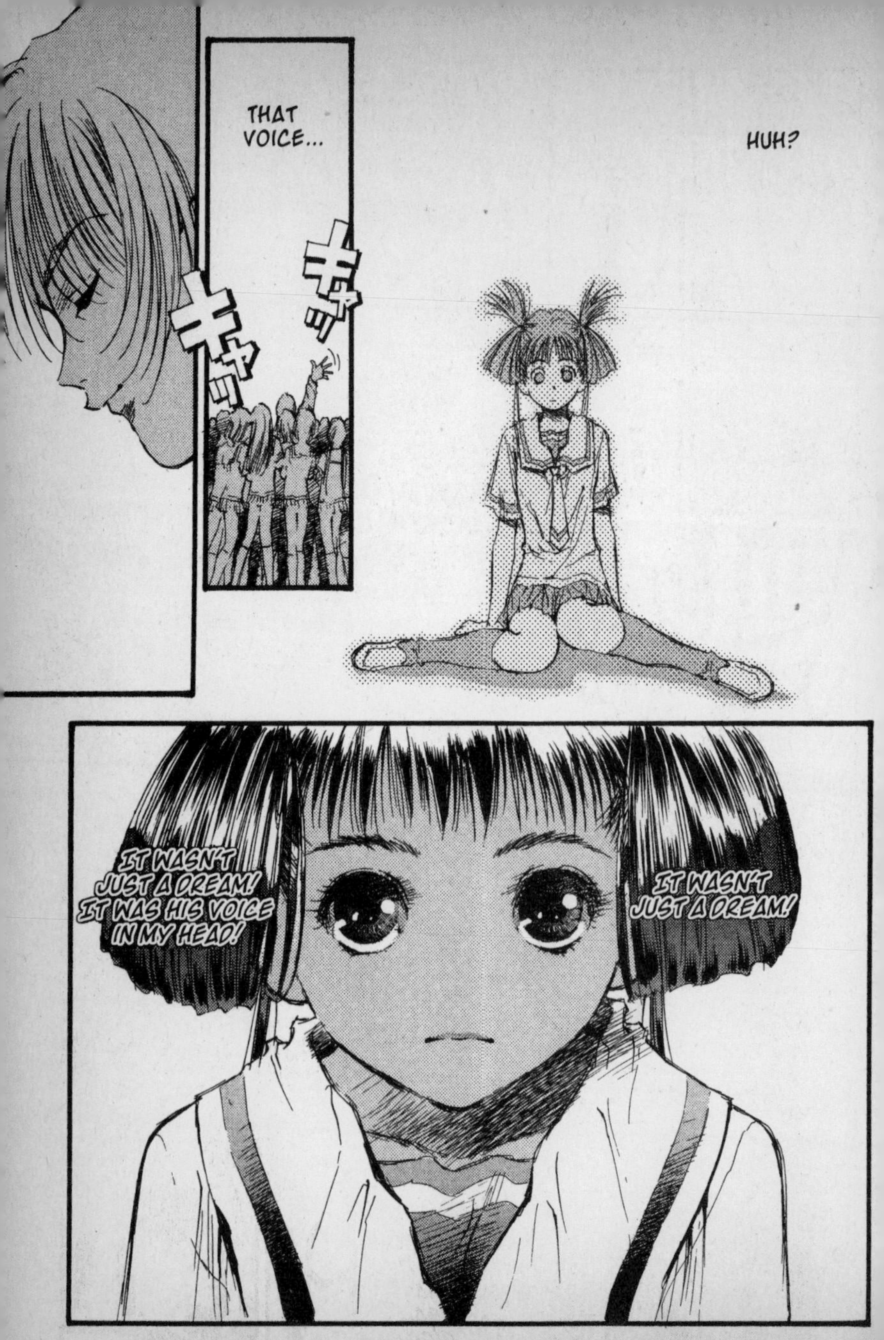
HUH?
THAT VOICE...
キャッ
キャッ
IT WASN'T JUST A DREAM!
IT WASN'T JUST A DREAM! IT WAS HIS VOICE IN MY HEAD!

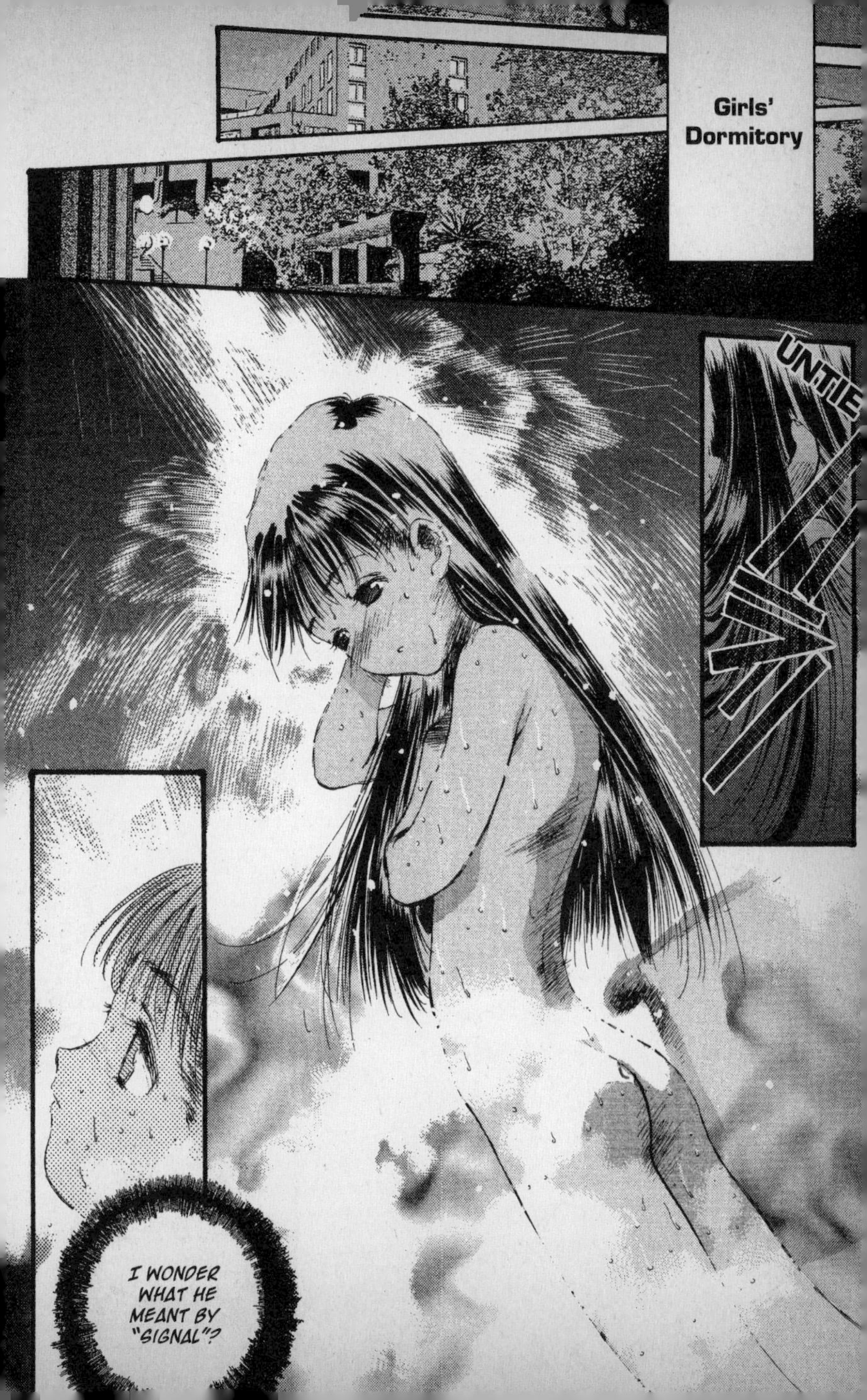
Girls' Dormitory
UNTIE
I WONDER WHAT HE MEANT BY "SIGNAL"?

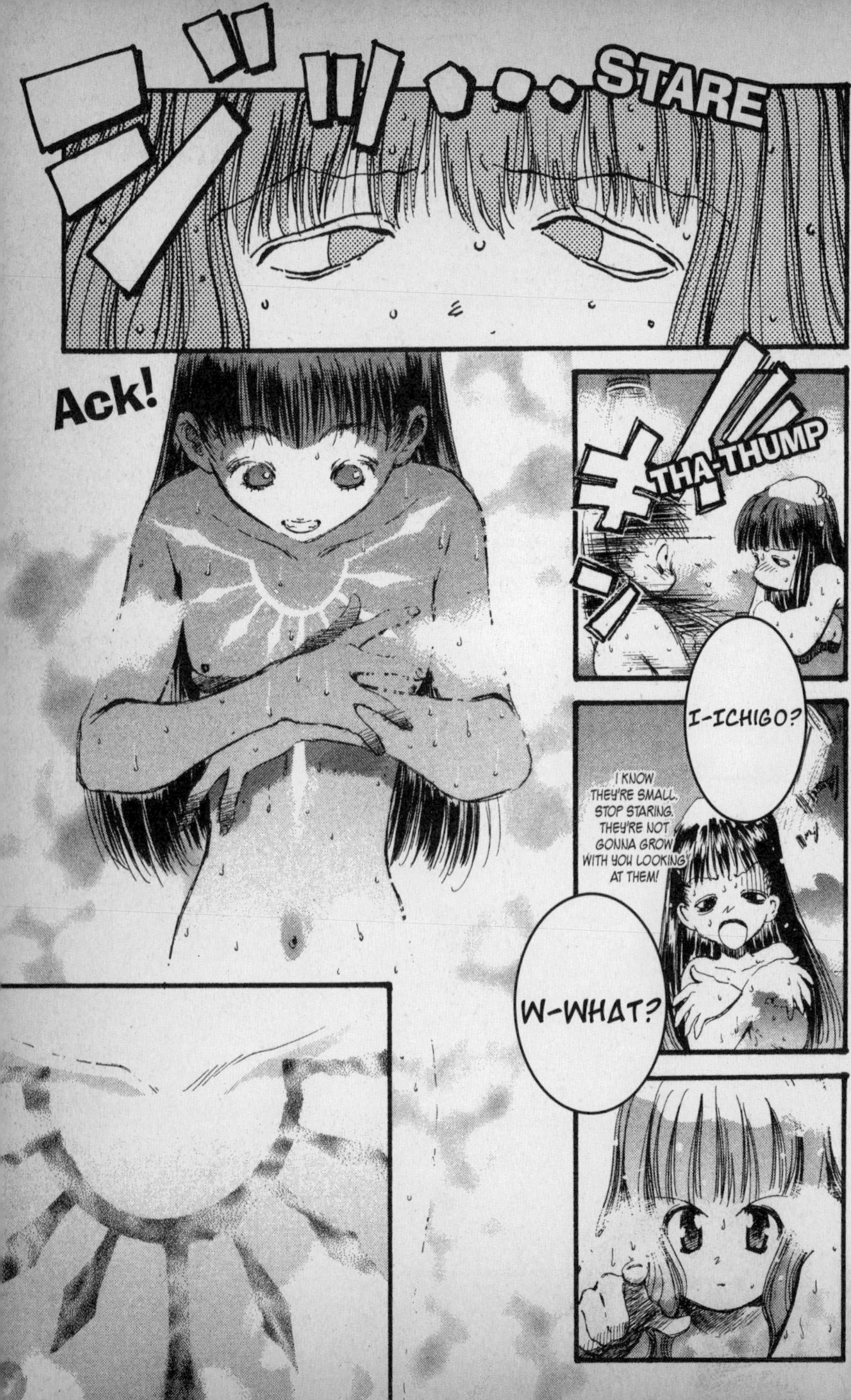
STARE
THA-THUMP
I-ICHIGO?
I KNOW THEY'RE SMALL. STOP STARING. THEY'RE NOT GONNA GROW WITH YOU LOOKING AT THEM!
W-WHAT?
Ack!

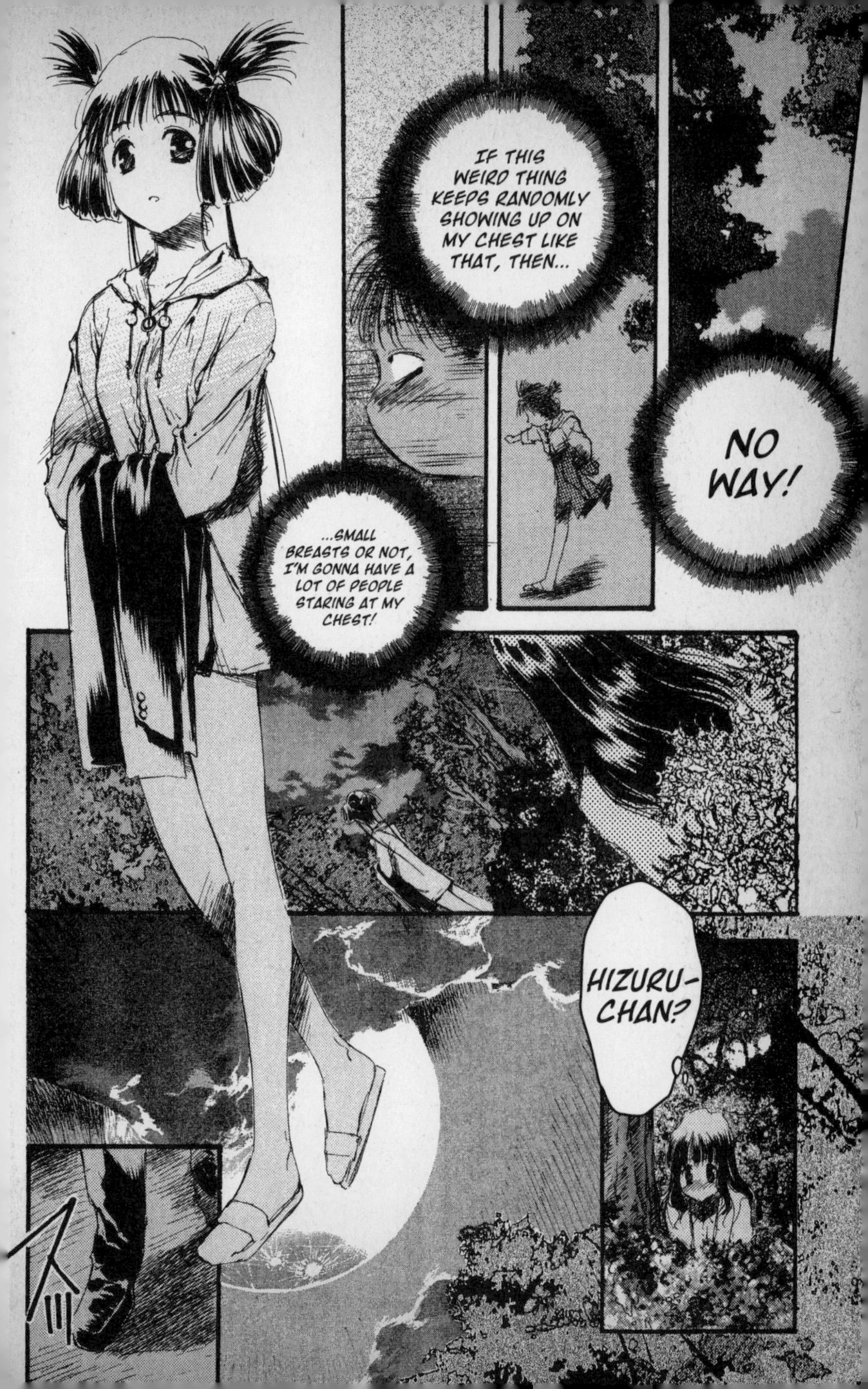
IF THIS WEIRD THING KEEPS RANDOMLY SHOWING UP ON MY CHEST LIKE THAT, THEN...
NO WAY!
...SMALL BREASTS OR NOT, I'M GONNA HAVE A LOT OF PEOPLE STARING AT MY CHEST!
HIZURU-CHAN?

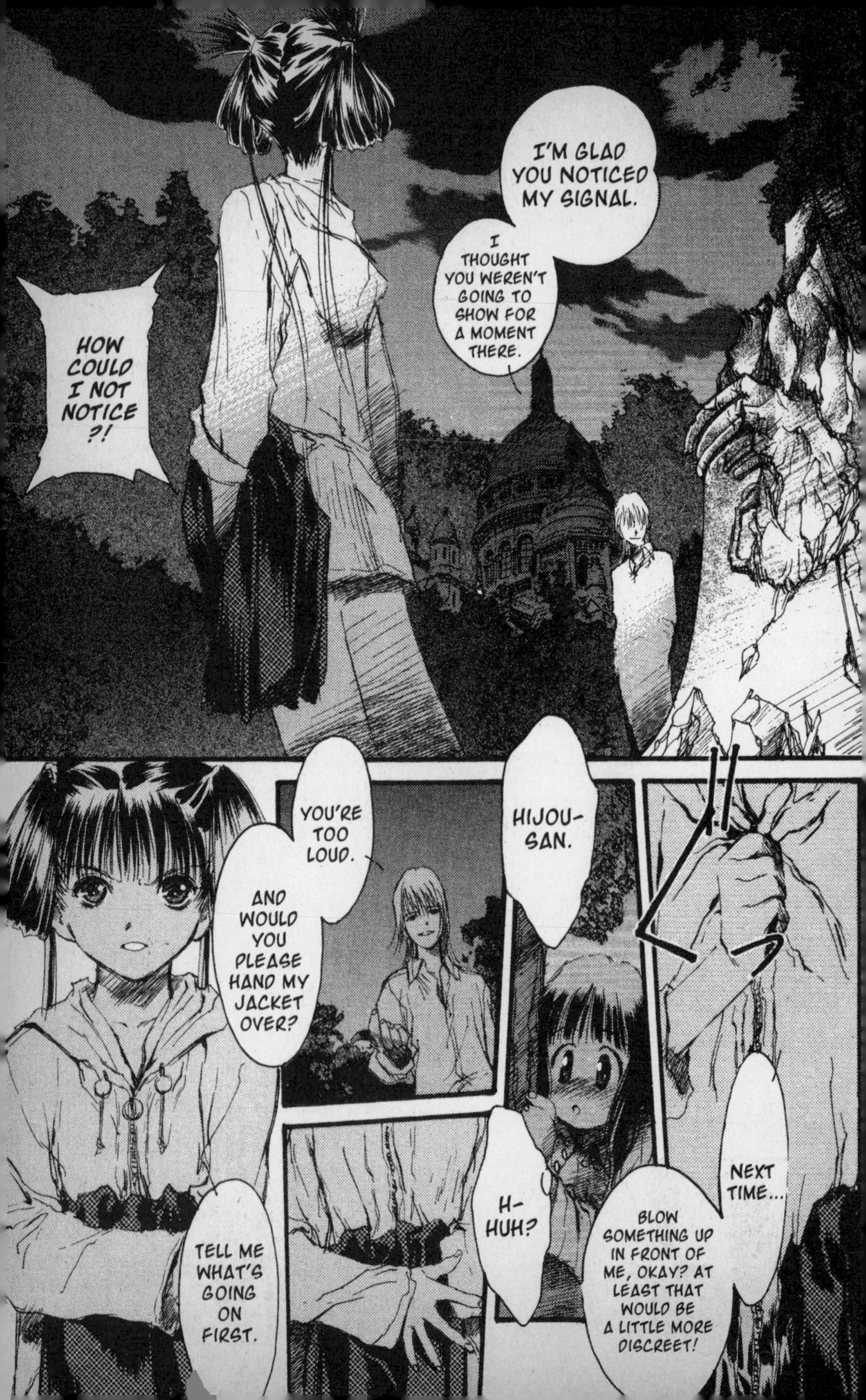
I'M GLAD YOU NOTICED MY SIGNAL.
I THOUGHT YOU WEREN'T GOING TO SHOW FOR A MOMENT THERE.
HOW COULD I NOT NOTICE ?!
HIJOU-SAN.
YOU'RE TOO LOUD.
AND WOULD YOU PLEASE HAND MY JACKET OVER?
H-HUH?
NEXT TIME...
BLOW SOMETHING UP IN FRONT OF ME, OKAY? AT LEAST THAT WOULD BE A LITTLE MORE DISCREET!
TELL ME WHAT'S GOING ON FIRST.

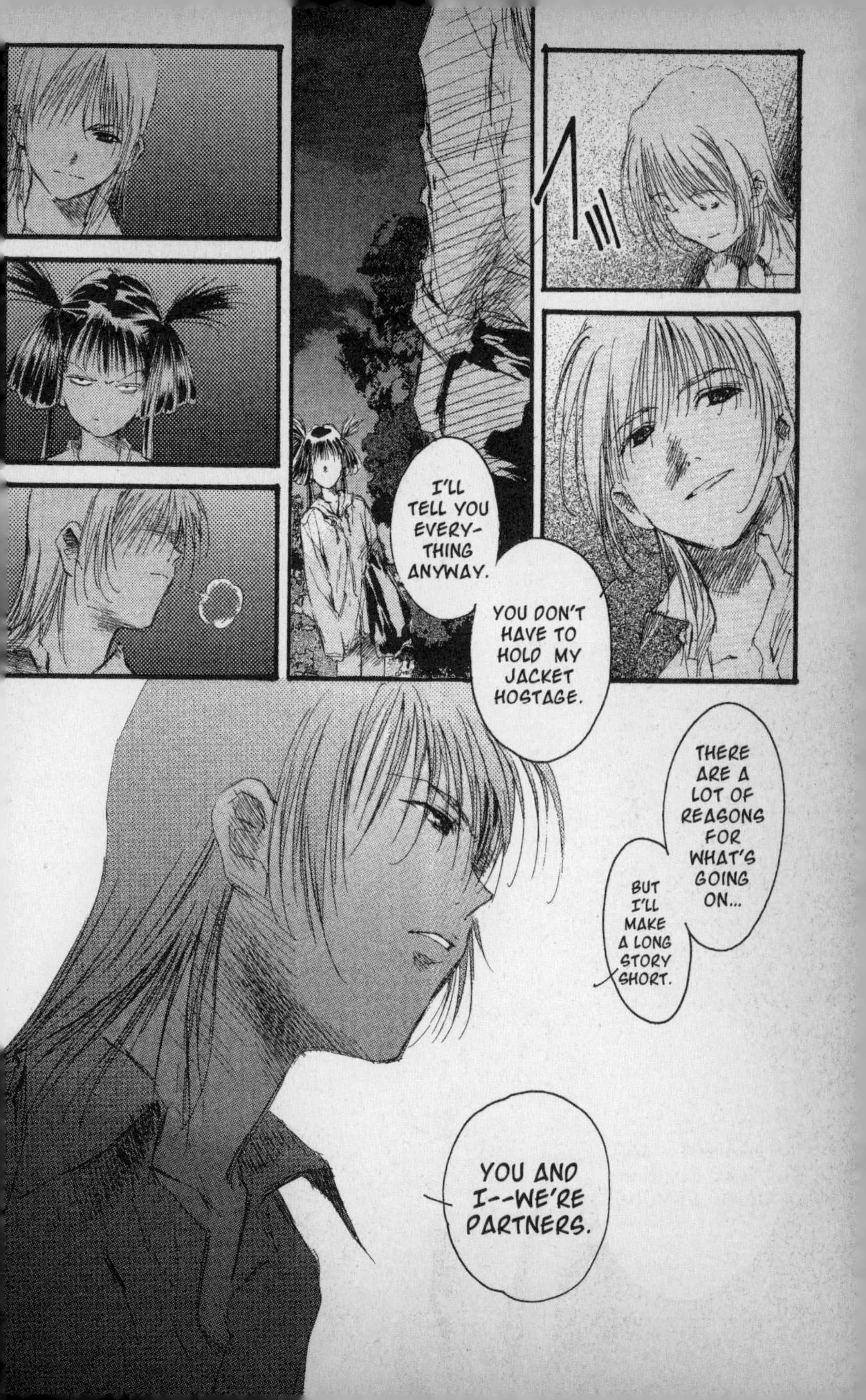
I'LL TELL YOU EVERY-THING ANYWAY.
YOU DON'T HAVE TO HOLD MY JACKET HOSTAGE.
THERE ARE A LOT OF REASONS FOR WHAT'S GOING ON...
BUT I'LL MAKE A LONG STORY SHORT.
YOU AND I--WE'RE PARTNERS.

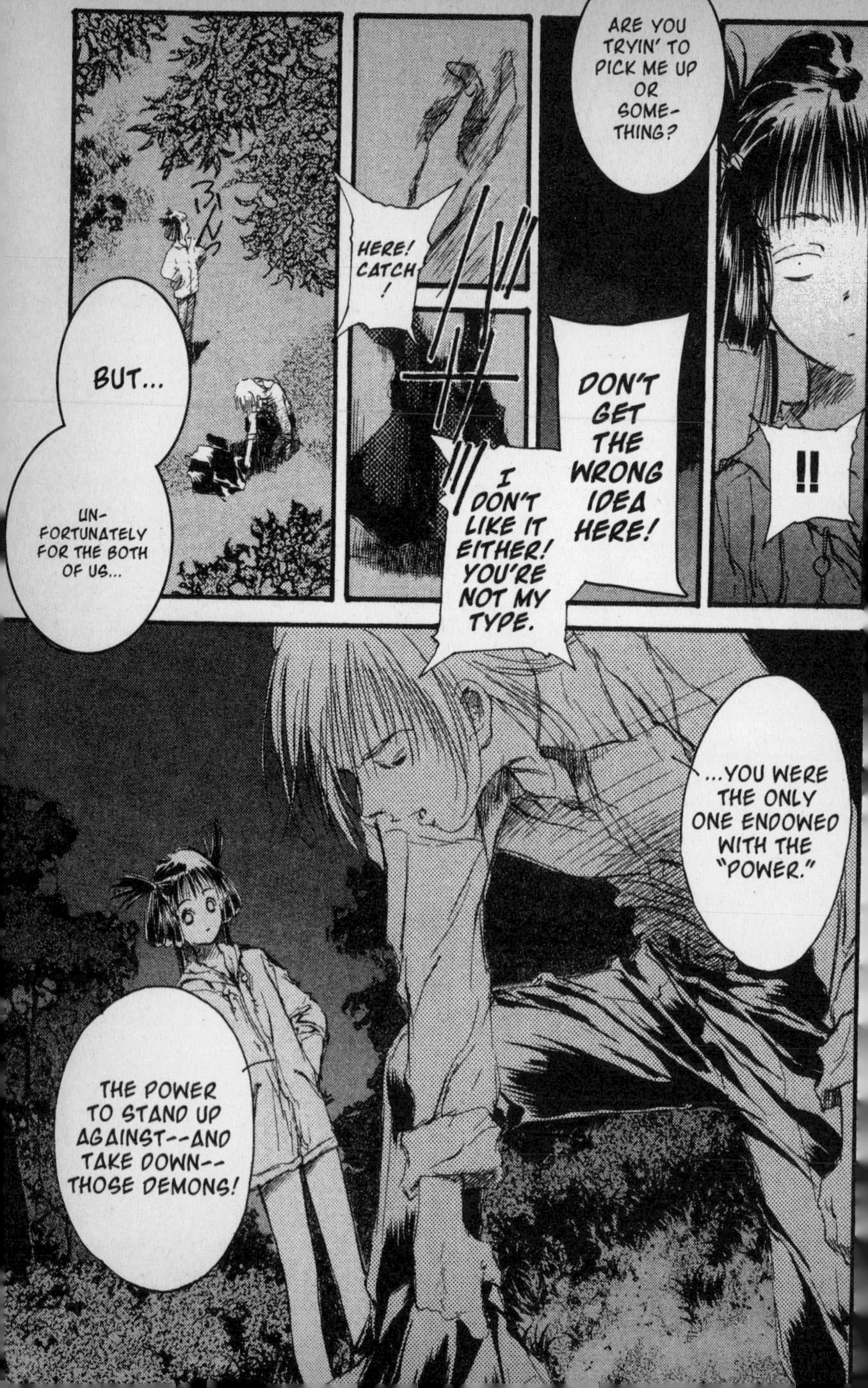
!!
ARE YOU TRYIN' TO PICK ME UP OR SOME-THING?
DON'T GET THE WRONG IDEA HERE!
I DON'T LIKE IT EITHER! YOU'RE NOT MY TYPE.
HERE! CATCH!
BUT...
UN-FORTUNATELY FOR THE BOTH OF US...
...YOU WERE THE ONLY ONE ENDOWED WITH THE "POWER."
THE POWER TO STAND UP AGAINST--AND TAKE DOWN--THOSE DEMONS!

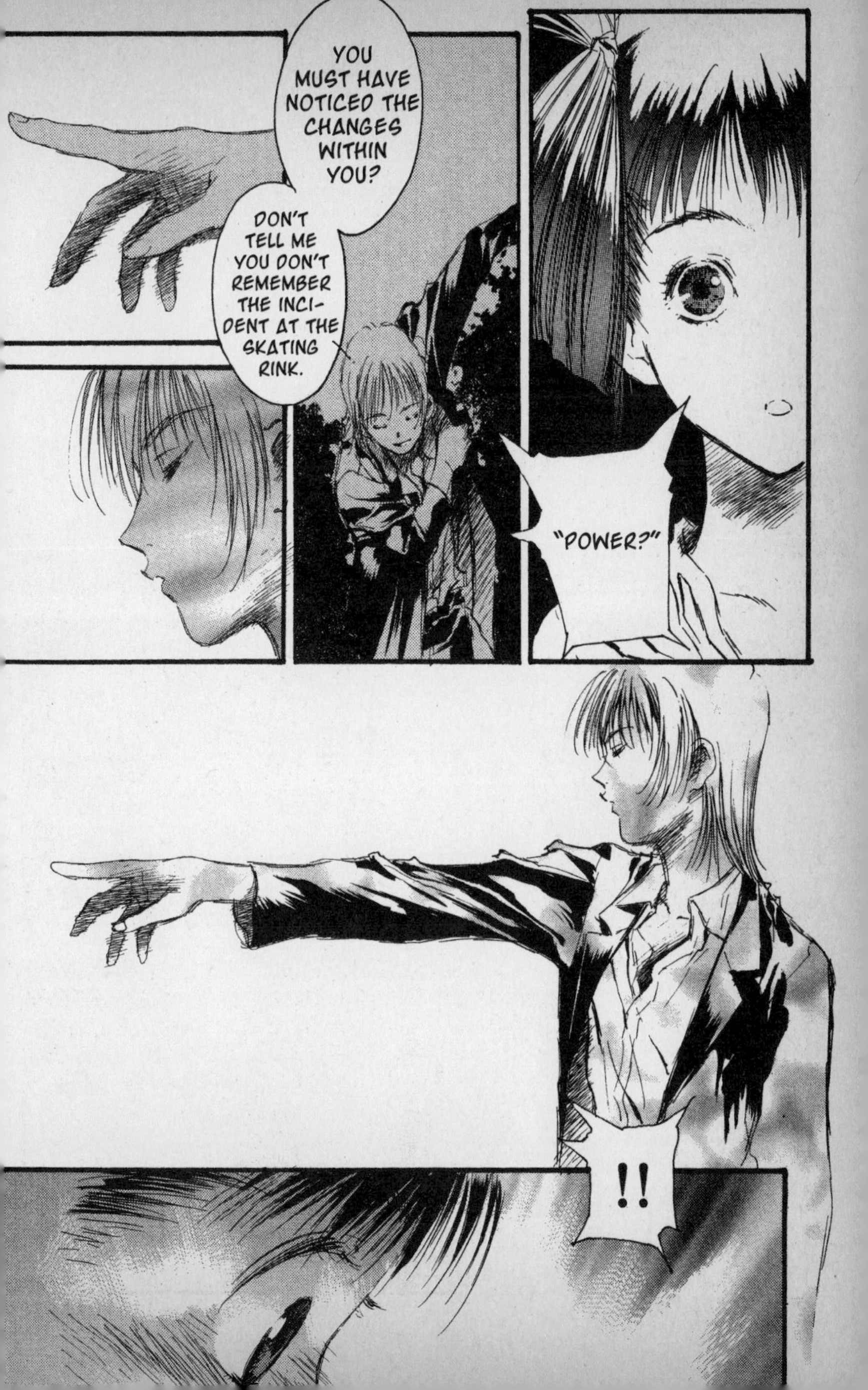
"POWER?"
YOU MUST HAVE NOTICED THE CHANGES WITHIN YOU?
DON'T TELL ME YOU DON'T REMEMBER THE INCI-DENT AT THE SKATING RINK.
!!

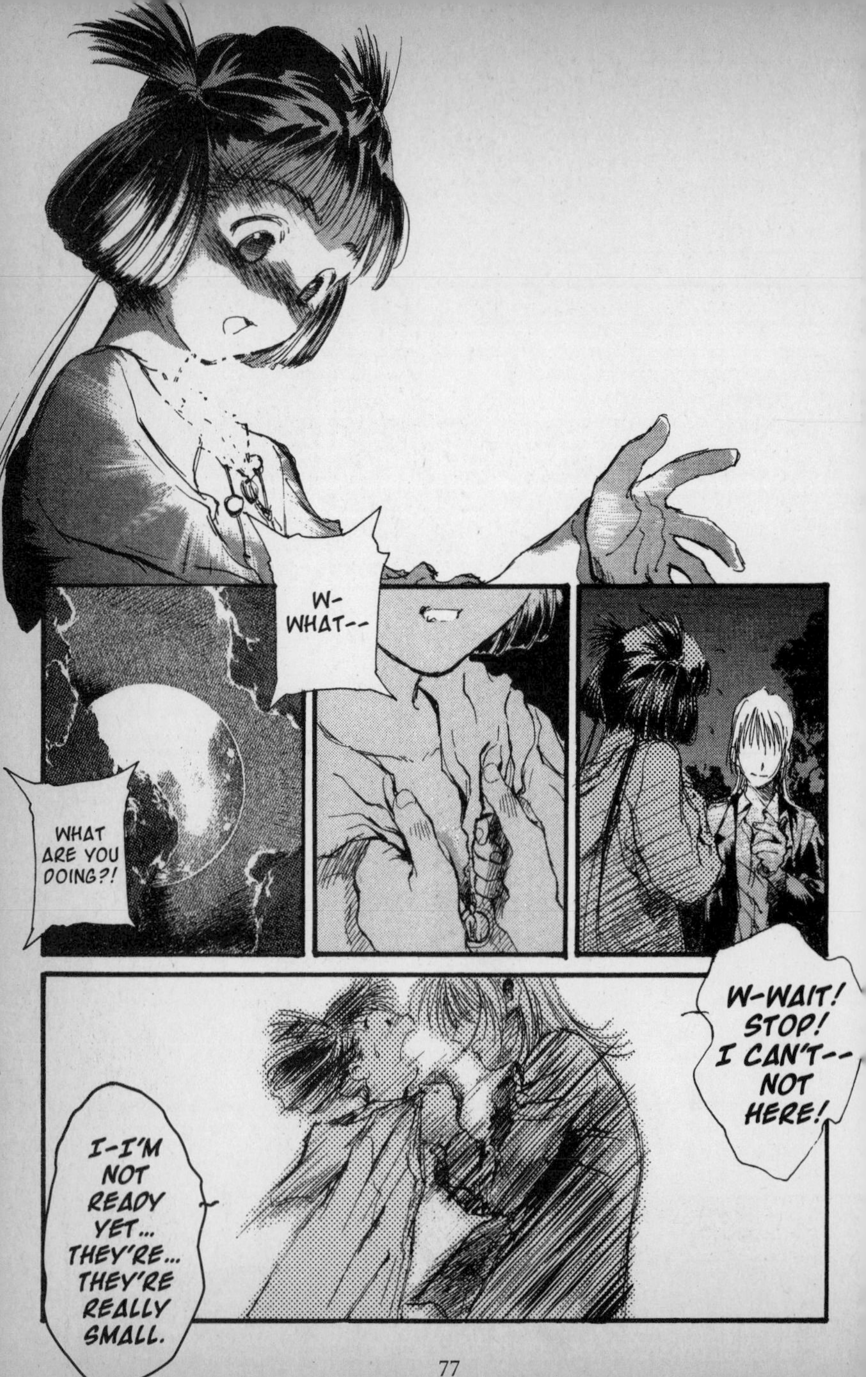
W- WHAT--
WHAT ARE YOU DOING?!
W-WAIT! STOP! I CAN'T-- NOT HERE!
I-I'M NOT READY YET... THEY'RE... THEY'RE REALLY SMALL.

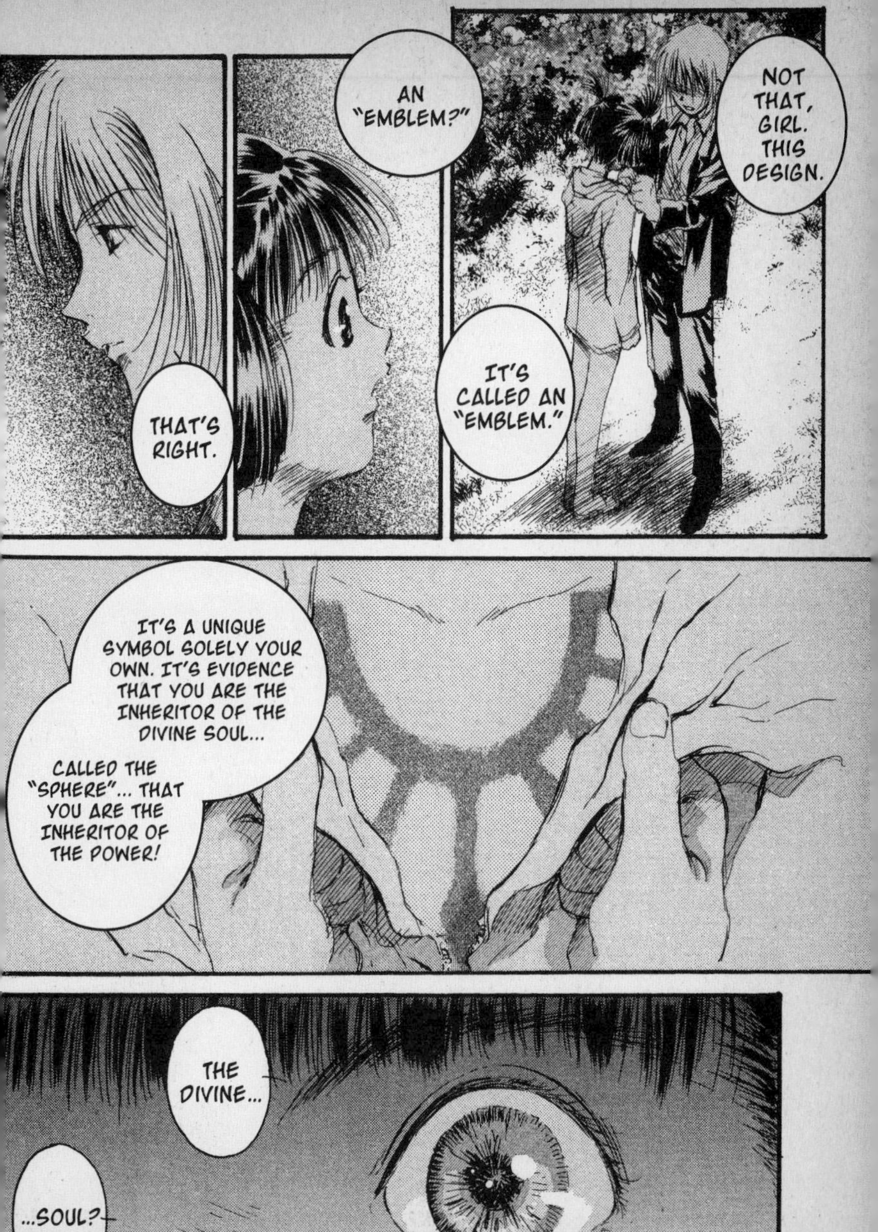
NOT THAT, GIRL. THIS DESIGN.
IT'S CALLED AN "EMBLEM."
AN "EMBLEM?"
THAT'S RIGHT.
IT'S A UNIQUE SYMBOL SOLELY YOUR OWN. IT'S EVIDENCE THAT YOU ARE THE INHERITOR OF THE DIVINE SOUL...
CALLED THE "SPHERE"... THAT YOU ARE THE INHERITOR OF THE POWER!
THE DIVINE...
...SOUL?

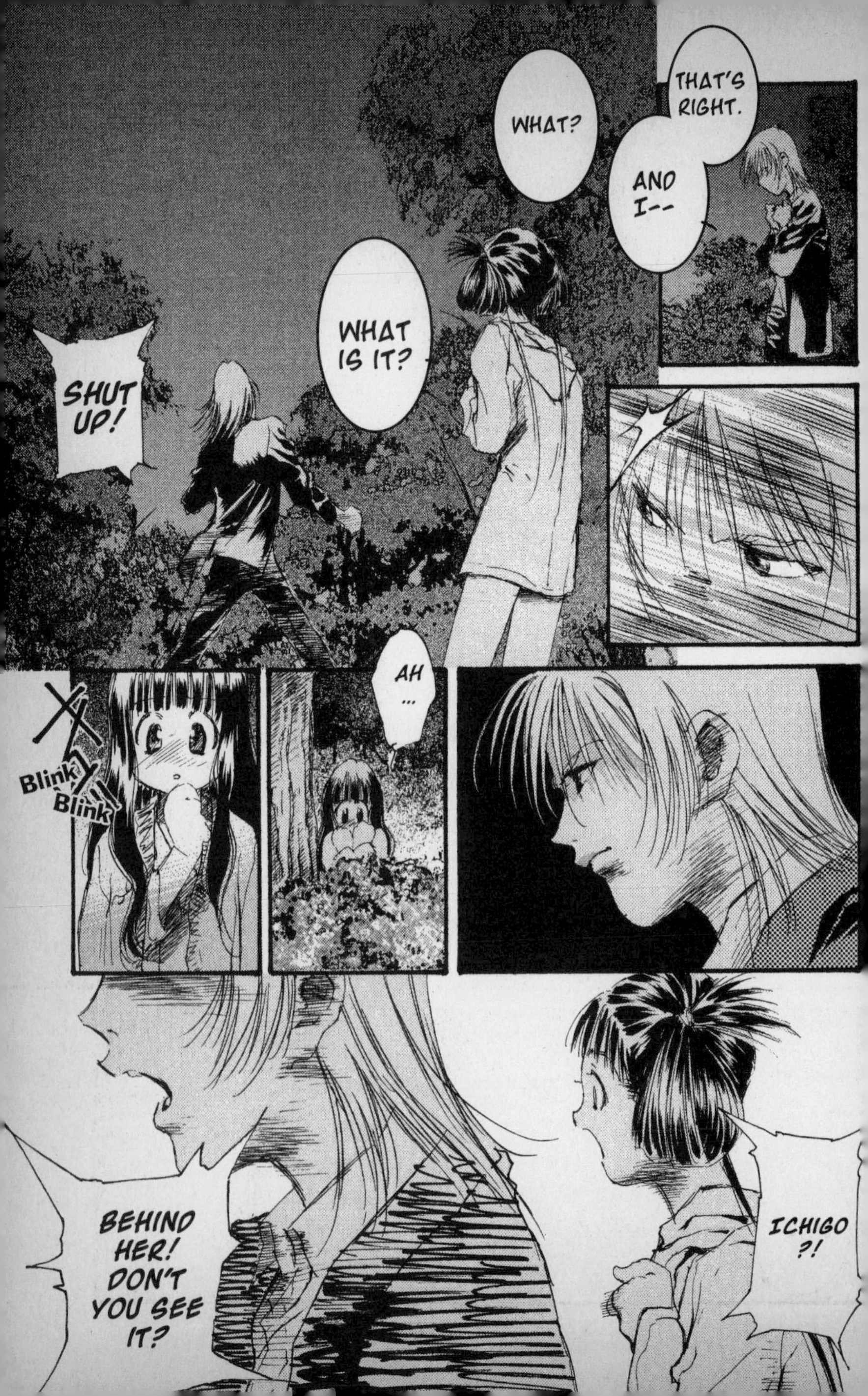
THAT'S RIGHT.
AND I--
WHAT?
WHAT IS IT?
SHUT UP!
AH ...
Blink Blink
ICHIGO ?!
BEHIND HER! DON'T YOU SEE IT?

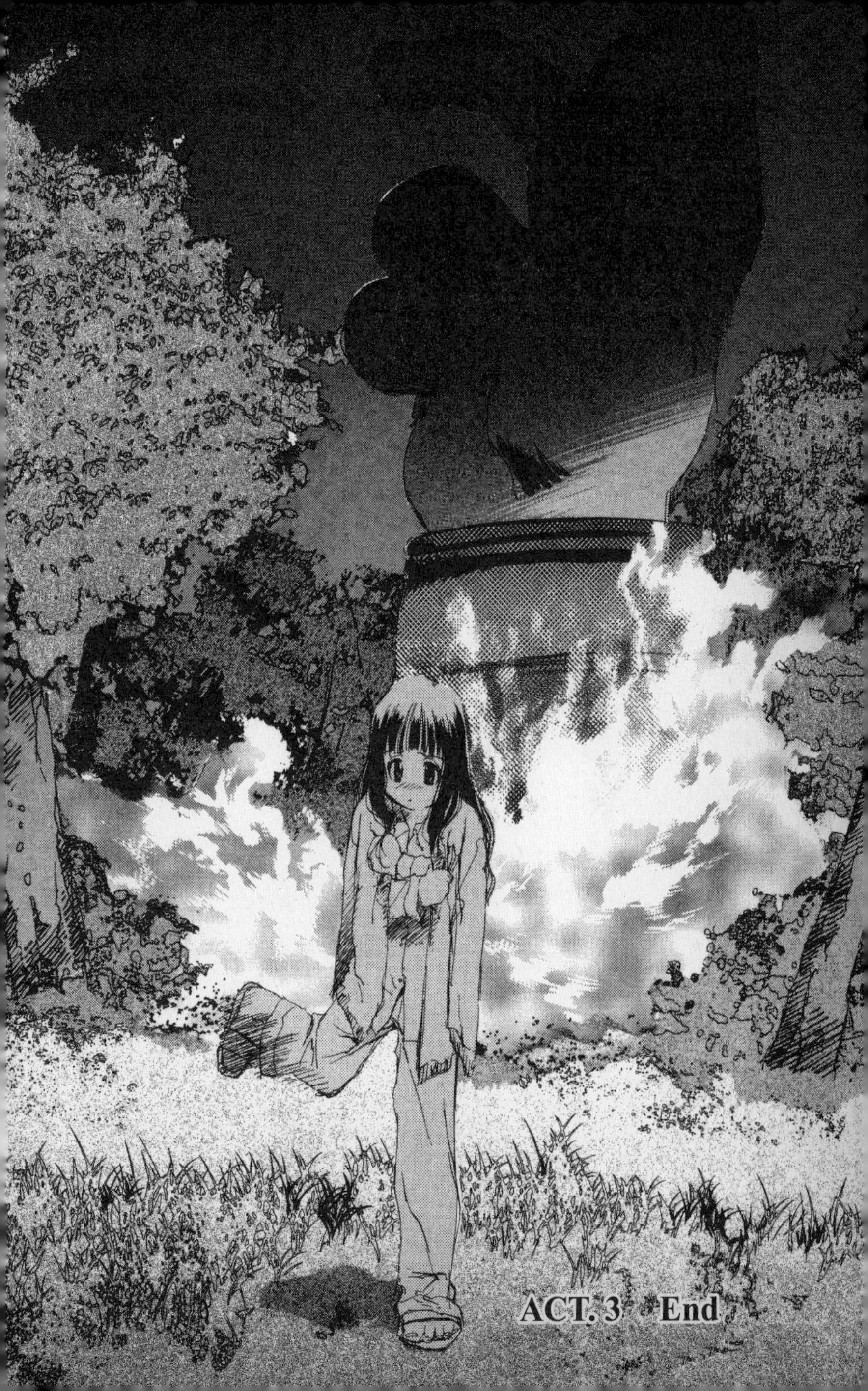
ACT. 3 End

ACT. 4 Revelations

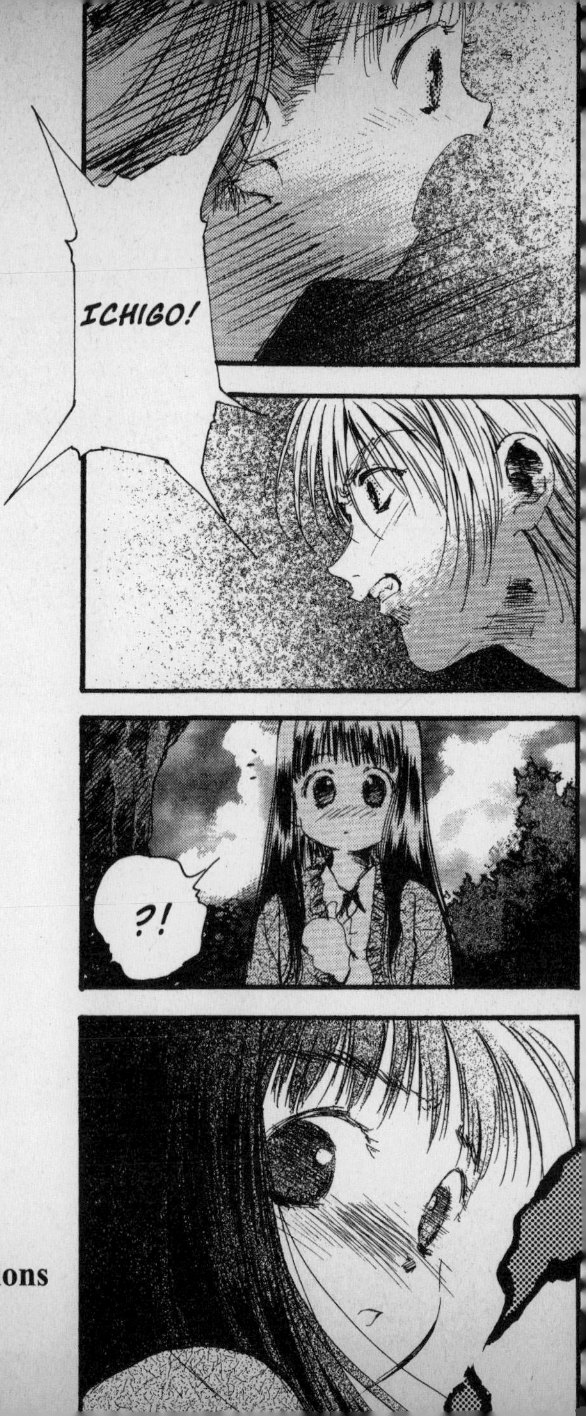
ICHIGO!
?!

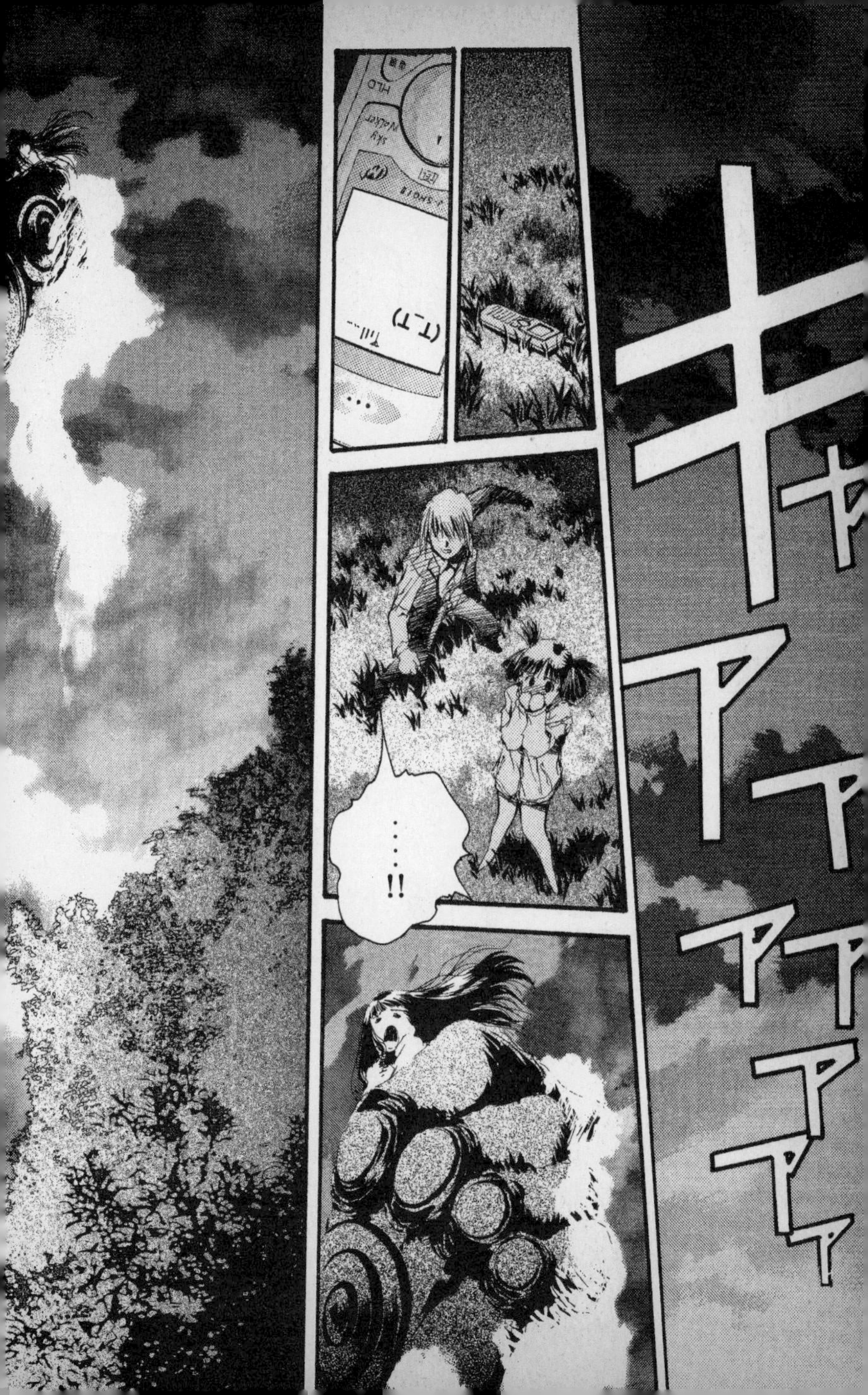
....!!

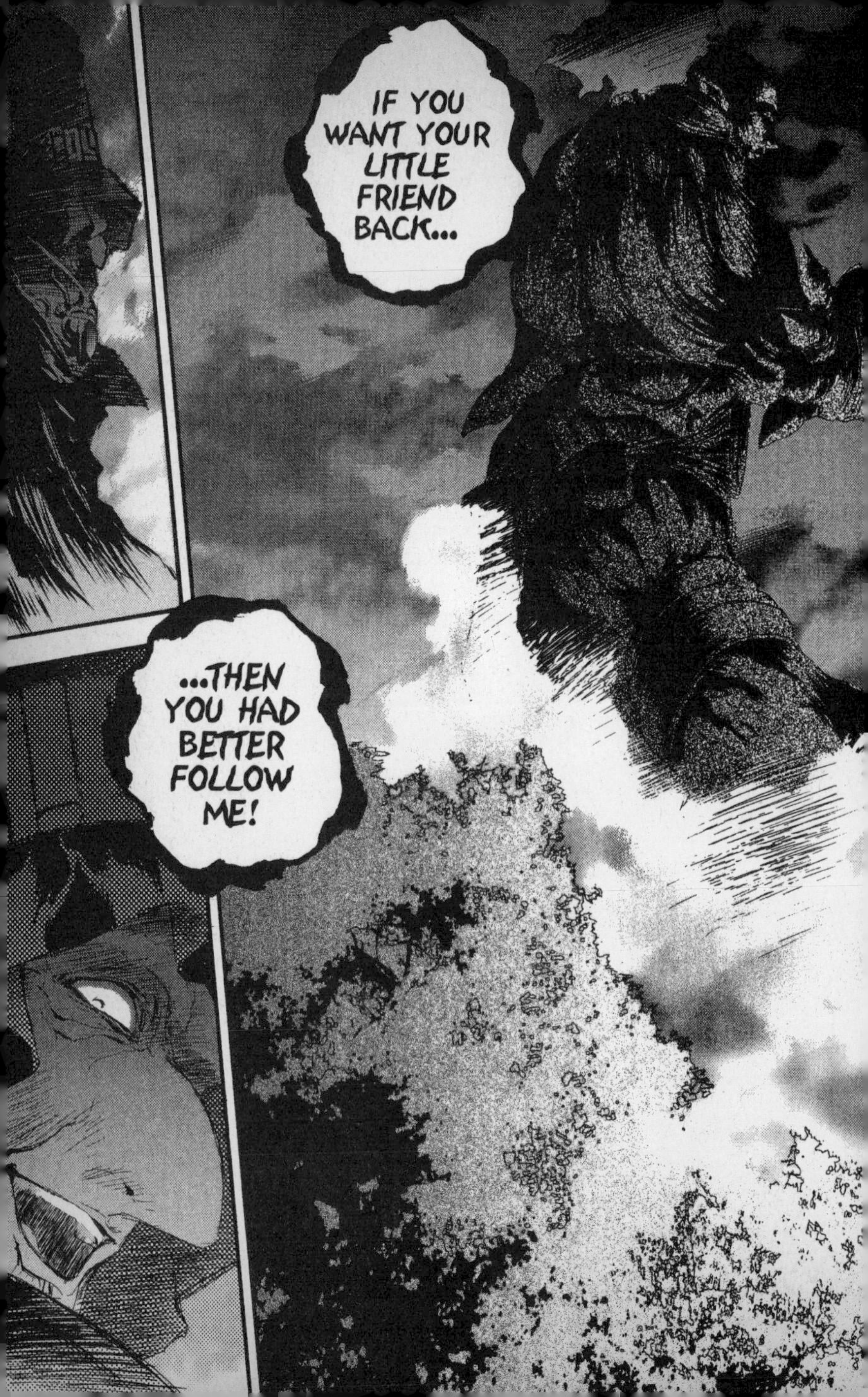
IF YOU WANT YOUR LITTLE FRIEND BACK...
...THEN YOU HAD BETTER FOLLOW ME!

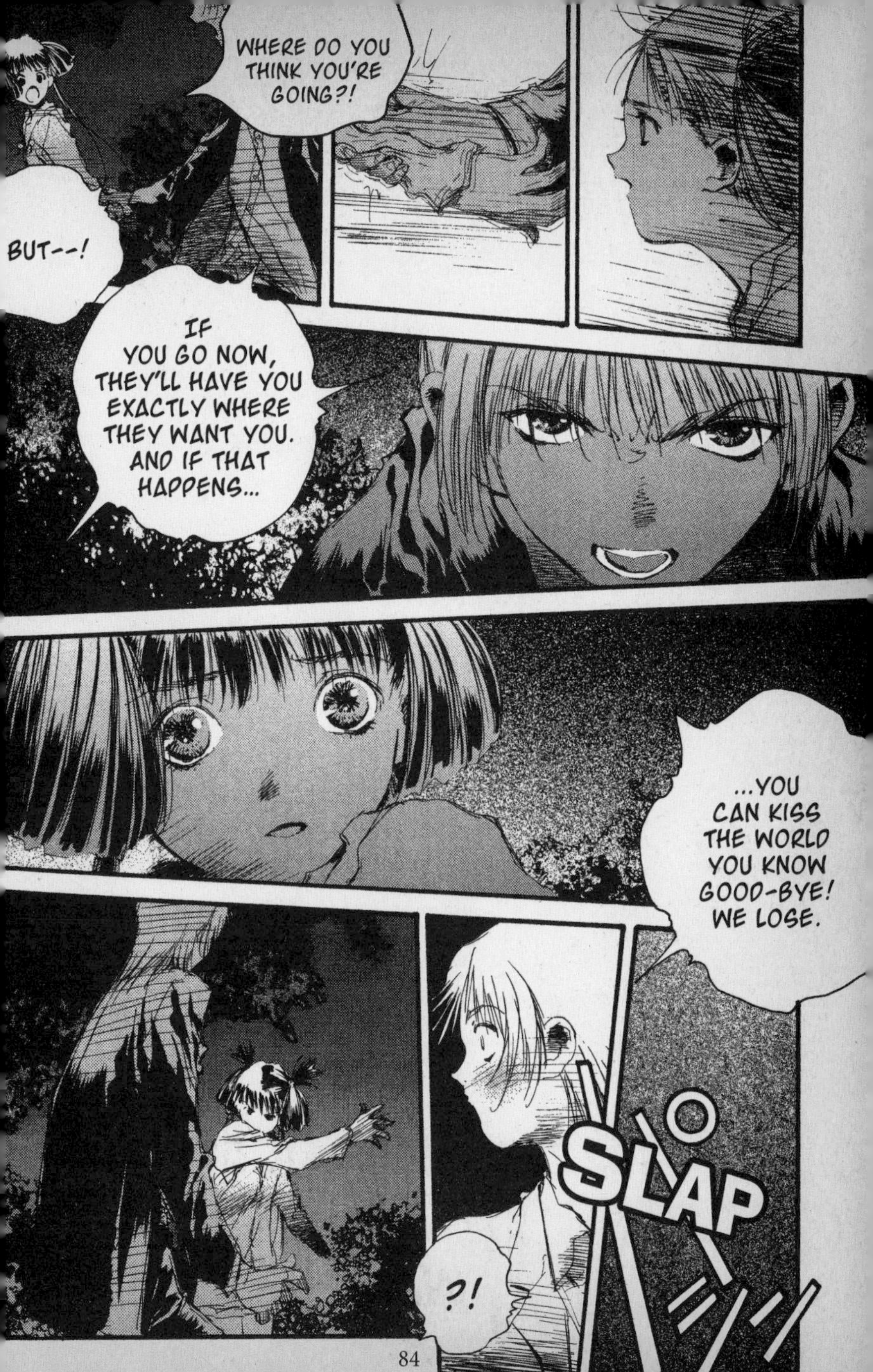
WHERE DO YOU THINK YOU'RE GOING?!
BUT--!
IF YOU GO NOW, THEY'LL HAVE YOU EXACTLY WHERE THEY WANT YOU. AND IF THAT HAPPENS...
...YOU CAN KISS THE WORLD YOU KNOW GOOD-BYE! WE LOSE.
SLAP
?!

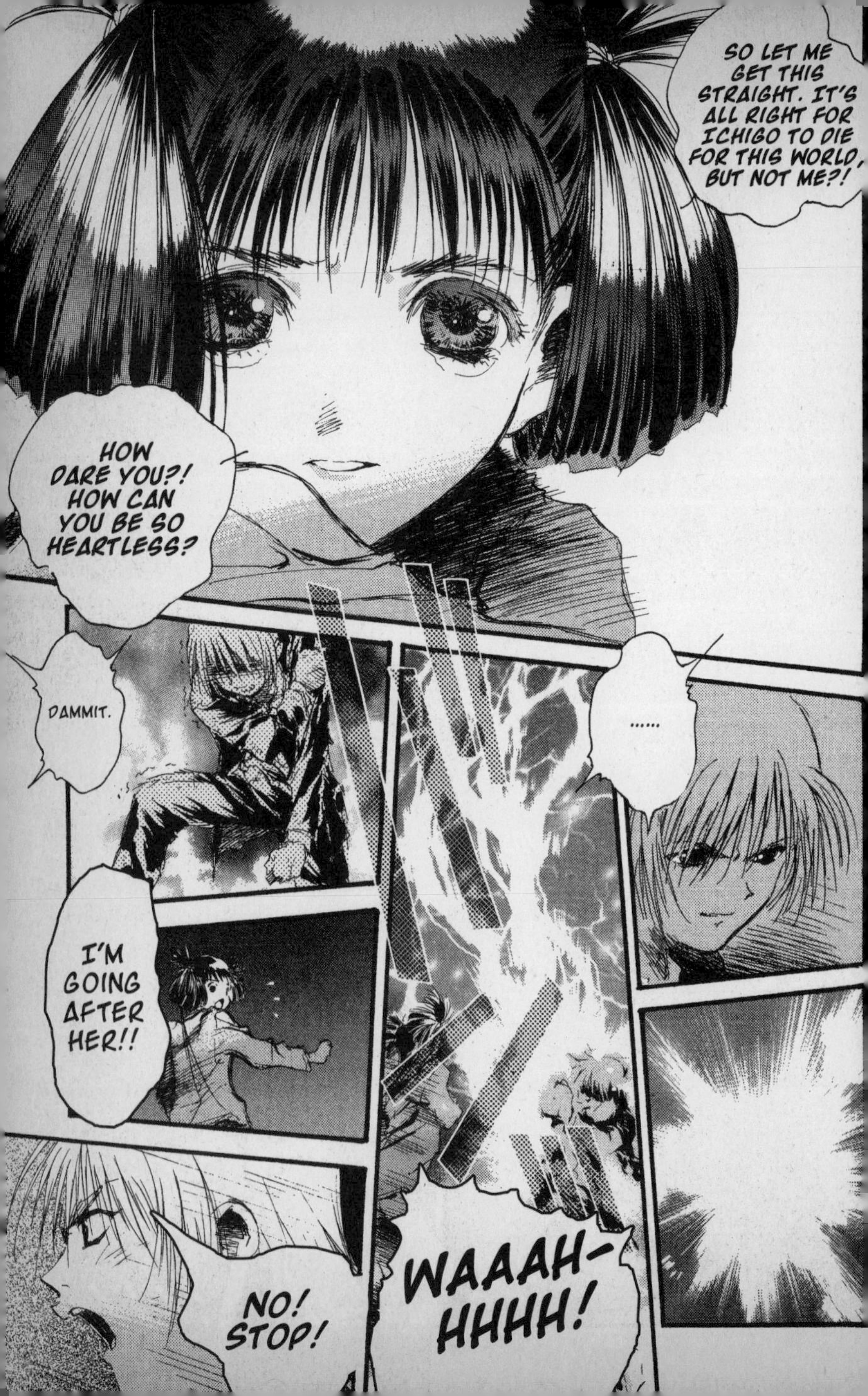
SO LET ME GET THIS STRAIGHT. IT'S ALL RIGHT FOR ICHIGO TO DIE FOR THIS WORLD, BUT NOT ME?!
HOW DARE YOU?! HOW CAN YOU BE SO HEARTLESS?
......
DAMMIT.
I'M GOING AFTER HER!!
WAAAH-HHHH!
NO! STOP!

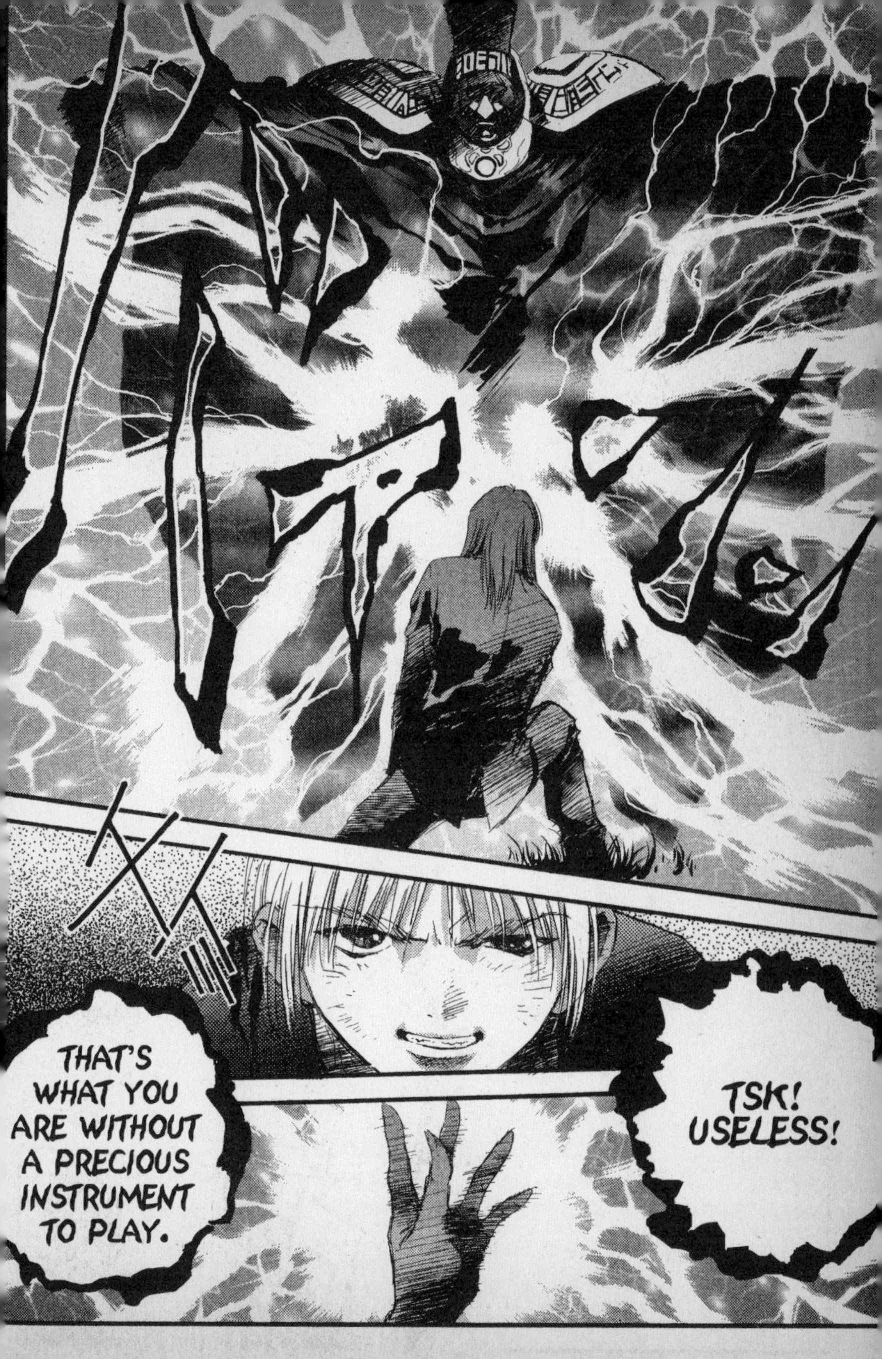
TSK! USELESS!
THAT'S WHAT YOU ARE WITHOUT A PRECIOUS INSTRUMENT TO PLAY.

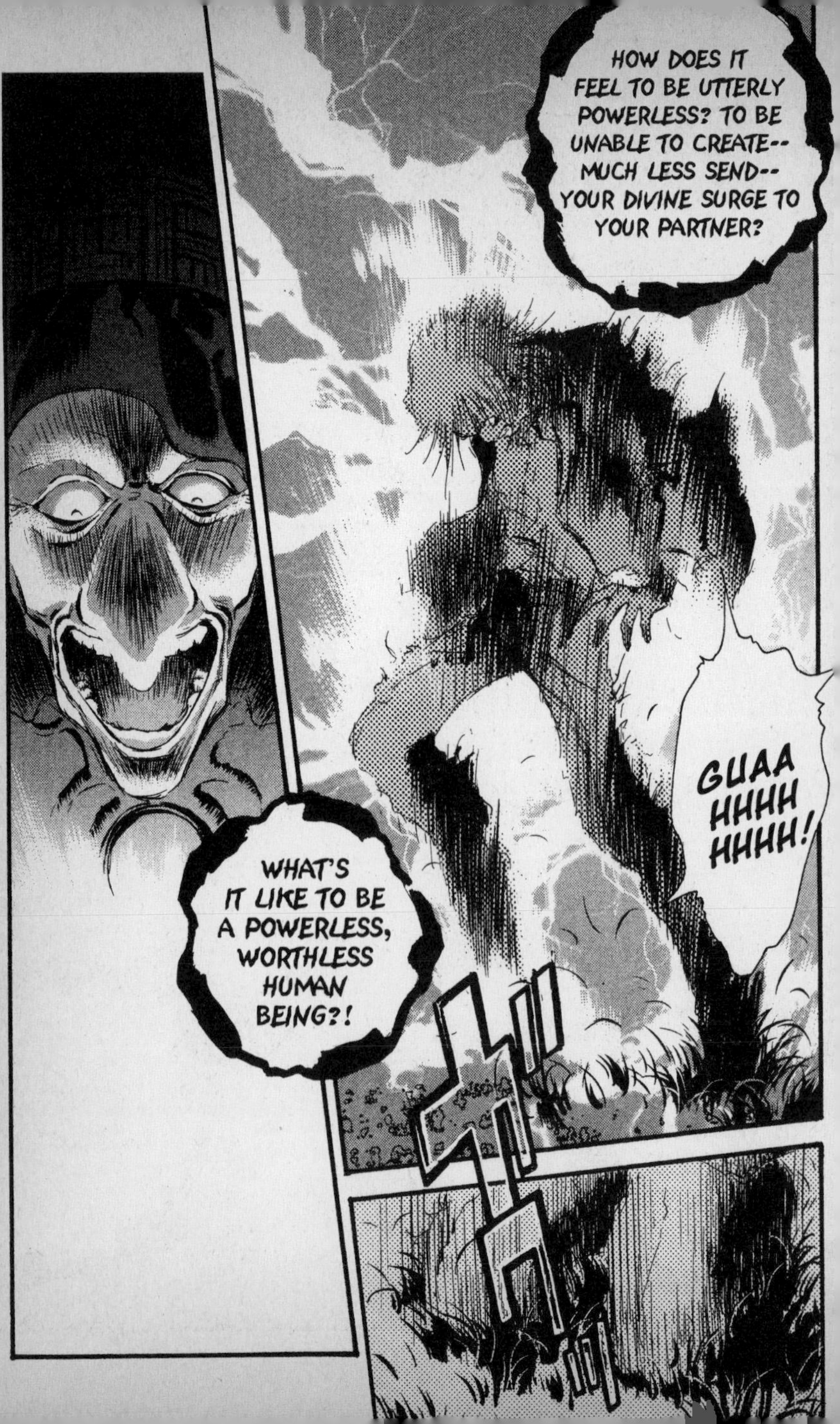
HOW DOES IT FEEL TO BE UTTERLY POWERLESS? TO BE UNABLE TO CREATE-- MUCH LESS SEND-- YOUR DIVINE SURGE TO YOUR PARTNER?
GUAA HHHH HHHH!
WHAT'S IT LIKE TO BE A POWERLESS, WORTHLESS HUMAN BEING?!

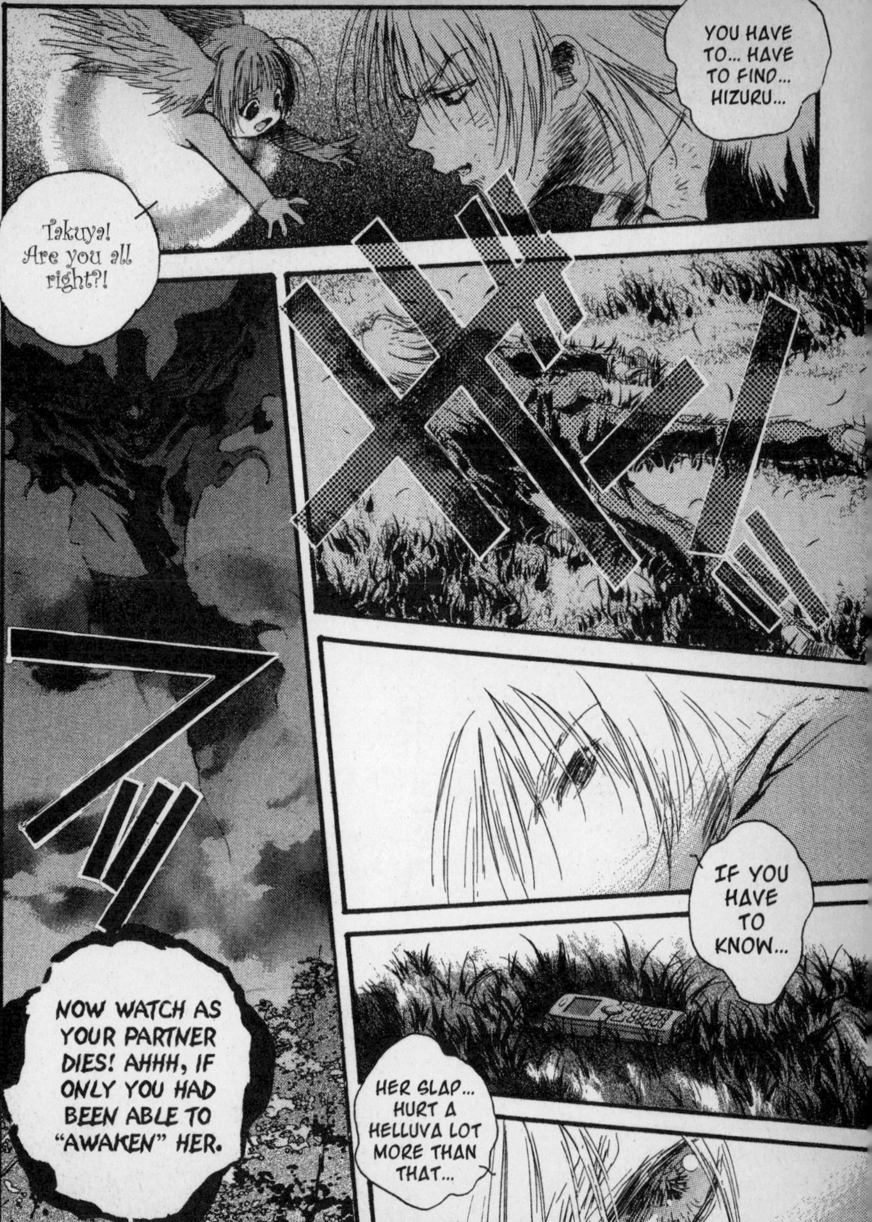
YOU HAVE TO... HAVE TO FIND... HIZURU...
Takuya! Are you all right?!
IF YOU HAVE TO KNOW...
HER SLAP... HURT A HELLUVA LOT MORE THAN THAT...
NOW WATCH AS YOUR PARTNER DIES! AHHH, IF ONLY YOU HAD BEEN ABLE TO "AWAKEN" HER.

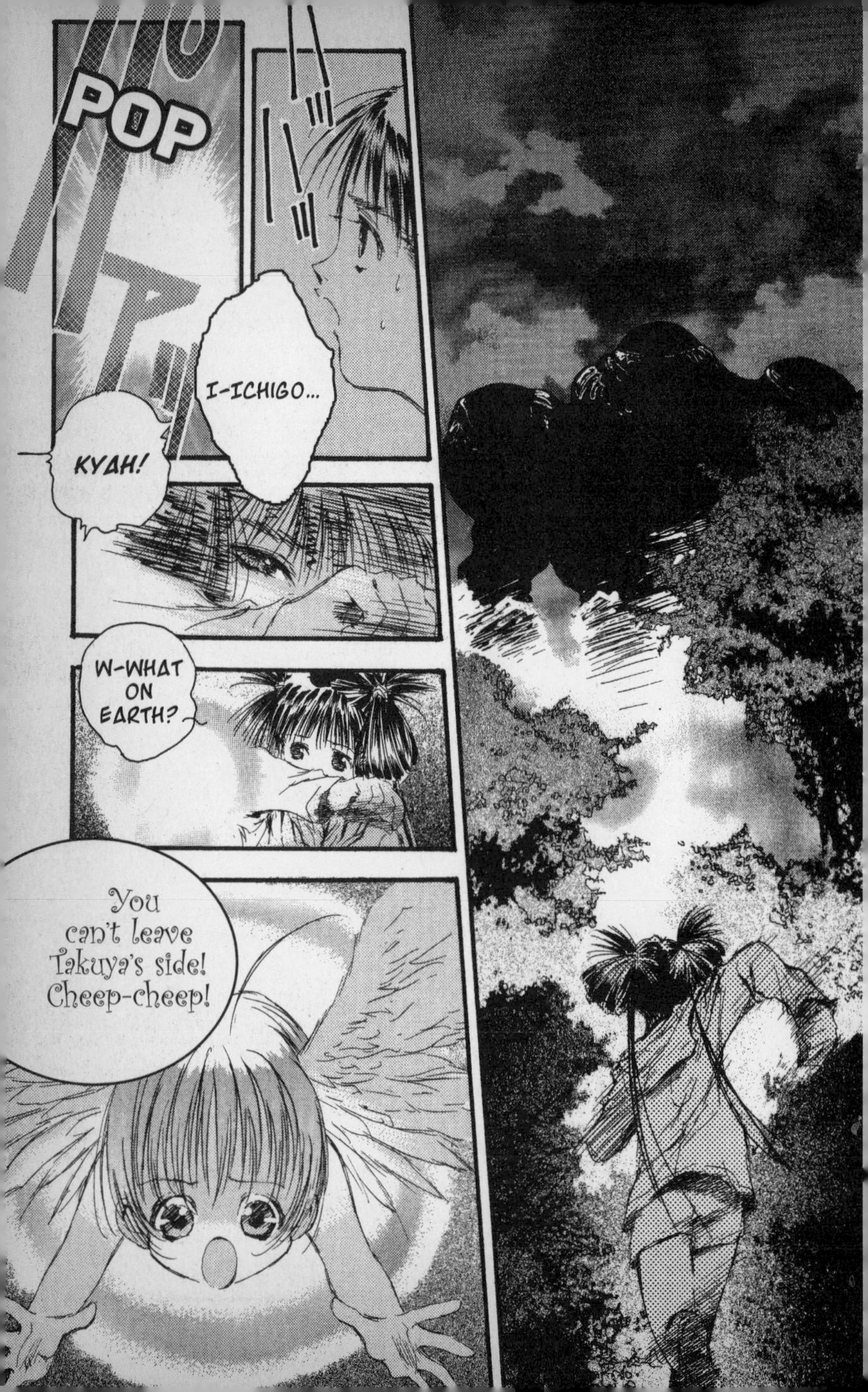
POP
I-ICHIGO...
KYAH!
W-WHAT ON EARTH?
You can't leave Takuya's side! Cheep-cheep!

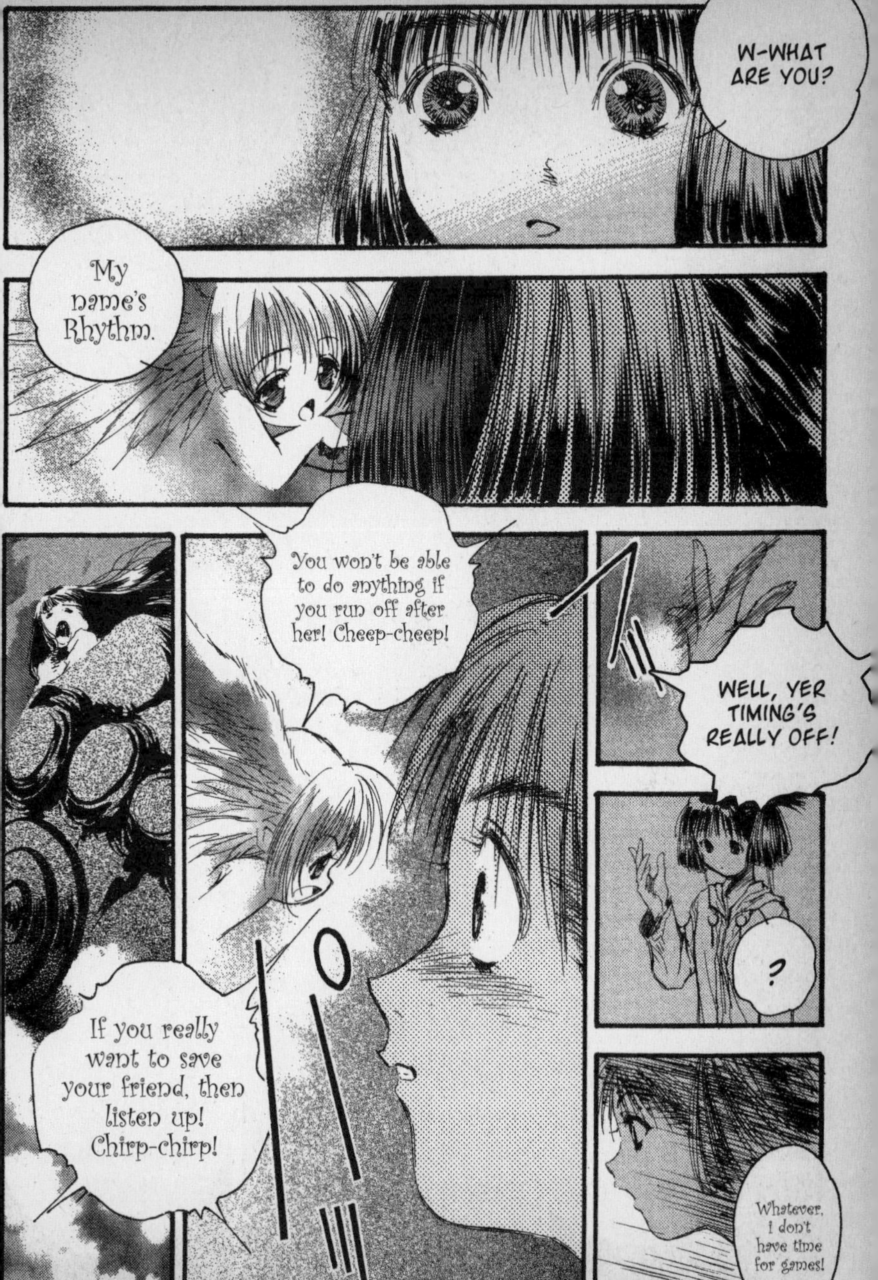
W-WHAT ARE YOU?
My name's Rhythm.
WELL, YER TIMING'S REALLY OFF!
You won't be able to do anything if you run off after her! Cheep-cheep!
?
Whatever, I don't have time for games!
If you really want to save your friend, then listen up! Chirp-chirp!

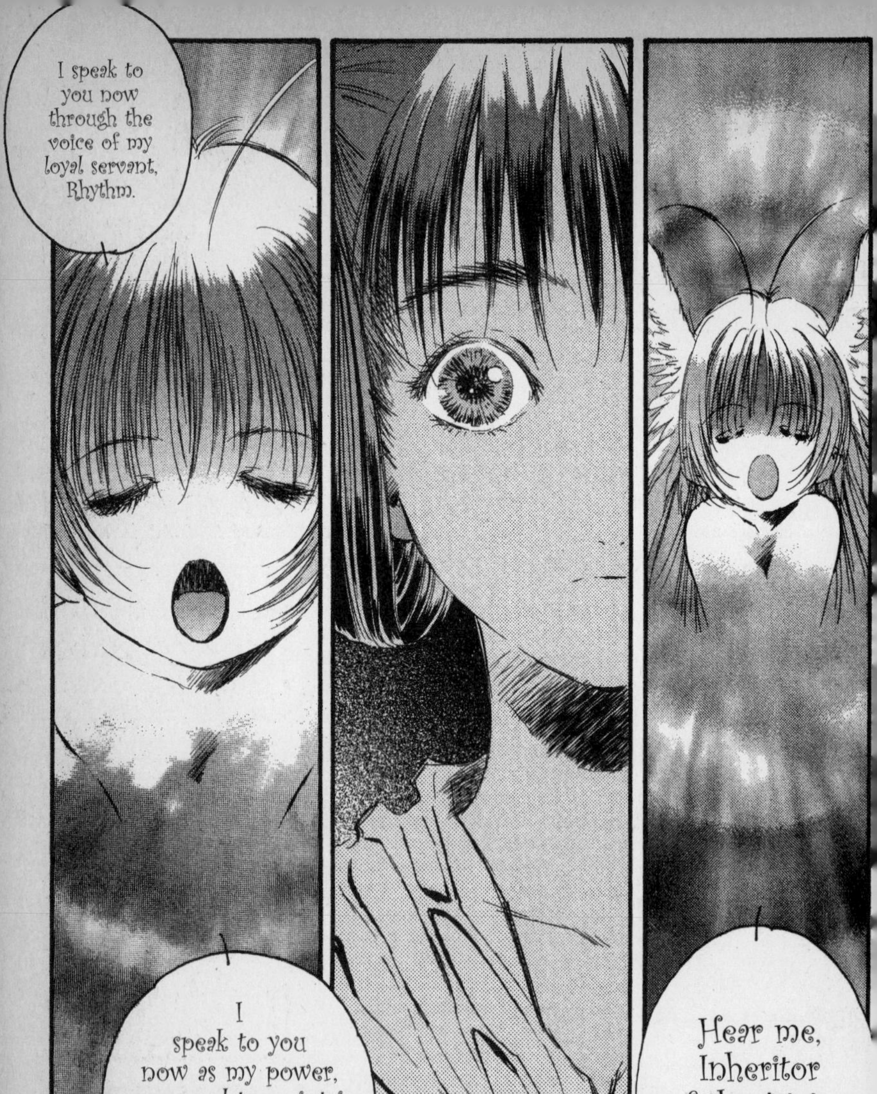
Hear me, Inheritor of the Divine Soul, Hizuru Oborozuki!
I speak to you now through the voice of my loyal servant, Rhythm.
I speak to you now as my power, once used to maintain the Equilibrium by banishing Demons into darkness, wanes.

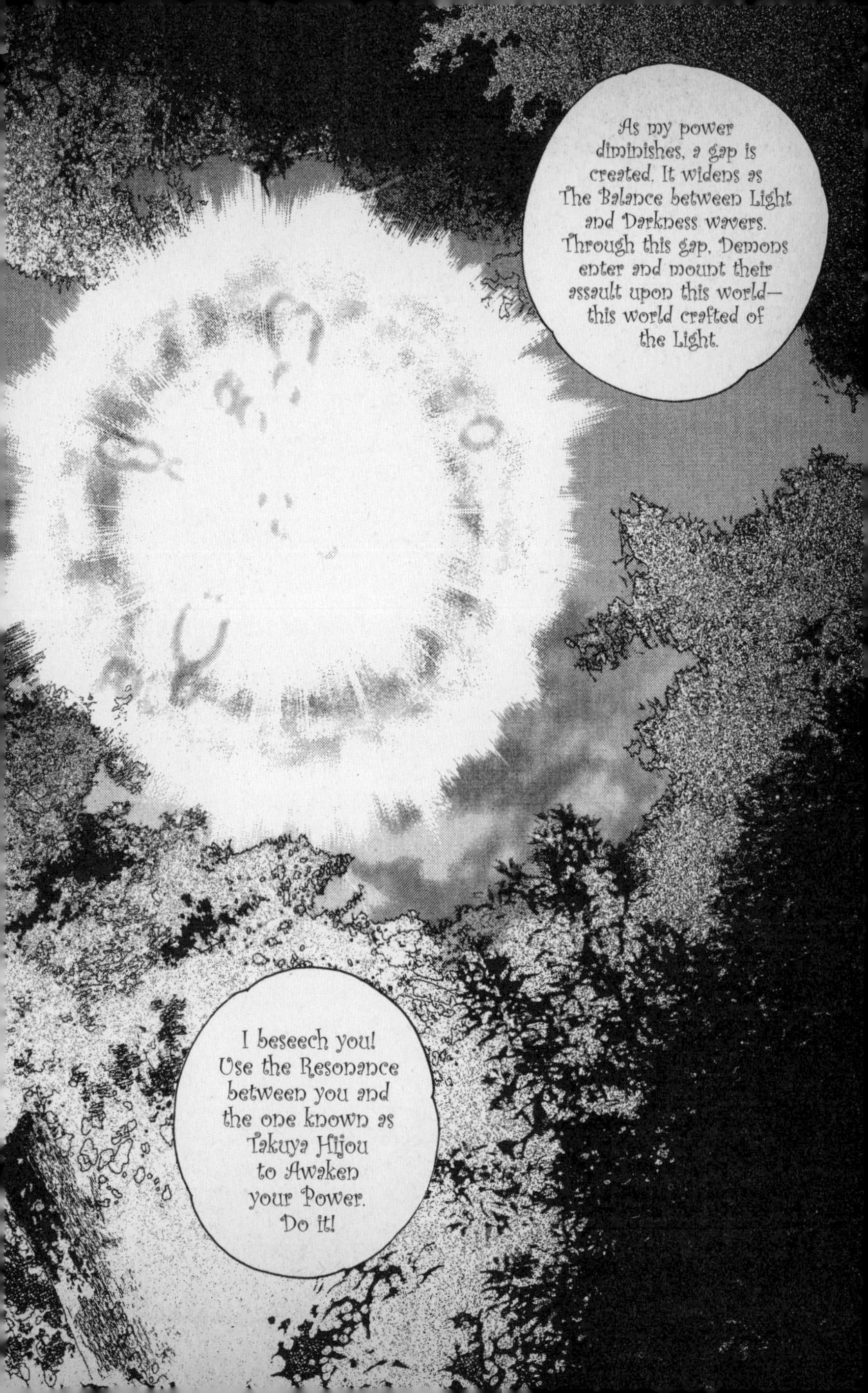
As my power diminishes, a gap is created. It widens as The Balance between Light and Darkness wavers. Through this gap, Demons enter and mount their assault upon this world—this world crafted of the Light.
I beseech you! Use the Resonance between you and the one known as Takuya Hijou to Awaken your Power. Do it!

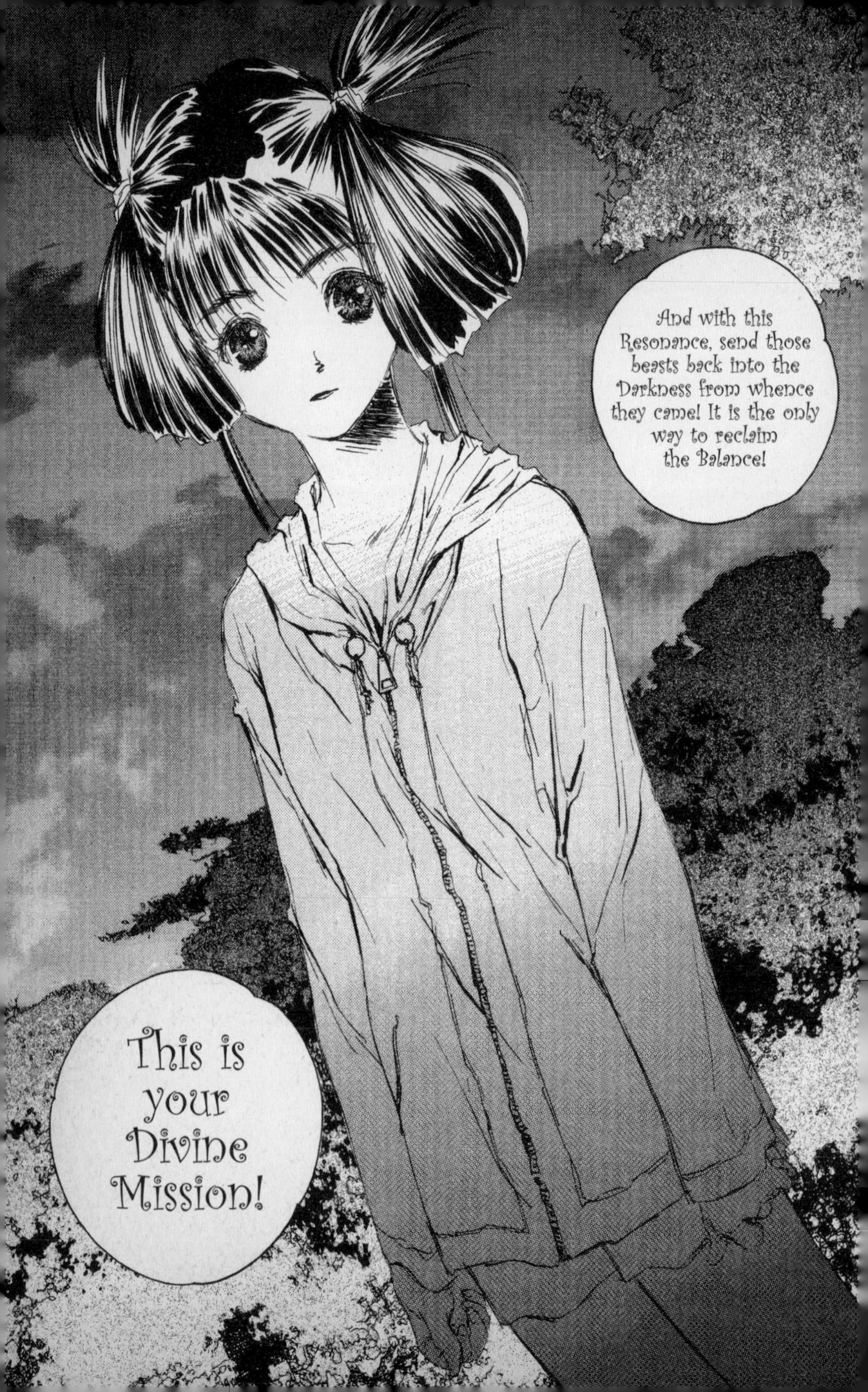
And with this Resonance, send those beasts back into the Darkness from whence they came! It is the only way to reclaim the Balance!
This is your Divine Mission!

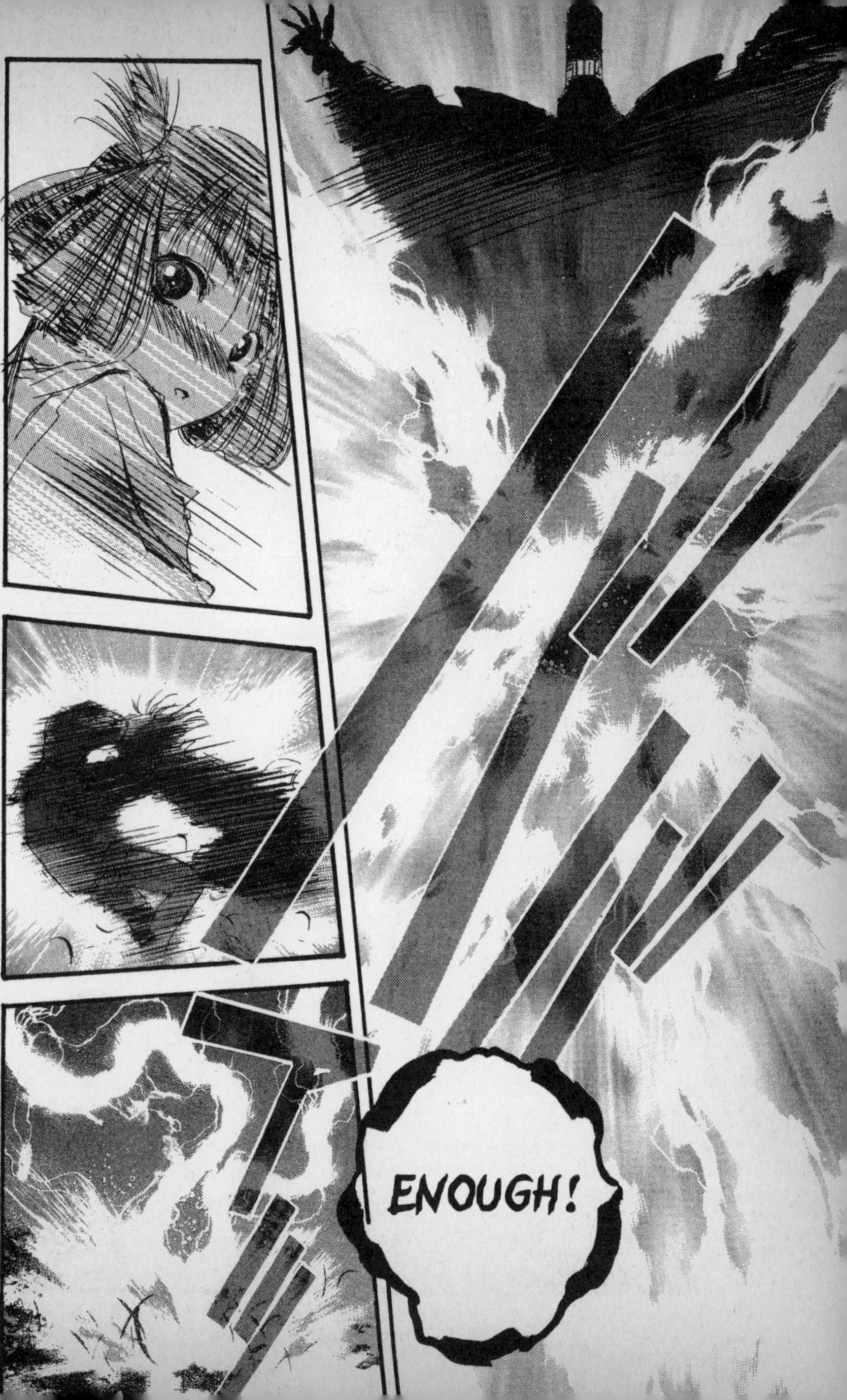
ENOUGH!

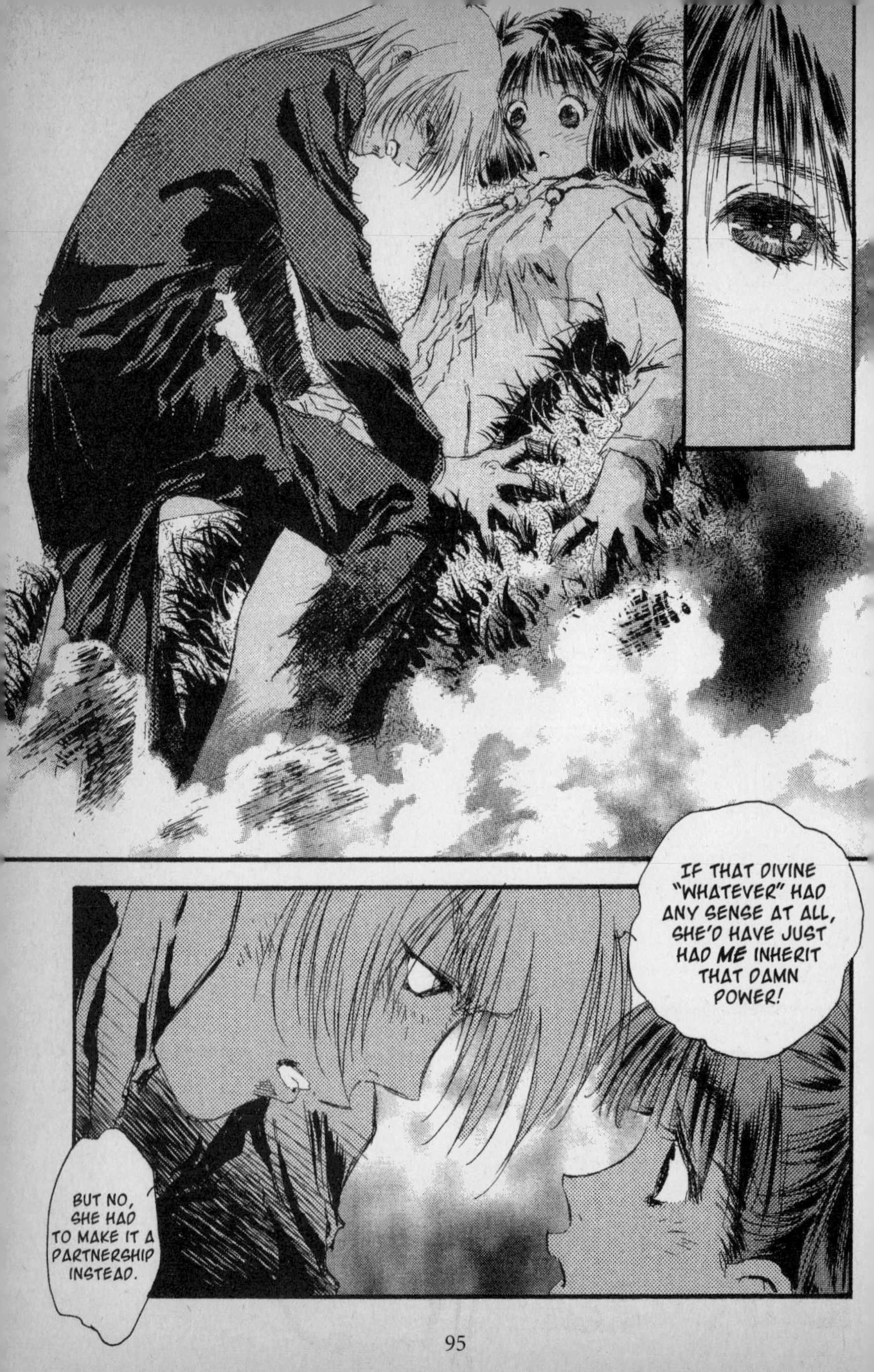
IF THAT DIVINE "WHATEVER" HAD ANY SENSE AT ALL, SHE'D HAVE JUST HAD ME INHERIT THAT DAMN POWER!
BUT NO, SHE HAD TO MAKE IT A PARTNERSHIP INSTEAD.

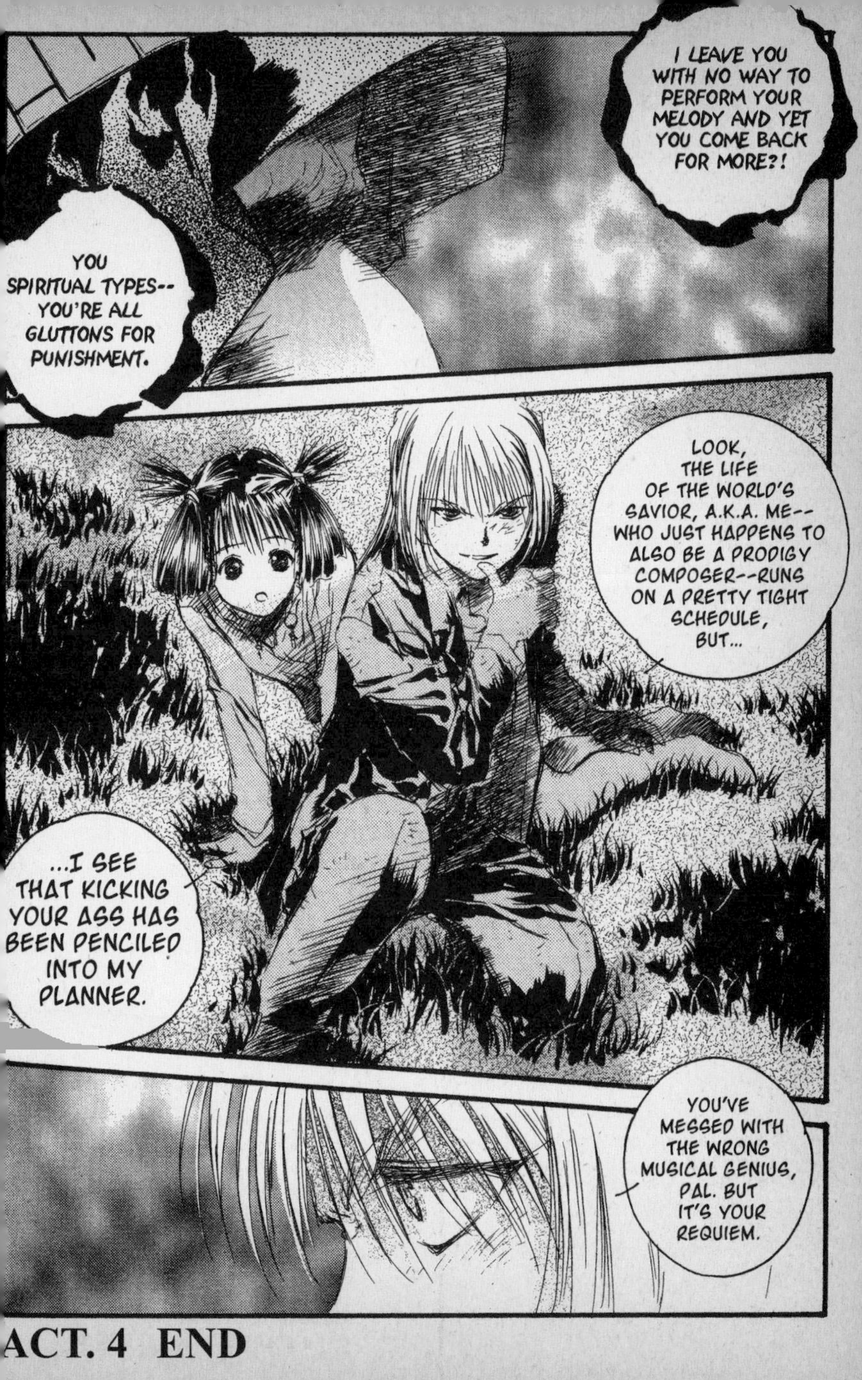
I LEAVE YOU WITH NO WAY TO PERFORM YOUR MELODY AND YET YOU COME BACK FOR MORE?!
YOU SPIRITUAL TYPES-- YOU'RE ALL GLUTTONS FOR PUNISHMENT.
LOOK, THE LIFE OF THE WORLD'S SAVIOR, A.K.A. ME-- WHO JUST HAPPENS TO ALSO BE A PRODIGY COMPOSER--RUNS ON A PRETTY TIGHT SCHEDULE, BUT...
...I SEE THAT KICKING YOUR ASS HAS BEEN PENCILED INTO MY PLANNER.
YOU'VE MESSED WITH THE WRONG MUSICAL GENIUS, PAL. BUT IT'S YOUR REQUIEM.

ACT. 4 END

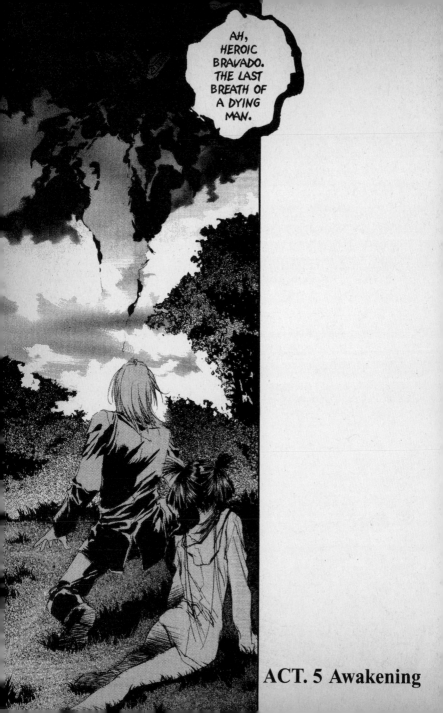

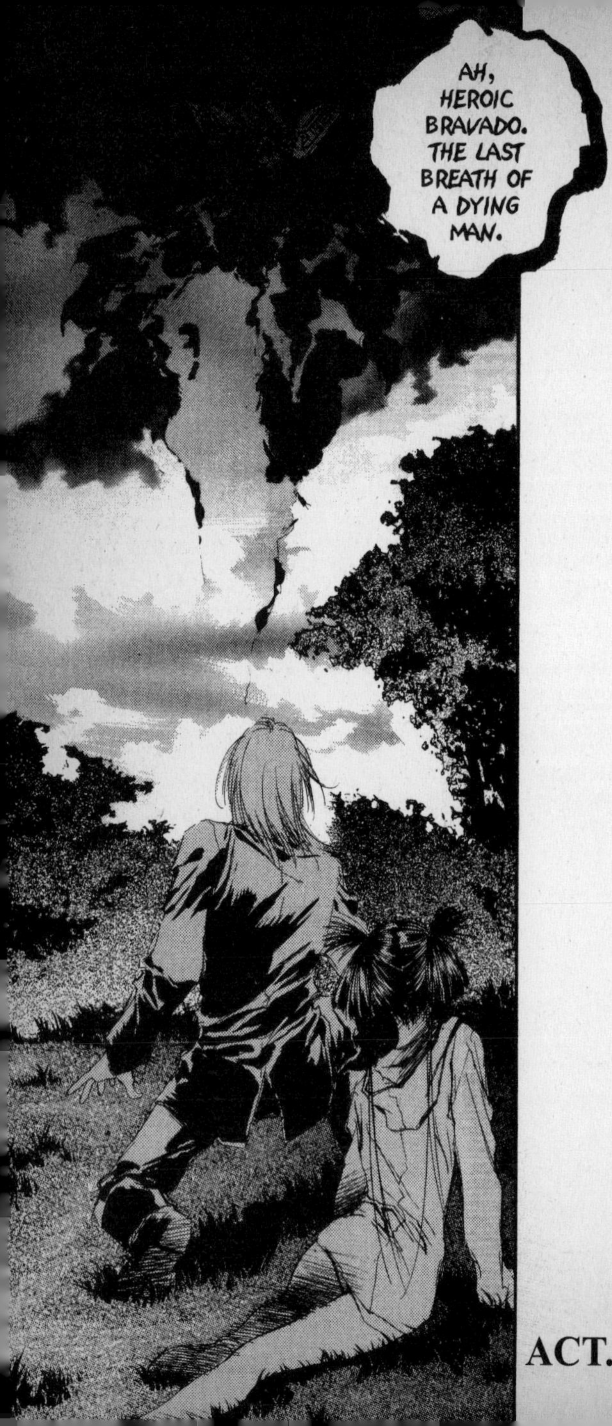
AH, HEROIC BRAVADO. THE LAST BREATH OF A DYING MAN.

ACT. 5 Awakening

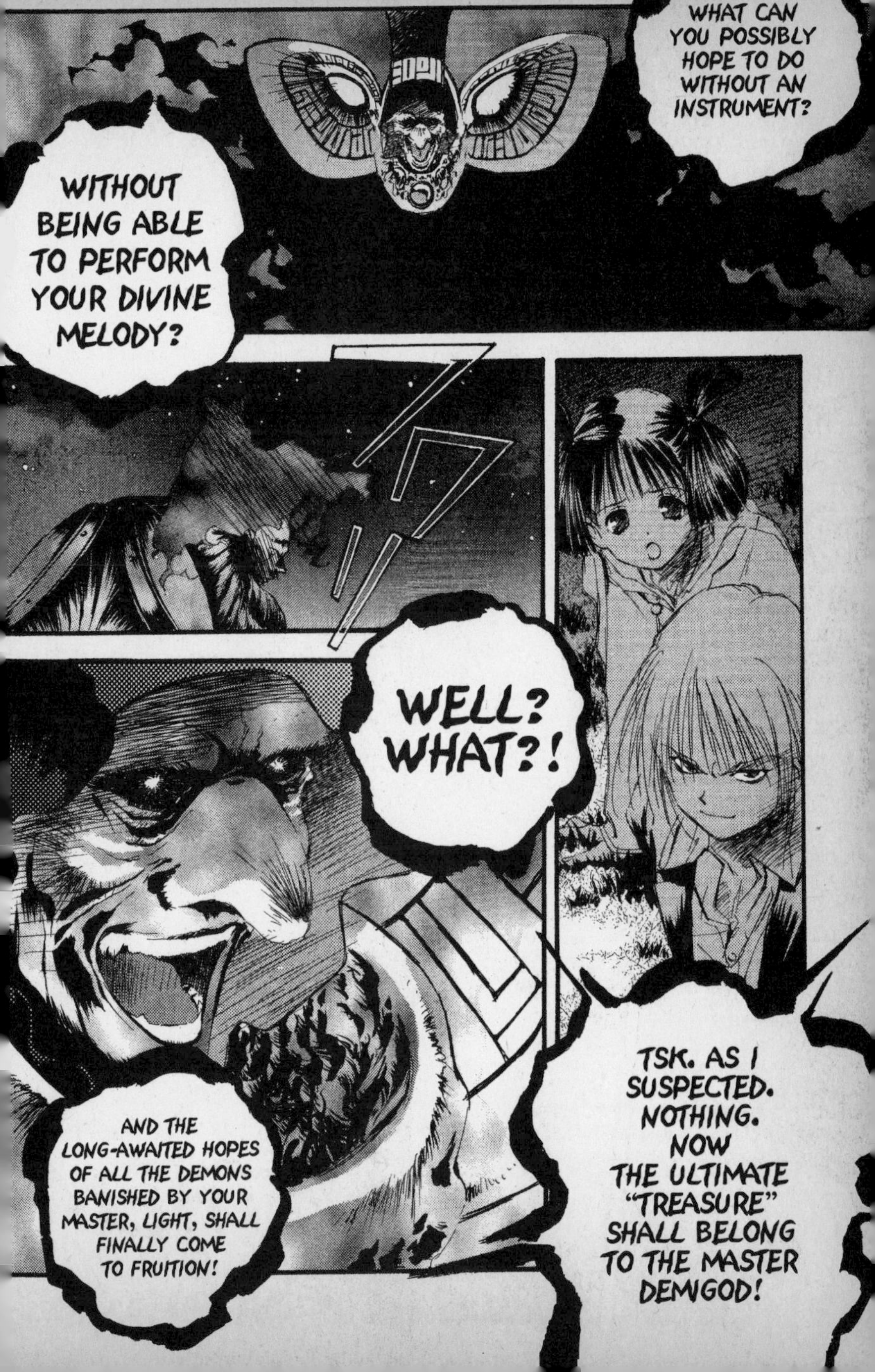
WHAT CAN YOU POSSIBLY HOPE TO DO WITHOUT AN INSTRUMENT?
WITHOUT BEING ABLE TO PERFORM YOUR DIVINE MELODY?
WELL? WHAT?!
TSK. AS I SUSPECTED. NOTHING. NOW THE ULTIMATE "TREASURE" SHALL BELONG TO THE MASTER DEMIGOD!
AND THE LONG-AWAITED HOPES OF ALL THE DEMONS BANISHED BY YOUR MASTER, LIGHT, SHALL FINALLY COME TO FRUITION!

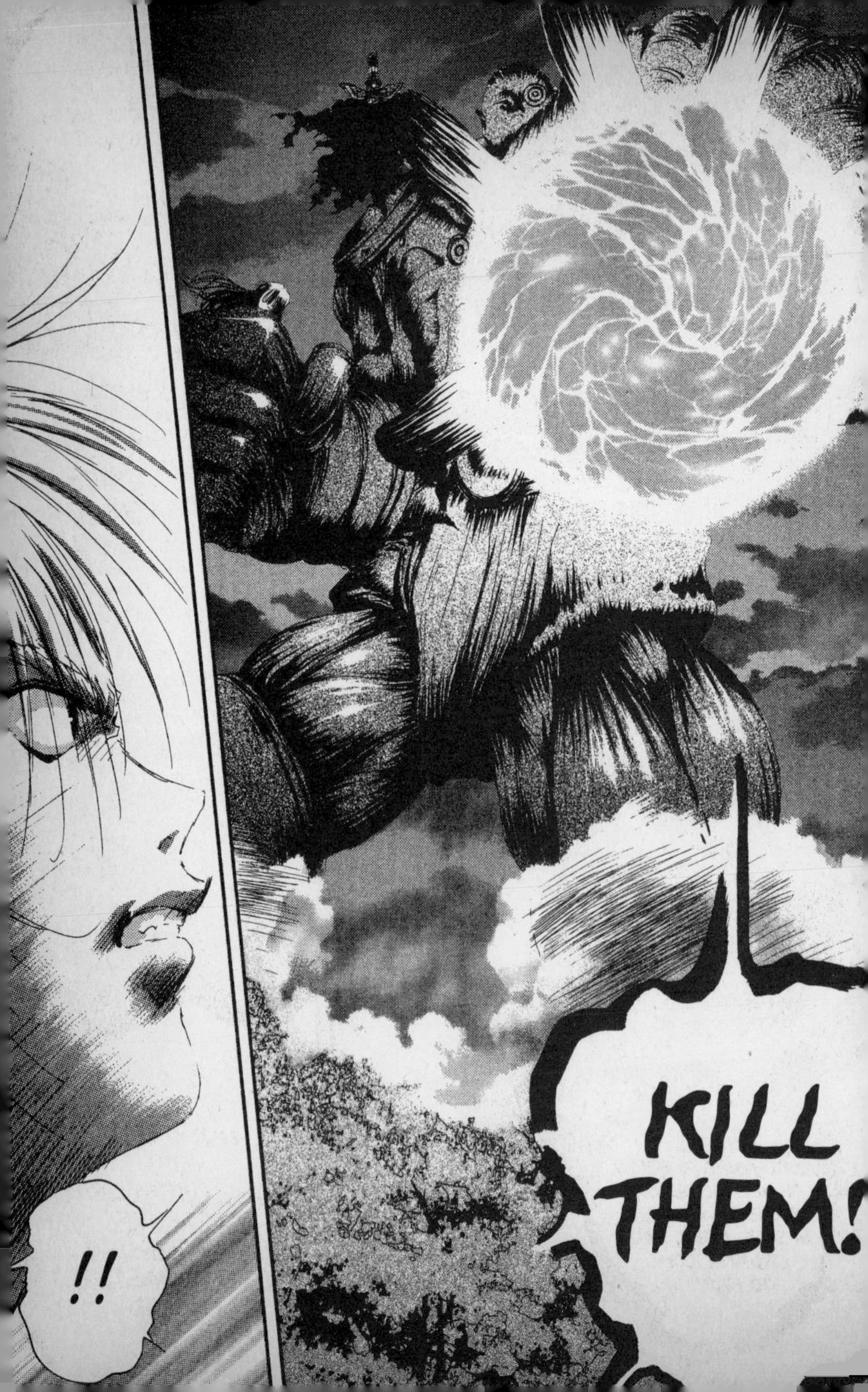
KILL THEM!
!!

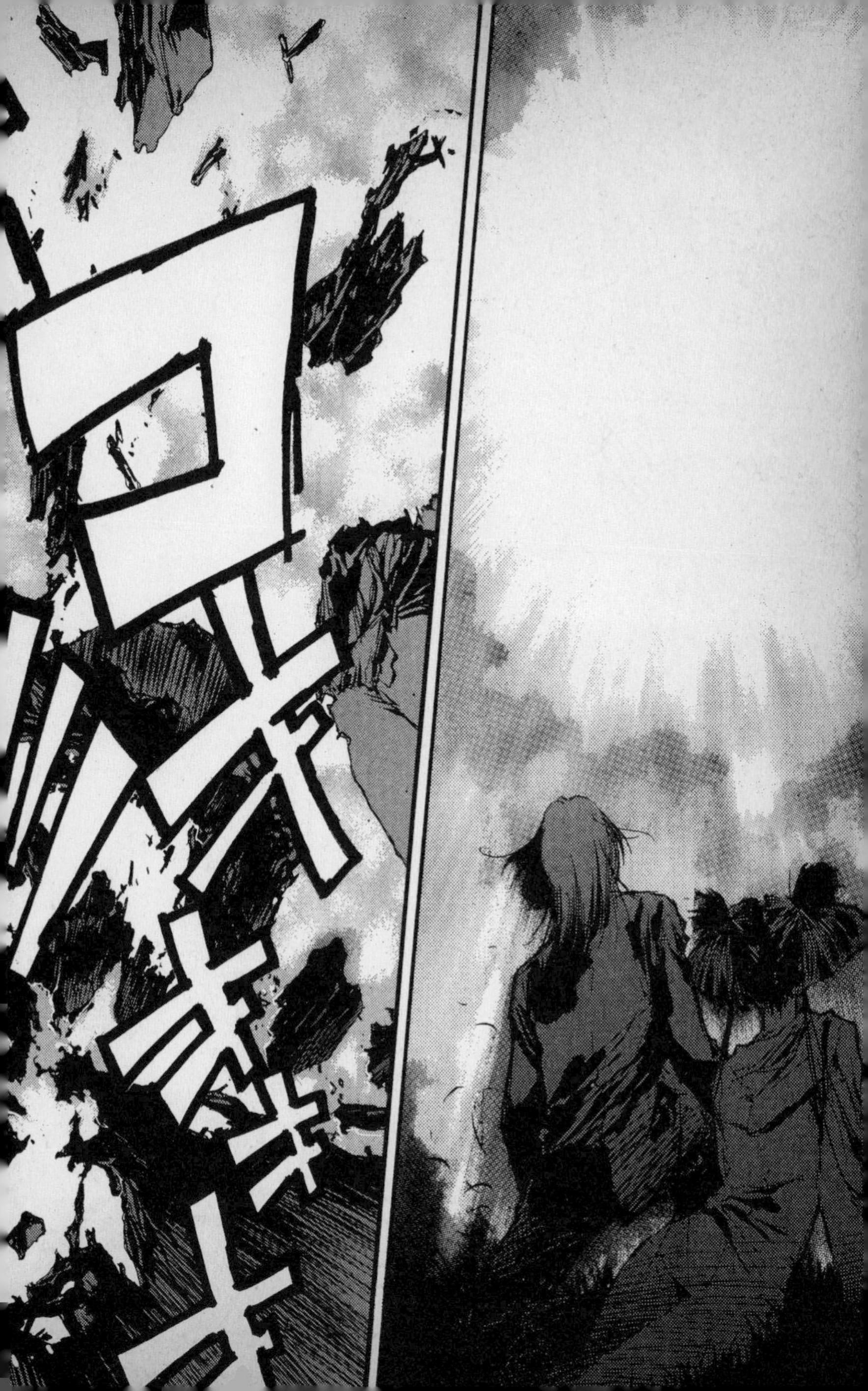

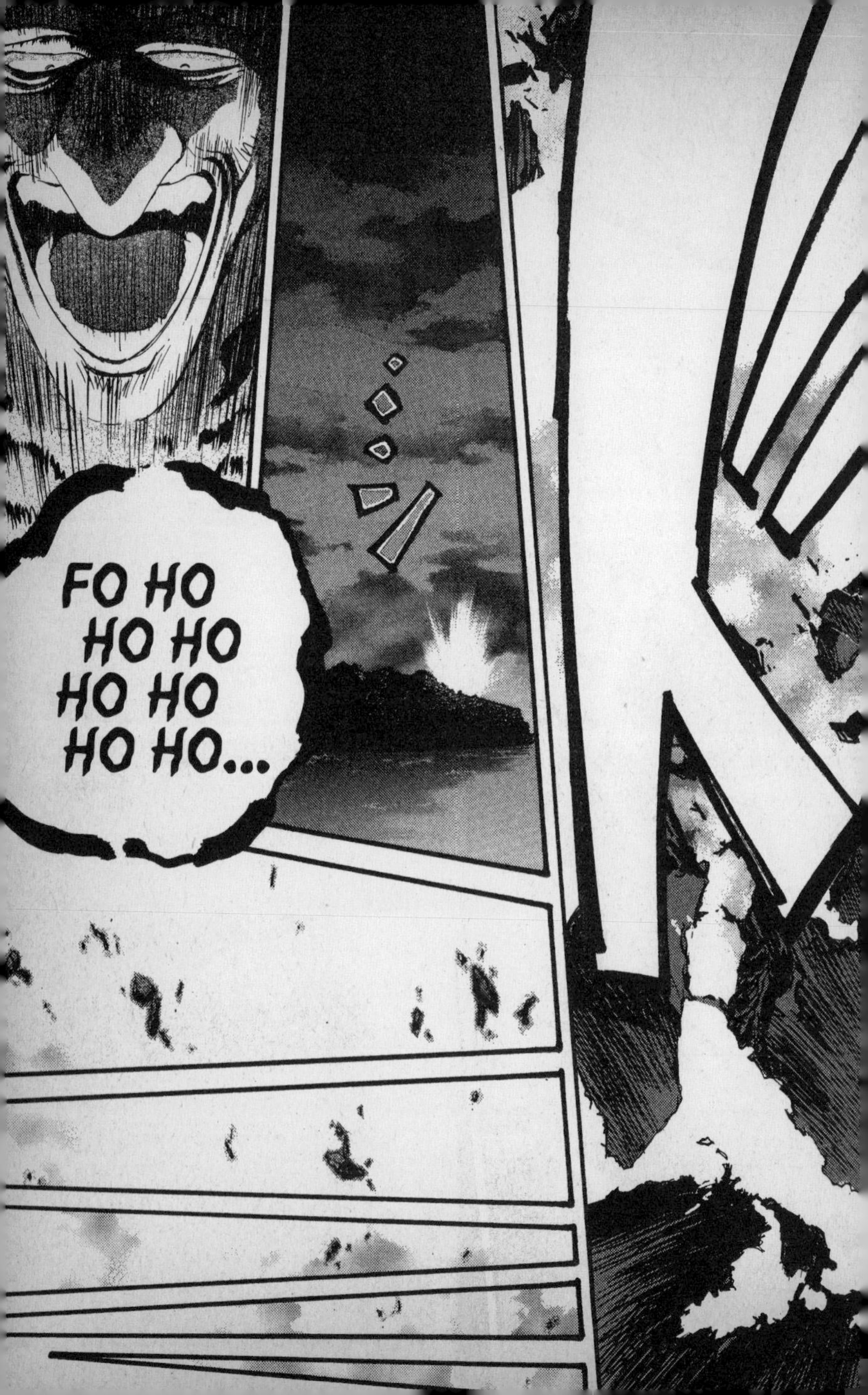
FO HO HO HO HO HO HO HO...

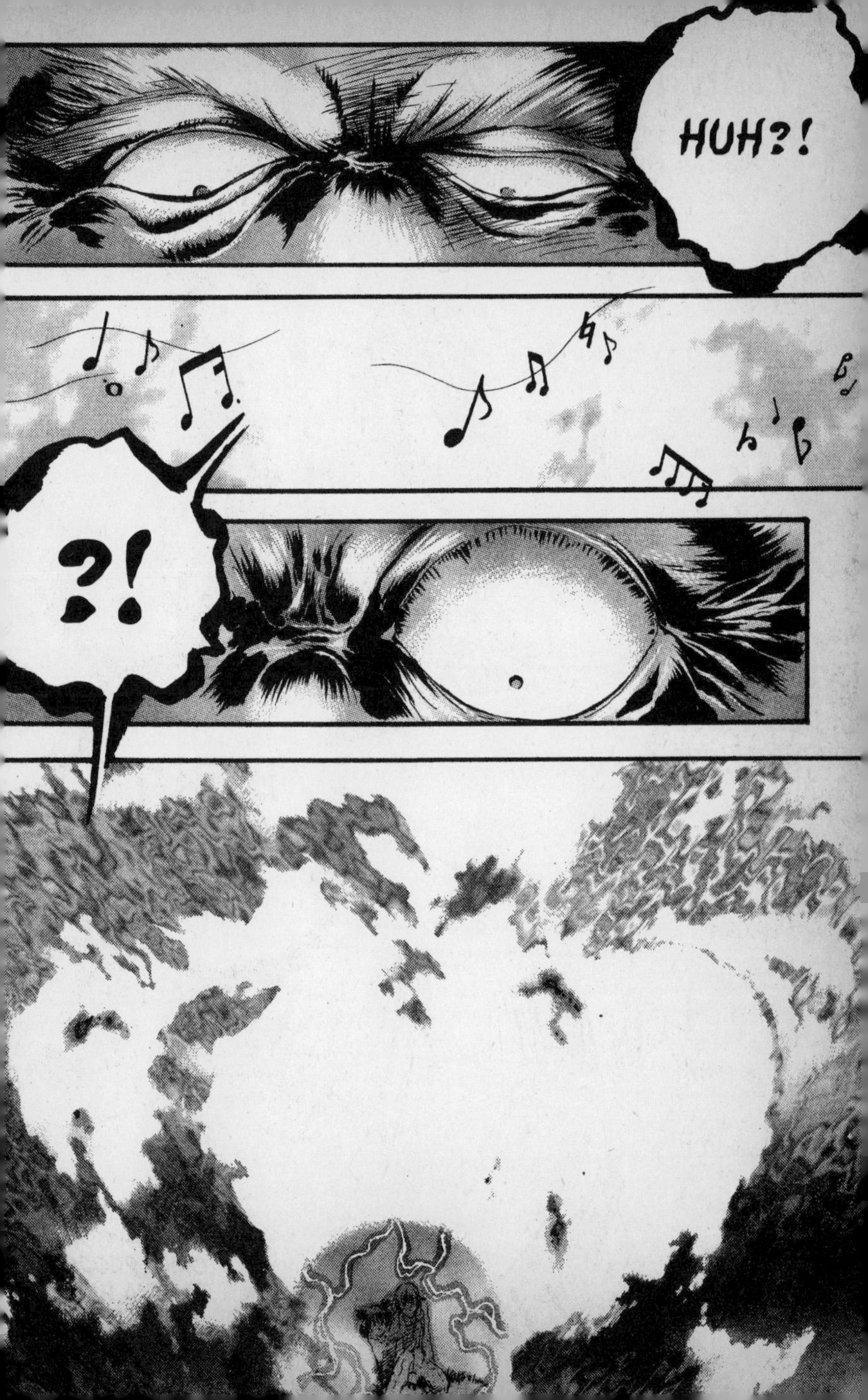
HUH?!
?!

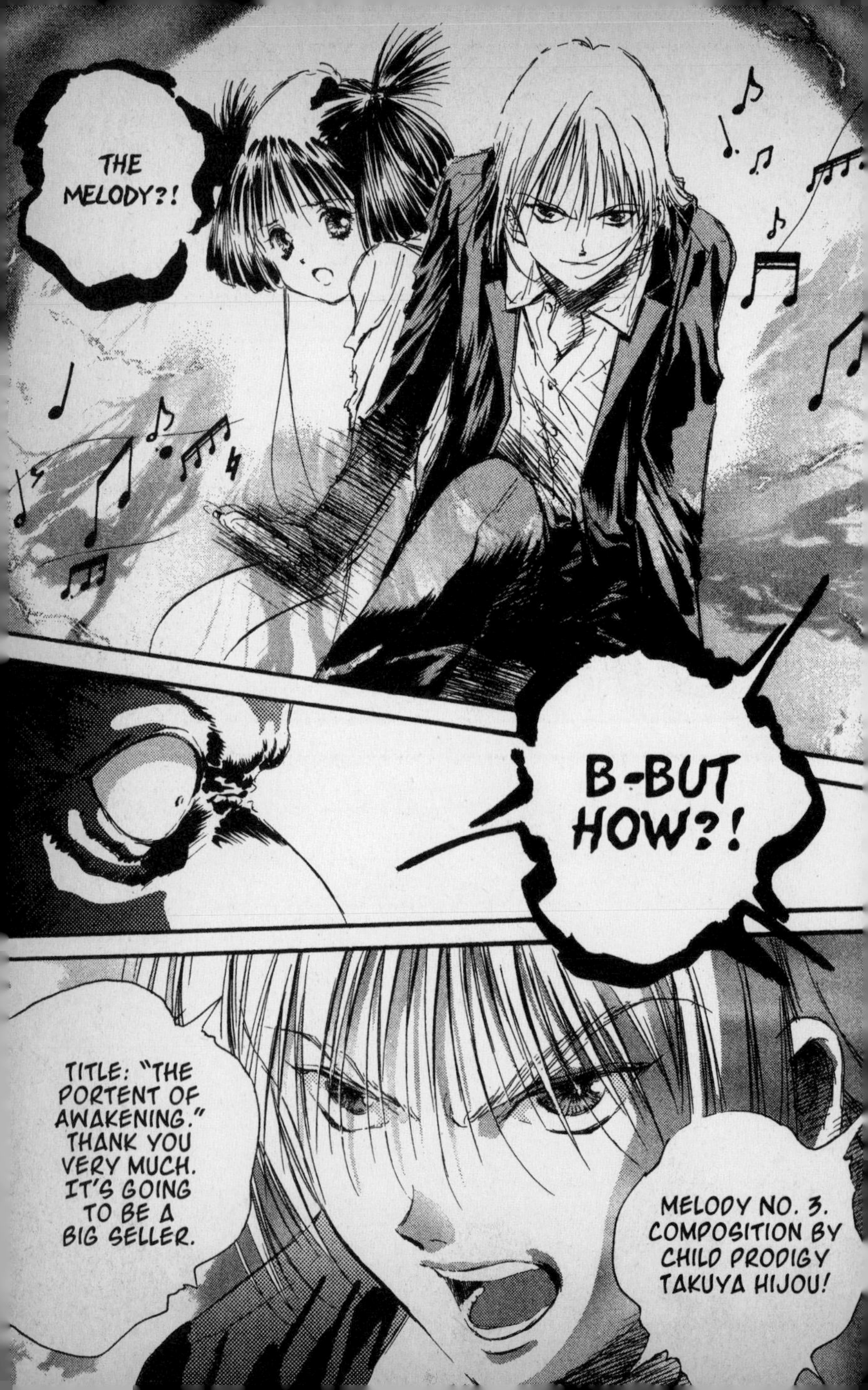
THE MELODY?!
B-BUT HOW?!
MELODY NO. 3. COMPOSITION BY CHILD PRODIGY TAKUYA HIJOU!
TITLE: "THE PORTENT OF AWAKENING." THANK YOU VERY MUCH. IT'S GOING TO BE A BIG SELLER.

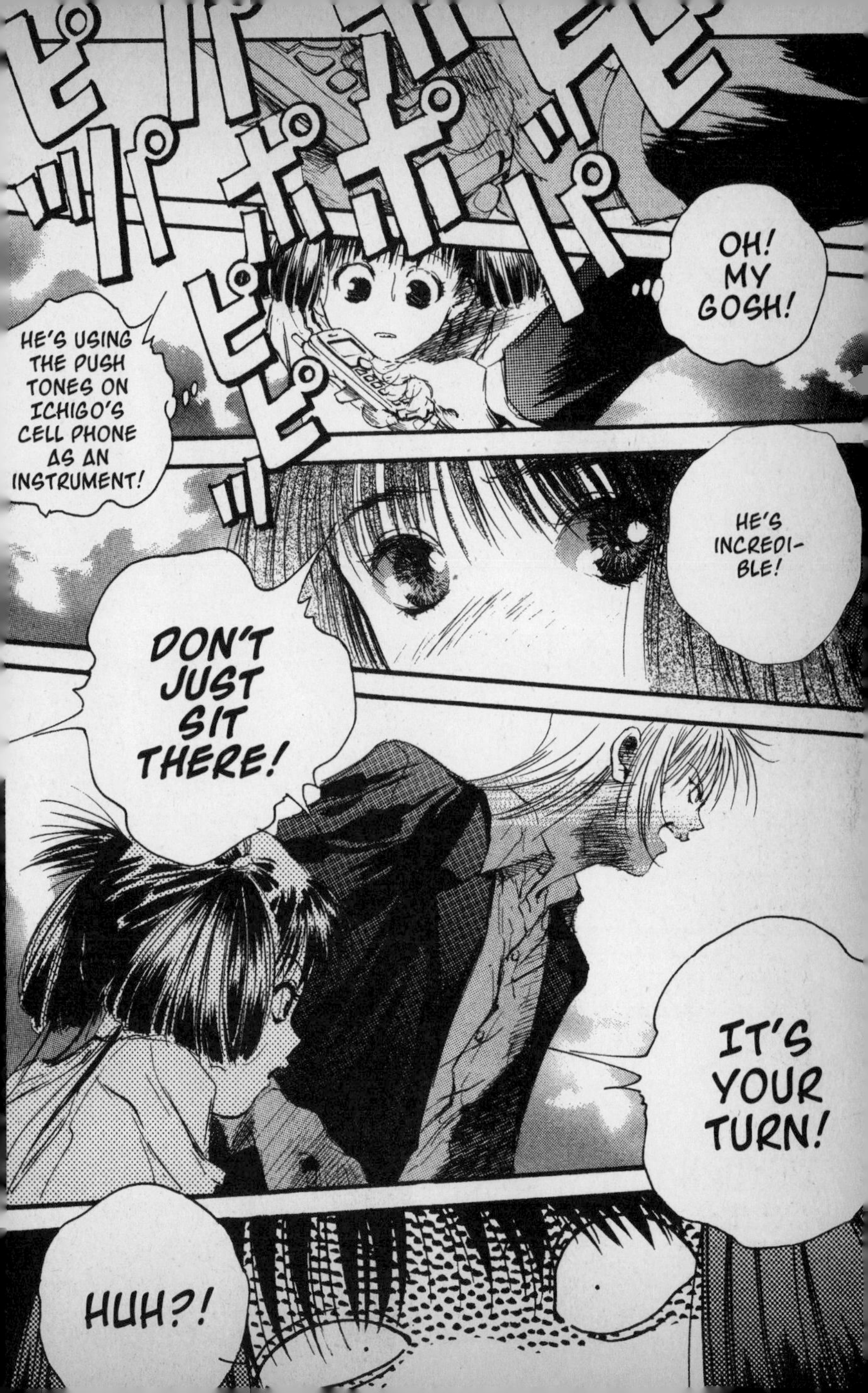
OH! MY GOSH!
HE'S USING THE PUSH TONES ON ICHIGO'S CELL PHONE AS AN INSTRUMENT!
HE'S INCREDI-BLE!
DON'T JUST SIT THERE!
IT'S YOUR TURN!
HUH?!

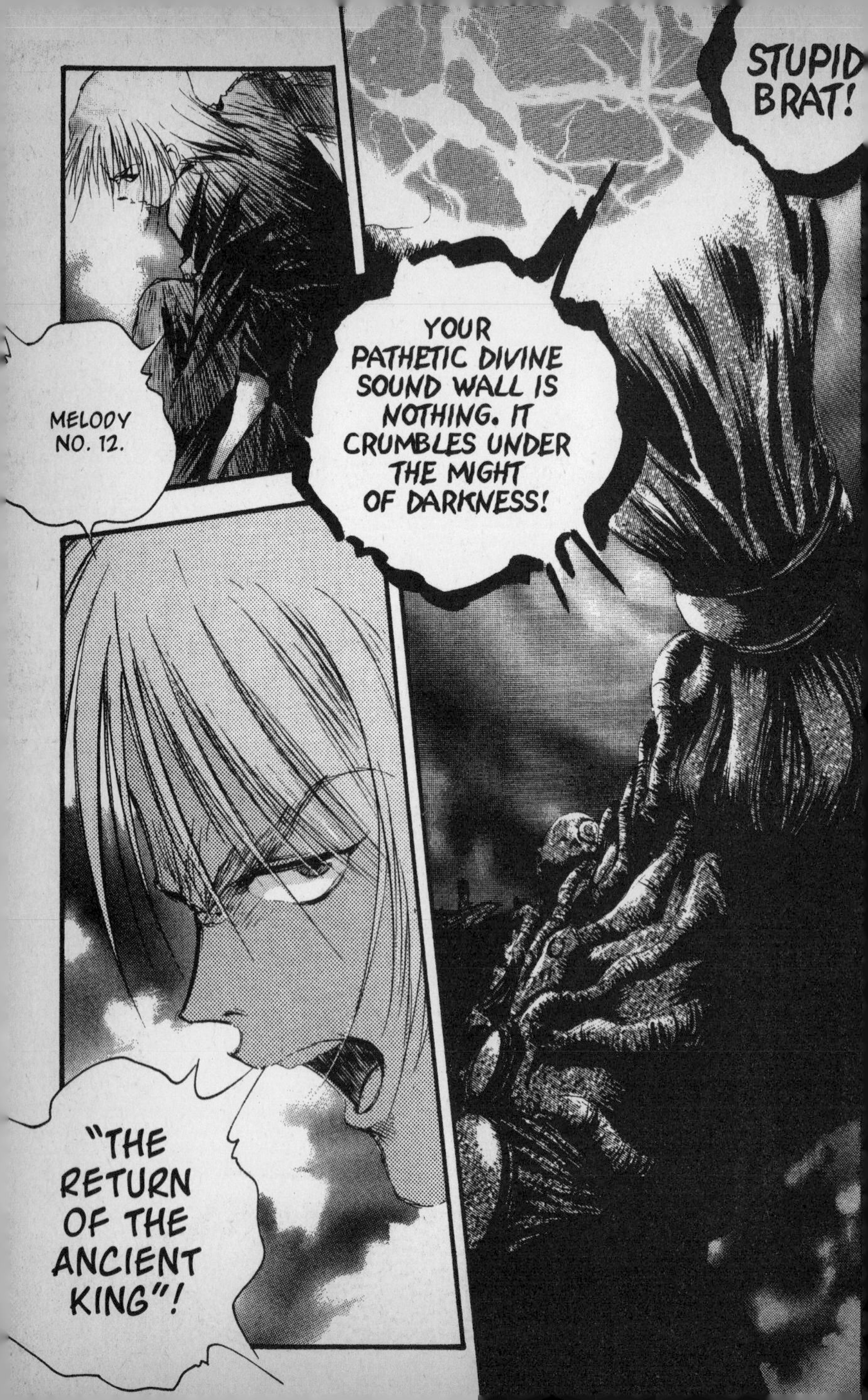
STUPID BRAT!
YOUR PATHETIC DIVINE SOUND WALL IS NOTHING. IT CRUMBLES UNDER THE MIGHT OF DARKNESS!
MELODY NO. 12.
"THE RETURN OF THE ANCIENT KING"!

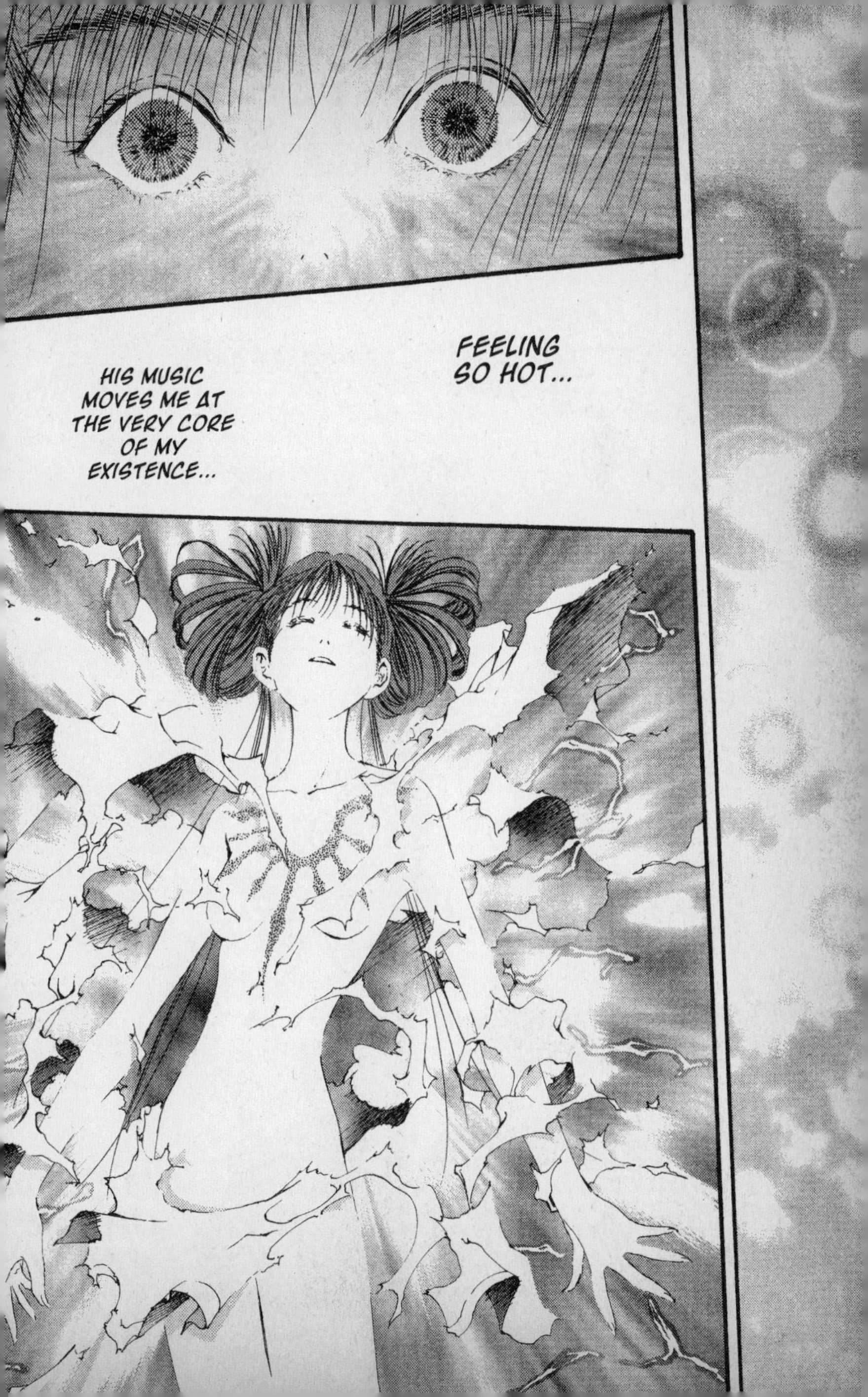
FEELING SO HOT...
HIS MUSIC MOVES ME AT THE VERY CORE OF MY EXISTENCE...

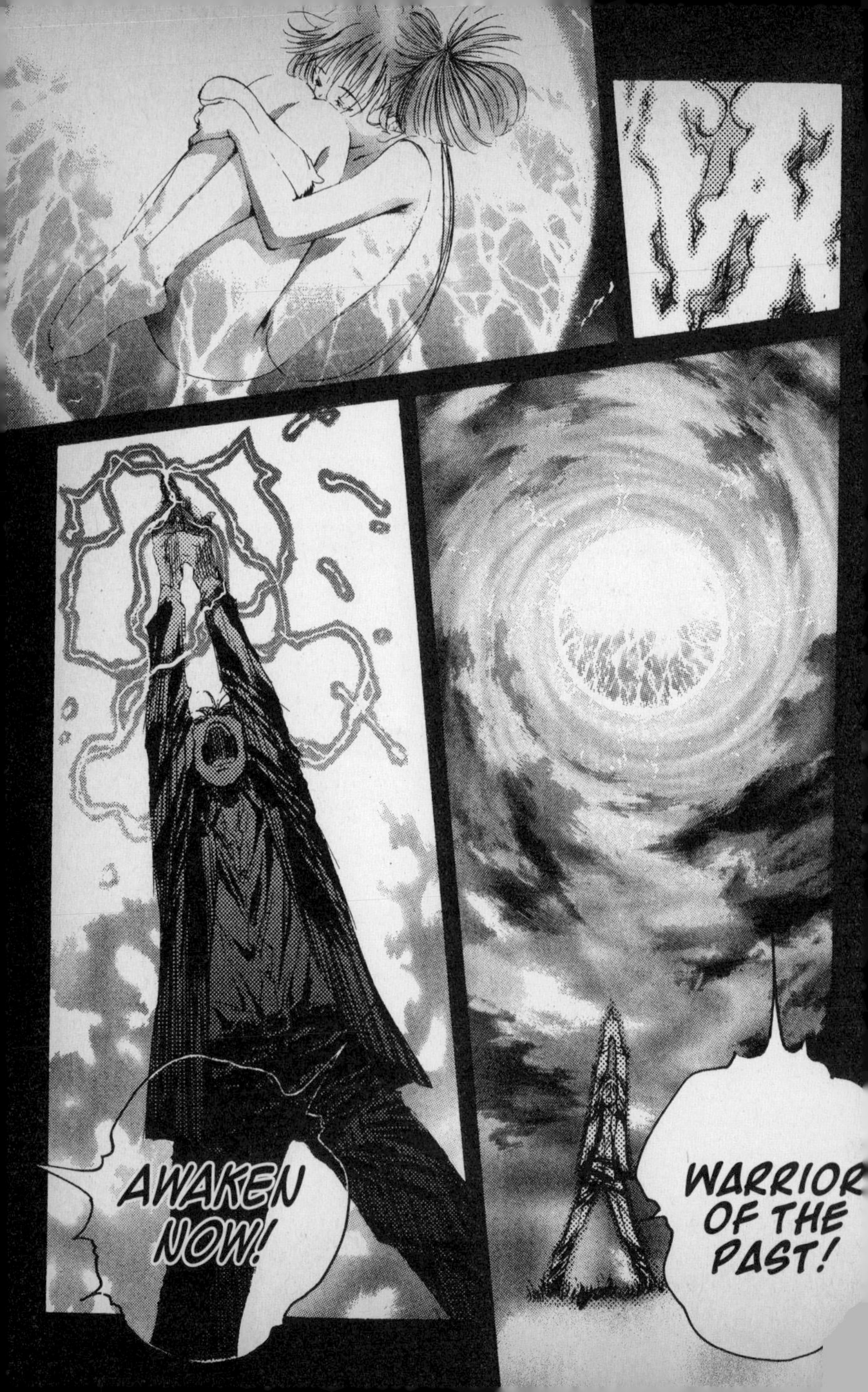
WARRIOR OF THE PAST!
AWAKEN NOW!

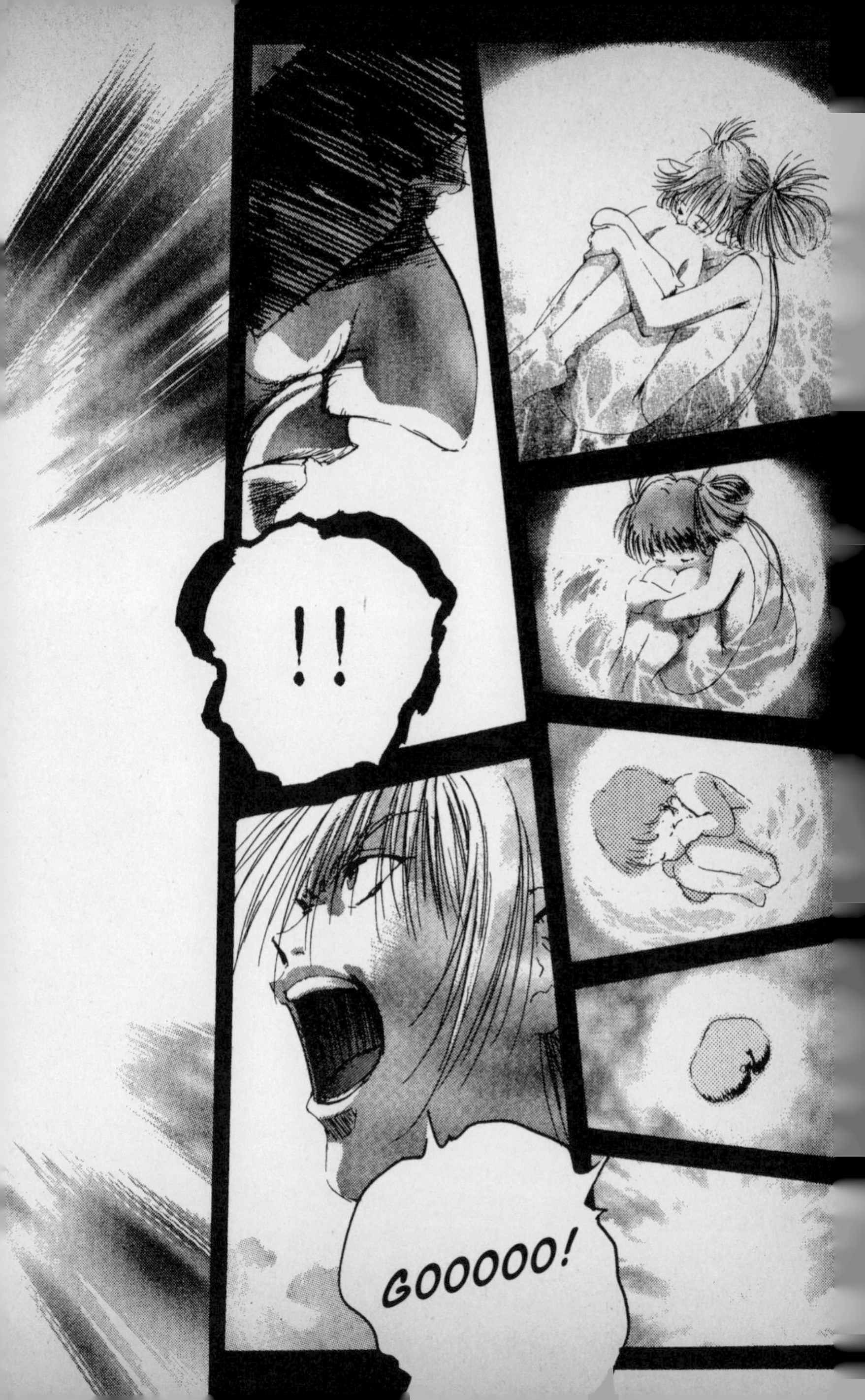
!!
GOOOOO!

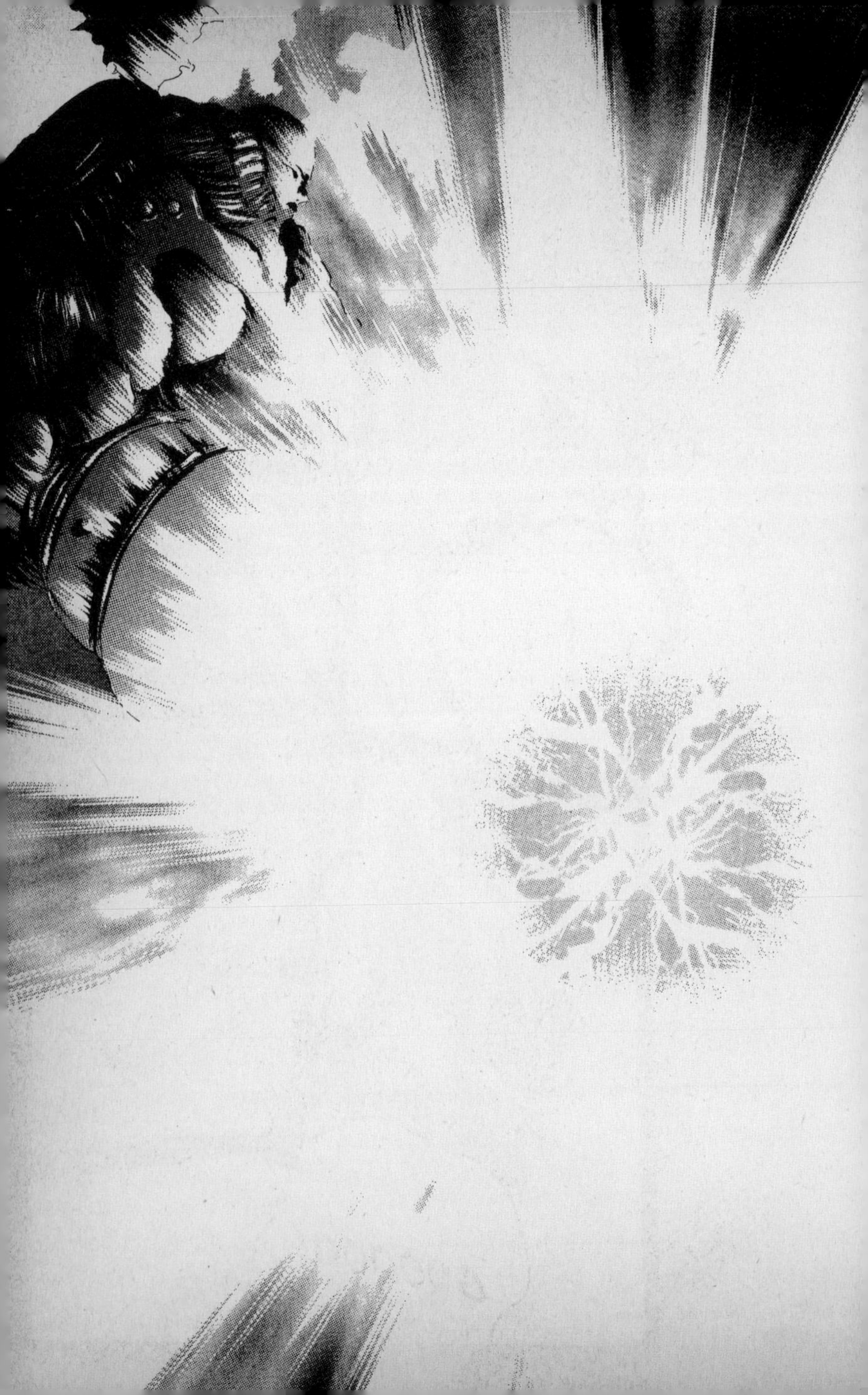

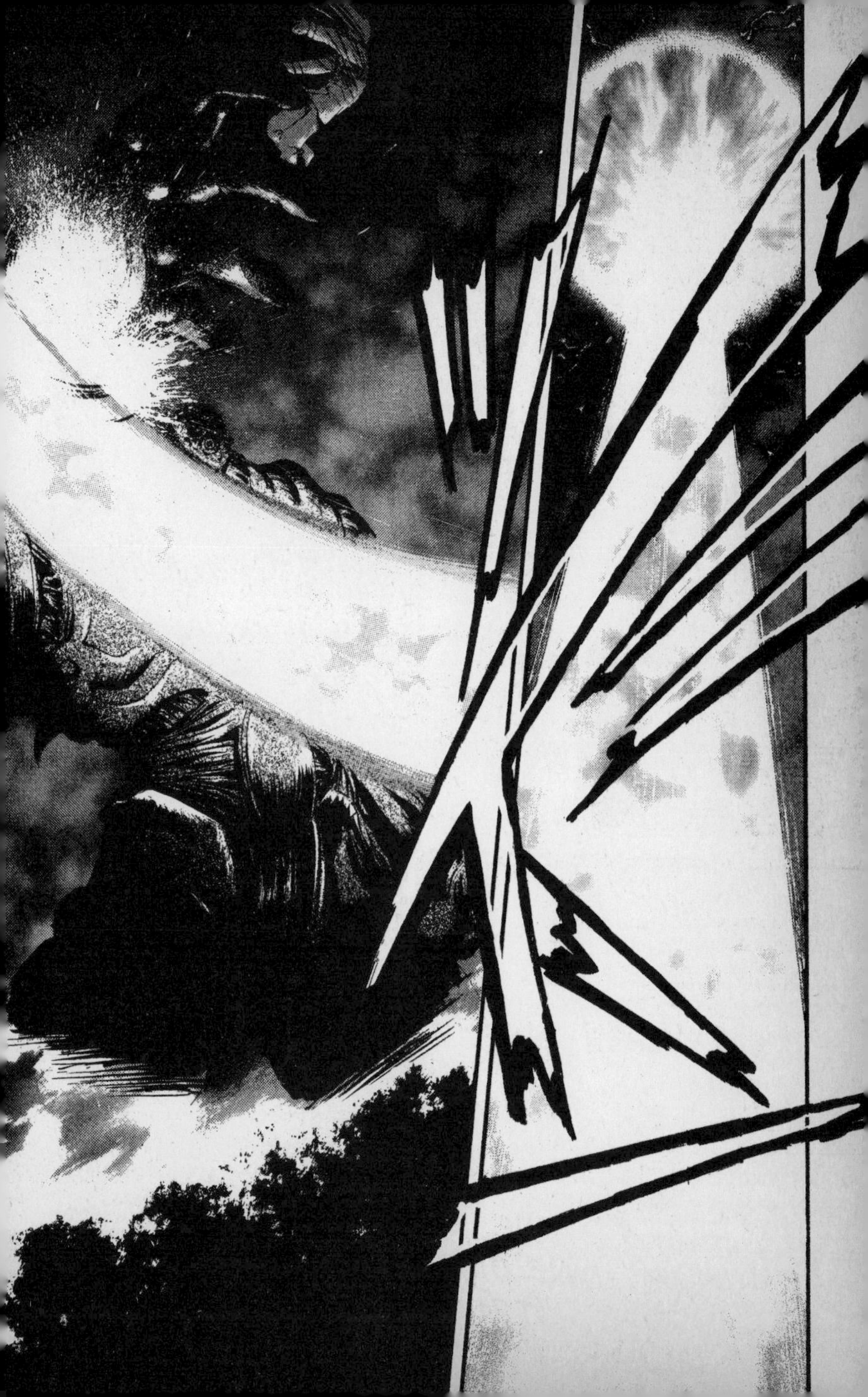

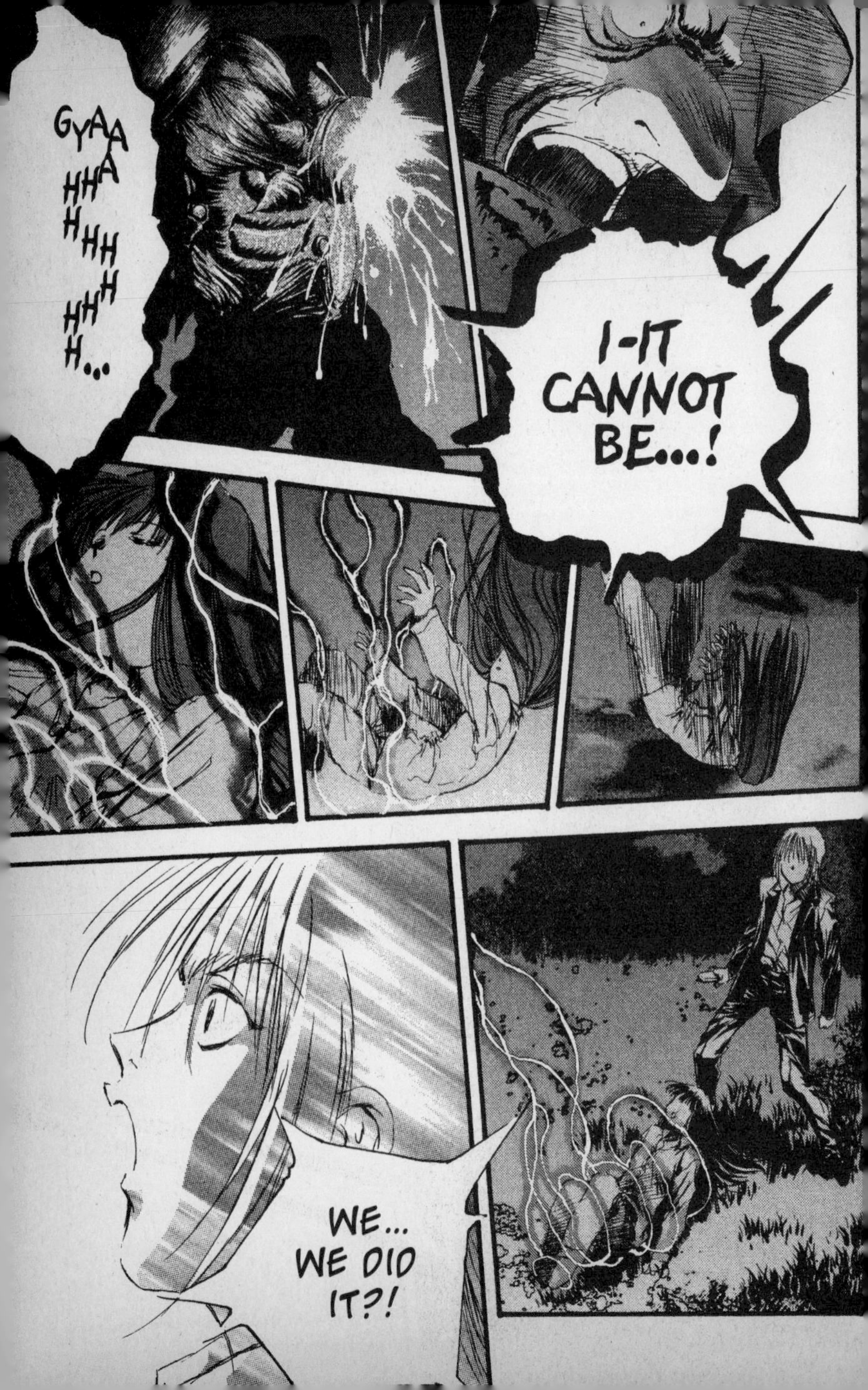
I-IT CANNOT BE...!
GYAAAAHHHHHHHHHHH...
WE... WE DID IT?!

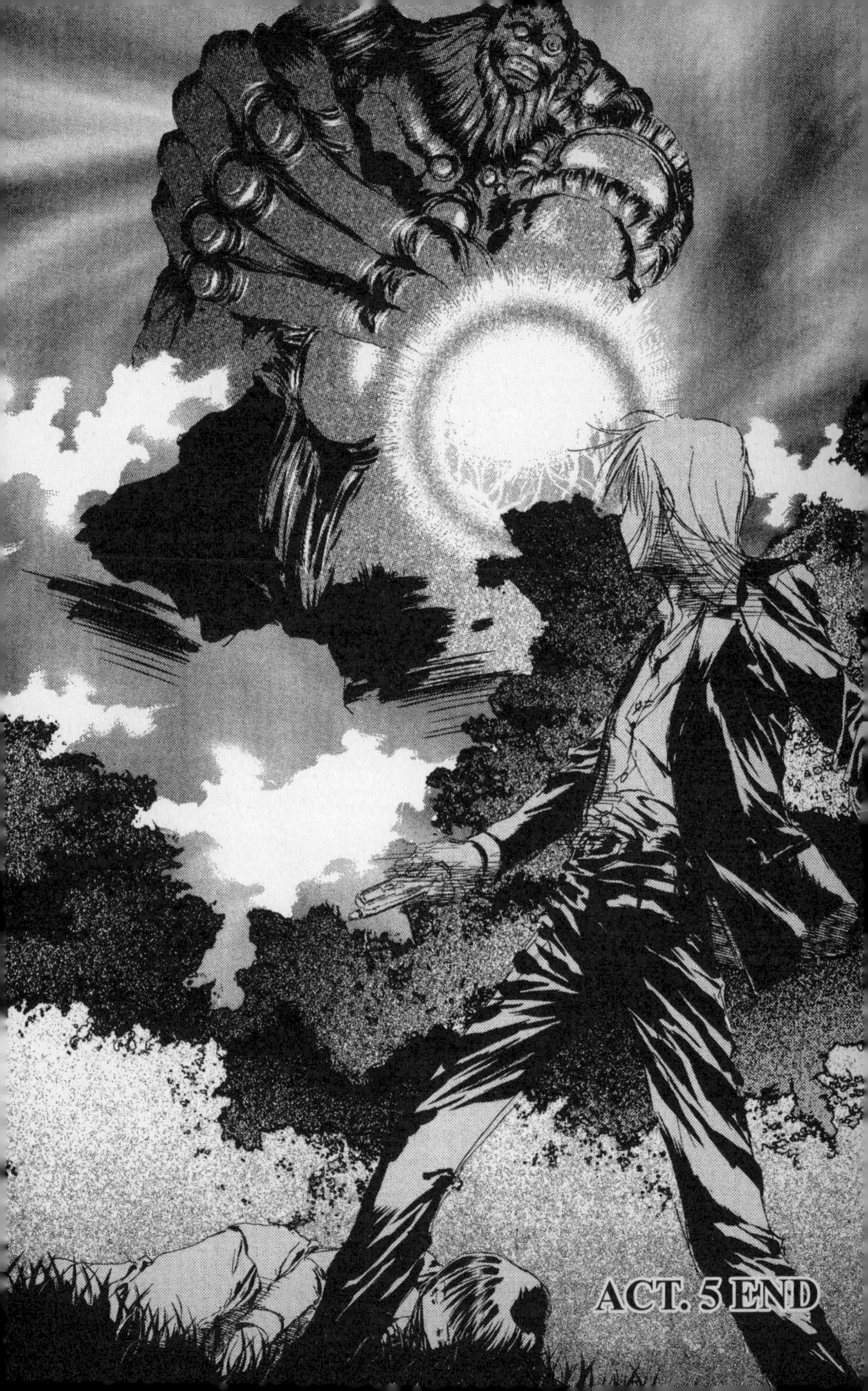
ACT. 5 END

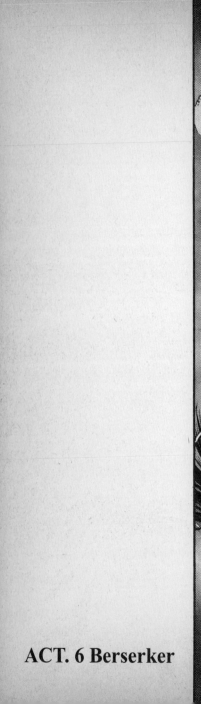

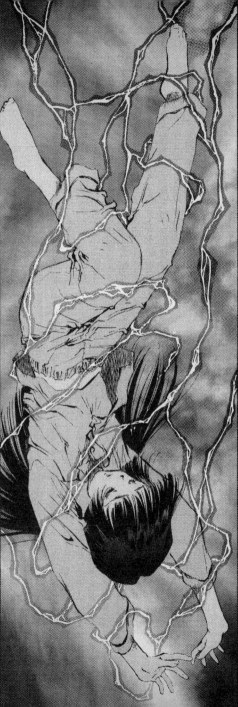

ACT. 6 Berserker

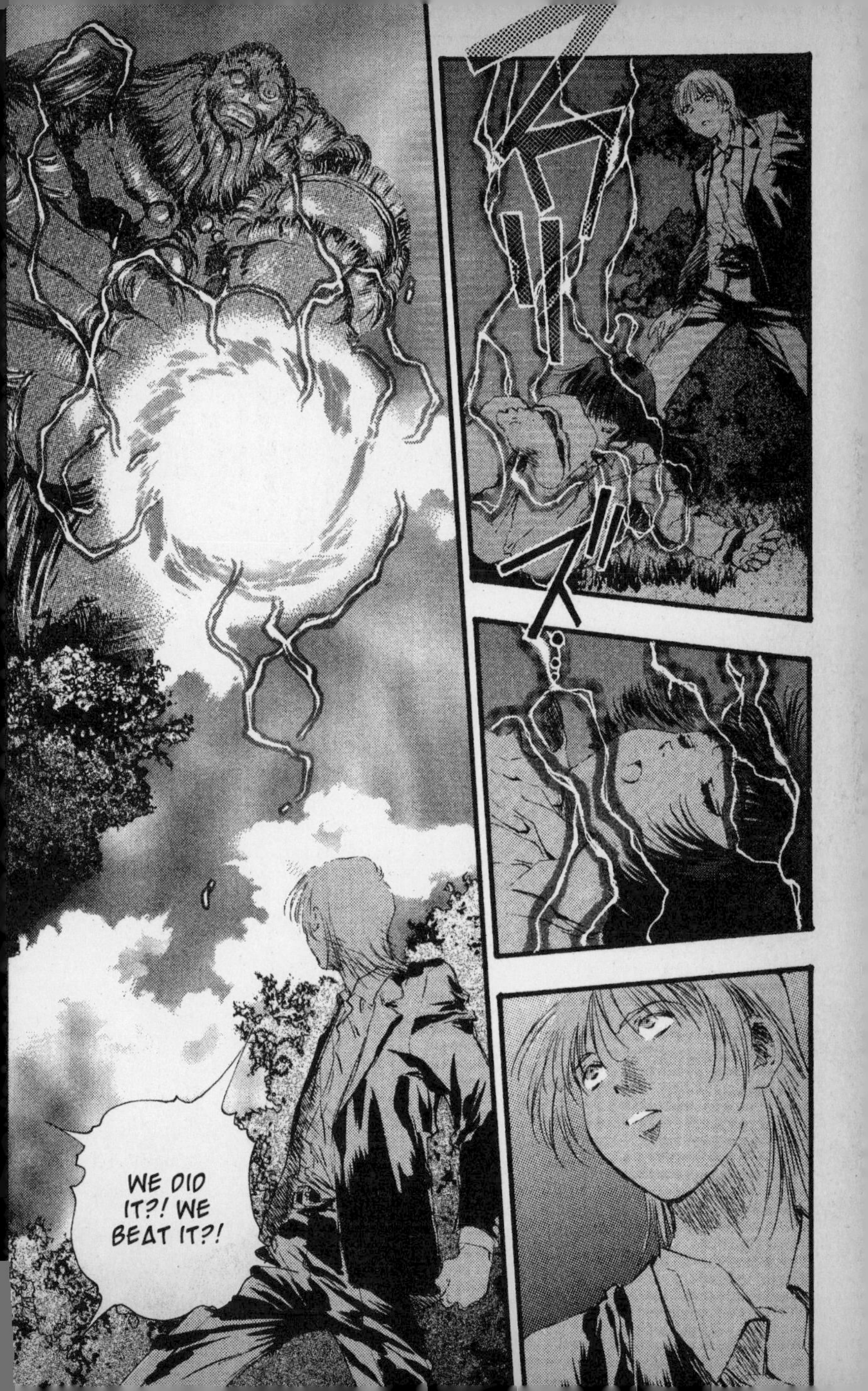
WE DID IT?! WE BEAT IT?!

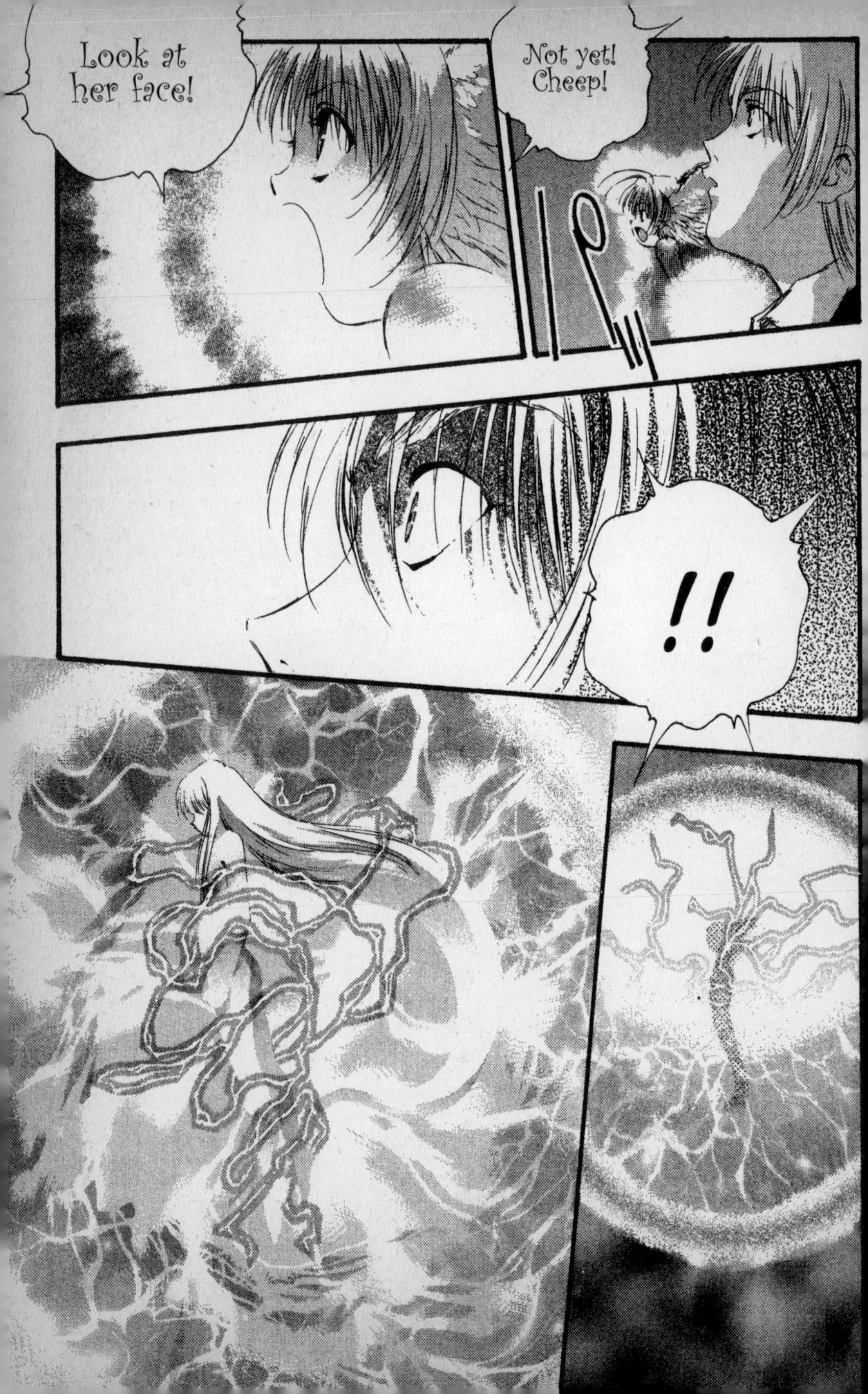
Not yet! Cheep!
Look at her face!
!!

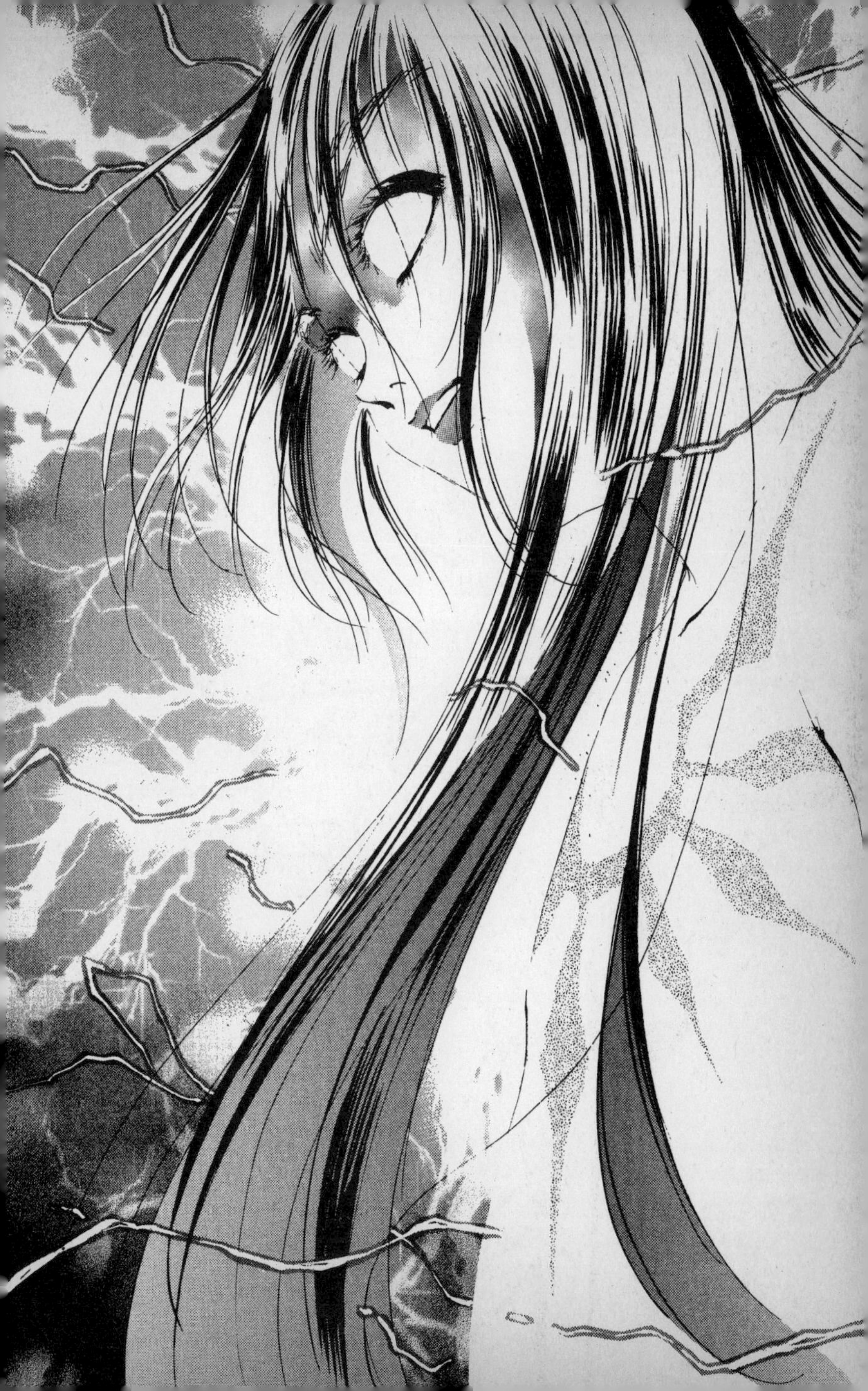

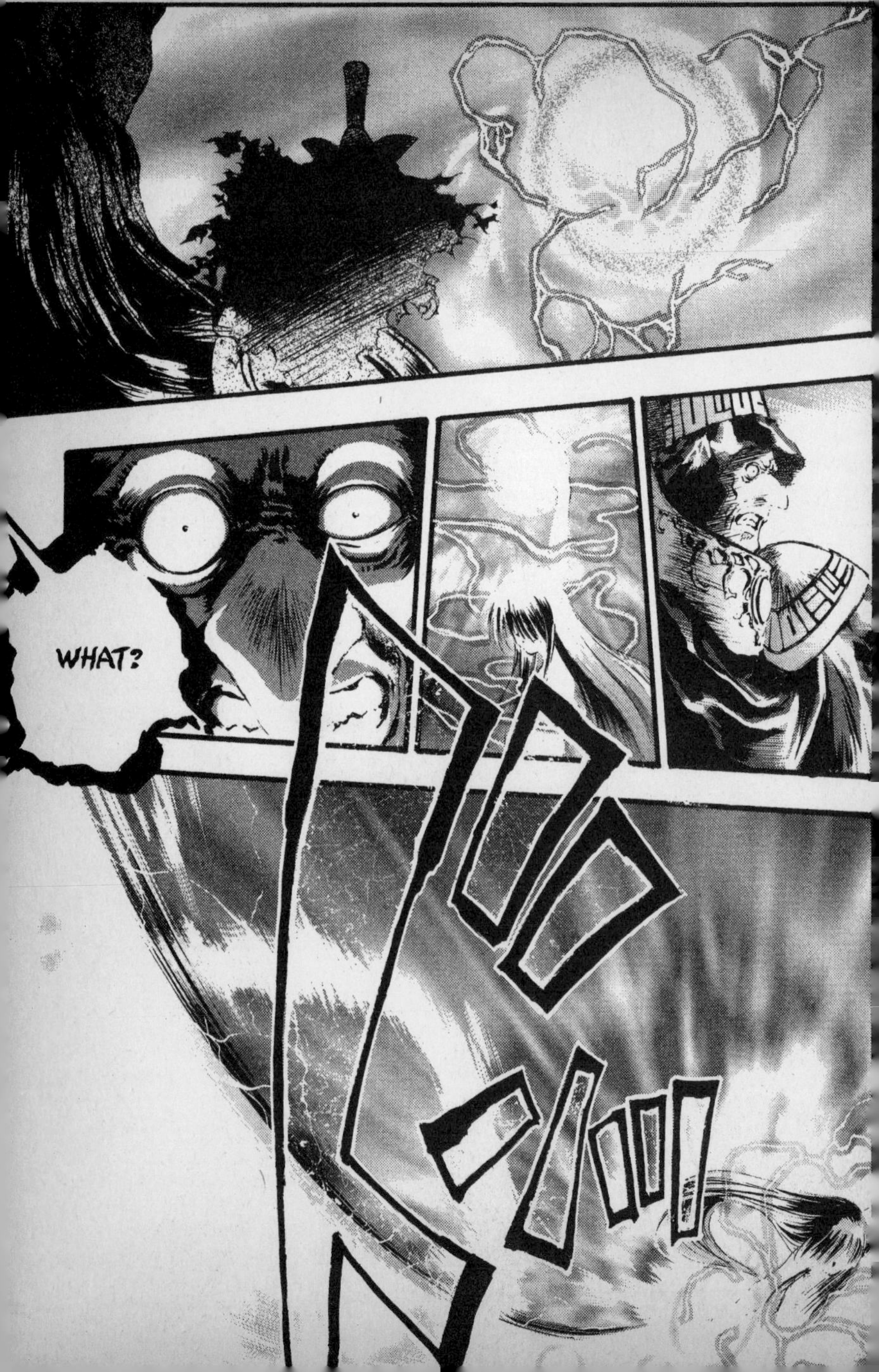
WHAT?

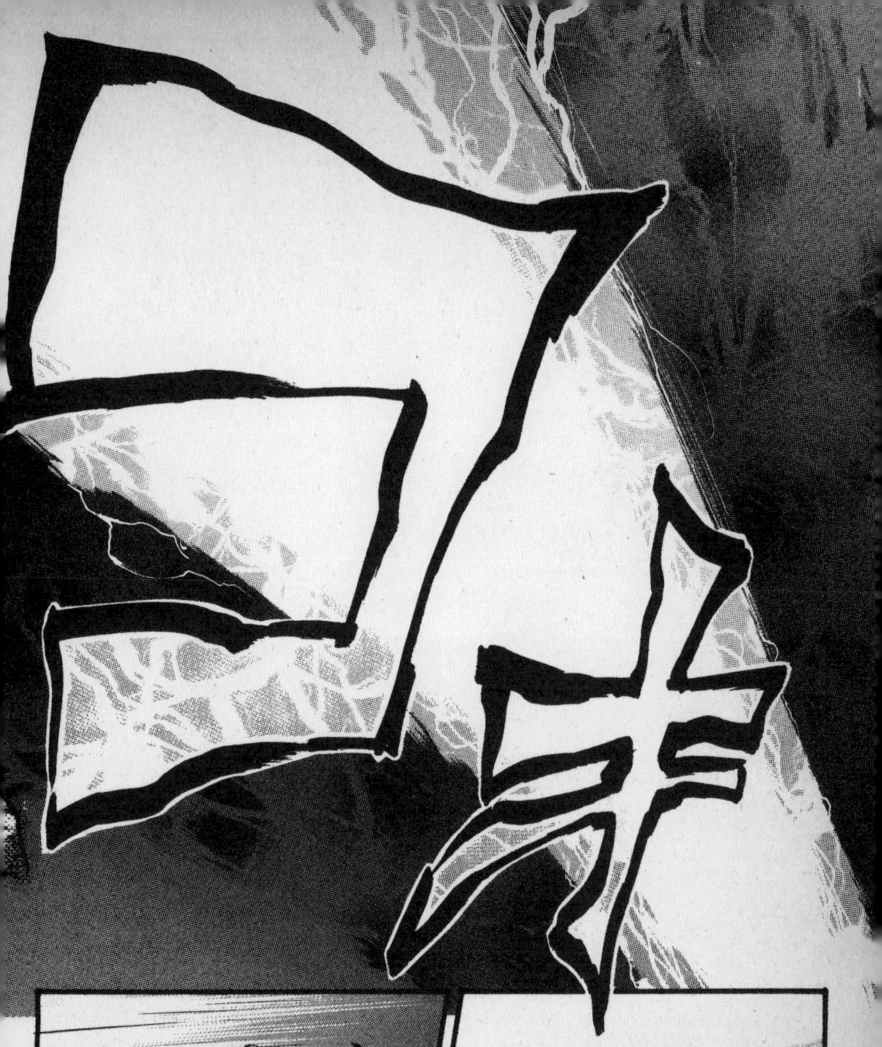
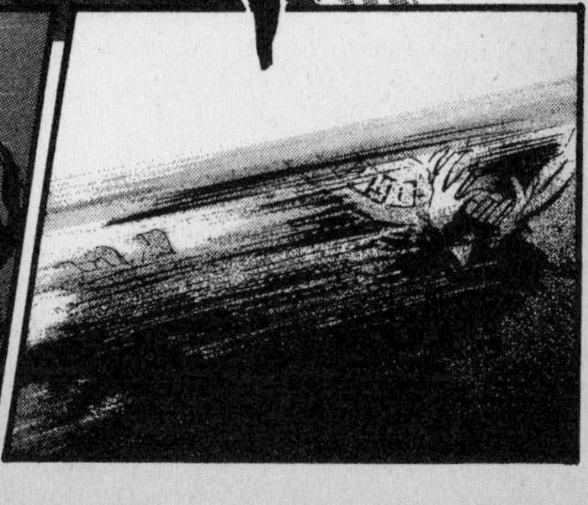
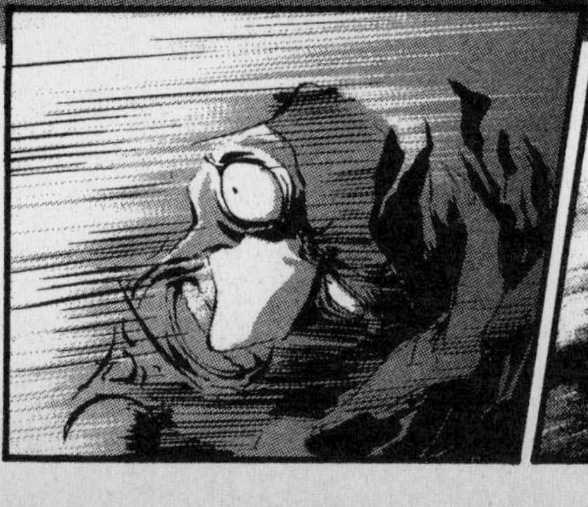

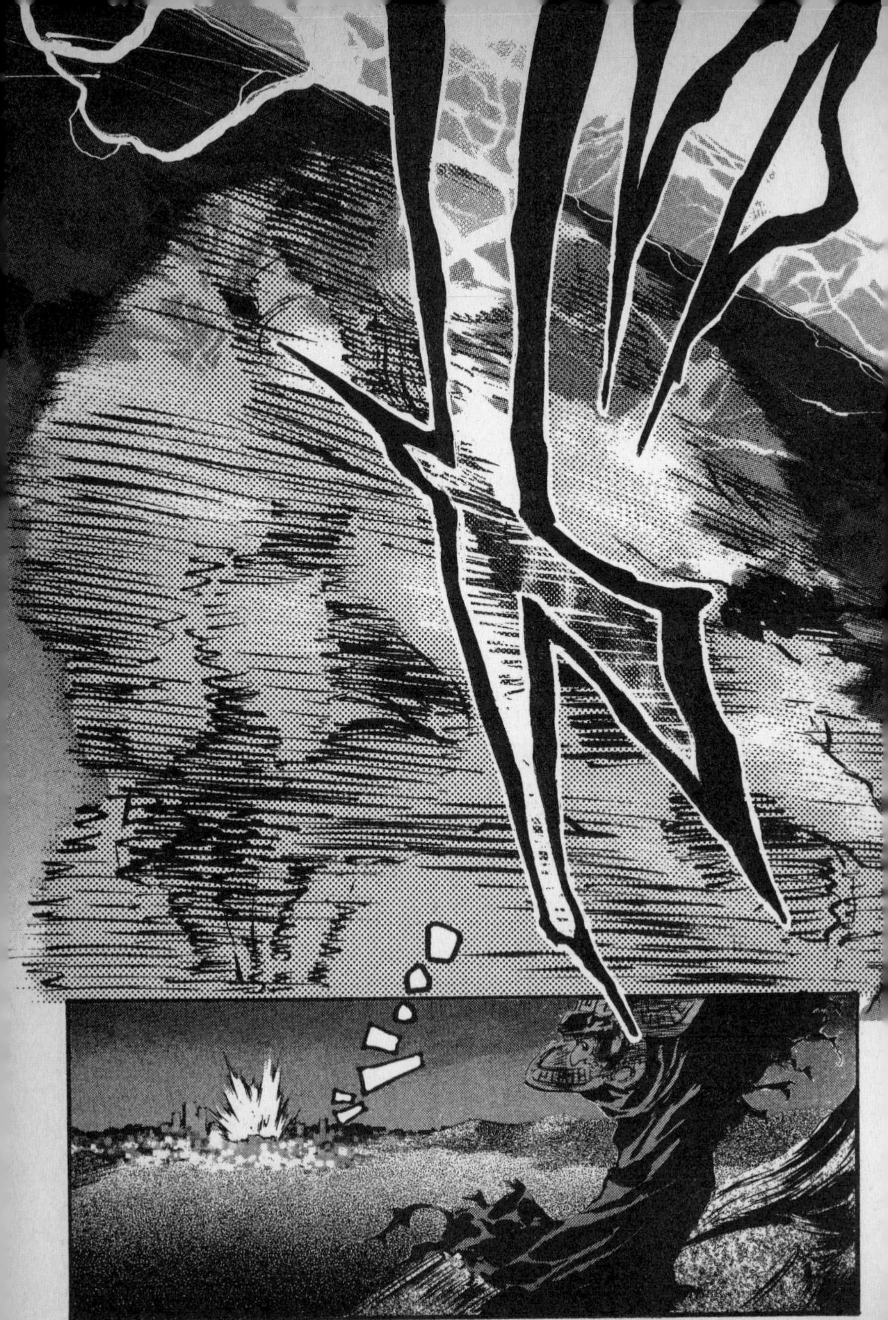

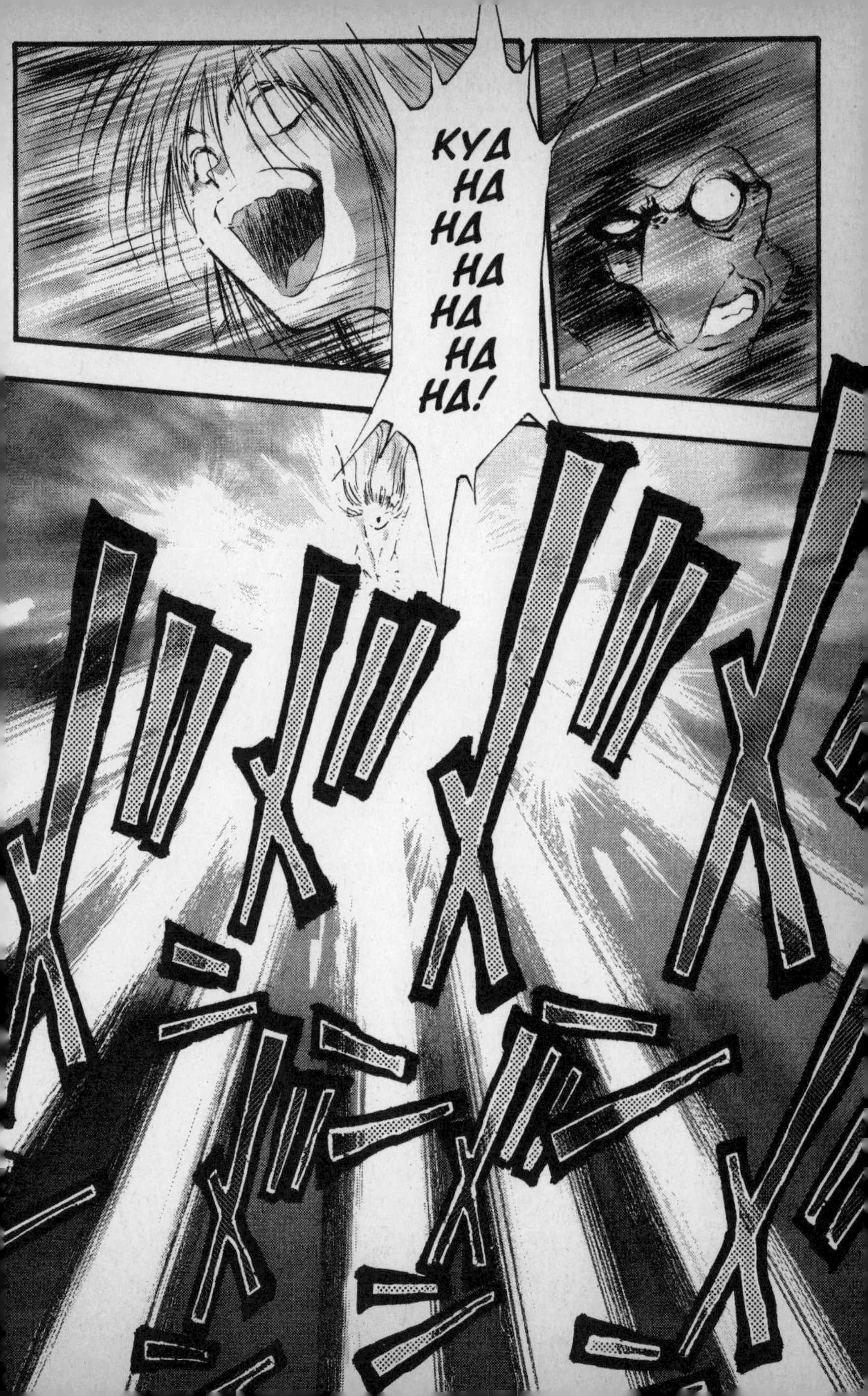
KYA HA HA HA HA HA HA!

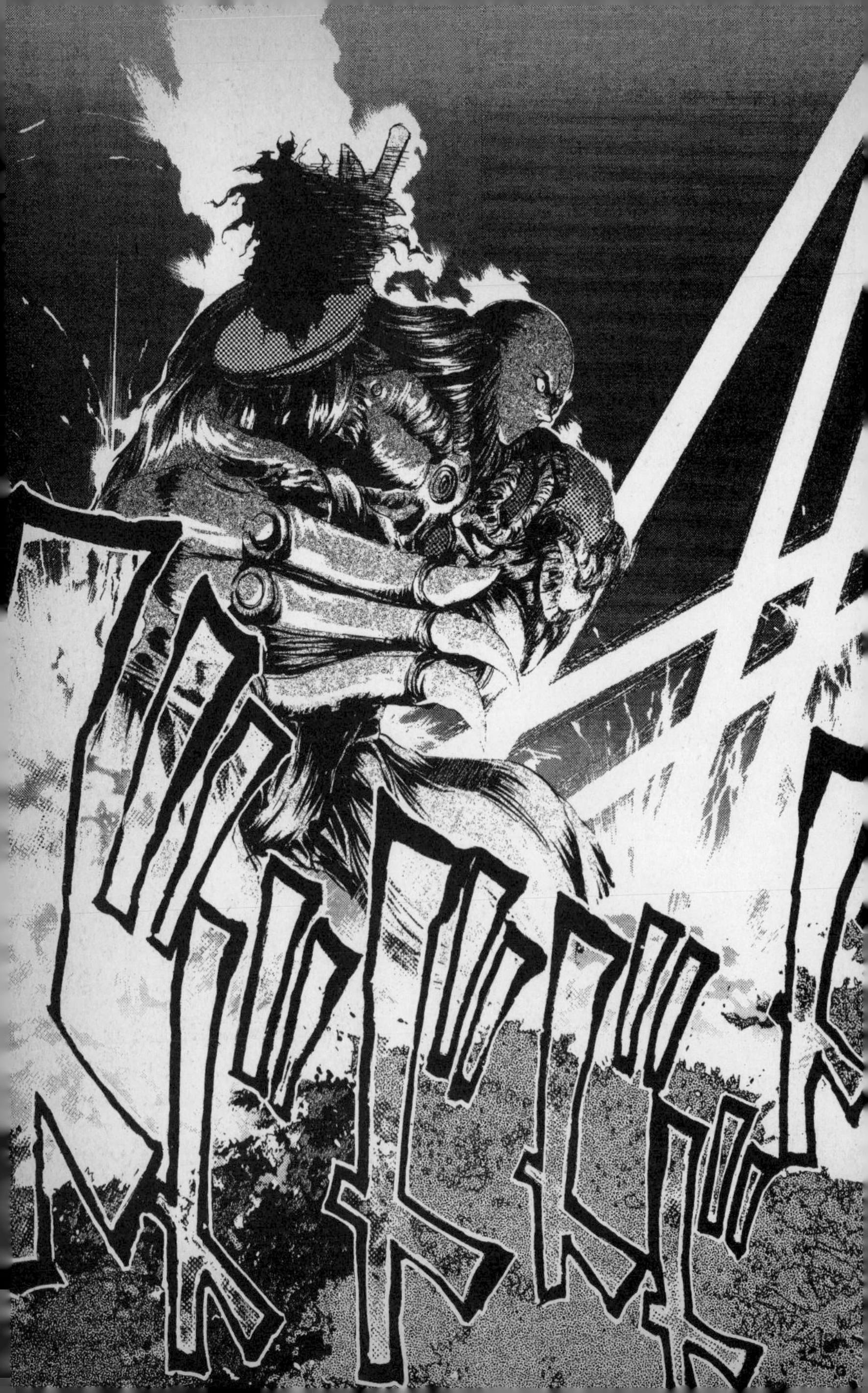

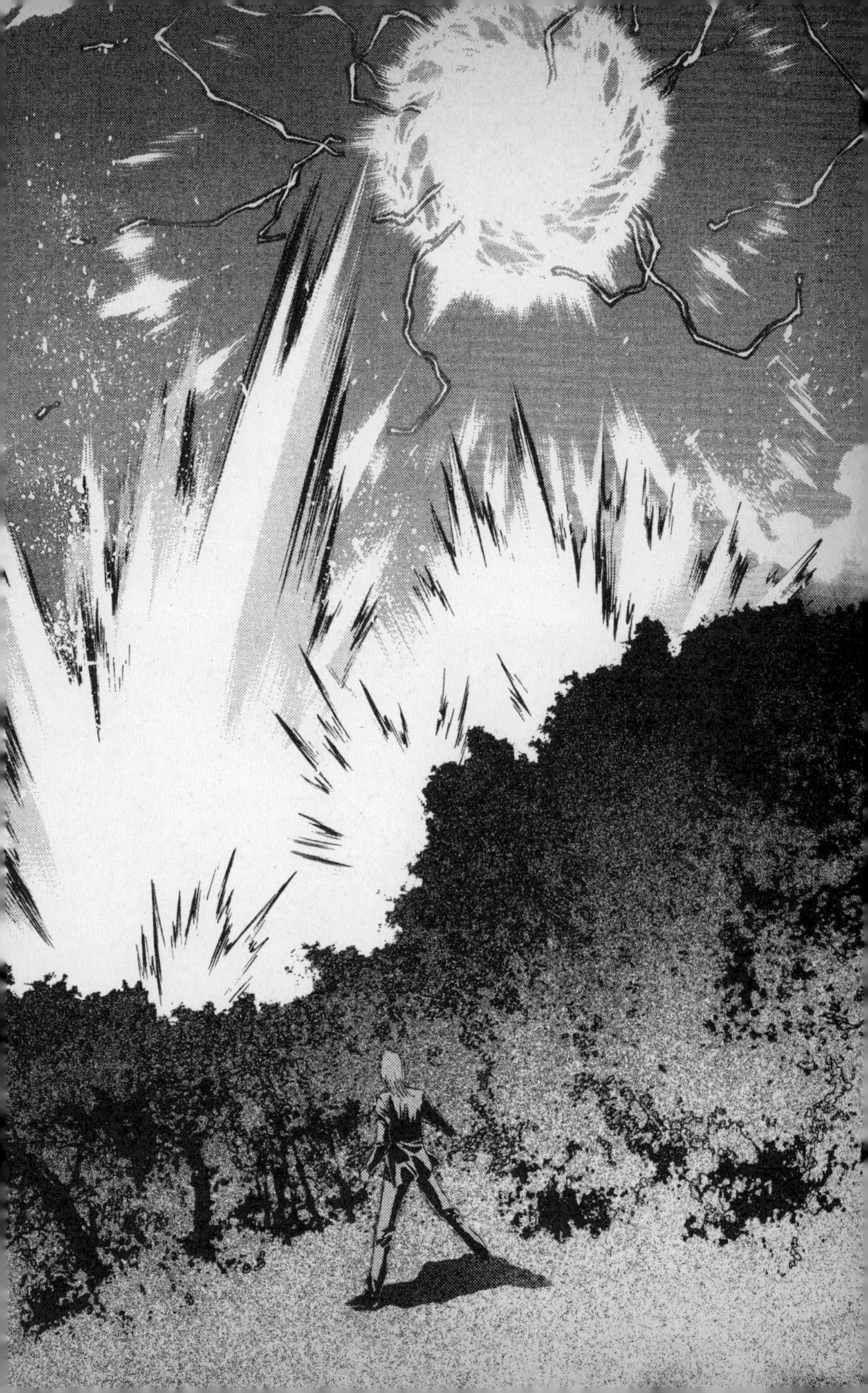

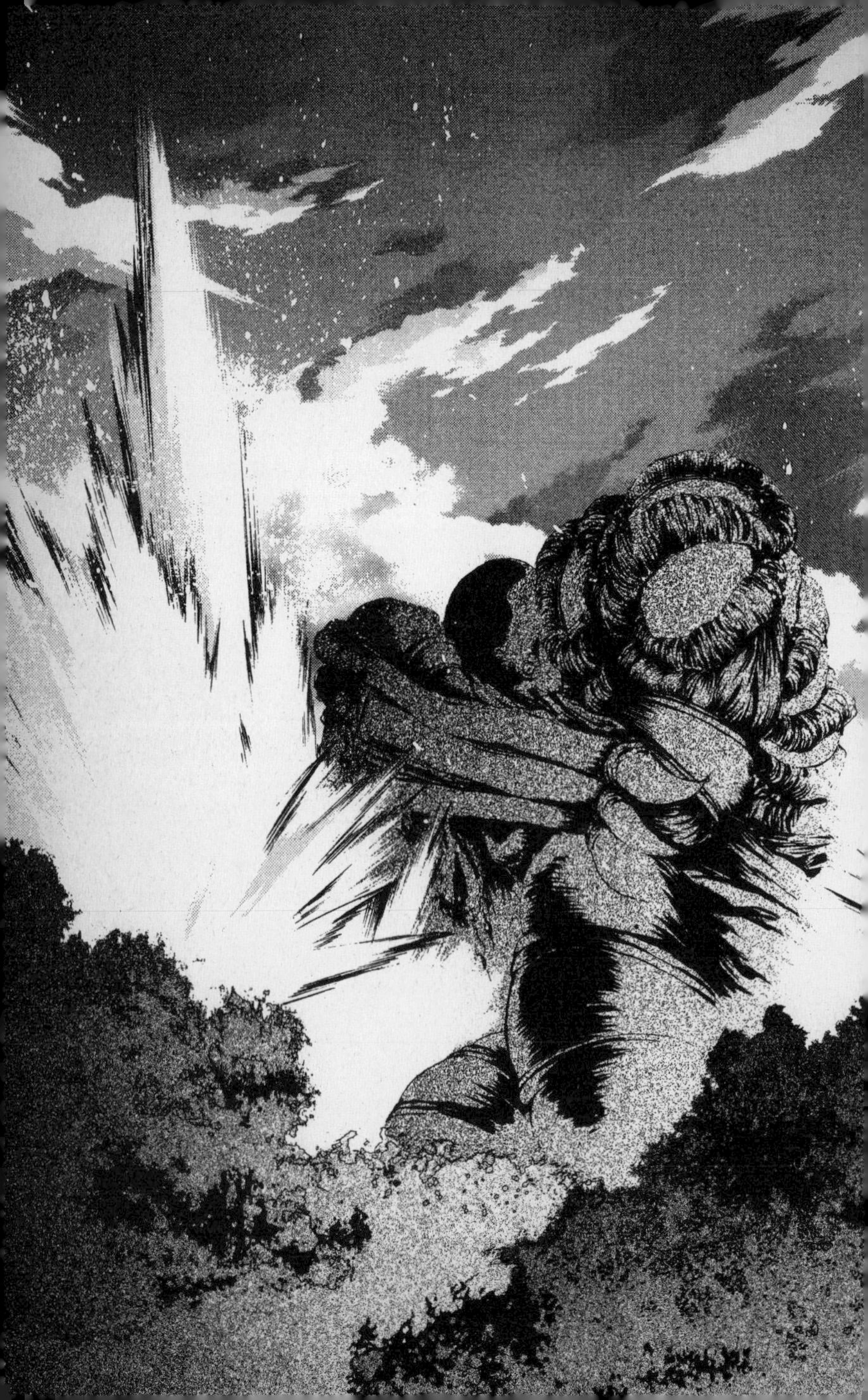

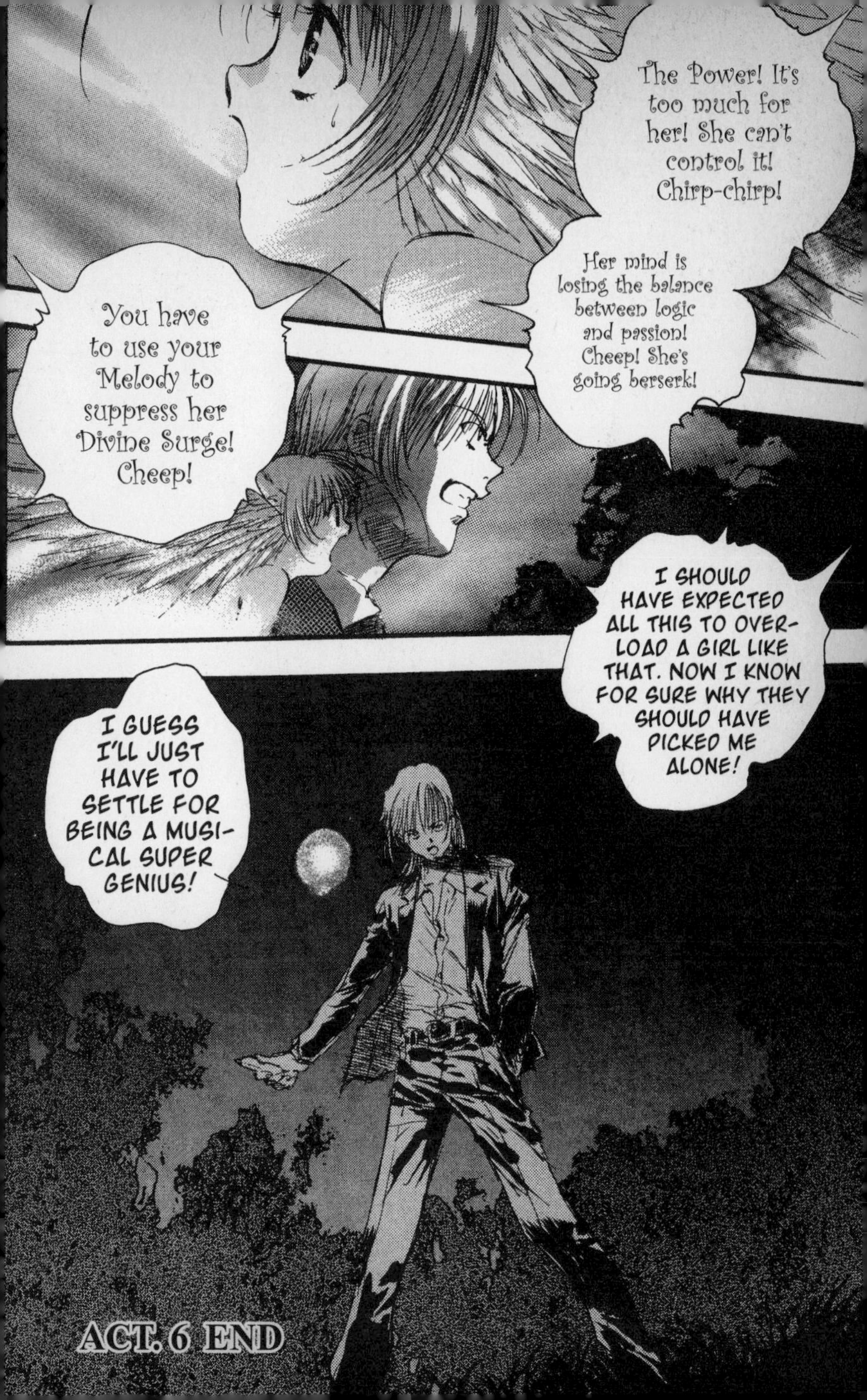
The Power! It's too much for her! She can't control it! Chirp-chirp!
Her mind is losing the balance between logic and passion! Cheep! She's going berserk!
You have to use your Melody to suppress her Divine Surge! Cheep!
I SHOULD HAVE EXPECTED ALL THIS TO OVER-LOAD A GIRL LIKE THAT. NOW I KNOW FOR SURE WHY THEY SHOULD HAVE PICKED ME ALONE!
I GUESS I'LL JUST HAVE TO SETTLE FOR BEING A MUSI-CAL SUPER GENIUS!
ACT. 6 END

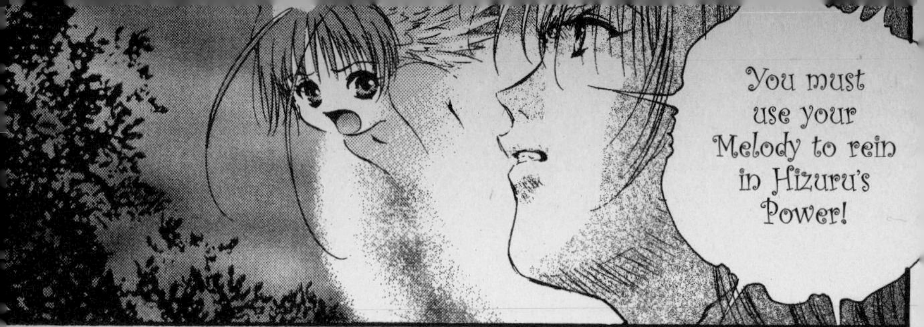
You must use your Melody to rein in Hizuru's Power!

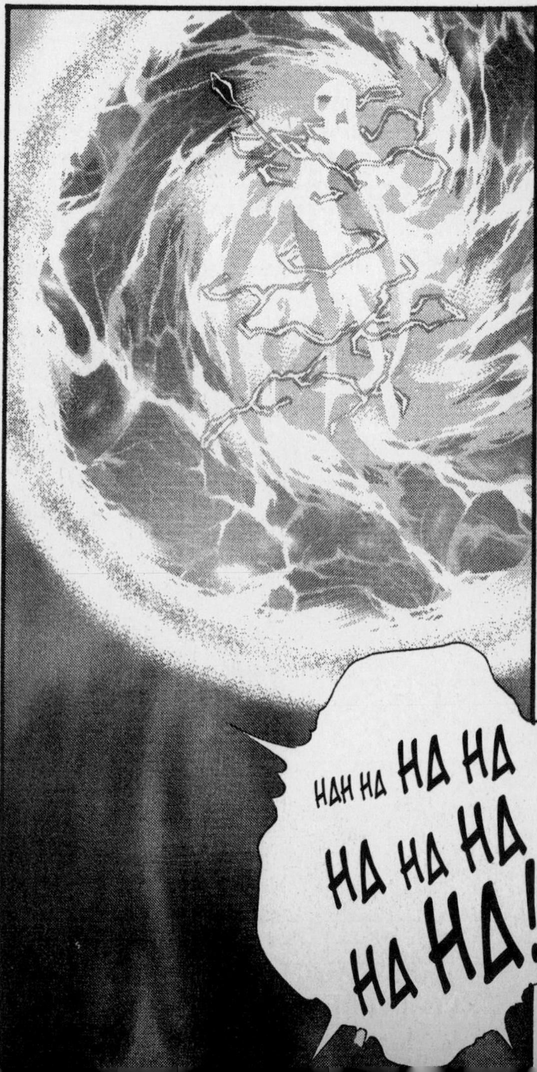
HAH HA HA HA HA HA HA HA HA!

ACT. 7 Warrior

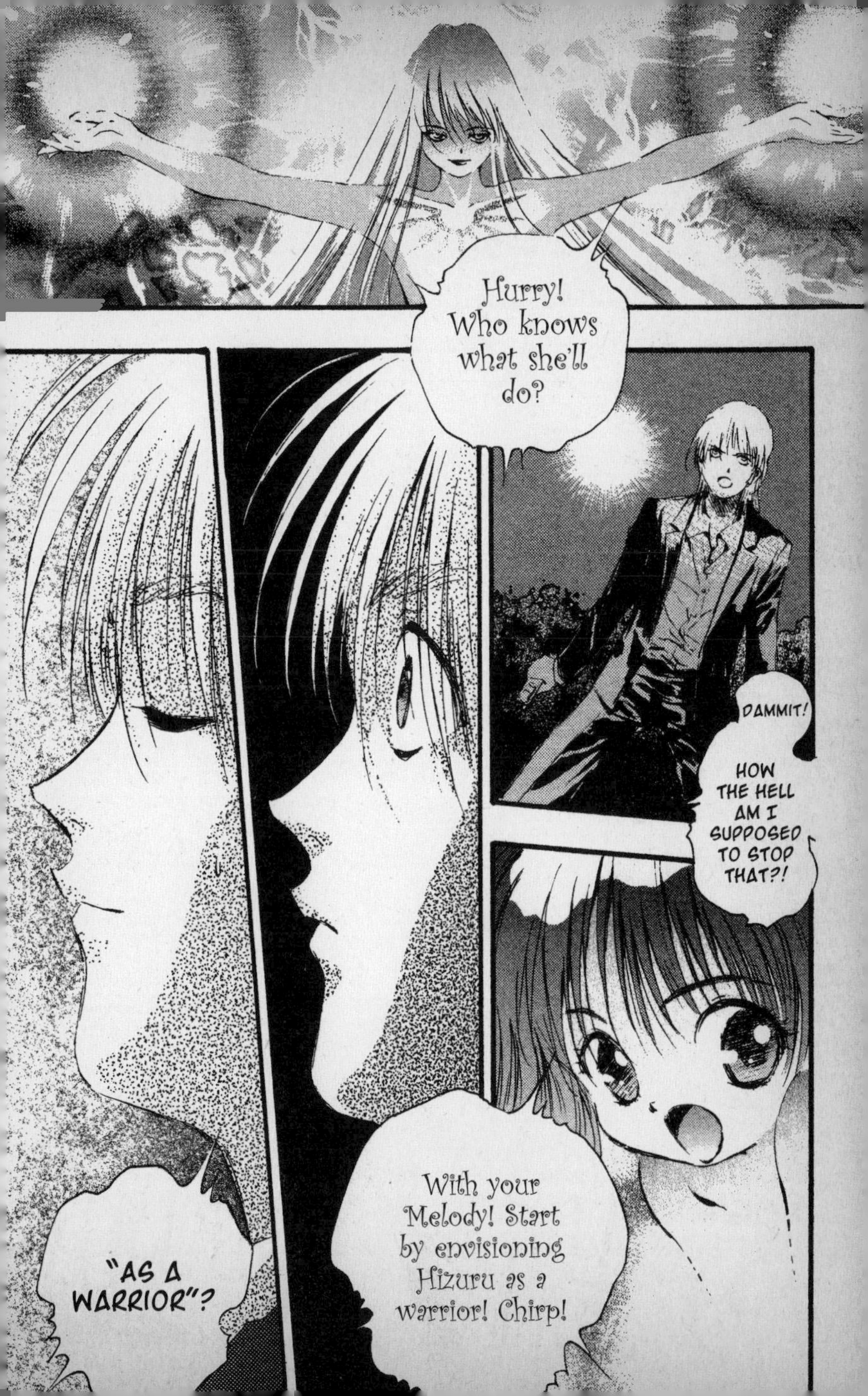
Hurry! Who knows what she'll do?
DAMMIT!
HOW THE HELL AM I SUPPOSED TO STOP THAT?!
With your Melody! Start by envisioning Hizuru as a warrior! Chirp!
"AS A WARRIOR"?

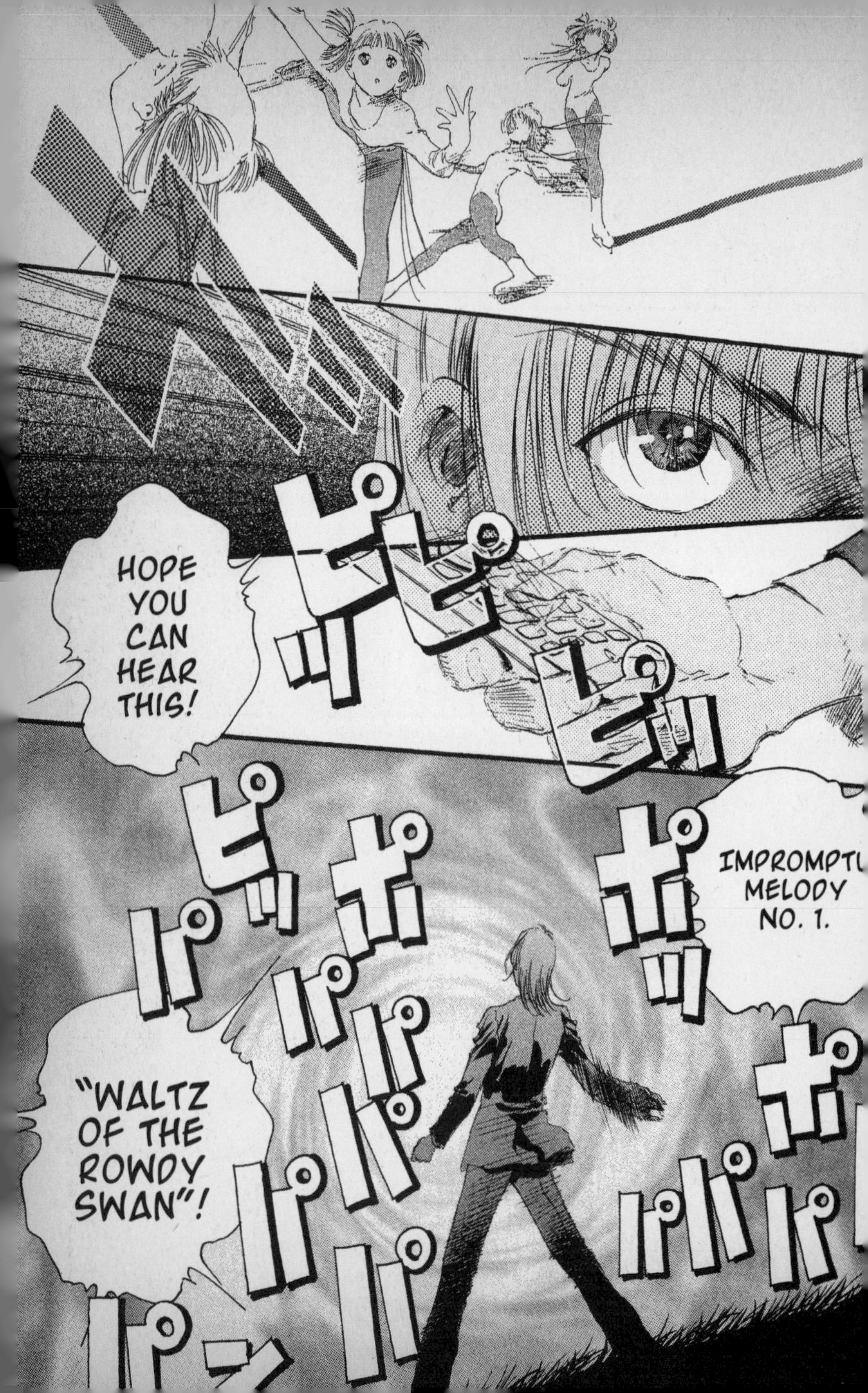
HOPE YOU CAN HEAR THIS!
IMPROMPTU MELODY NO. 1.
"WALTZ OF THE ROWDY SWAN"!

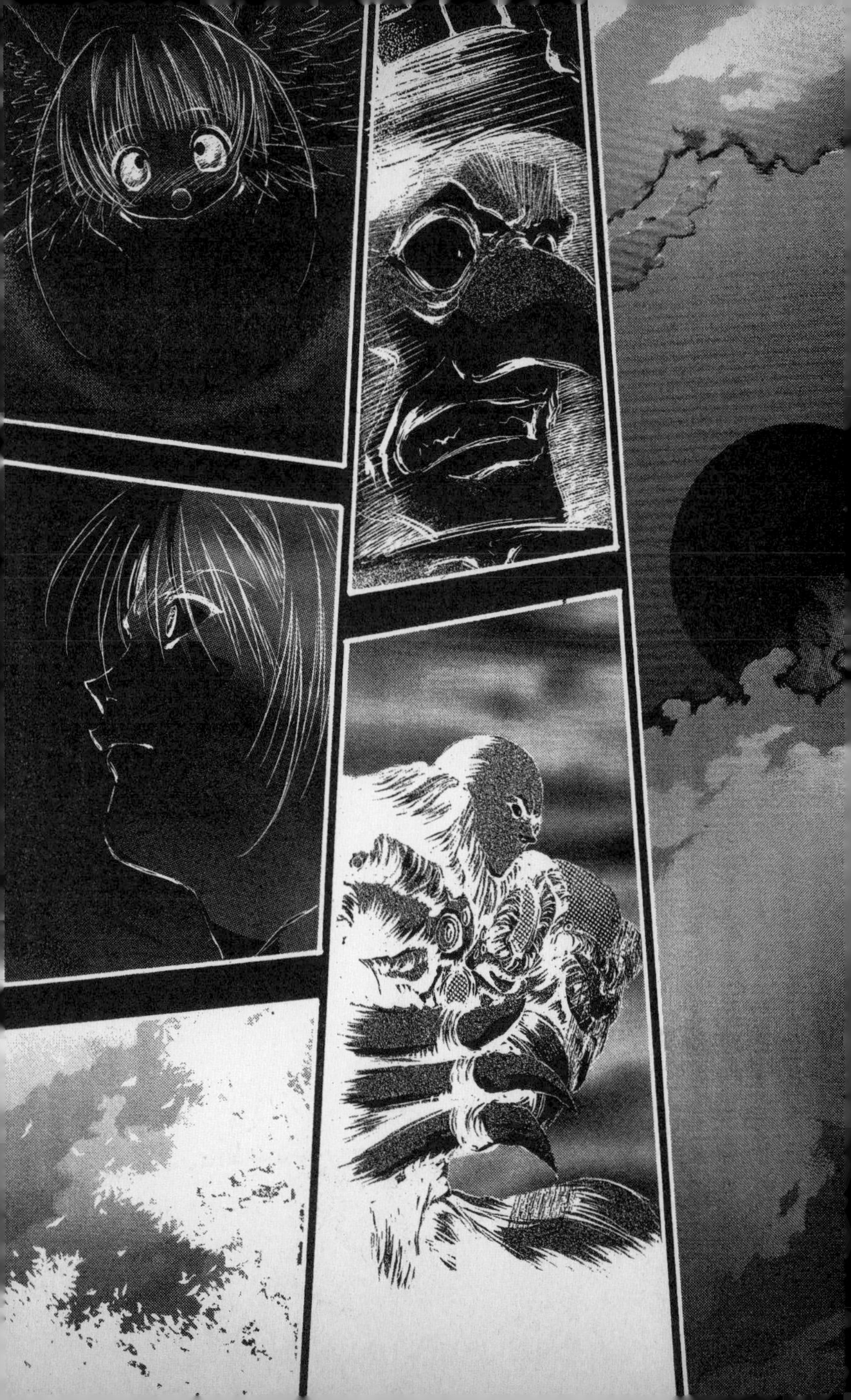

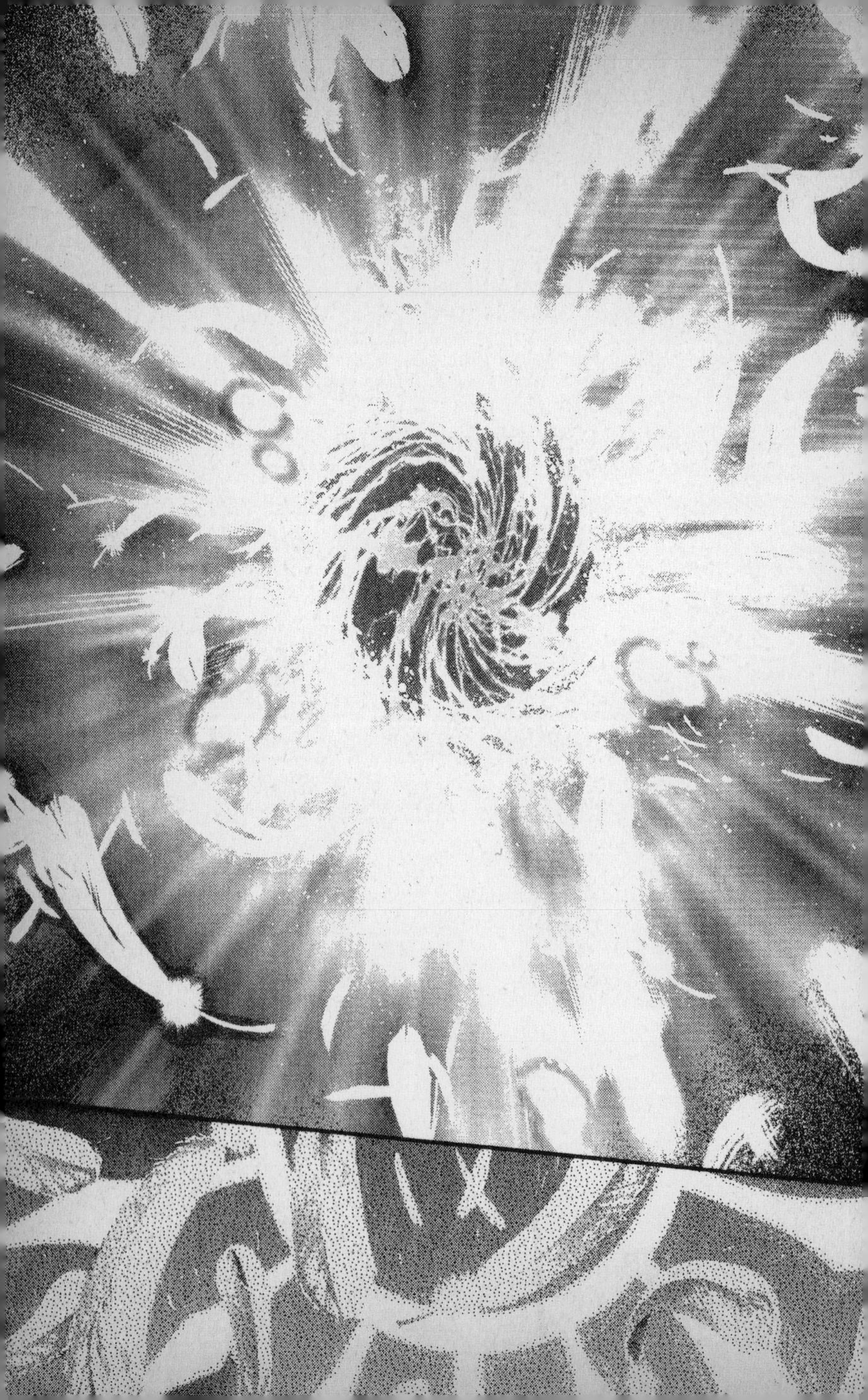

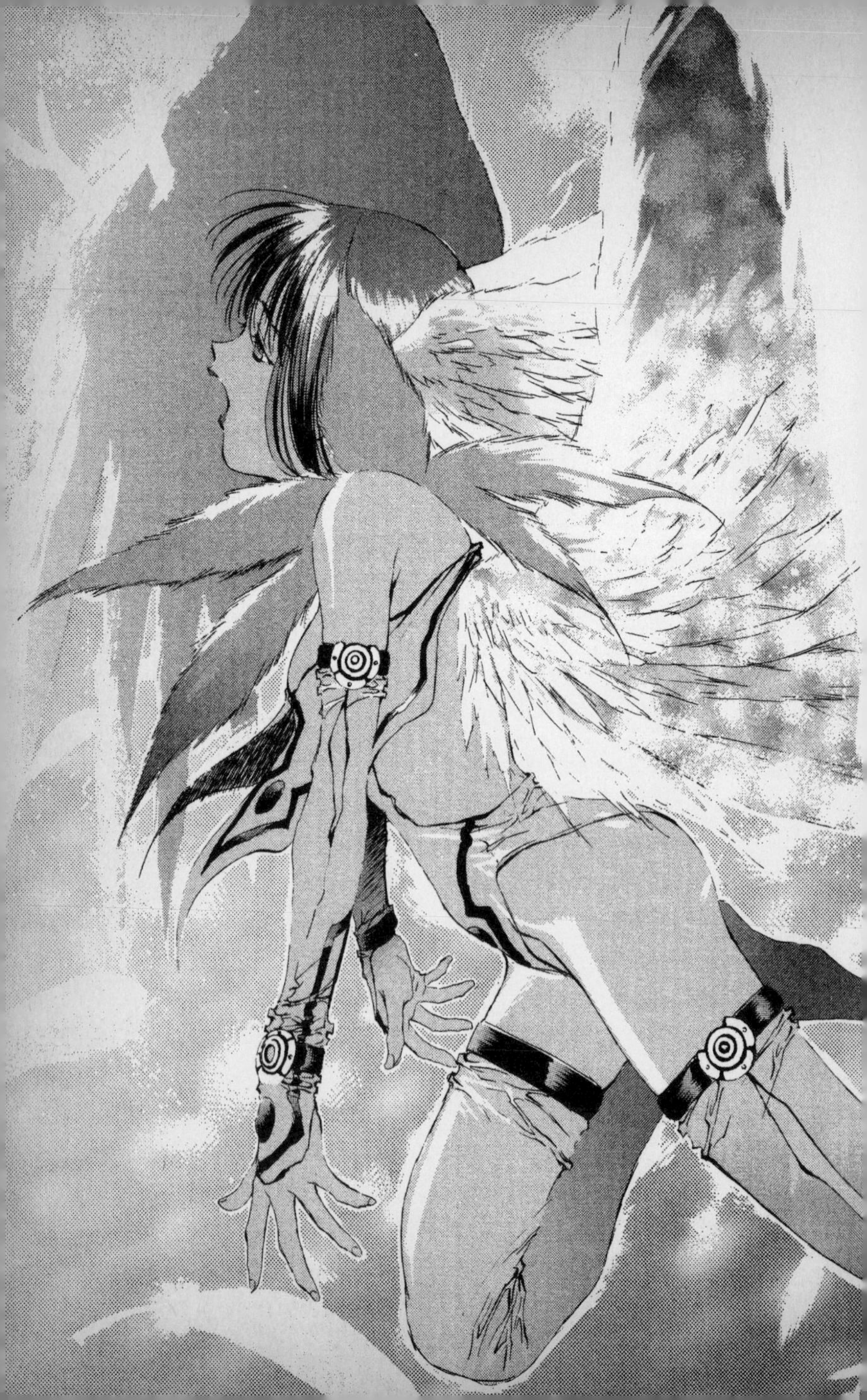

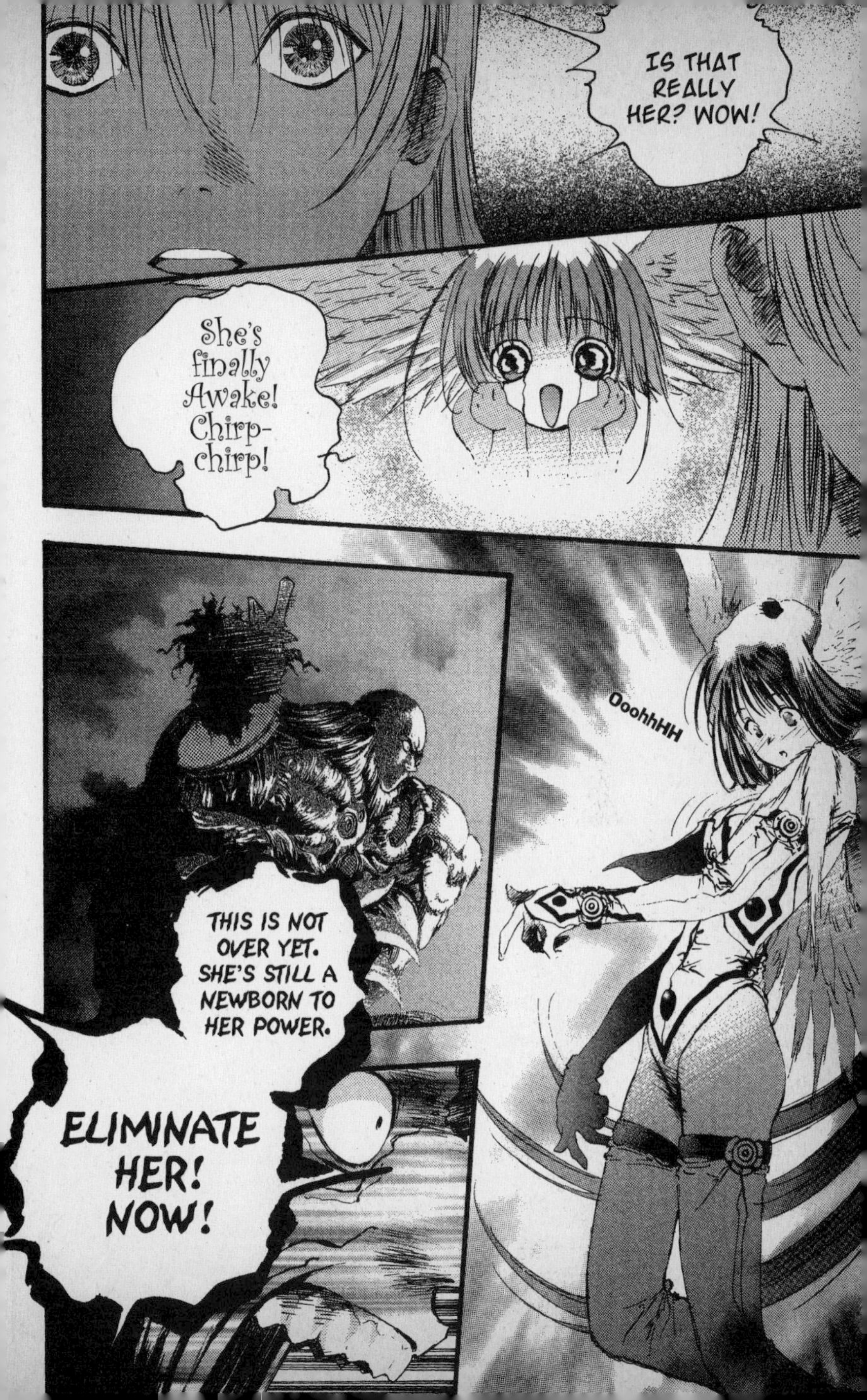
IS THAT REALLY HER? WOW!
She's finally Awake! Chirp-chirp!
OoohhHH
THIS IS NOT OVER YET. SHE'S STILL A NEWBORN TO HER POWER.
ELIMINATE HER! NOW!

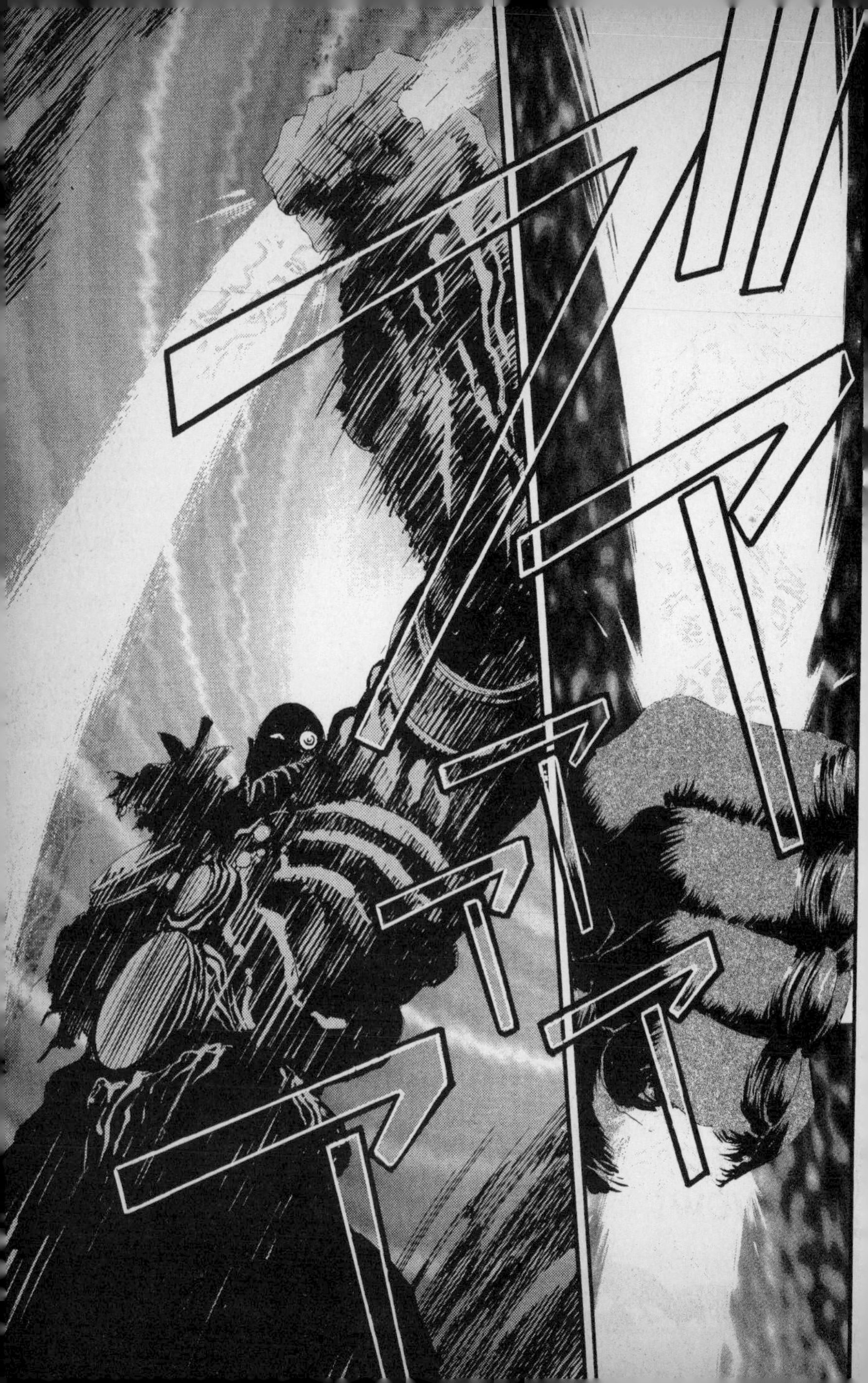

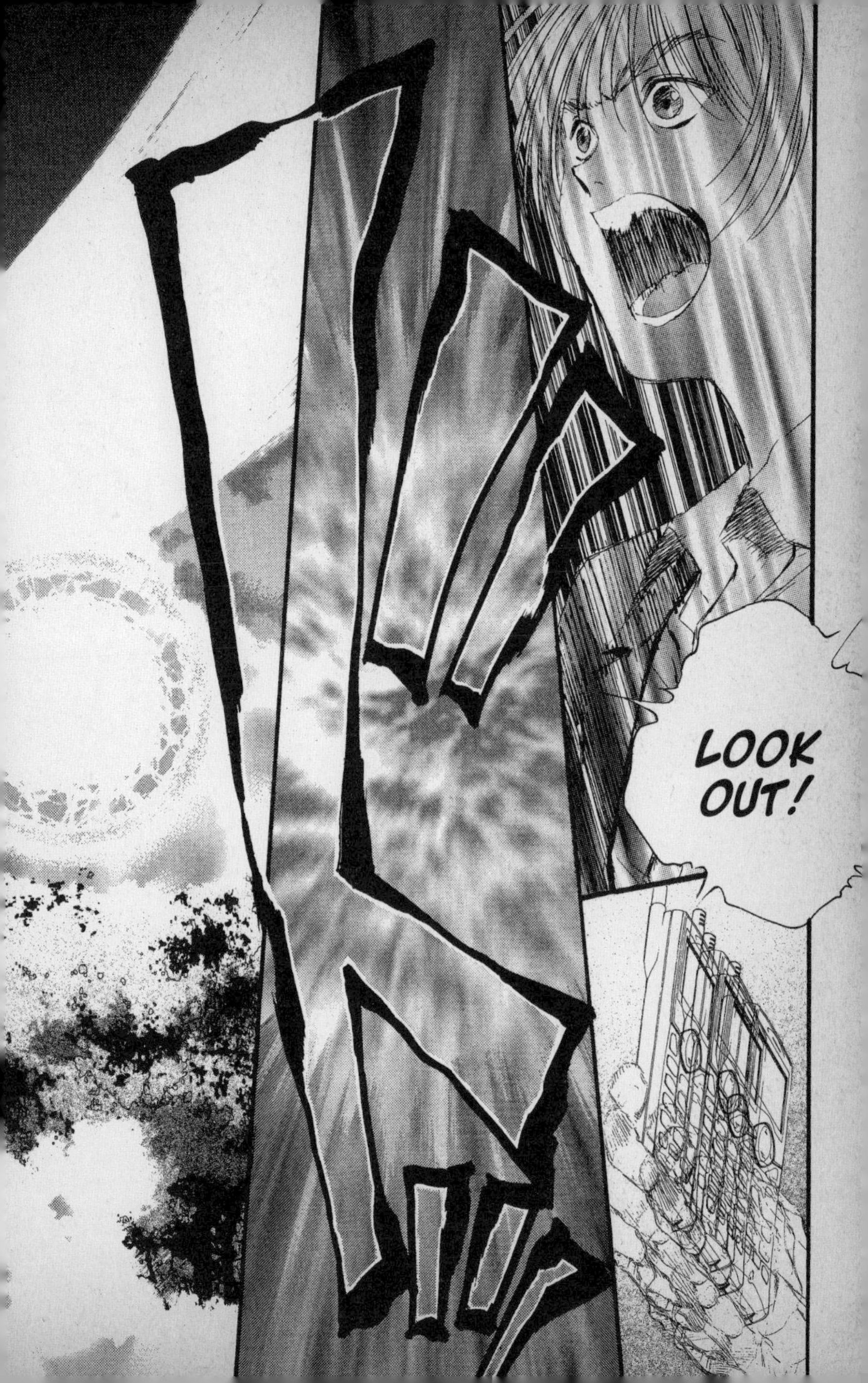
LOOK OUT!

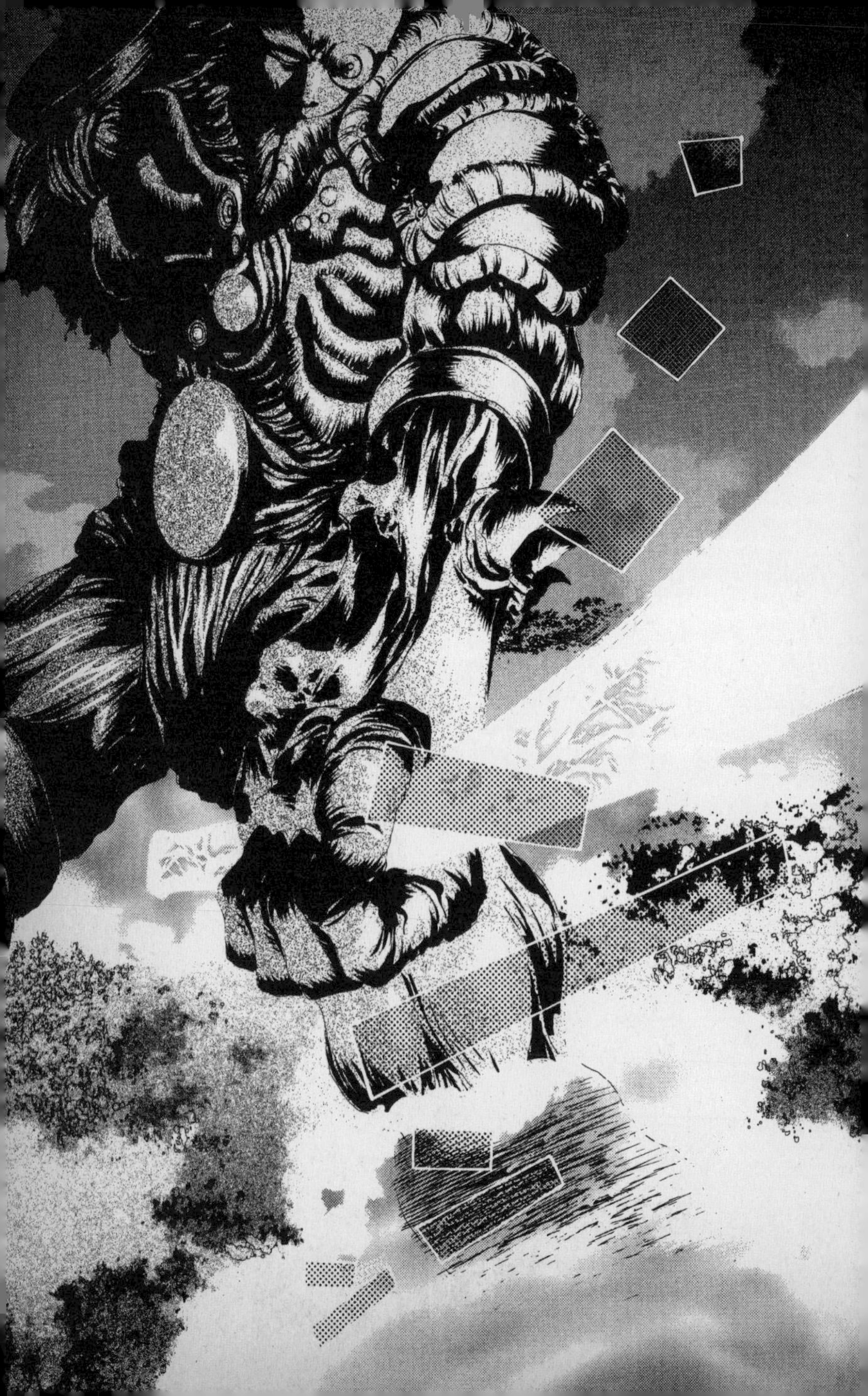

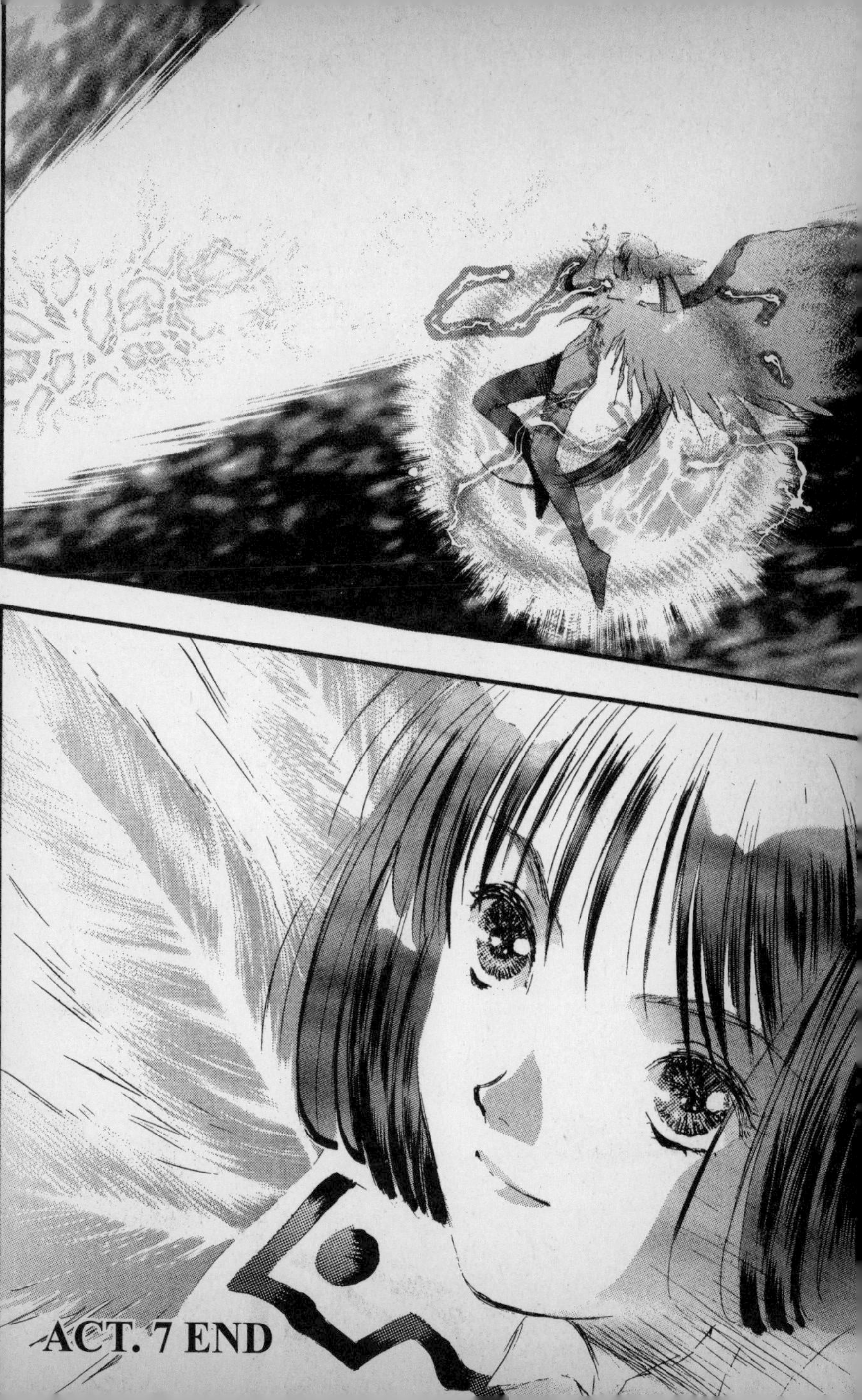
ACT. 7 END

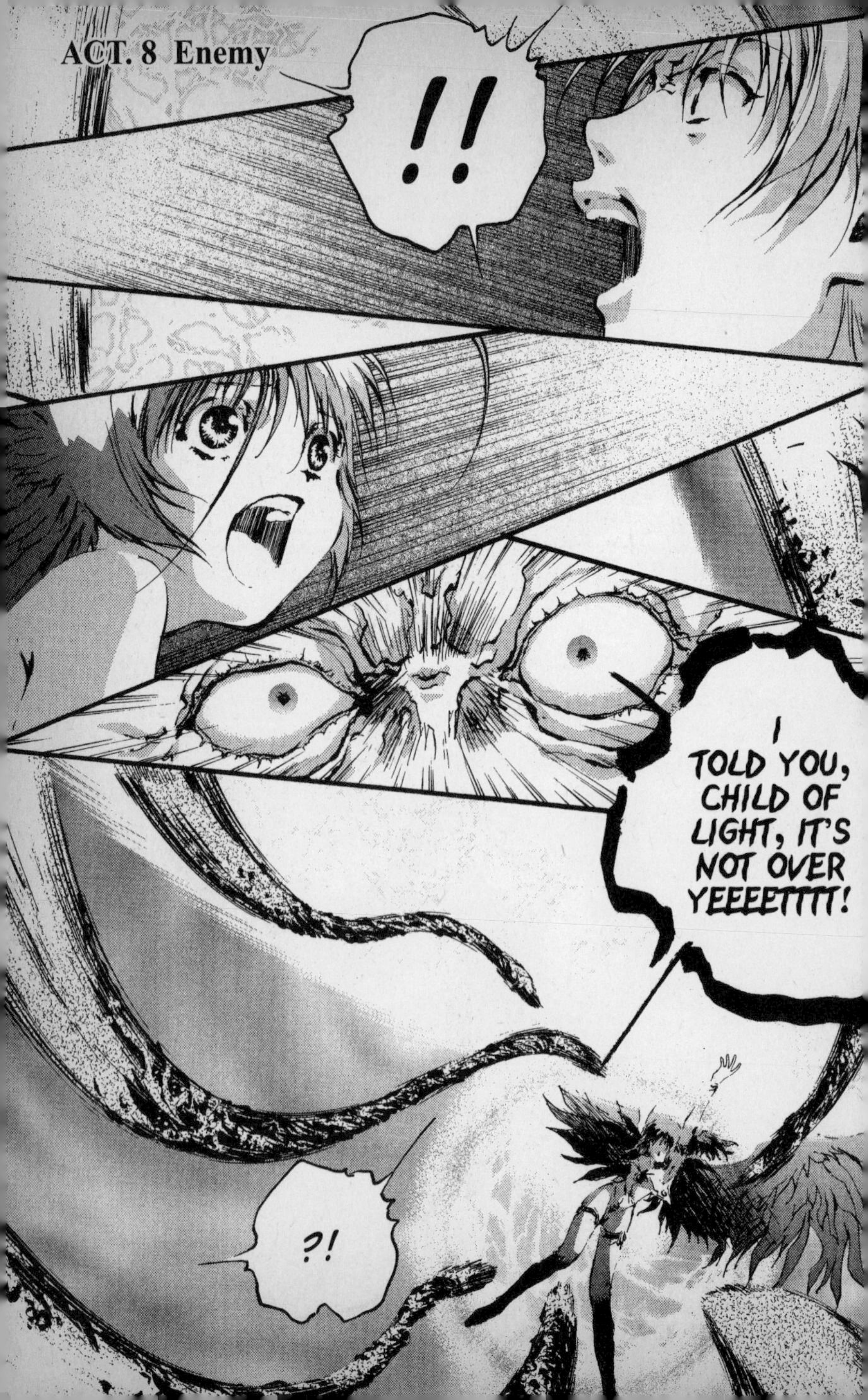
!!
I TOLD YOU, CHILD OF LIGHT, IT'S NOT OVER YEEEETTTT!
?!

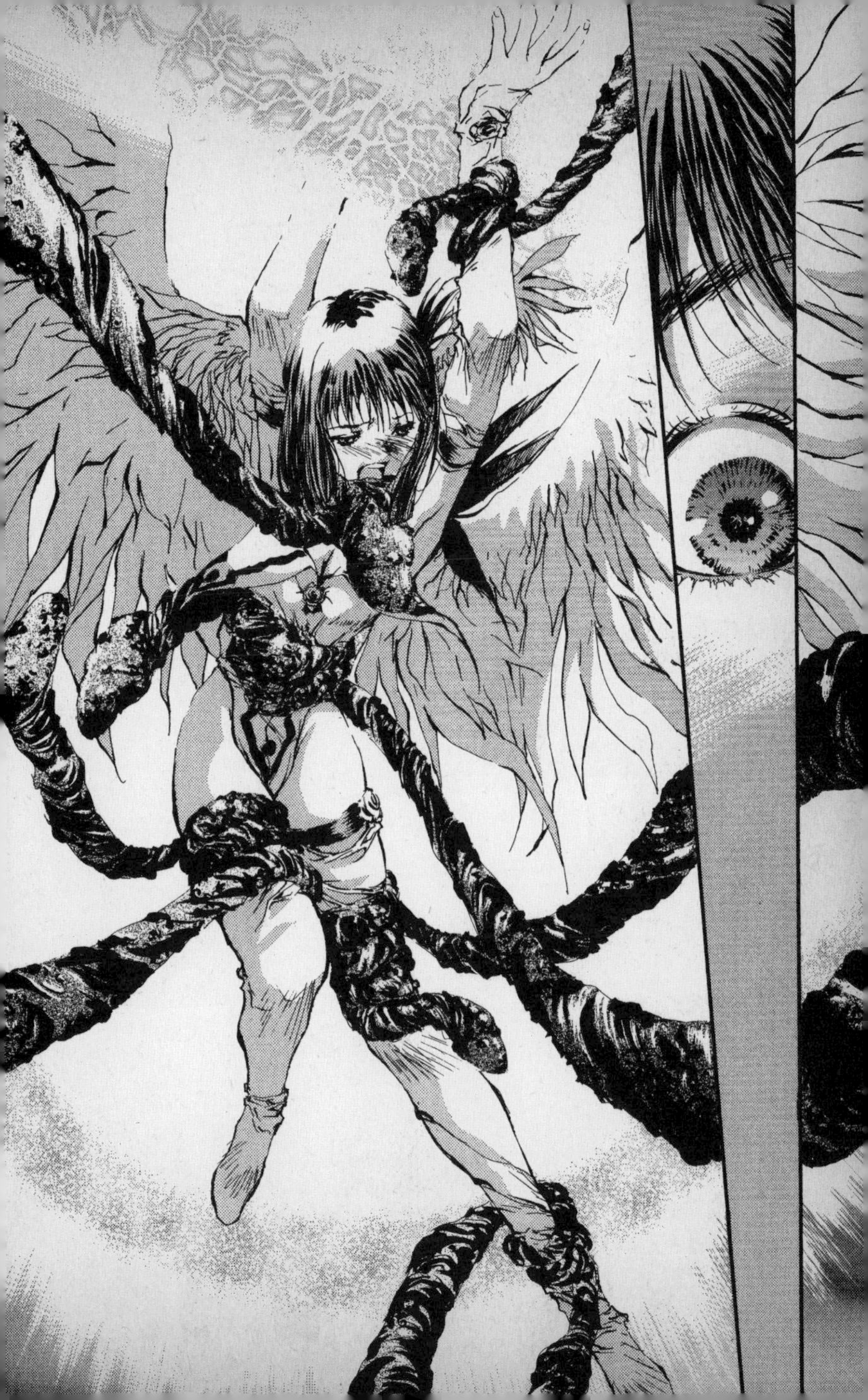

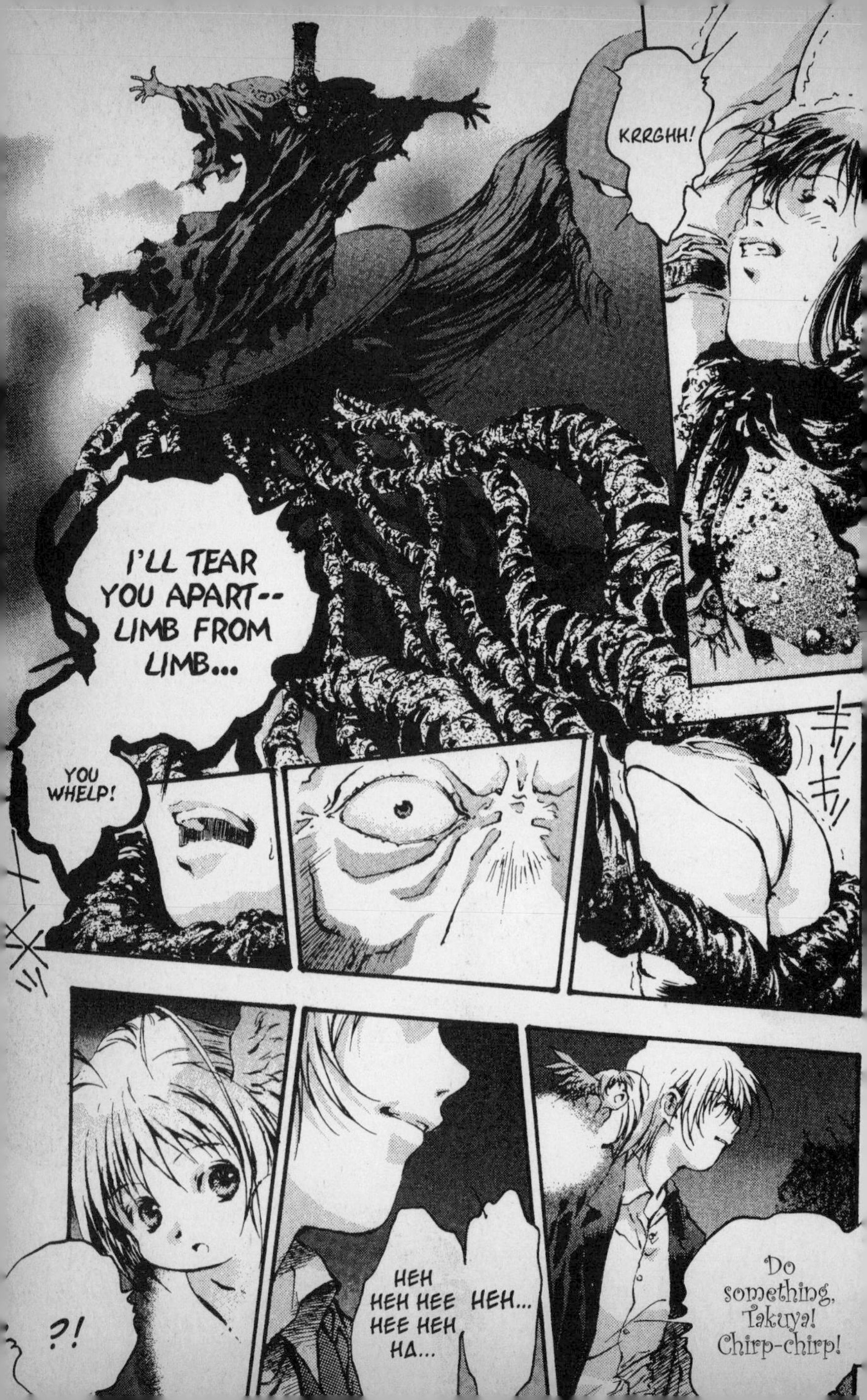
KRRGHH!
I'LL TEAR YOU APART-- LIMB FROM LIMB...
YOU WHELP!
Do something, Takuya! Chirp-chirp!
HEH HEH HEE HEH... HEE HEH HA...
?!

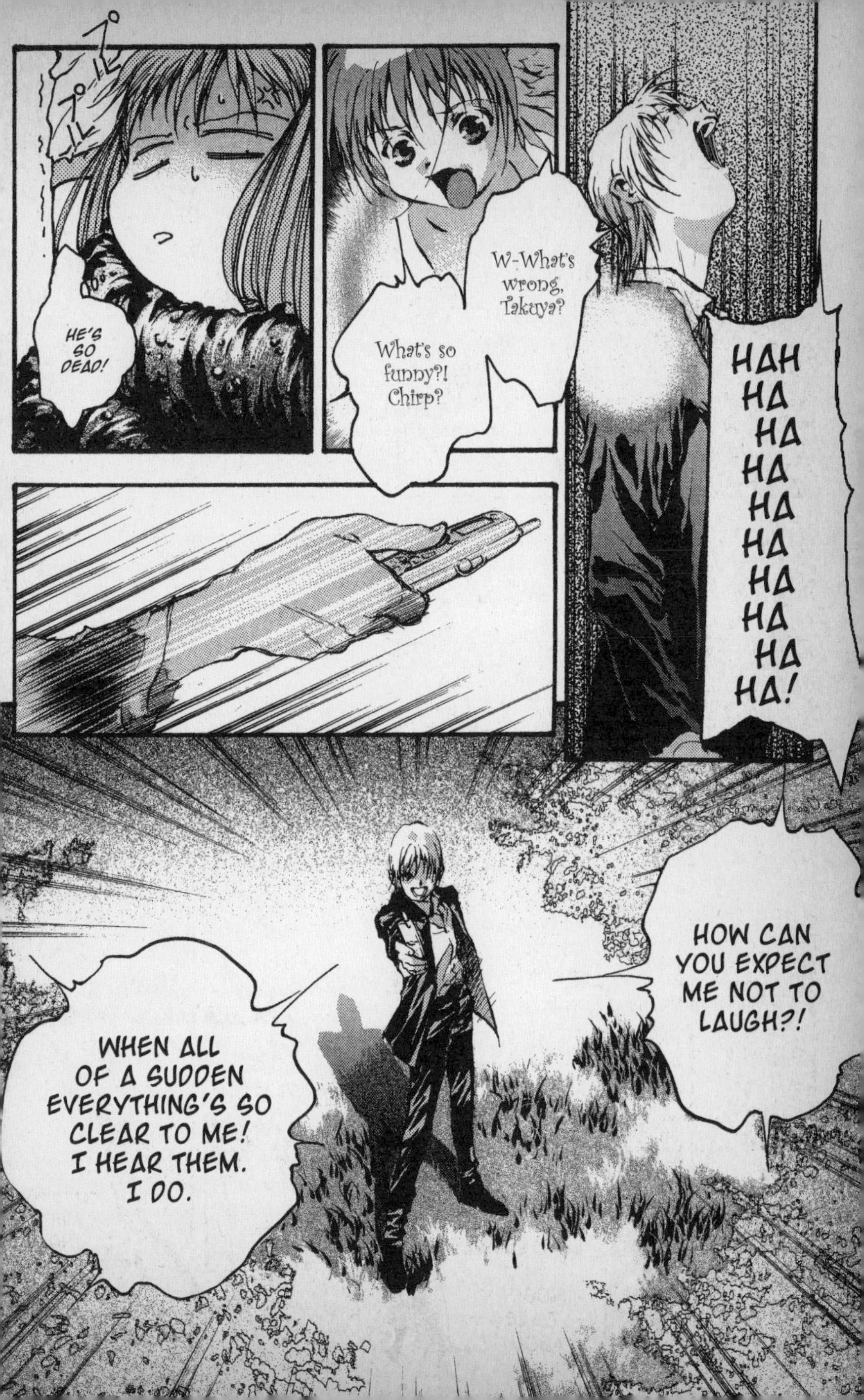
HAH HA HA HA HA HA HA HA HA HA!
W-What's wrong, Takuya?
What's so funny?! Chirp?
HE'S SO DEAD!
HOW CAN YOU EXPECT ME NOT TO LAUGH?!
WHEN ALL OF A SUDDEN EVERYTHING'S SO CLEAR TO ME! I HEAR THEM. I DO.

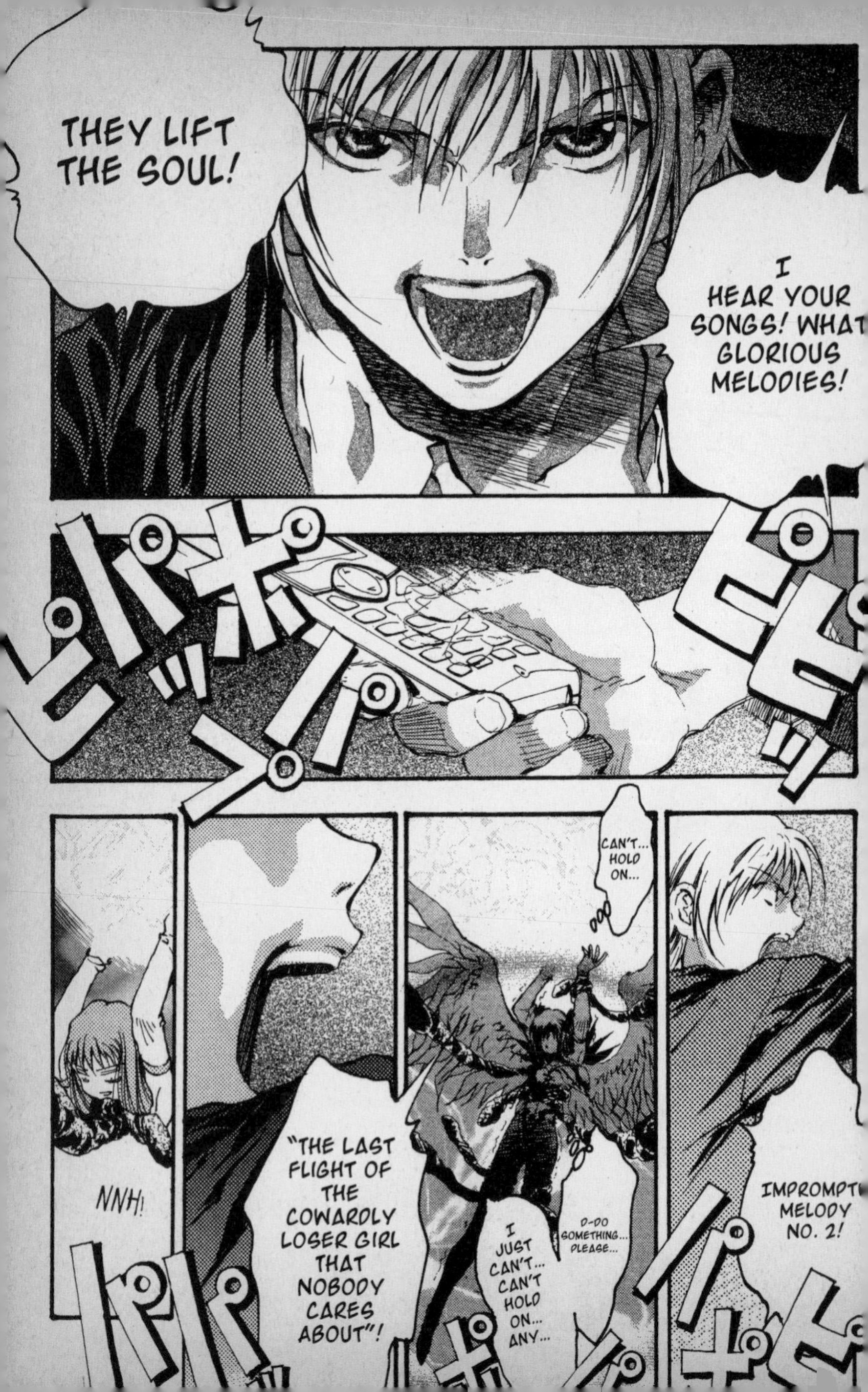
I HEAR YOUR SONGS! WHAT GLORIOUS MELODIES!
THEY LIFT THE SOUL!
IMPROMPTU MELODY NO. 2!
CAN'T... HOLD ON...
D-DO SOMETHING... PLEASE...
I JUST CAN'T... CAN'T HOLD ON... ANY...
"THE LAST FLIGHT OF THE COWARDLY LOSER GIRL THAT NOBODY CARES ABOUT"!
NNH!

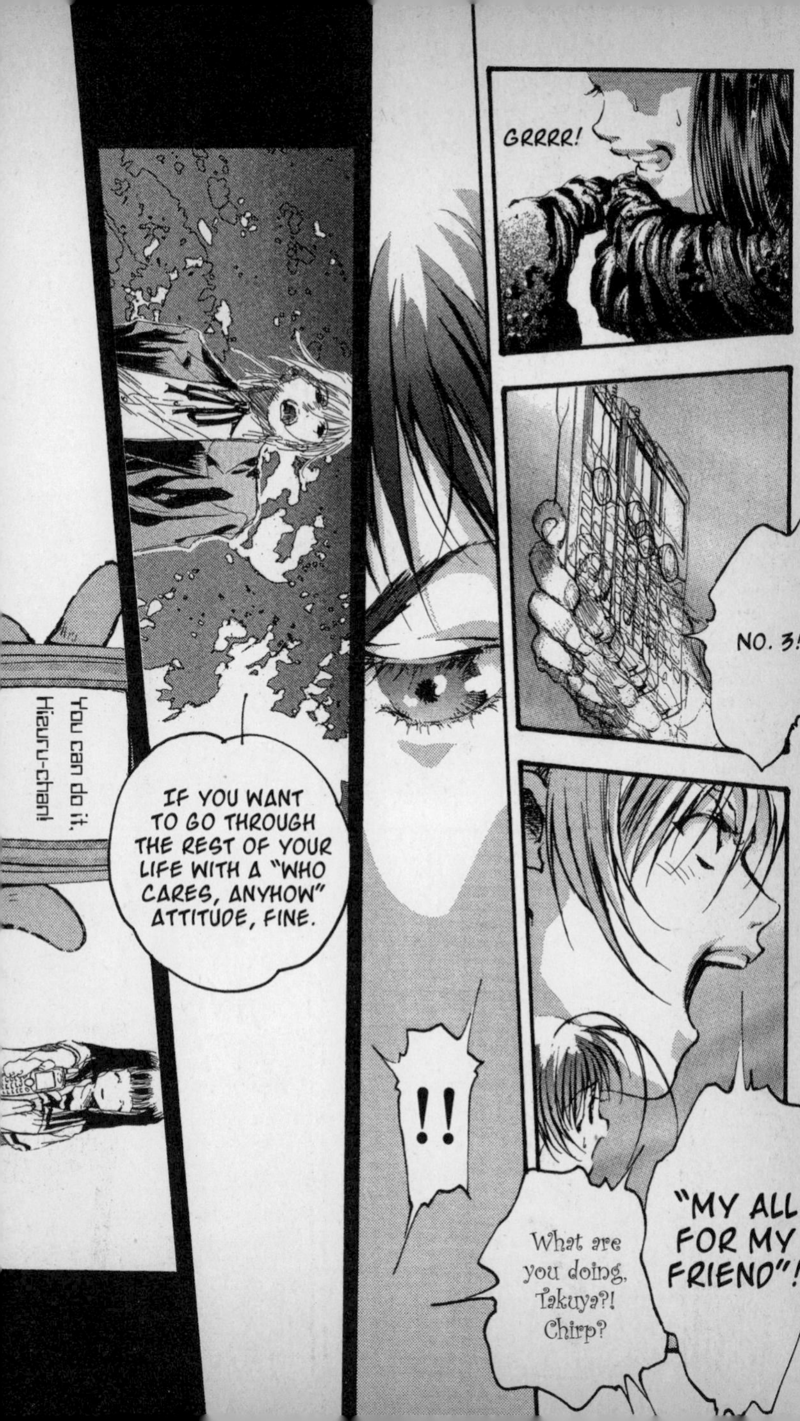
GRRRR!
NO. 3!
"MY ALL FOR MY FRIEND"!
What are you doing, Takuya?! Chirp?
!!
IF YOU WANT TO GO THROUGH THE REST OF YOUR LIFE WITH A "WHO CARES, ANYHOW" ATTITUDE, FINE.
You can do it, Hizuru-chan!

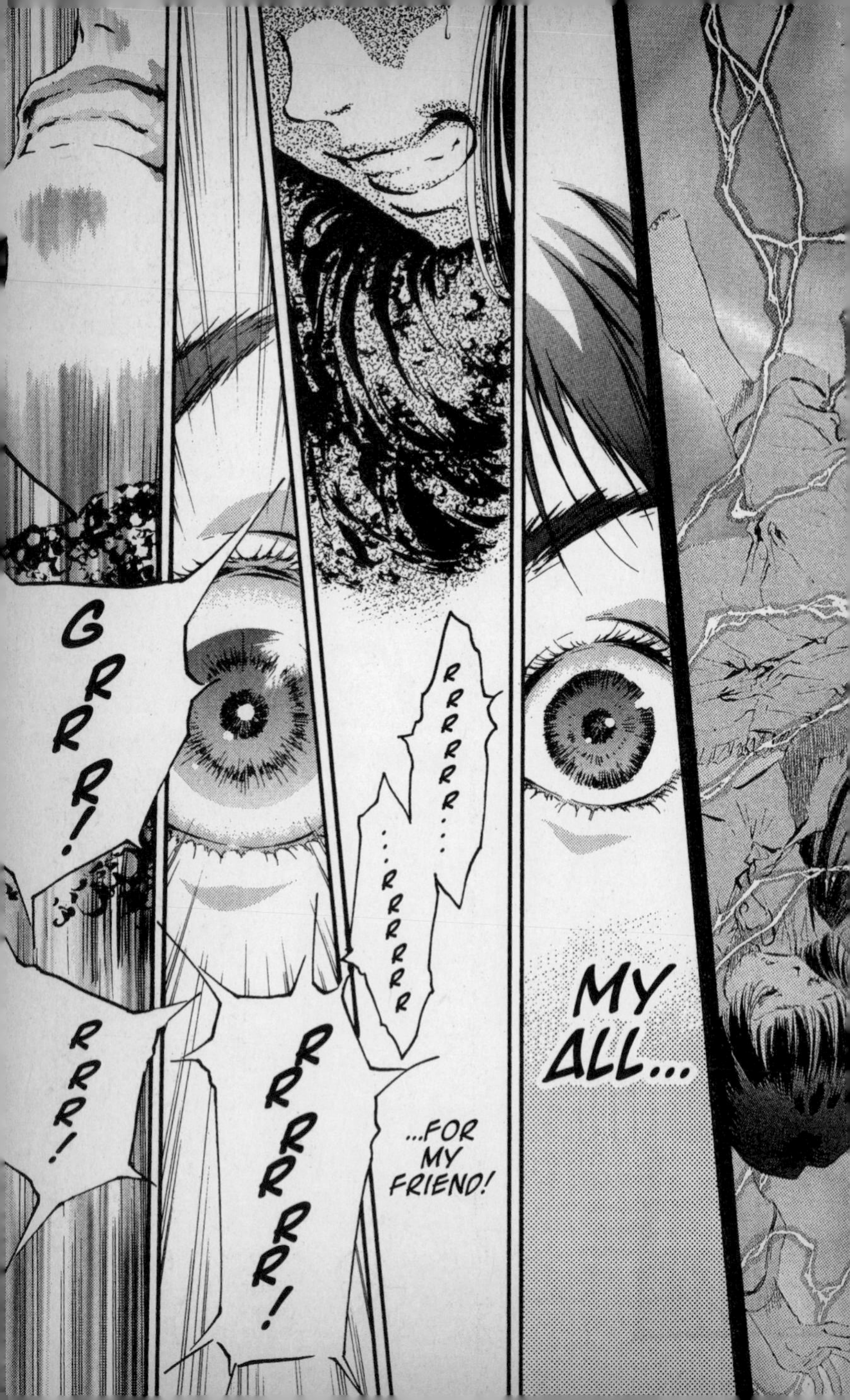
MY ALL...
RRRRRR...
...RRRRRR
...FOR MY FRIEND!
RRRRRR!
GRRR!
RRR!

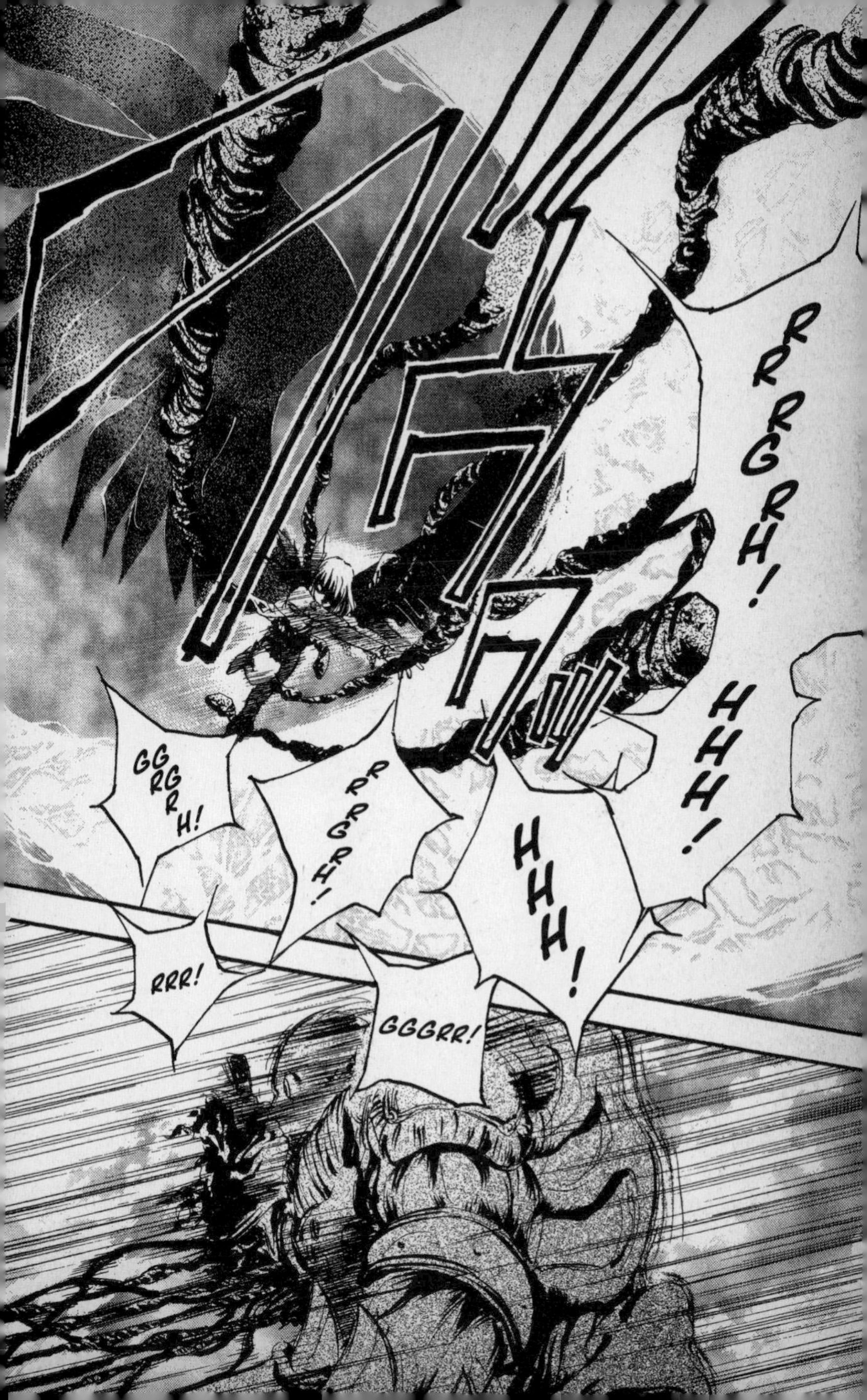
RRRGRH!
HHH!
HHHH!
RRRGRH!
GGRGRH!
GGGRR!
RRR!

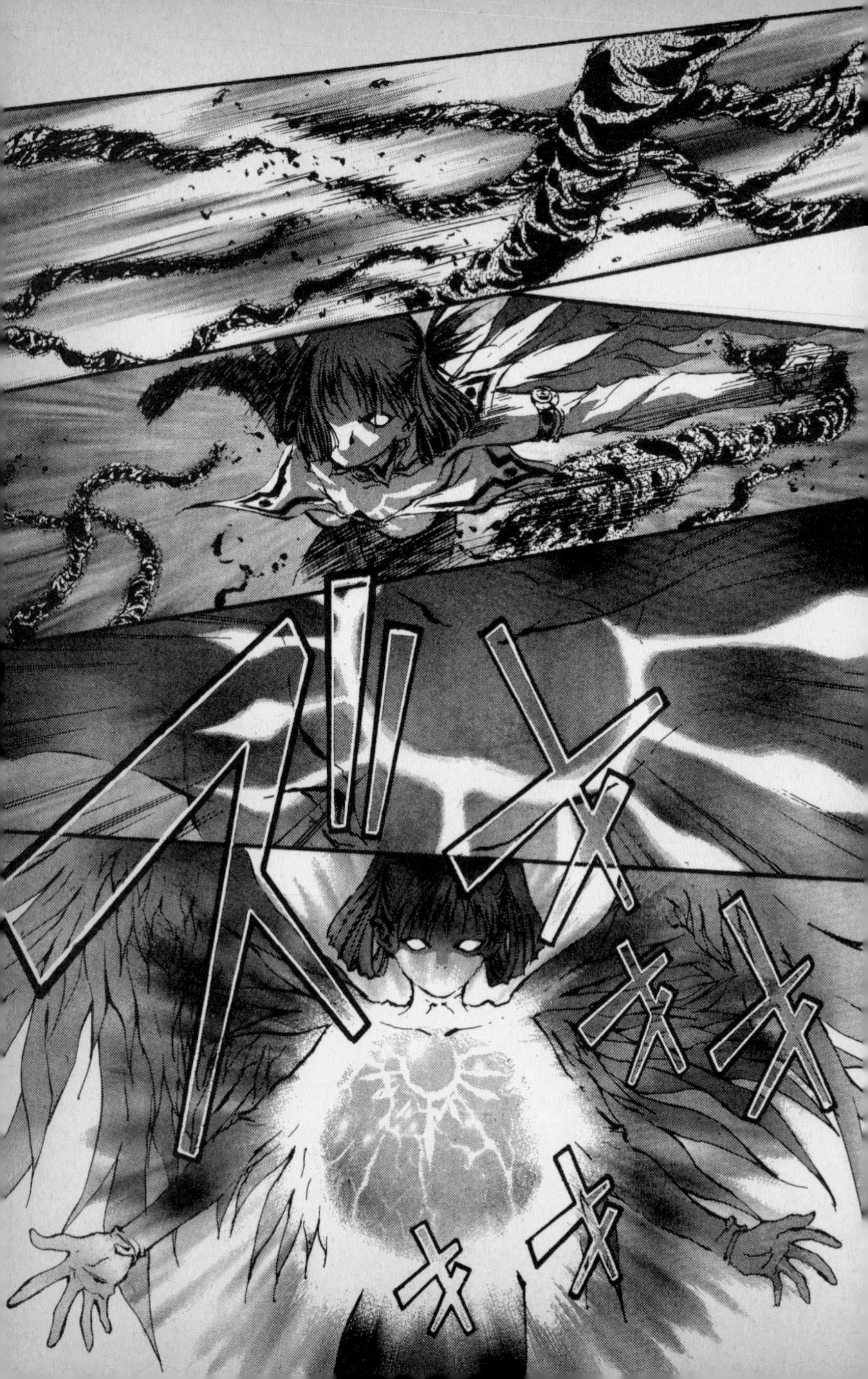
ズオォォォォ

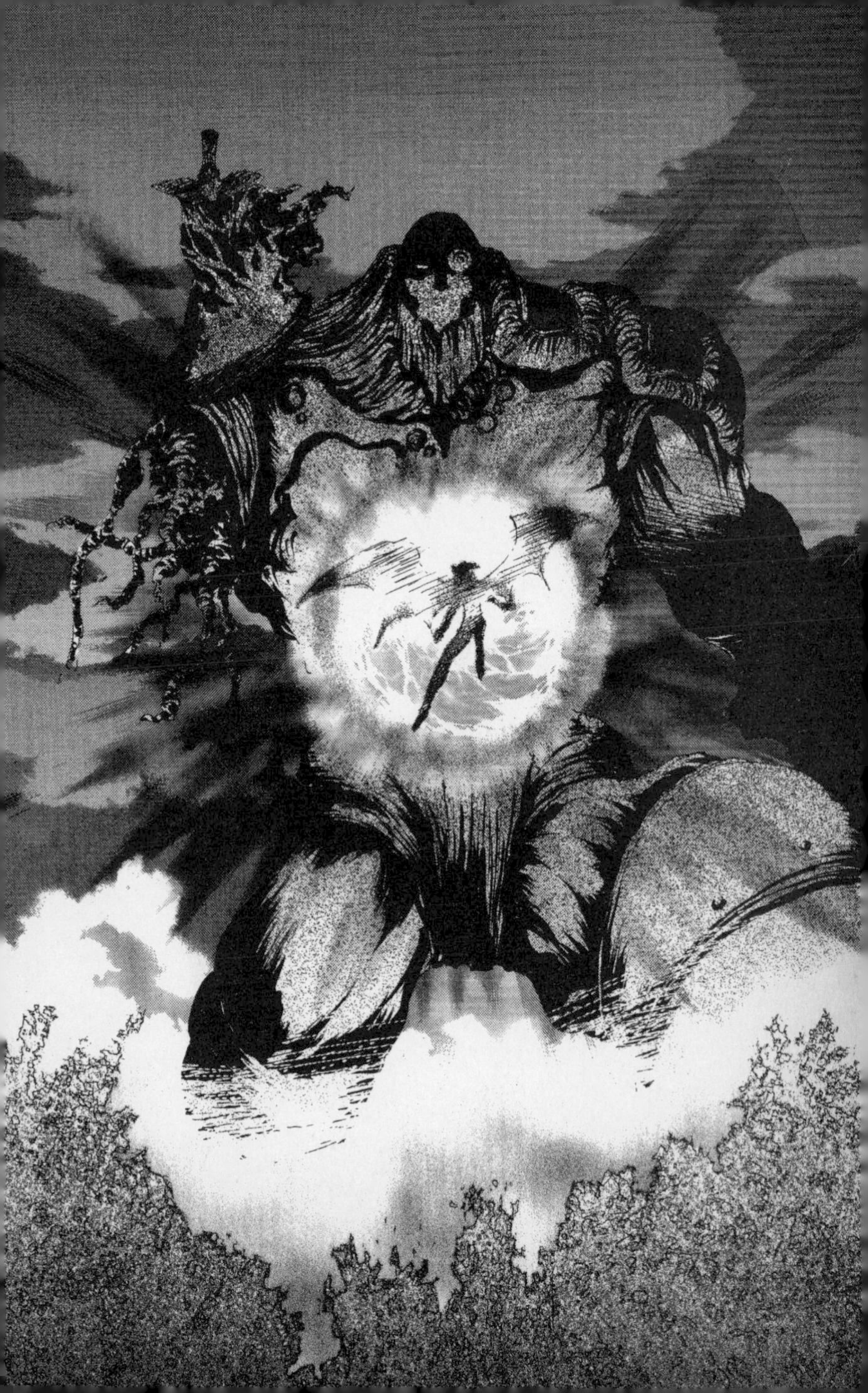

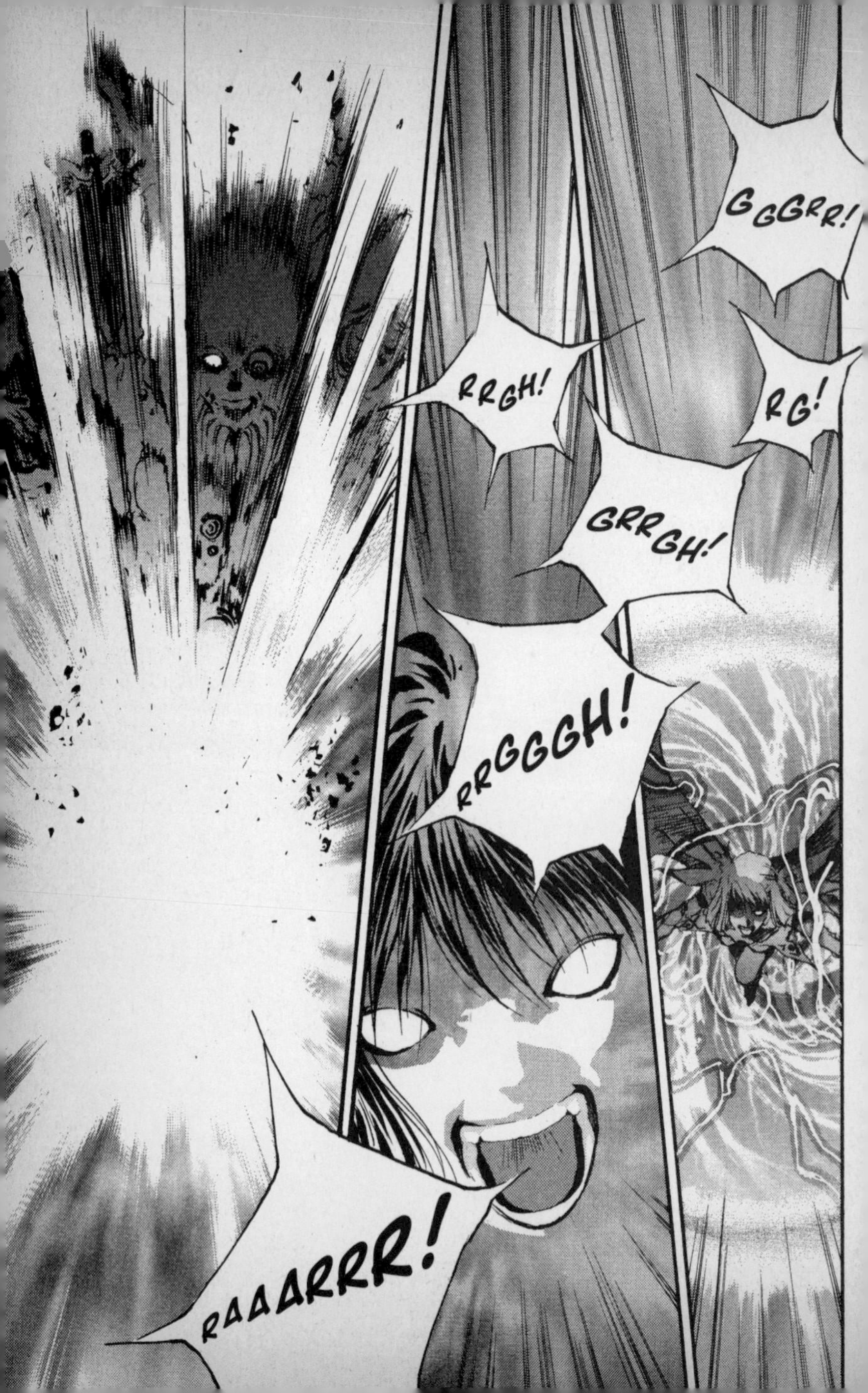
GGGRRR!
RG!
RRGH!
GRRRGH!
RRGGGH!
RAAARRR!

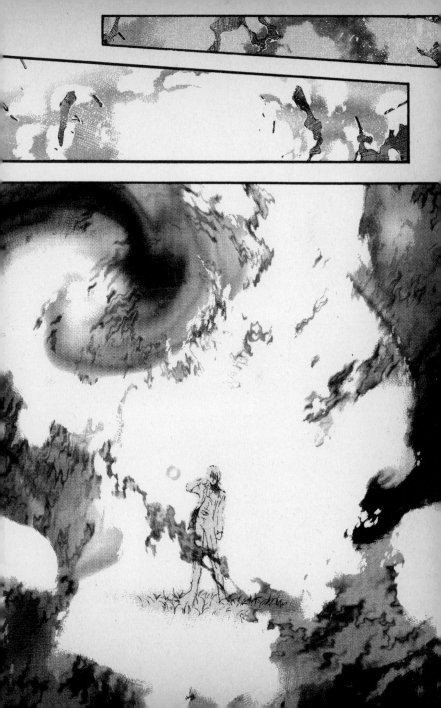

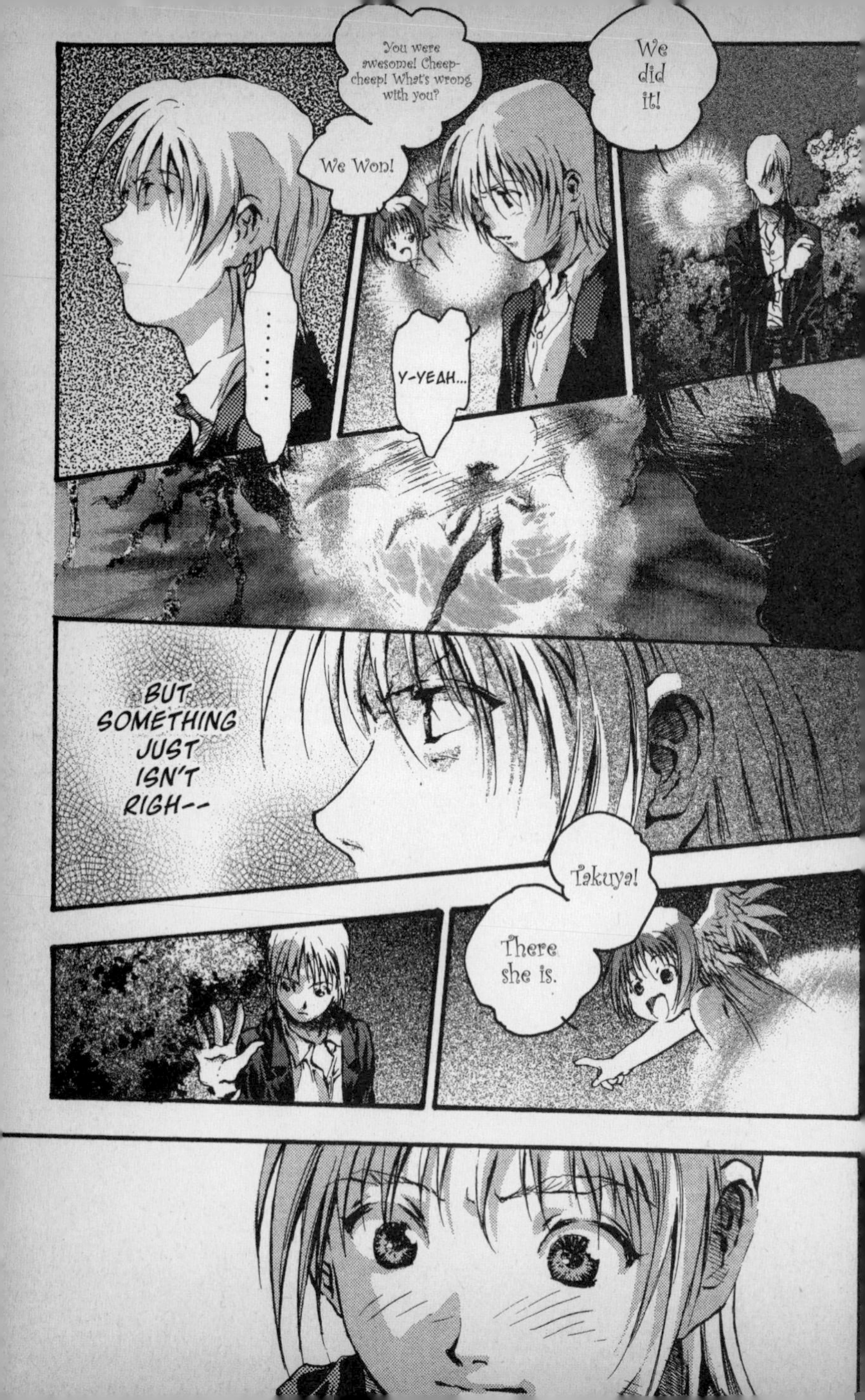
We did it!
You were awesome! Cheep-cheep! What's wrong with you?
We Won!
Y-YEAH...
......
BUT SOMETHING JUST ISN'T RIGH--
Takuya!
There she is.

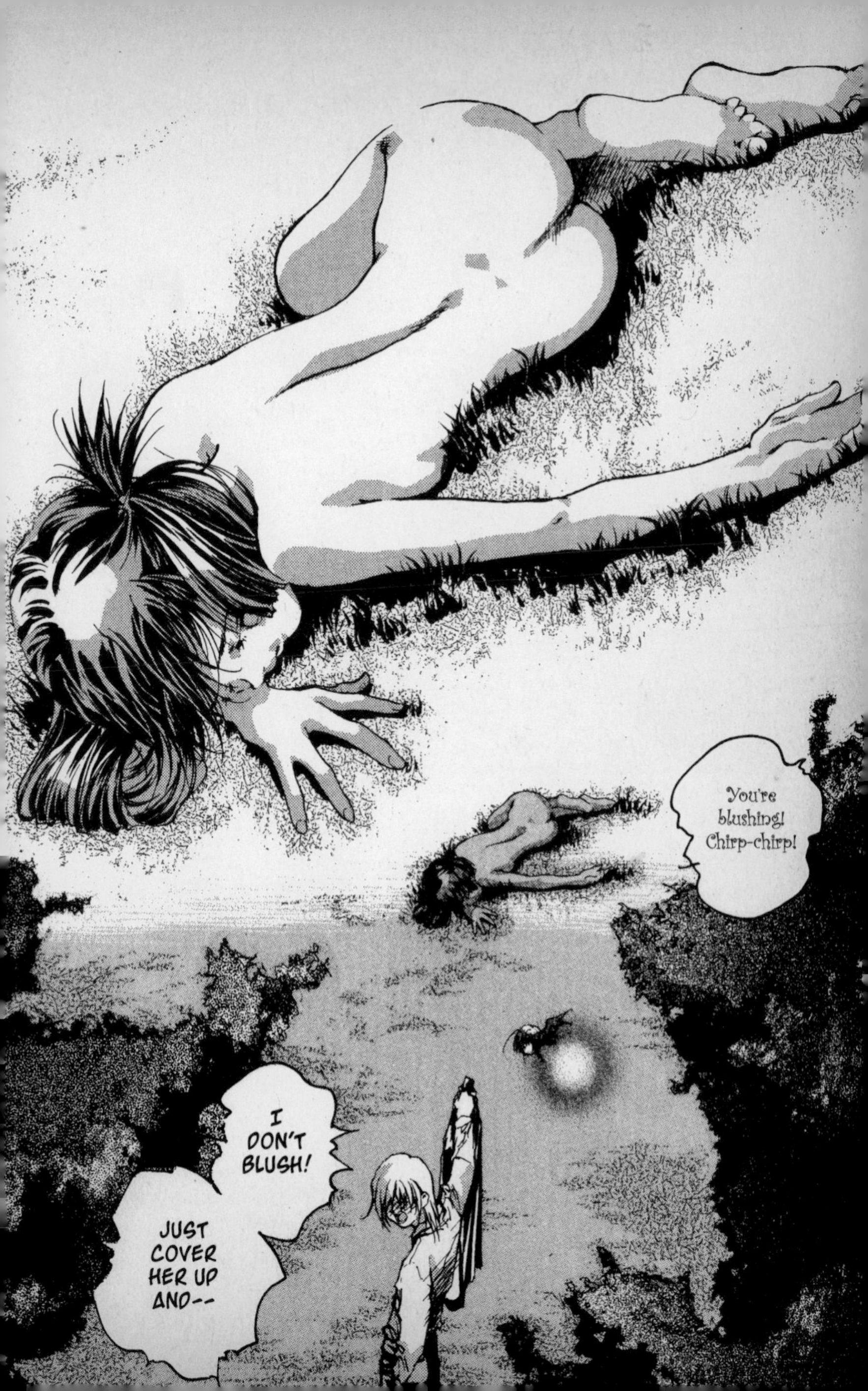
You're blushing! Chirp-chirp!
I DON'T BLUSH!
JUST COVER HER UP AND--

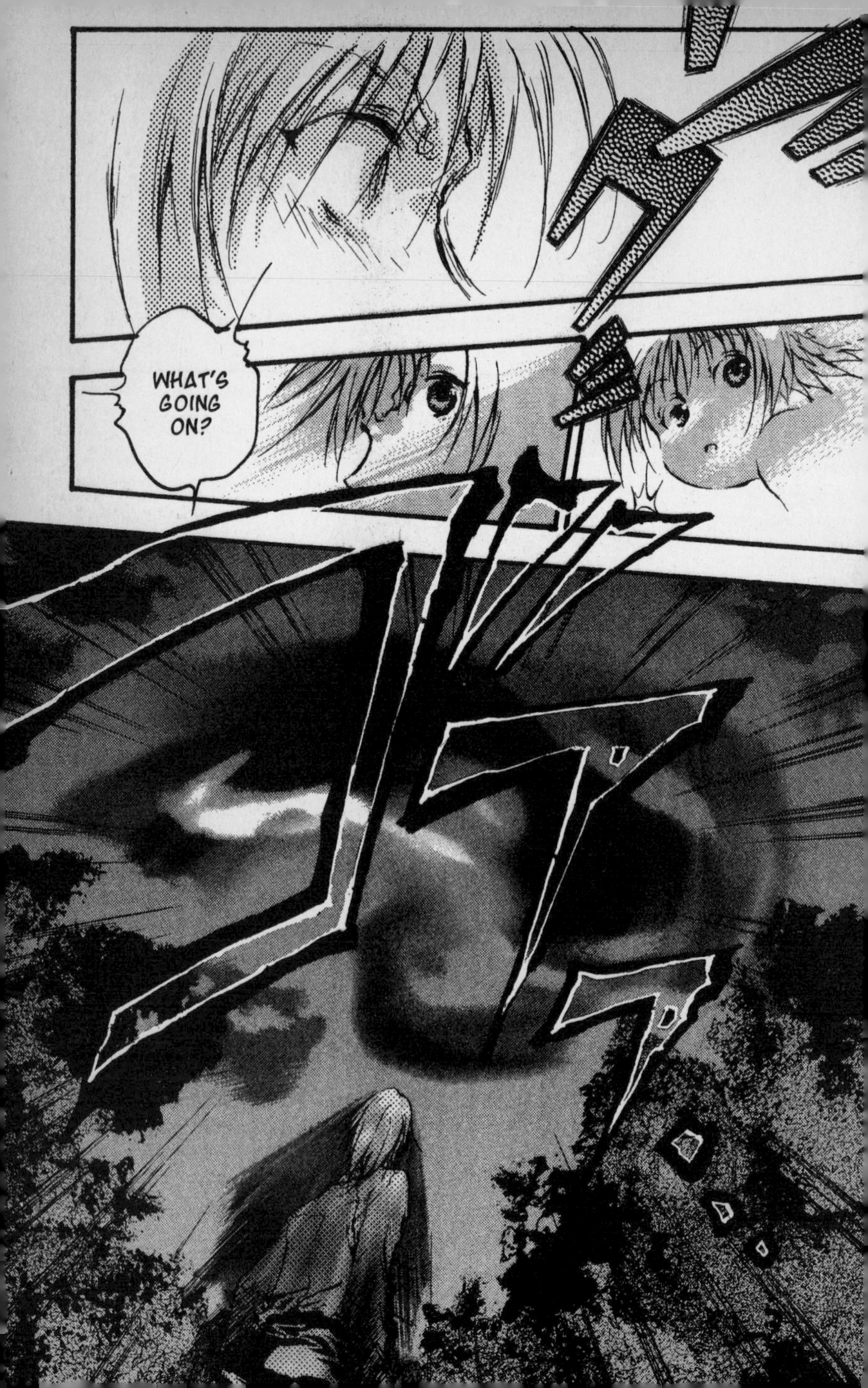
WHAT'S GOING ON?

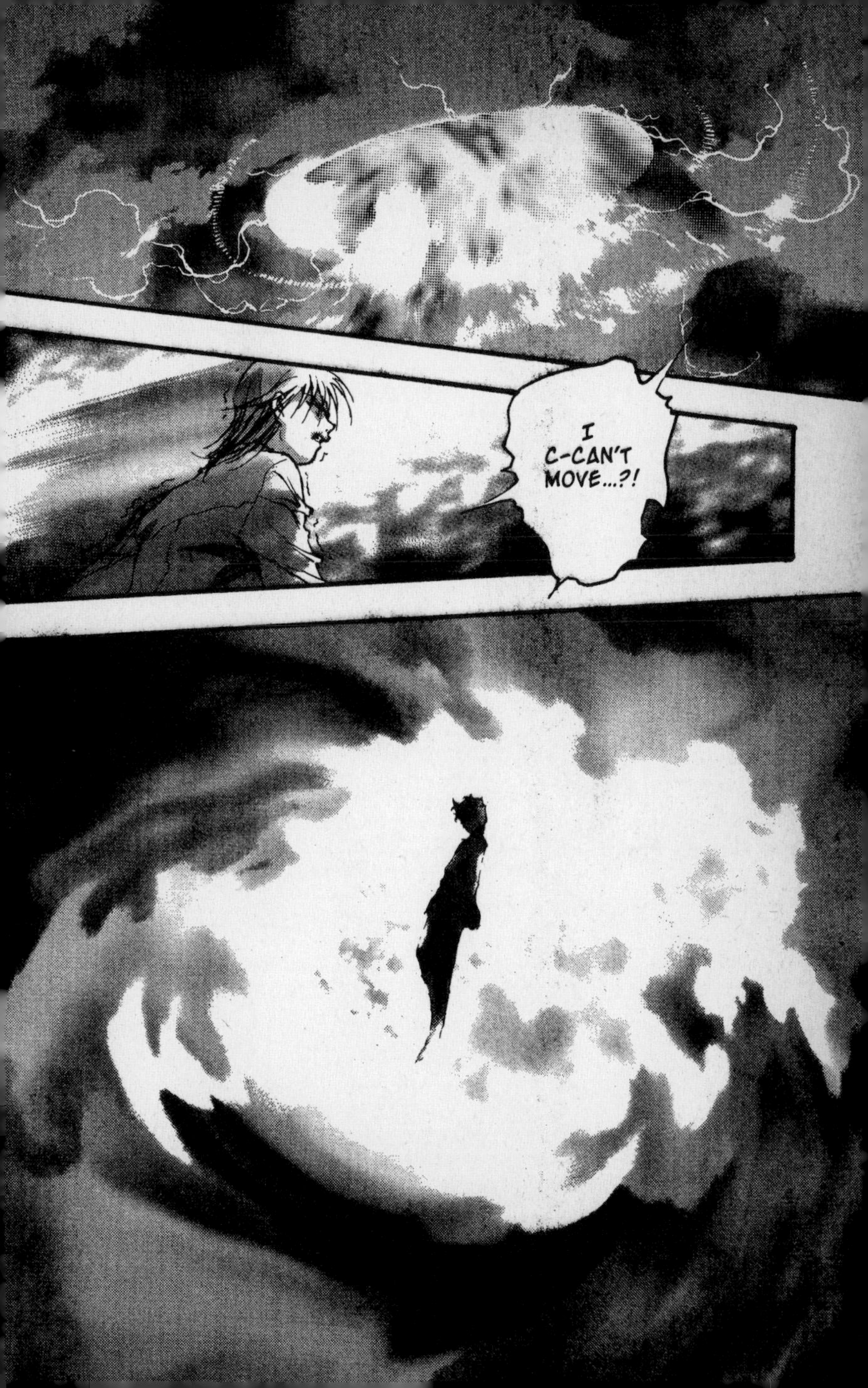
I C-CAN'T MOVE...?!

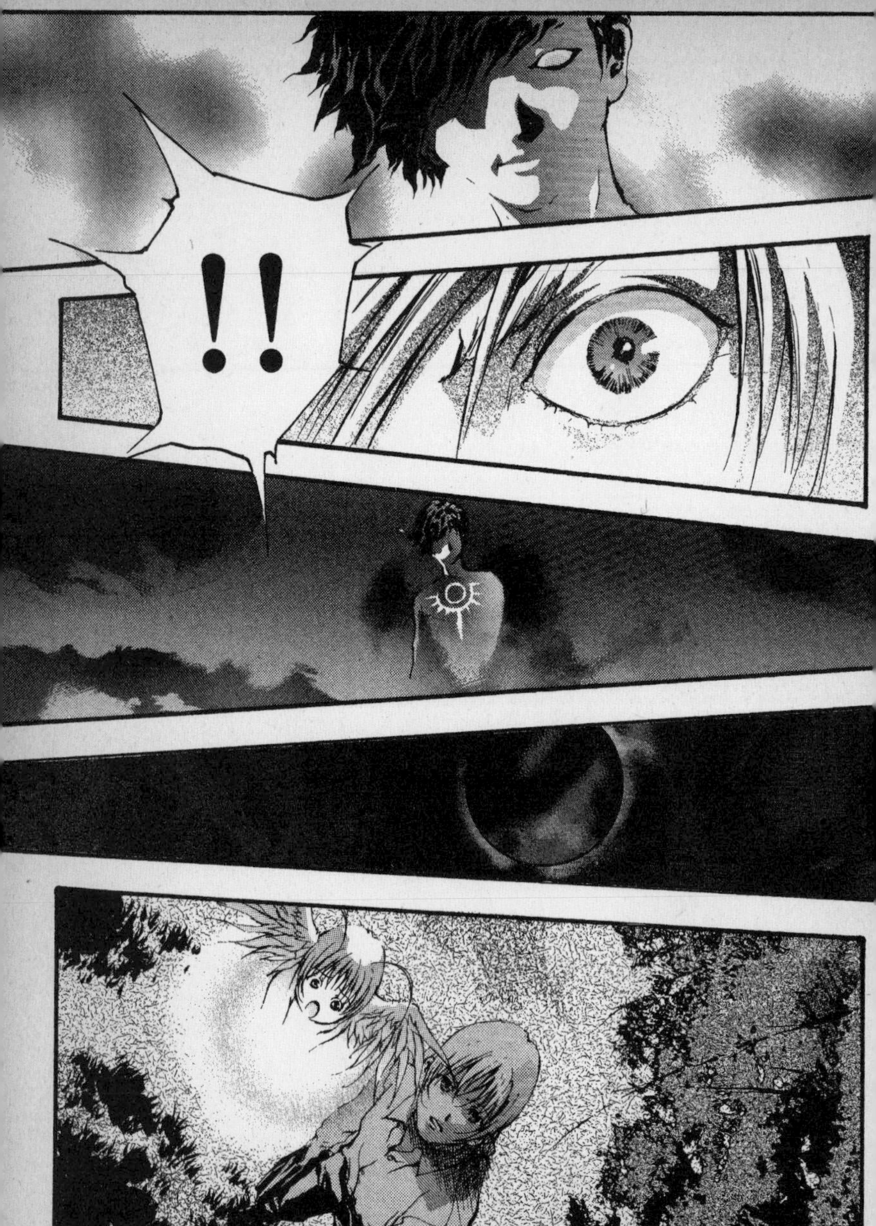
!!

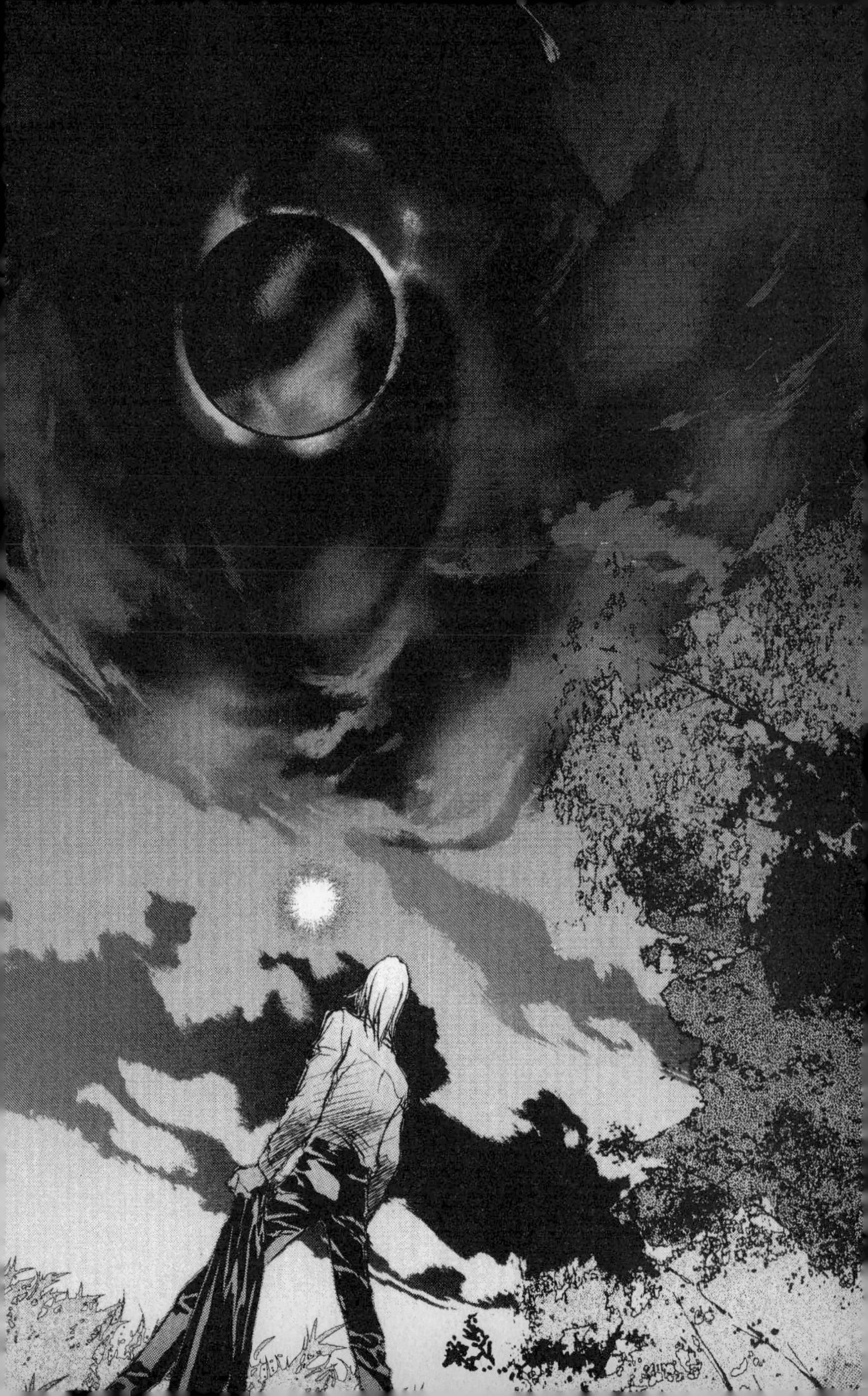

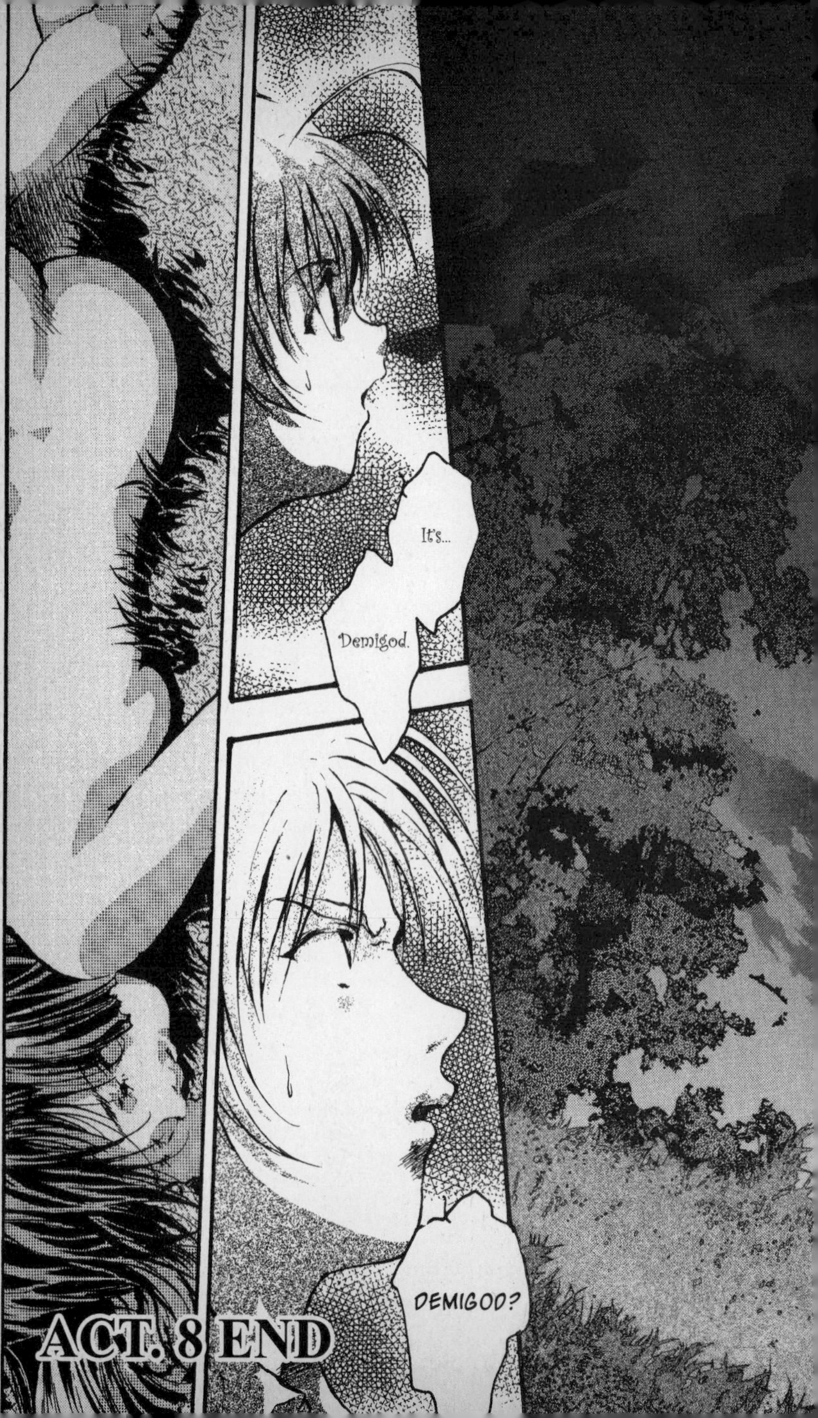
It's...
Demigod.
DEMIGOD?
ACT. 8 END

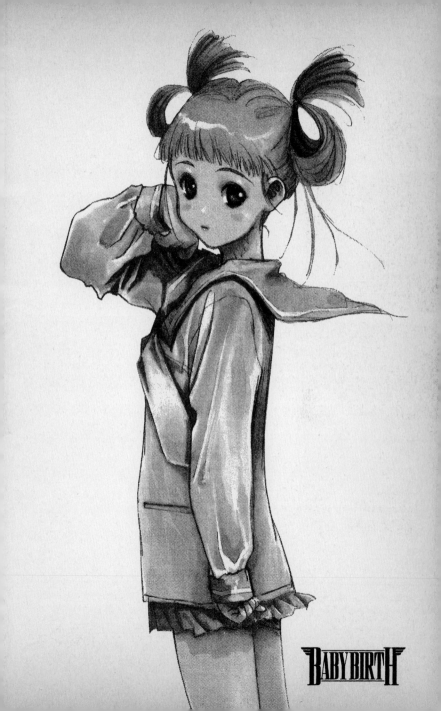

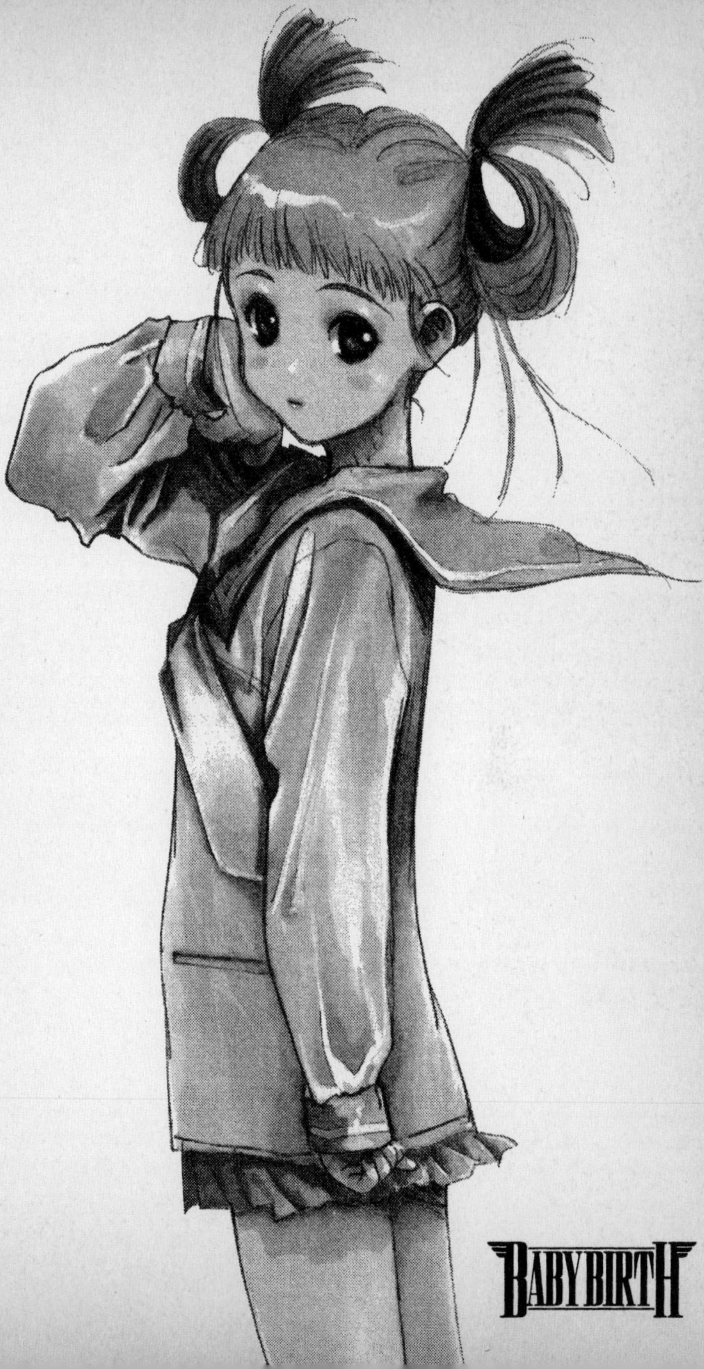
BABY BIRTH

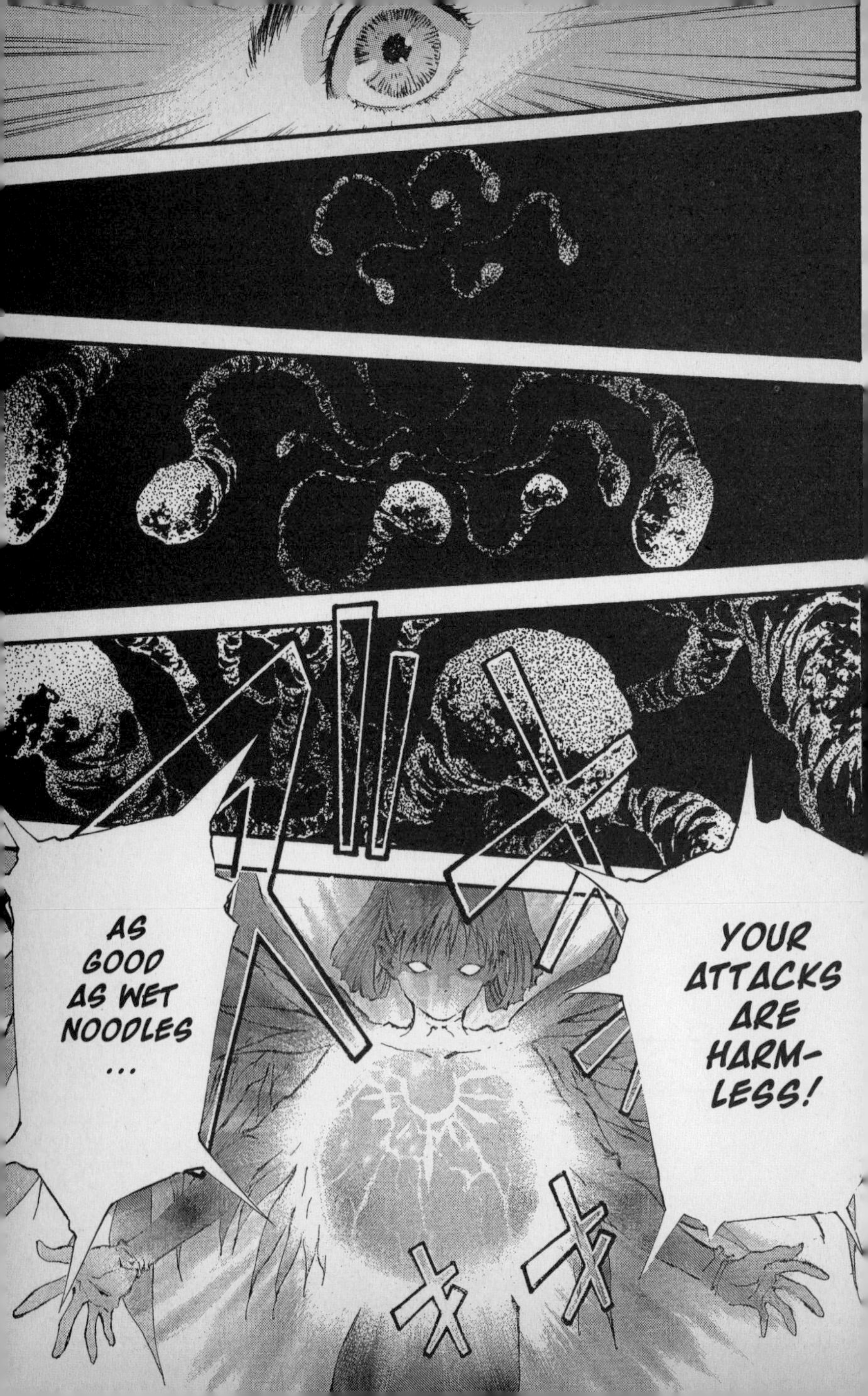
YOUR ATTACKS ARE HARM-LESS!
AS GOOD AS WET NOODLES ...

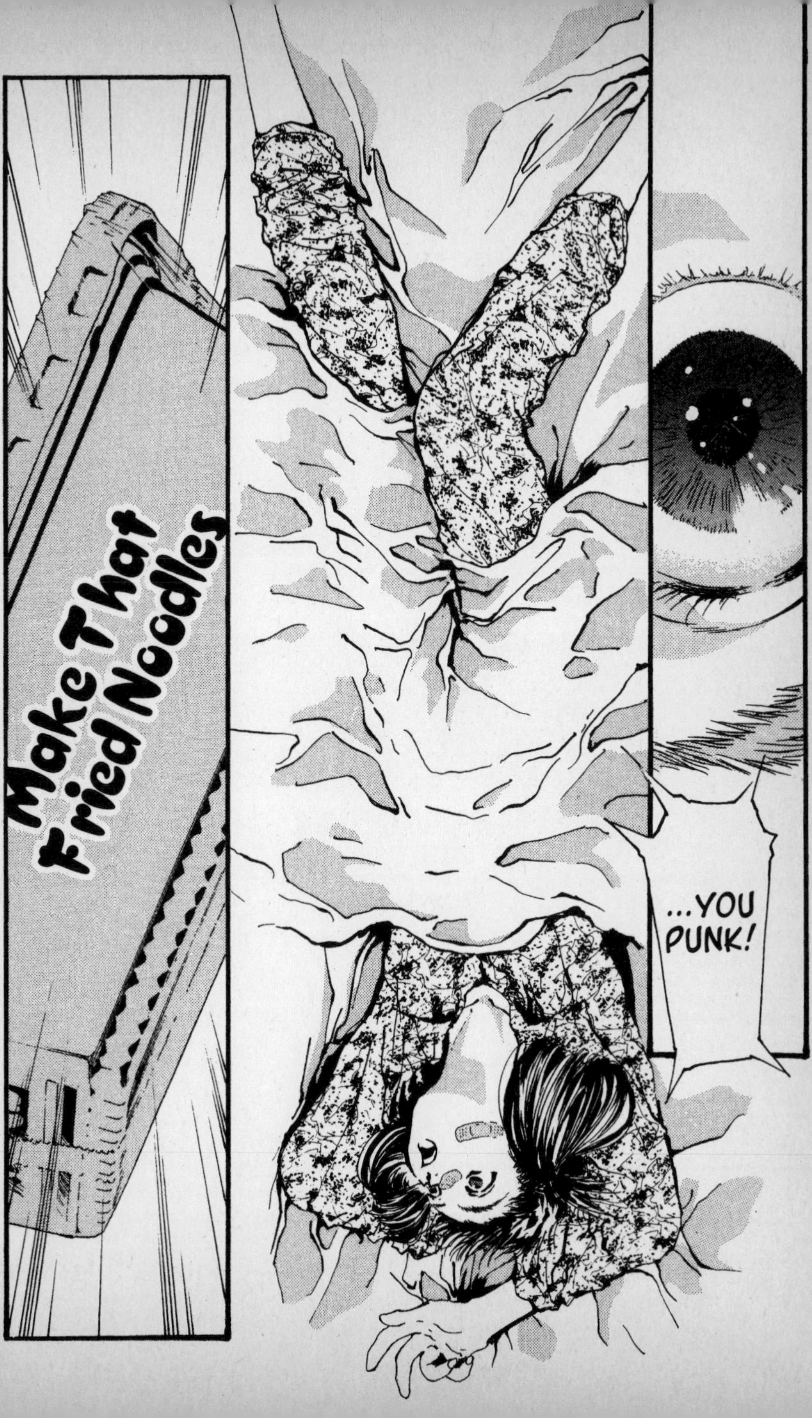
...YOU PUNK!
Make That Fried Noodles

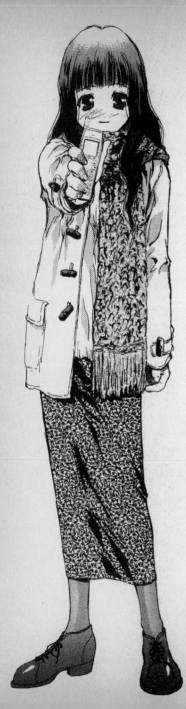

ACT. 9 The Ancient Miracle

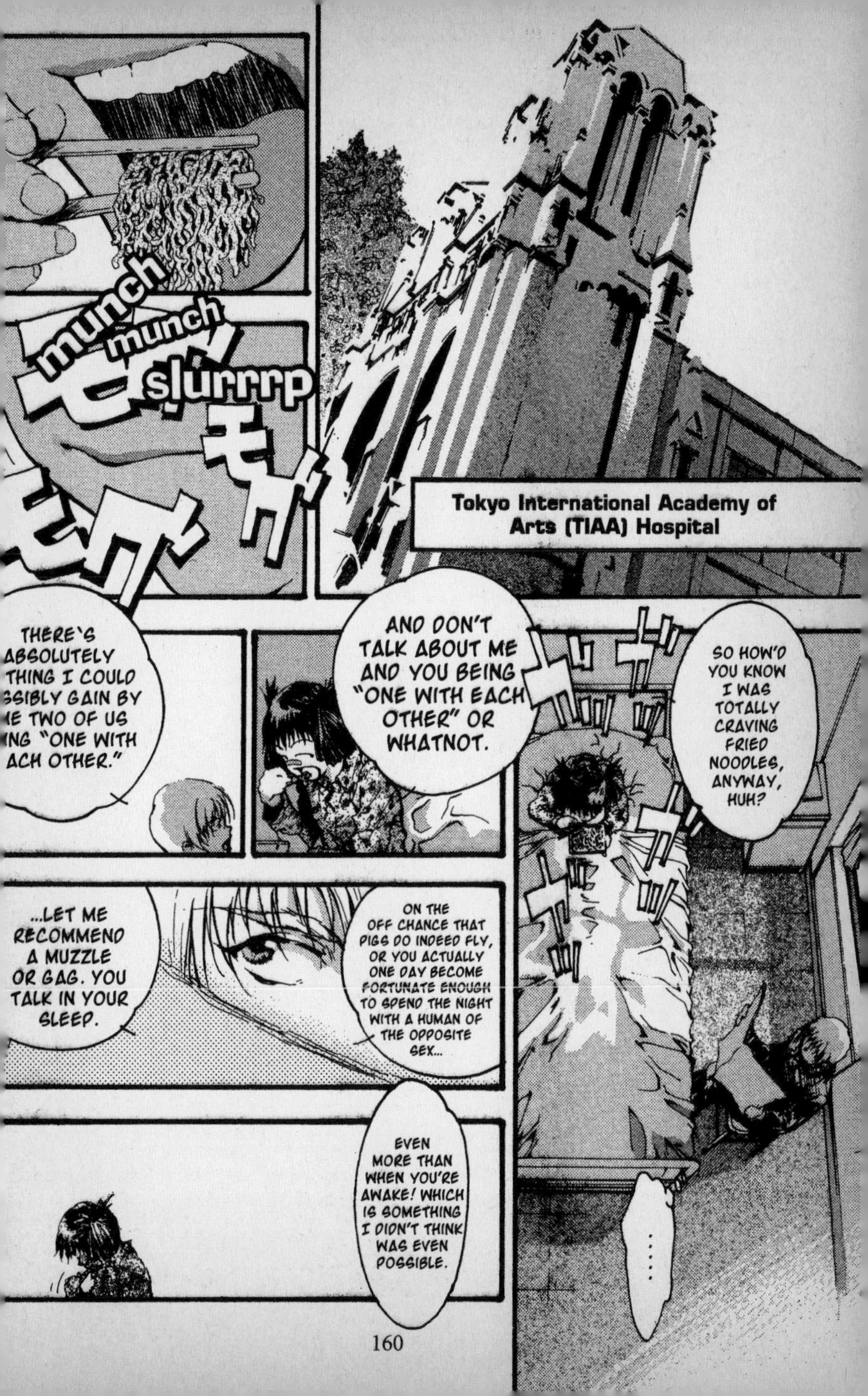
Tokyo International Academy of Arts (TIAA) Hospital
munch munch
slurrrp
SO HOW'D YOU KNOW I WAS TOTALLY CRAVING FRIED NOODLES, ANYWAY, HUH?
AND DON'T TALK ABOUT ME AND YOU BEING "ONE WITH EACH OTHER" OR WHATNOT.
THERE'S ABSOLUTELY THING I COULD SSIBLY GAIN BY IE TWO OF US NG "ONE WITH ACH OTHER."
ON THE OFF CHANCE THAT PIGS DO INDEED FLY, OR YOU ACTUALLY ONE DAY BECOME FORTUNATE ENOUGH TO SPEND THE NIGHT WITH A HUMAN OF THE OPPOSITE SEX...
...LET ME RECOMMEND A MUZZLE OR GAG. YOU TALK IN YOUR SLEEP.
EVEN MORE THAN WHEN YOU'RE AWAKE! WHICH IS SOMETHING I DIDN'T THINK WAS EVEN POSSIBLE.
......

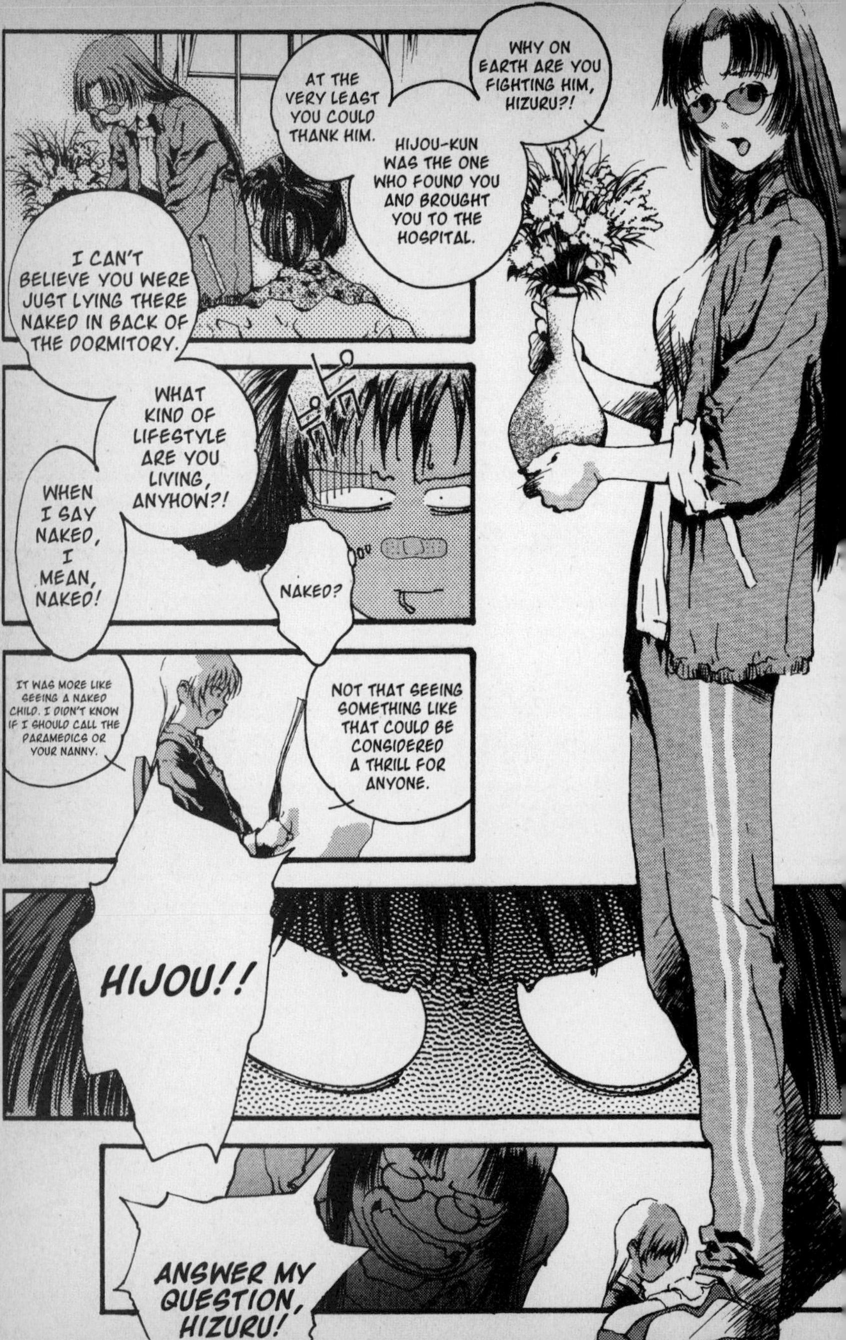
WHY ON EARTH ARE YOU FIGHTING HIM, HIZURU?!
AT THE VERY LEAST YOU COULD THANK HIM.
HIJOU-KUN WAS THE ONE WHO FOUND YOU AND BROUGHT YOU TO THE HOSPITAL.
I CAN'T BELIEVE YOU WERE JUST LYING THERE NAKED IN BACK OF THE DORMITORY.
WHAT KIND OF LIFESTYLE ARE YOU LIVING, ANYHOW?!
WHEN I SAY NAKED, I MEAN, NAKED!
NAKED?
NOT THAT SEEING SOMETHING LIKE THAT COULD BE CONSIDERED A THRILL FOR ANYONE.
IT WAS MORE LIKE SEEING A NAKED CHILD. I DIDN'T KNOW IF I SHOULD CALL THE PARAMEDICS OR YOUR NANNY.
HIJOU!!
ANSWER MY QUESTION, HIZURU!

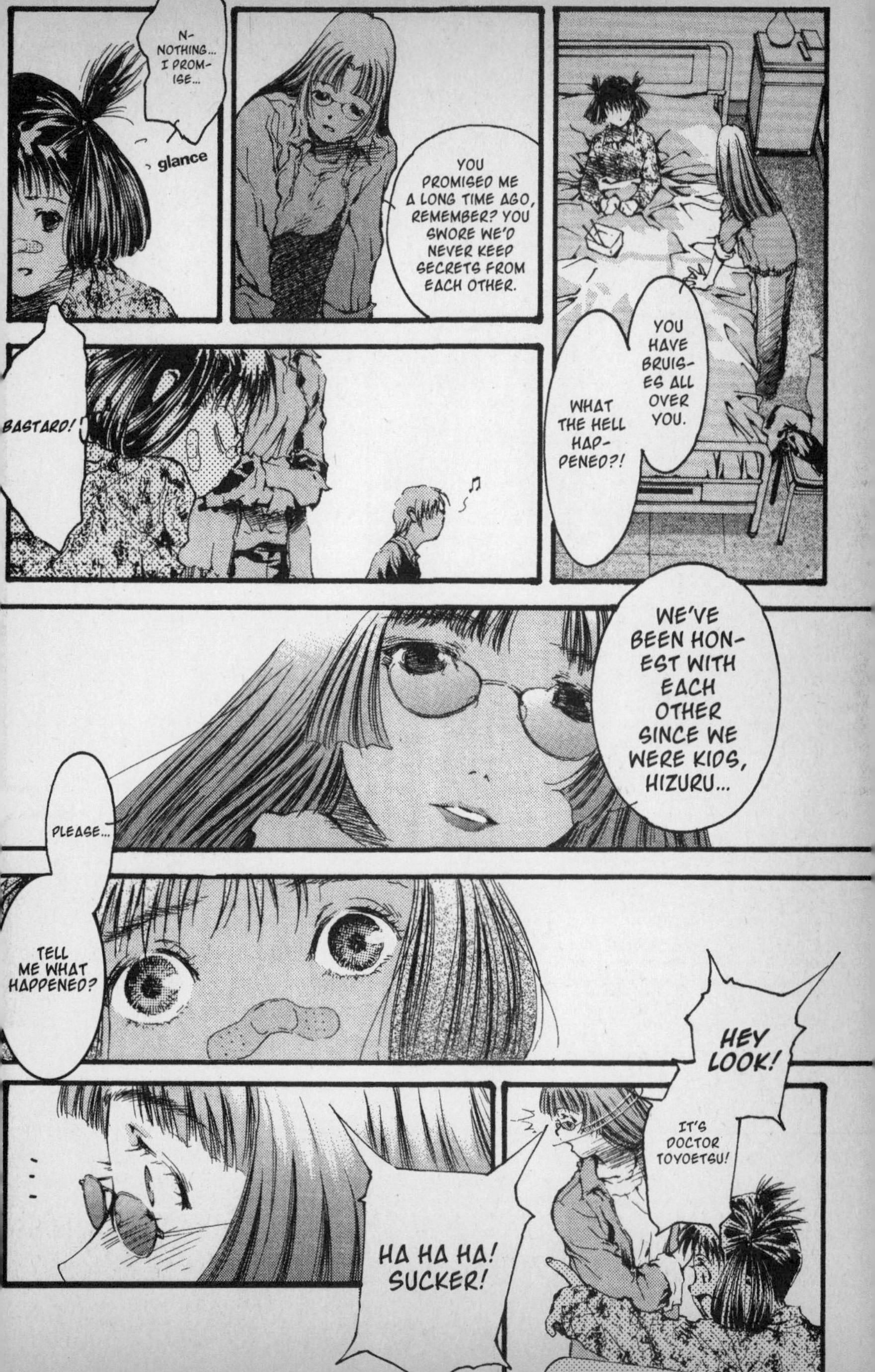
YOU HAVE BRUISES ALL OVER YOU.
WHAT THE HELL HAPPENED?!
YOU PROMISED ME A LONG TIME AGO, REMEMBER? YOU SWORE WE'D NEVER KEEP SECRETS FROM EACH OTHER.
N-NOTHING... I PROMISE...
glance
BASTARD!
♪
WE'VE BEEN HONEST WITH EACH OTHER SINCE WE WERE KIDS, HIZURU...
PLEASE...
TELL ME WHAT HAPPENED?
HEY LOOK!
IT'S DOCTOR TOYOETSU!
HA HA HA! SUCKER!
...

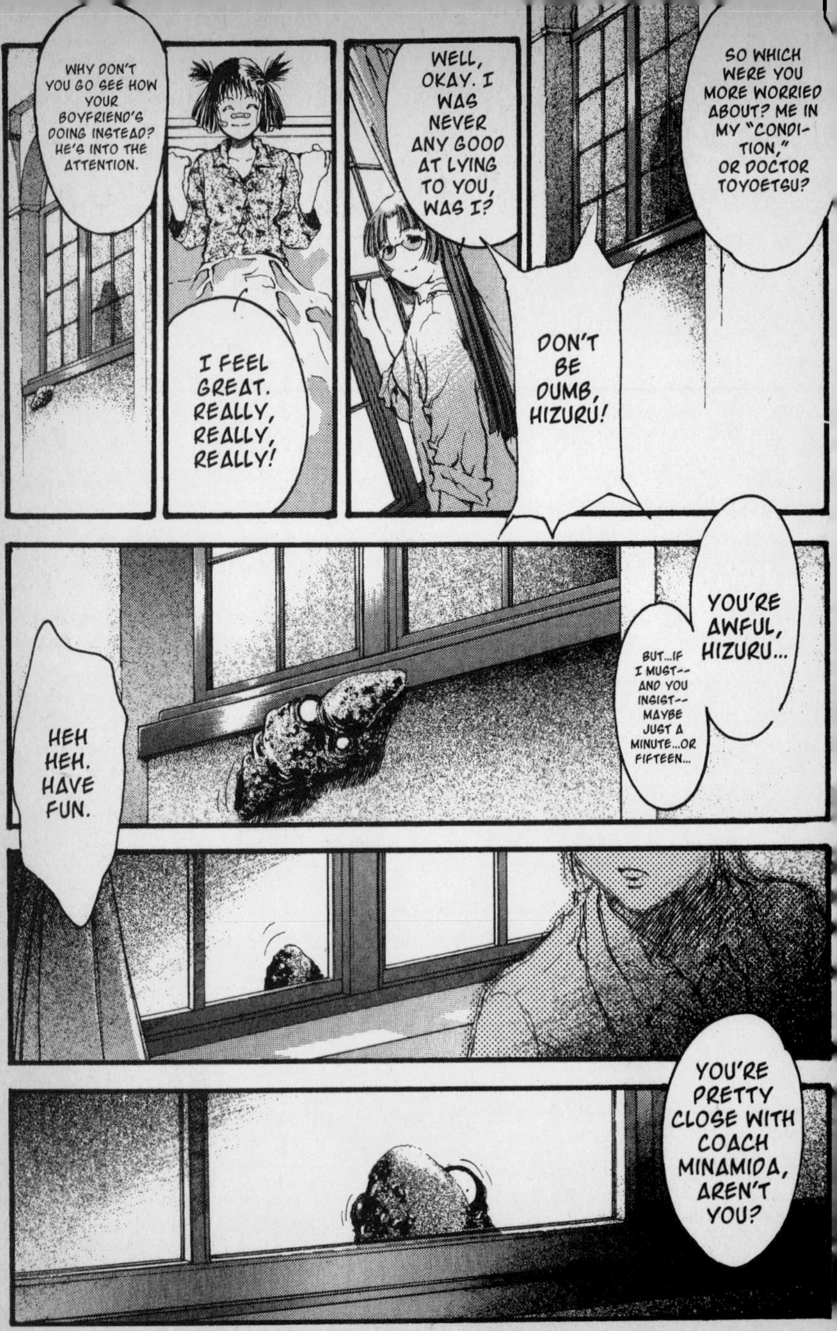
SO WHICH WERE YOU MORE WORRIED ABOUT? ME IN MY "CONDITION," OR DOCTOR TOYOETSU?
DON'T BE DUMB, HIZURU!
WELL, OKAY. I WAS NEVER ANY GOOD AT LYING TO YOU, WAS I?
I FEEL GREAT. REALLY, REALLY, REALLY!
WHY DON'T YOU GO SEE HOW YOUR BOYFRIEND'S DOING INSTEAD? HE'S INTO THE ATTENTION.
YOU'RE AWFUL, HIZURU...
BUT...IF I MUST--AND YOU INSIST--MAYBE JUST A MINUTE...OR FIFTEEN...
HEH HEH. HAVE FUN.
YOU'RE PRETTY CLOSE WITH COACH MINAMIDA, AREN'T YOU?

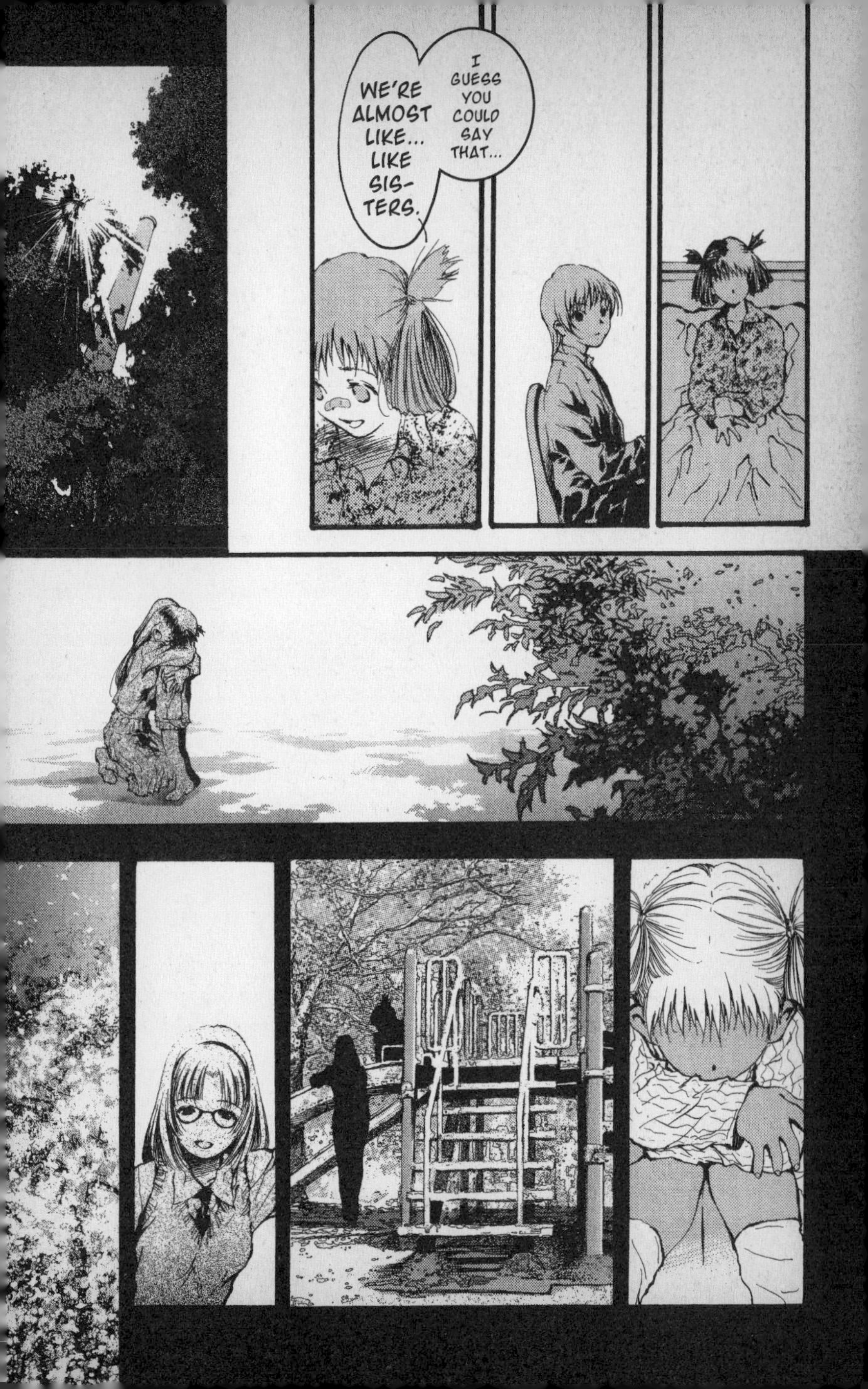
WE'RE ALMOST LIKE... LIKE SIS-TERS.
I GUESS YOU COULD SAY THAT...

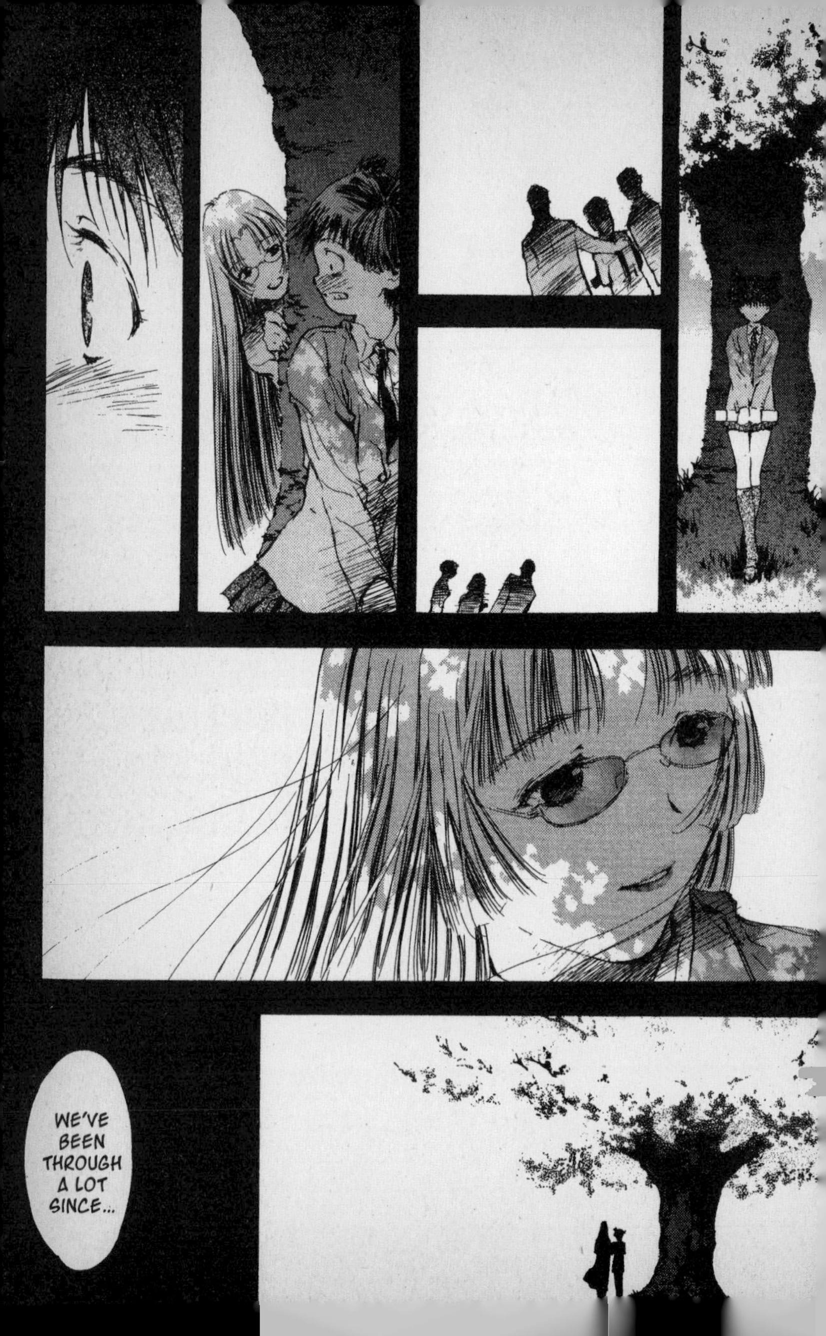
WE'VE BEEN THROUGH A LOT SINCE...

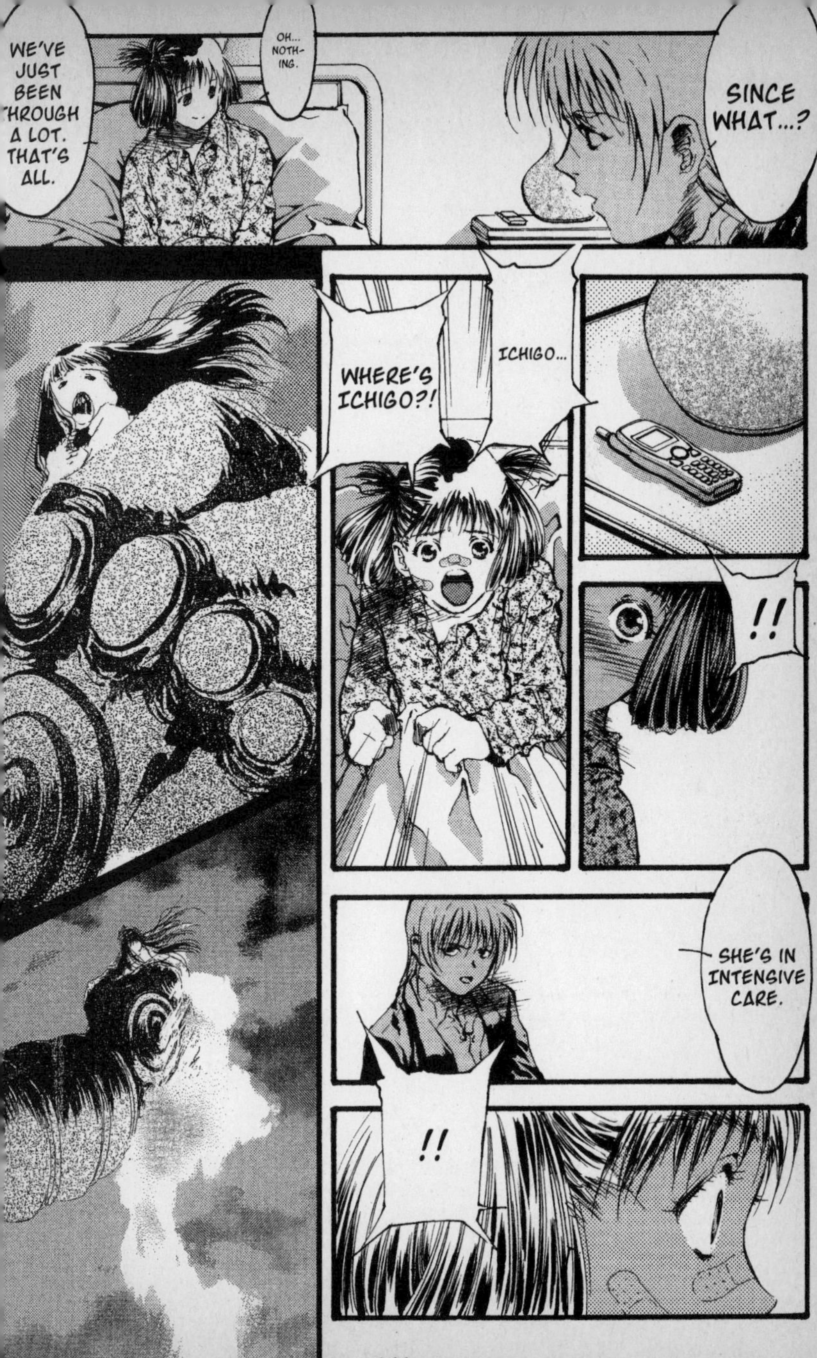
SINCE WHAT...?
OH... NOTHING.
WE'VE JUST BEEN THROUGH A LOT. THAT'S ALL.
ICHIGO...
!!
WHERE'S ICHIGO?!
SHE'S IN INTENSIVE CARE.
!!

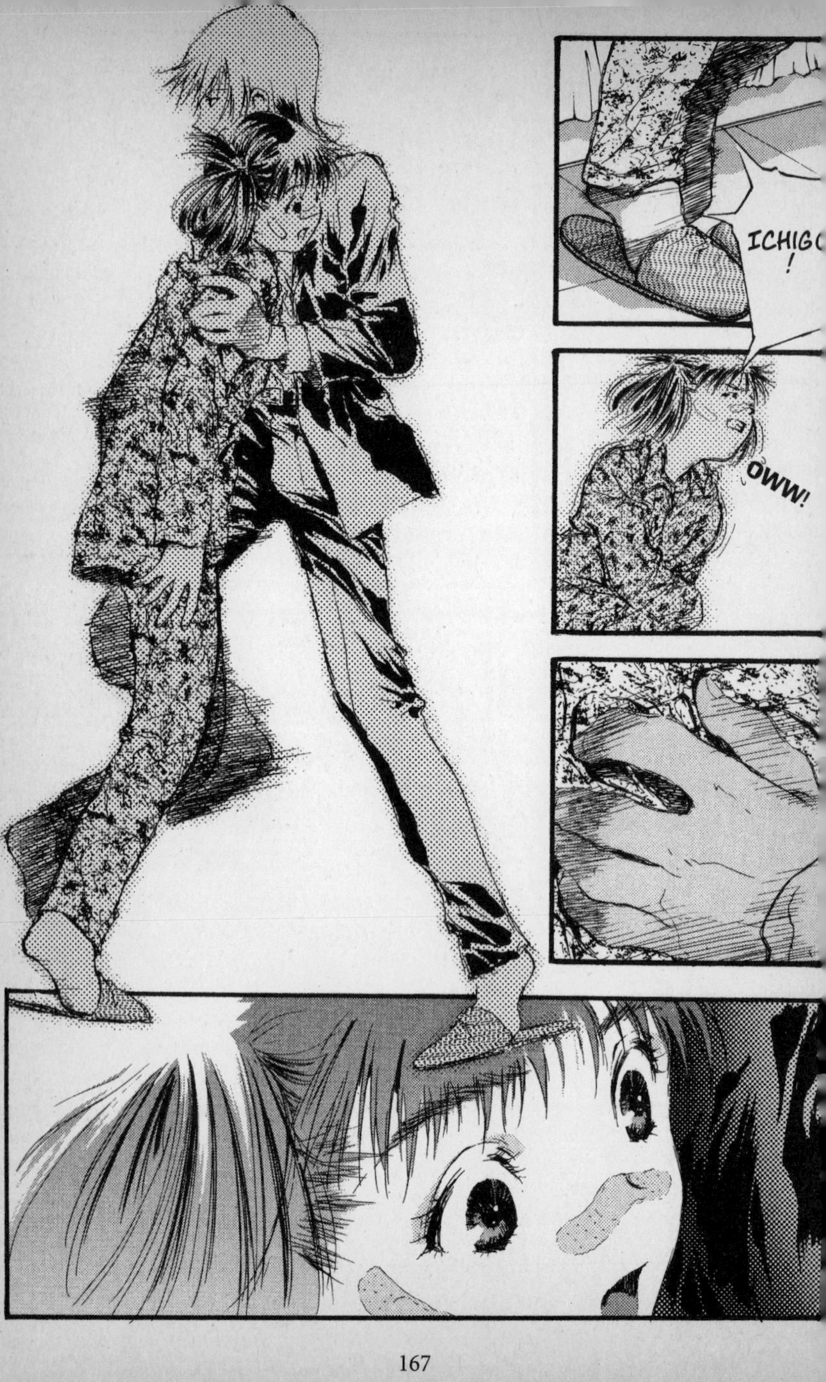
ICHIGO
!
OWW!

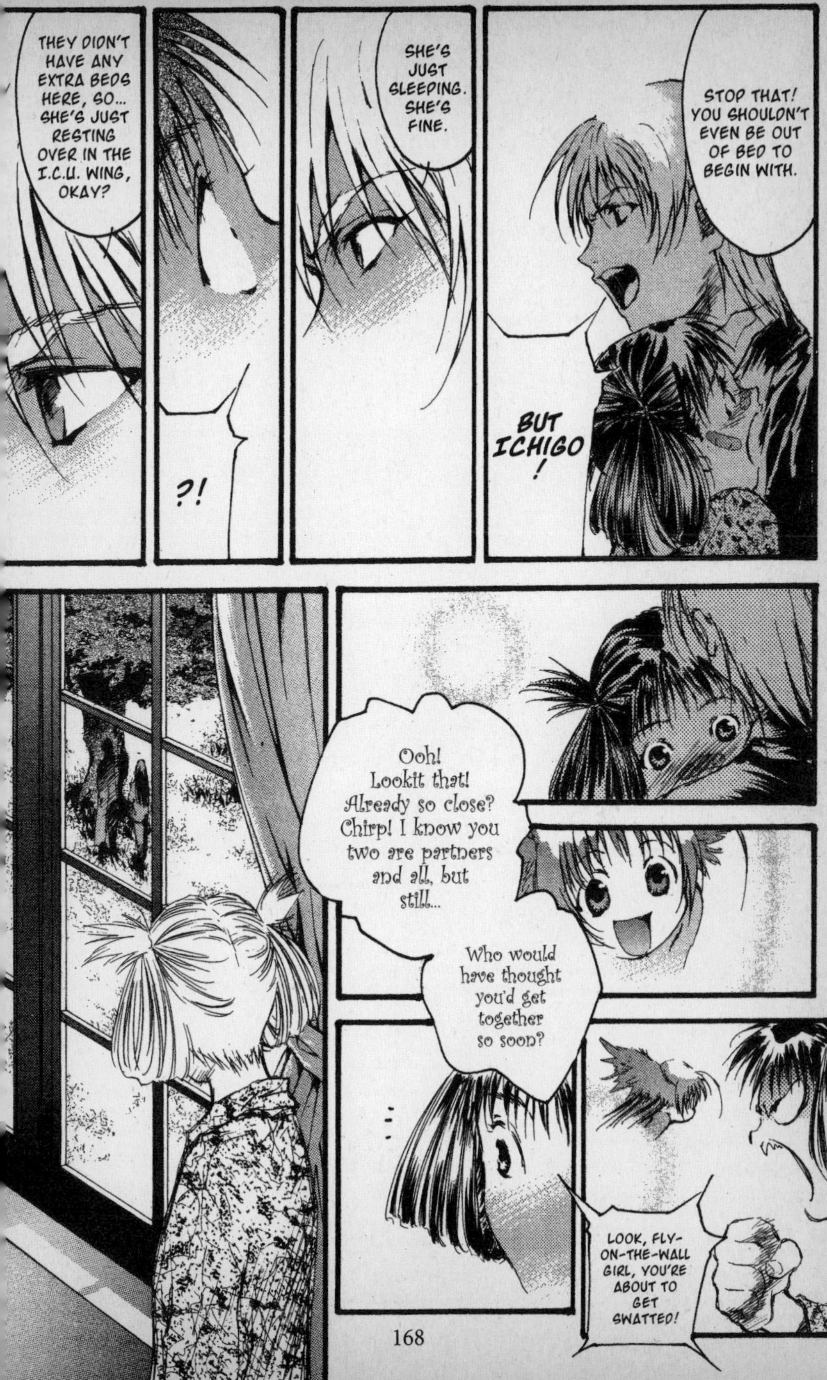
STOP THAT! YOU SHOULDN'T EVEN BE OUT OF BED TO BEGIN WITH.
BUT ICHIGO!
SHE'S JUST SLEEPING. SHE'S FINE.
?!
THEY DIDN'T HAVE ANY EXTRA BEDS HERE, SO... SHE'S JUST RESTING OVER IN THE I.C.U. WING, OKAY?
Ooh! Lookit that! Already so close? Chirp! I know you two are partners and all, but still...
Who would have thought you'd get together so soon?
LOOK, FLY-ON-THE-WALL GIRL, YOU'RE ABOUT TO GET SWATTED!
...

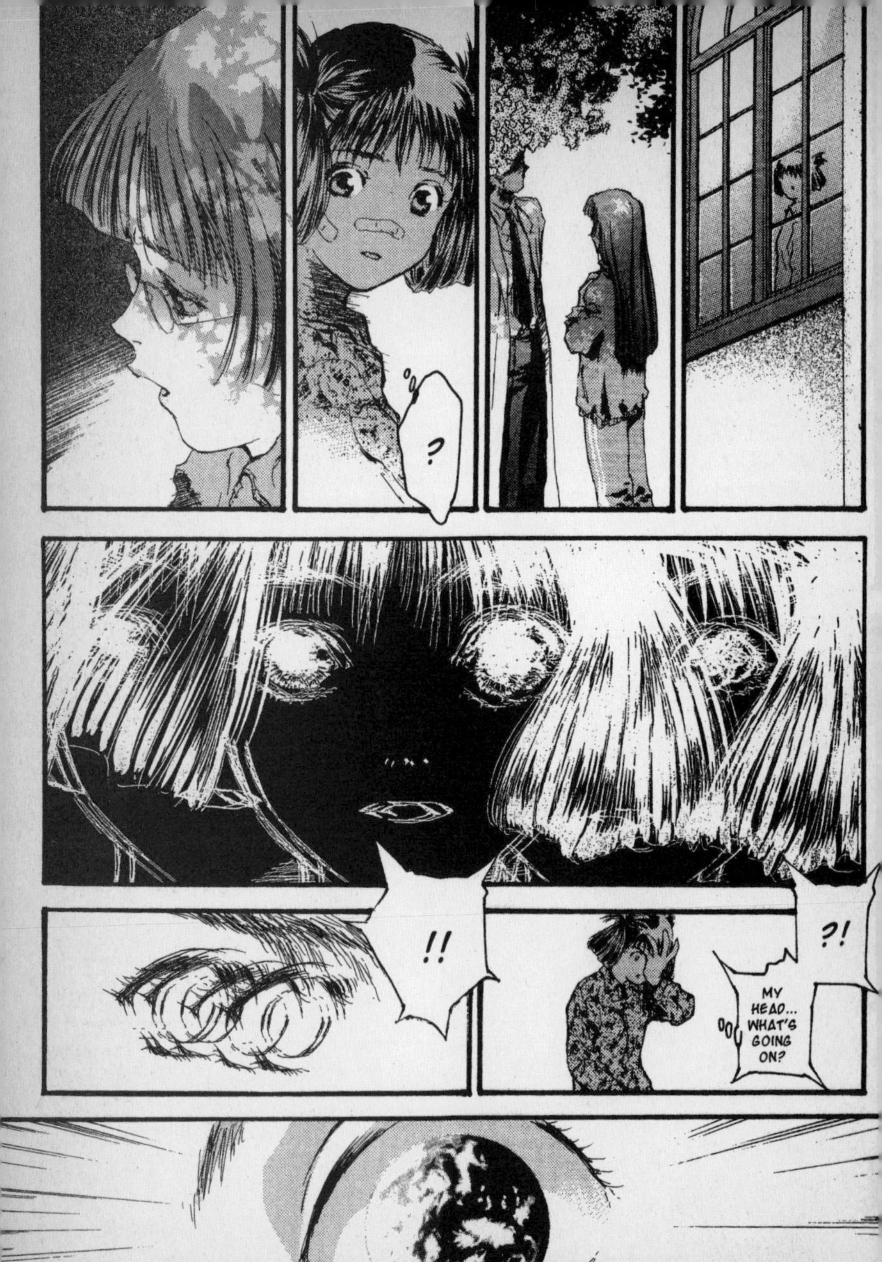

?
!!
?!
MY HEAD... WHAT'S GOING ON?

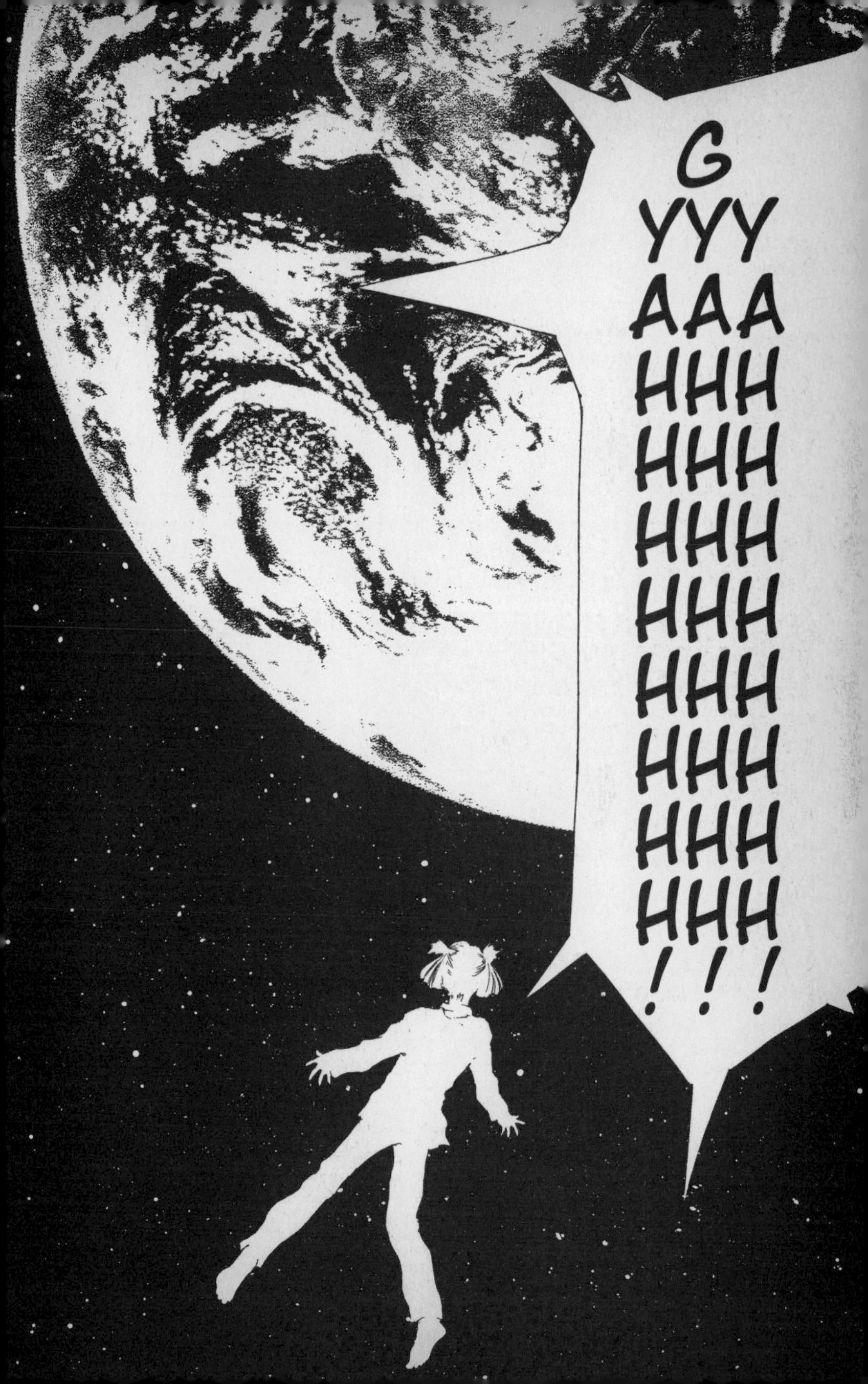
GYYYAAAHHHHHHHHHHHHHHHHHHHHHHHHHHH!!!

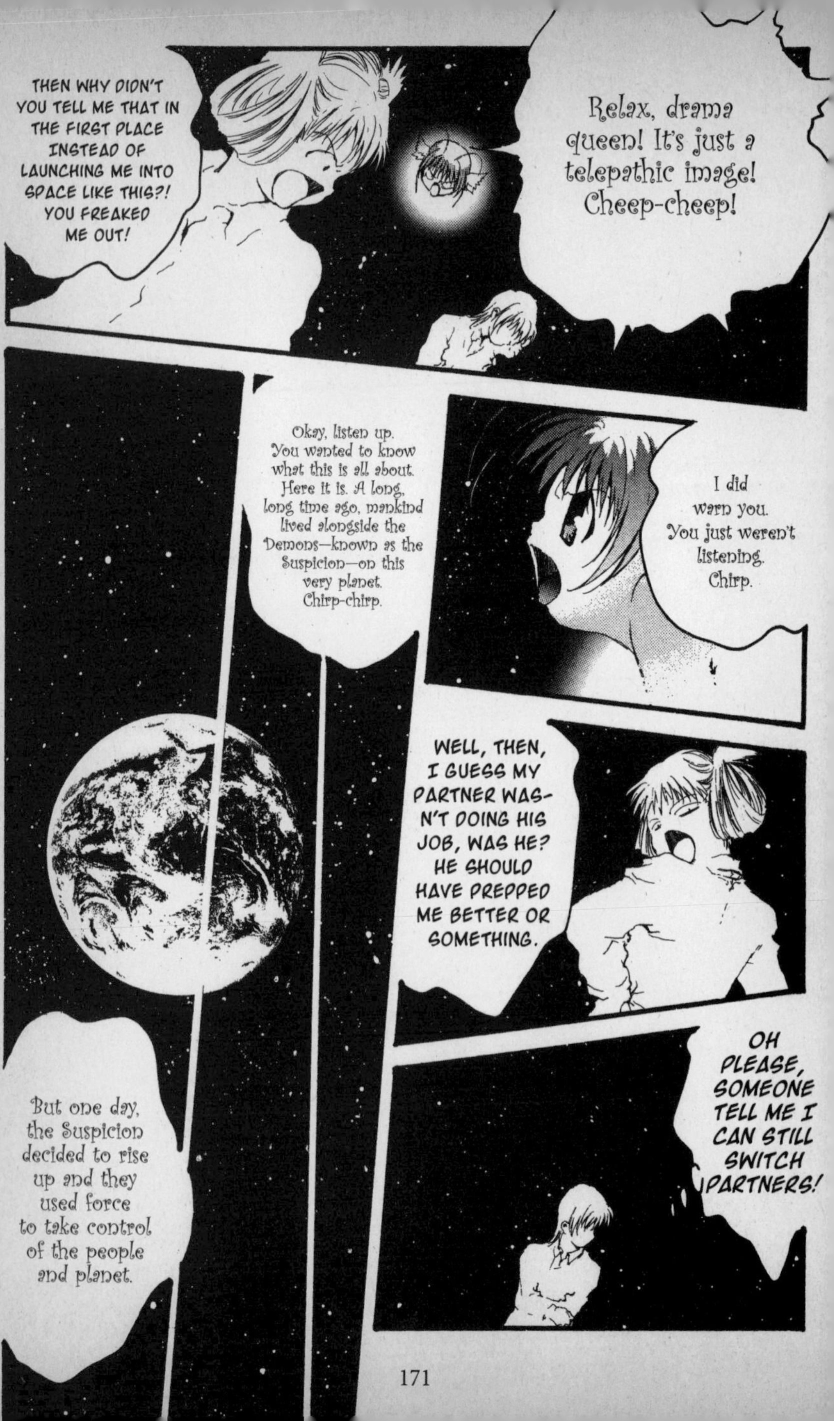
Relax, drama queen! It's just a telepathic image! Cheep-cheep!
THEN WHY DIDN'T YOU TELL ME THAT IN THE FIRST PLACE INSTEAD OF LAUNCHING ME INTO SPACE LIKE THIS?! YOU FREAKED ME OUT!
I did warn you. You just weren't listening. Chirp.
WELL, THEN, I GUESS MY PARTNER WASN'T DOING HIS JOB, WAS HE? HE SHOULD HAVE PREPPED ME BETTER OR SOMETHING.
OH PLEASE, SOMEONE TELL ME I CAN STILL SWITCH PARTNERS!
Okay, listen up. You wanted to know what this is all about. Here it is. A long, long time ago, mankind lived alongside the Demons—known as the Suspicion—on this very planet. Chirp-chirp.
But one day, the Suspicion decided to rise up and they used force to take control of the people and planet.

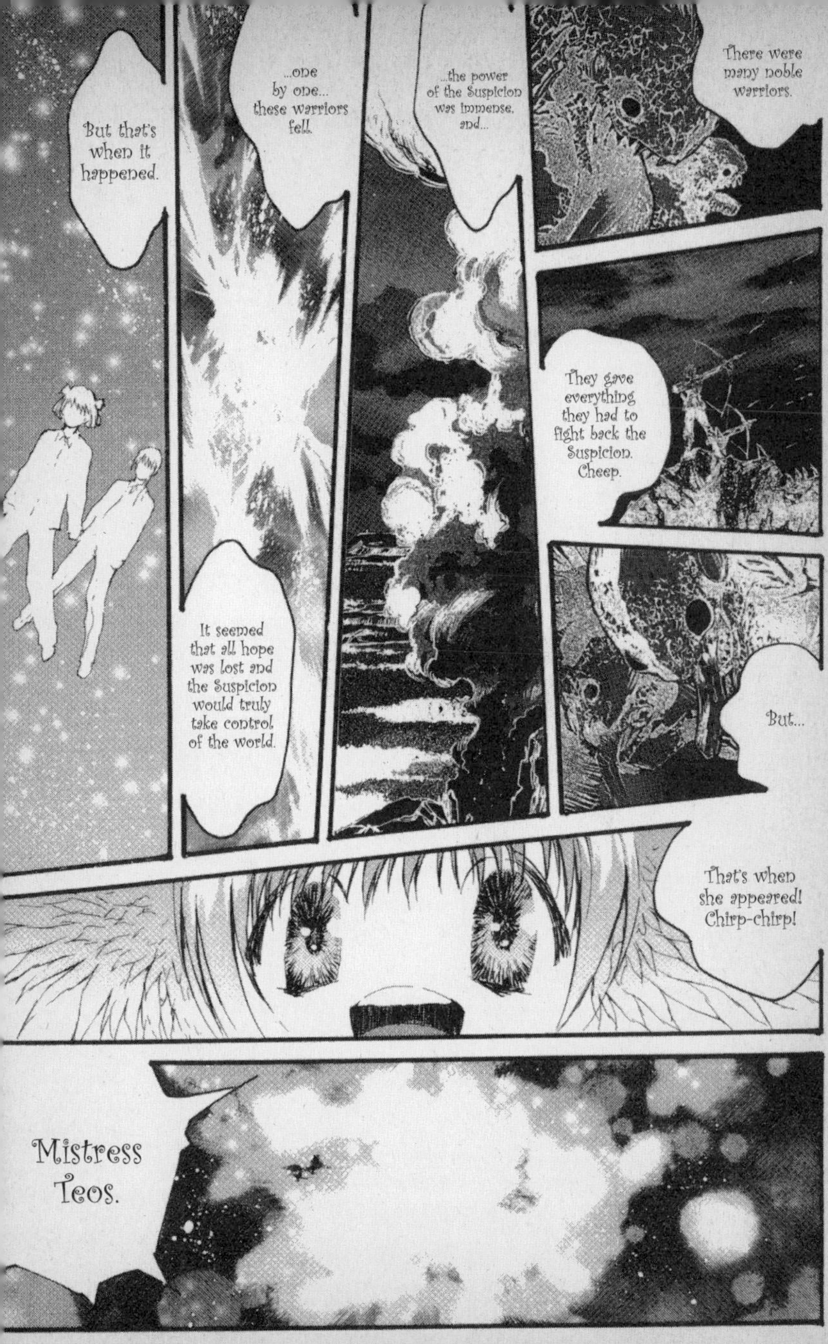
There were many noble warriors.
They gave everything they had to fight back the Suspicion. Cheep.
But...
...the power of the Suspicion was immense, and...
...one by one... these warriors fell.
It seemed that all hope was lost and the Suspicion would truly take control of the world.
But that's when it happened.
That's when she appeared! Chirp-chirp!
Mistress Teos.

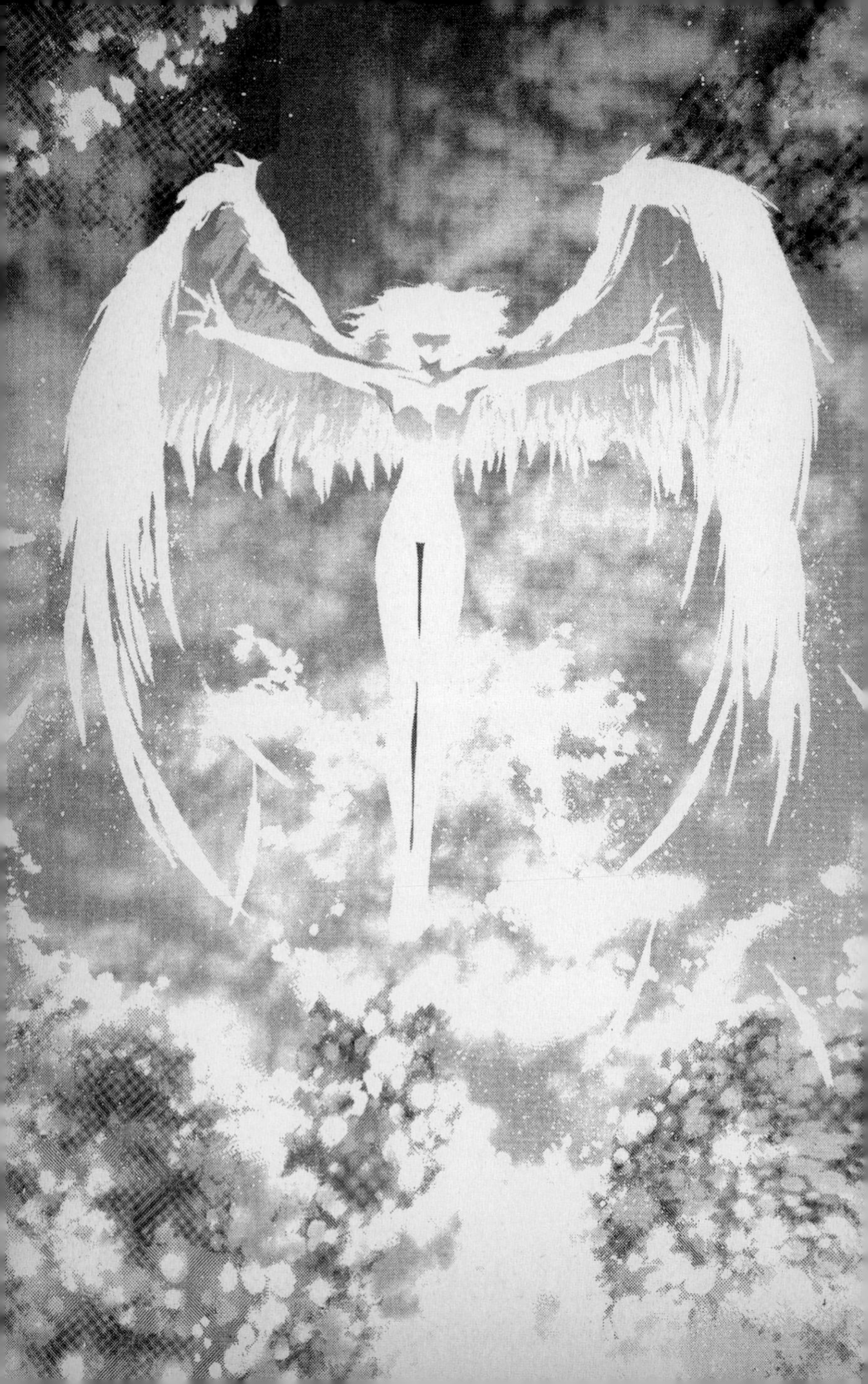

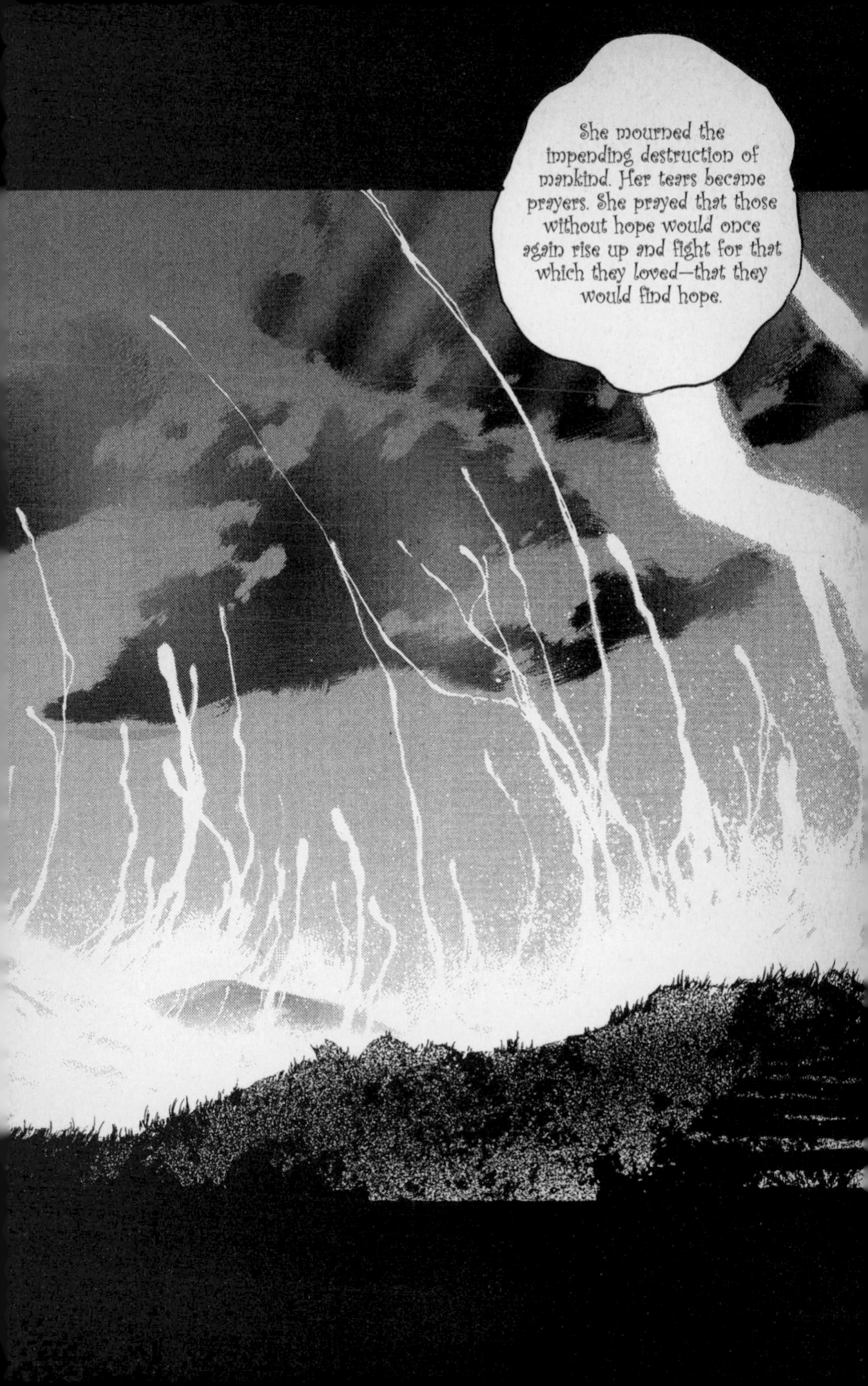
She mourned the impending destruction of mankind. Her tears became prayers. She prayed that those without hope would once again rise up and fight for that which they loved—that they would find hope.

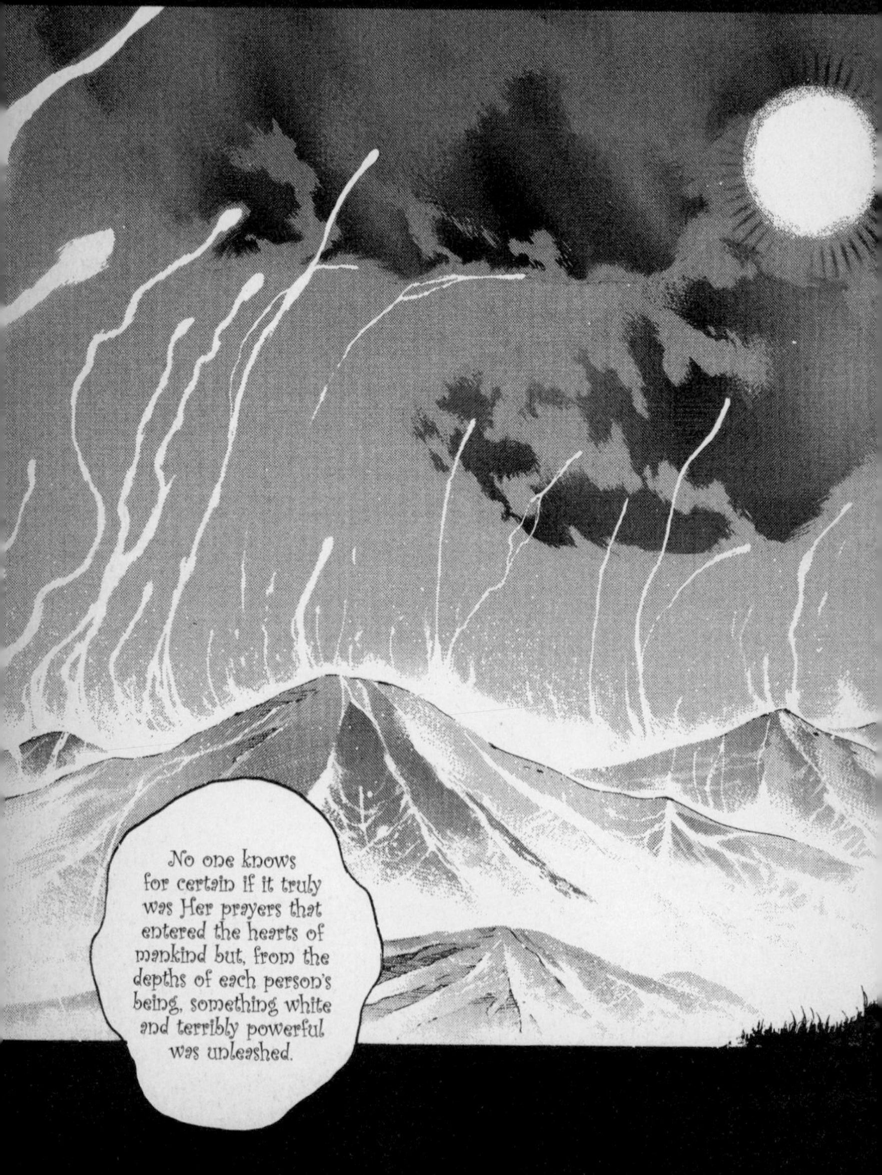
No one knows for certain if it truly was Her prayers that entered the hearts of mankind but, from the depths of each person's being, something white and terribly powerful was unleashed.

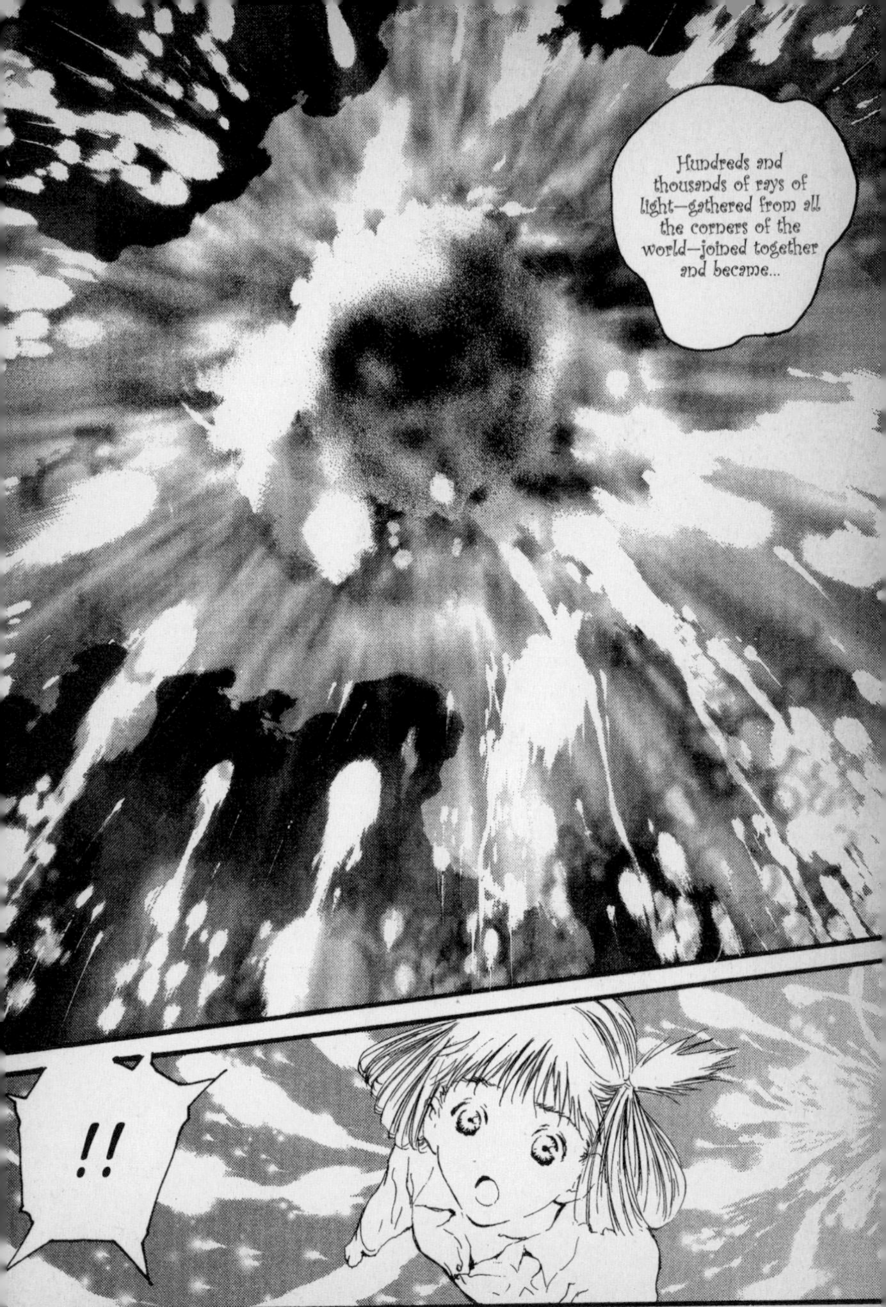
Hundreds and thousands of rays of light—gathered from all the corners of the world—joined together and became...
!!

ACT. 9 END

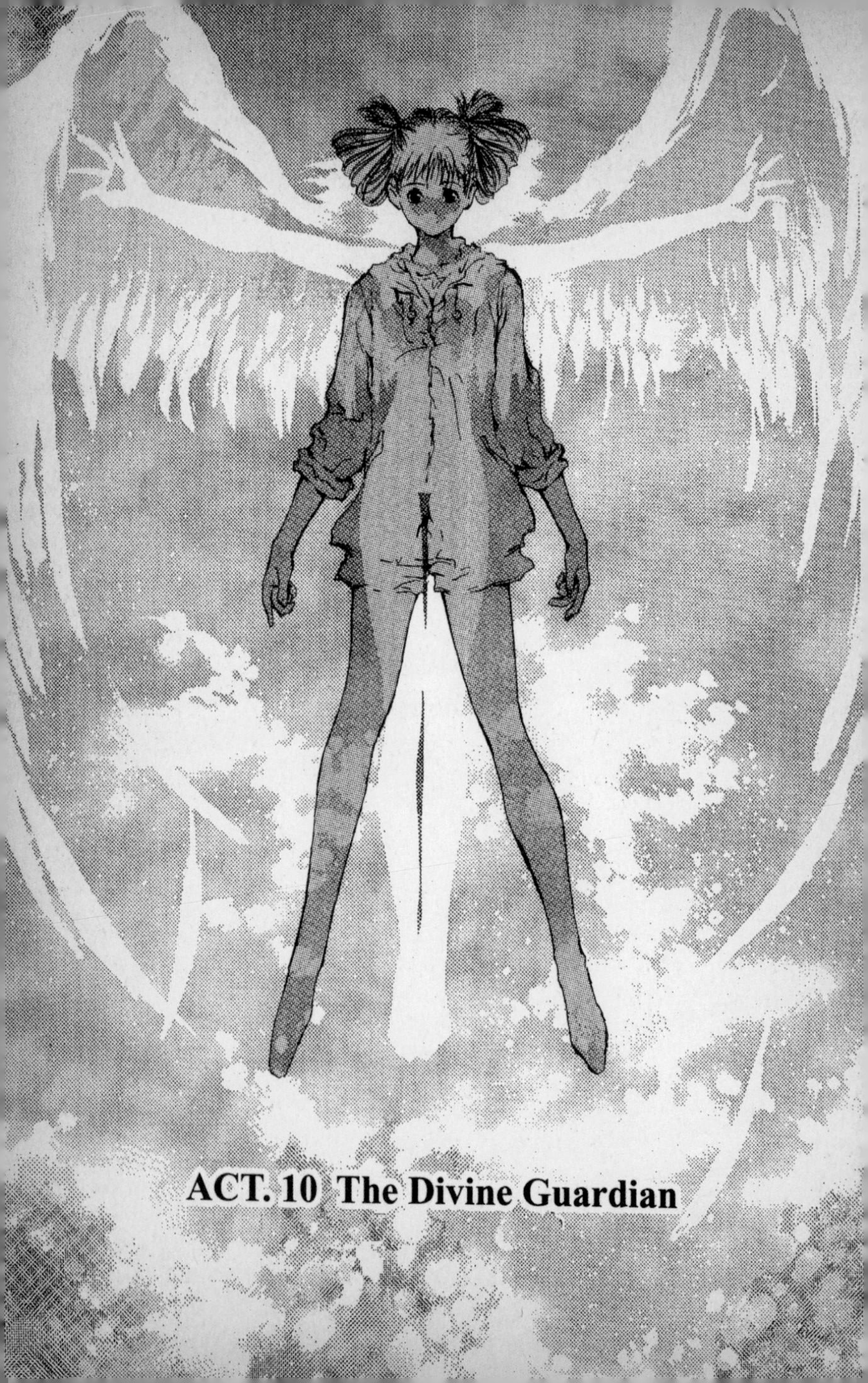
ACT. 10 The Divine Guardian

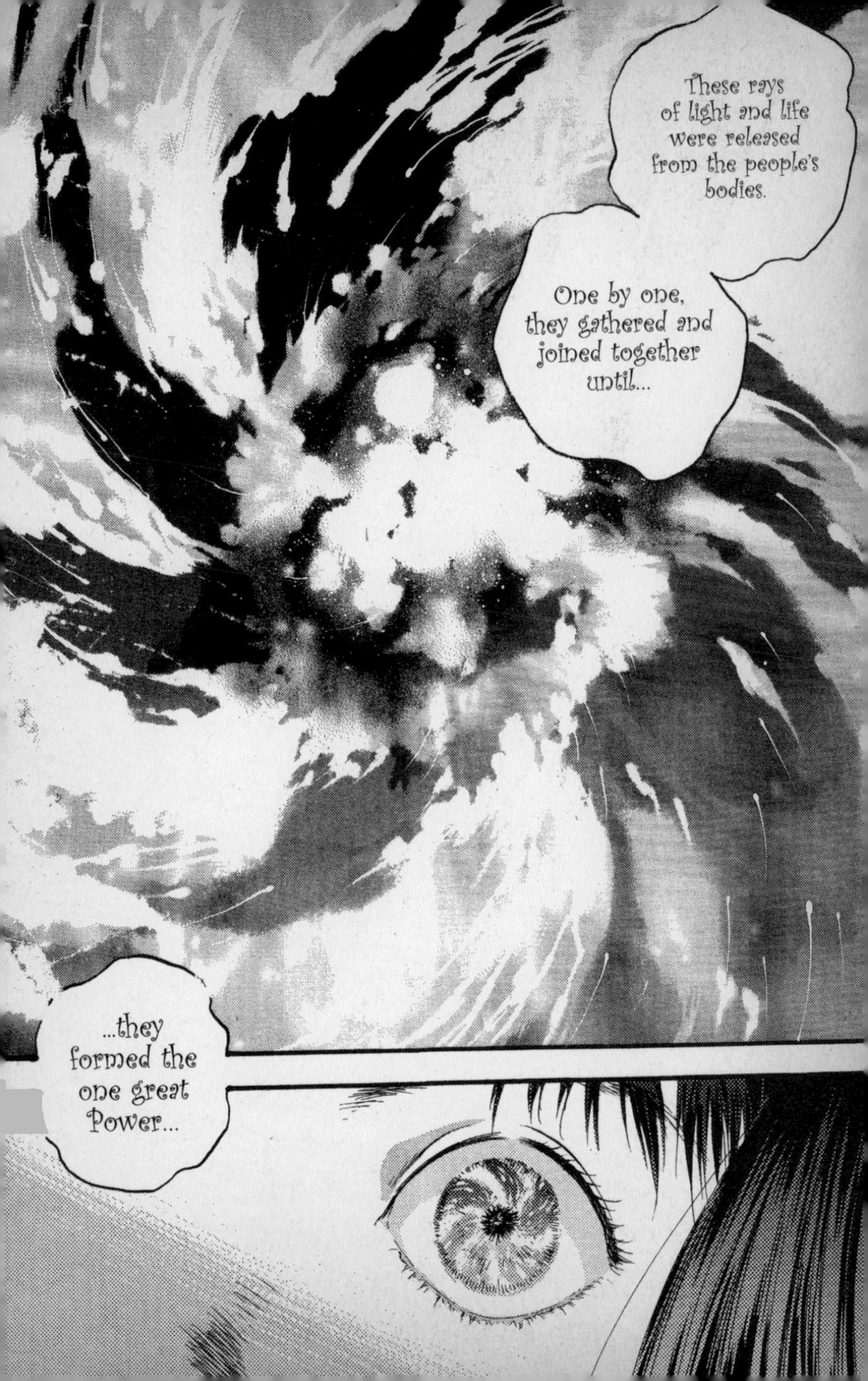
These rays of light and life were released from the people's bodies.
One by one, they gathered and joined together until...
...they formed the one great Power...

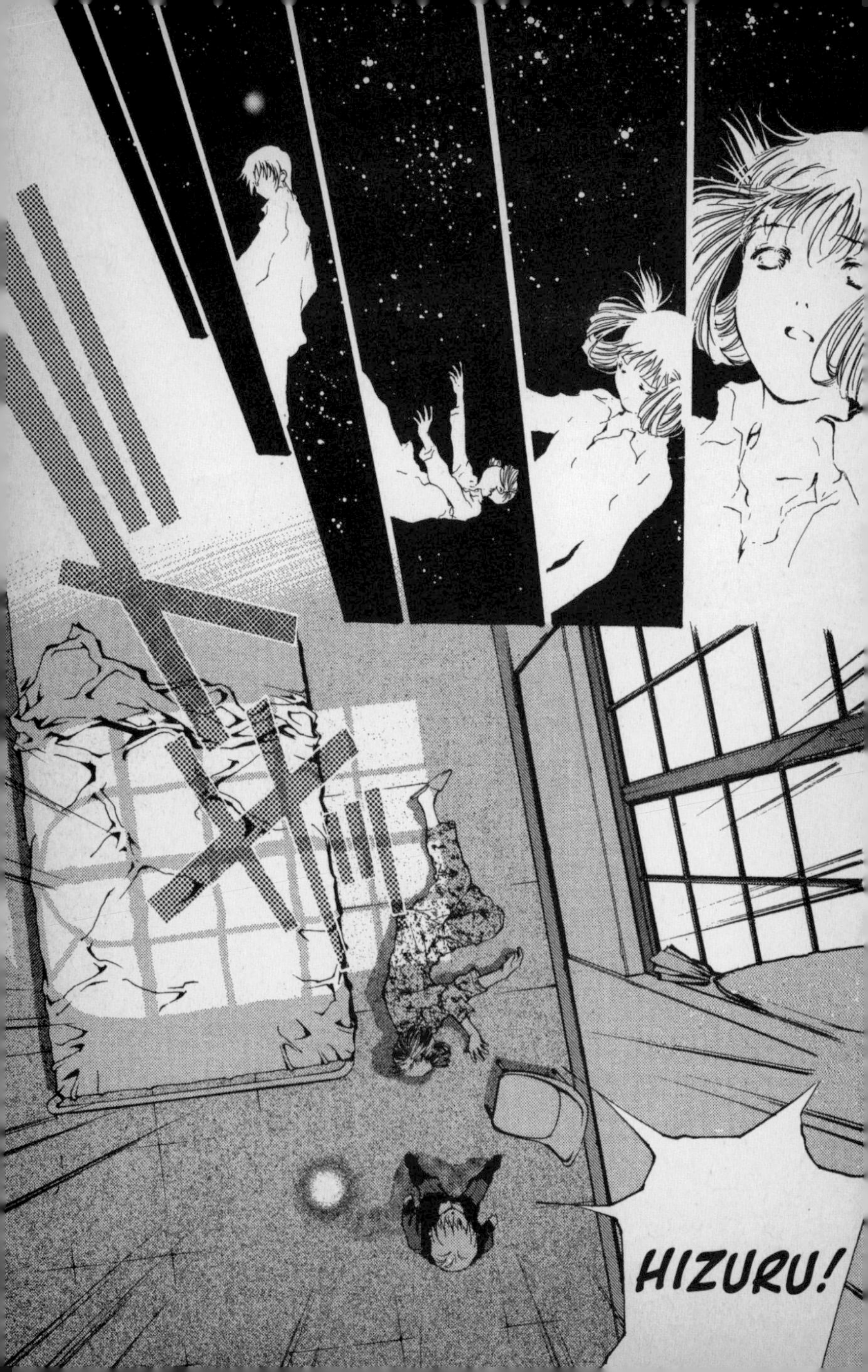
HIZURU!

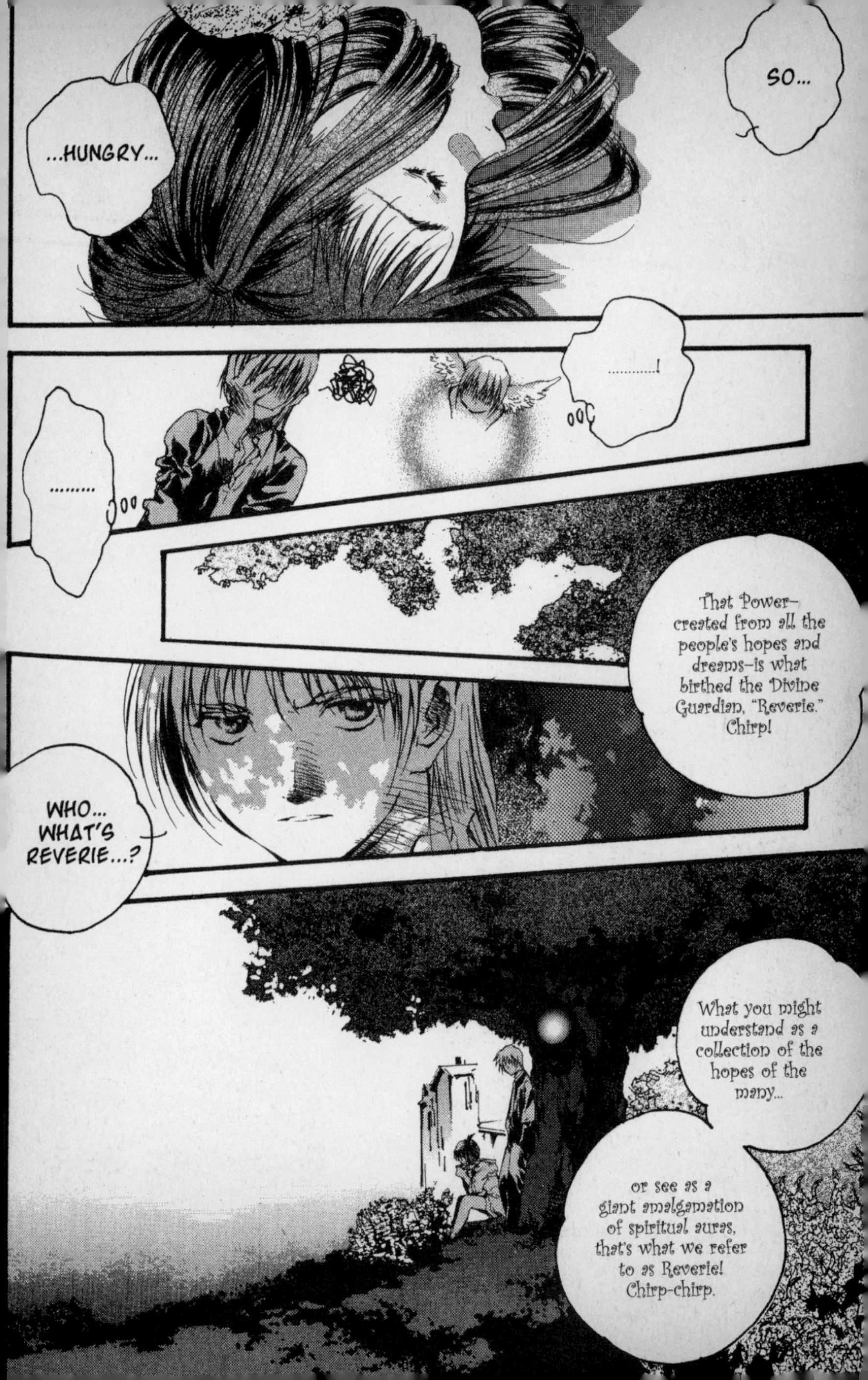
SO...
...HUNGRY...
..........!
....
That Power—created from all the people's hopes and dreams—is what birthed the Divine Guardian, "Reverie." Chirp!
WHO... WHAT'S REVERIE...?
What you might understand as a collection of the hopes of the many...
or see as a giant amalgamation of spiritual auras, that's what we refer to as Reverie! Chirp-chirp.

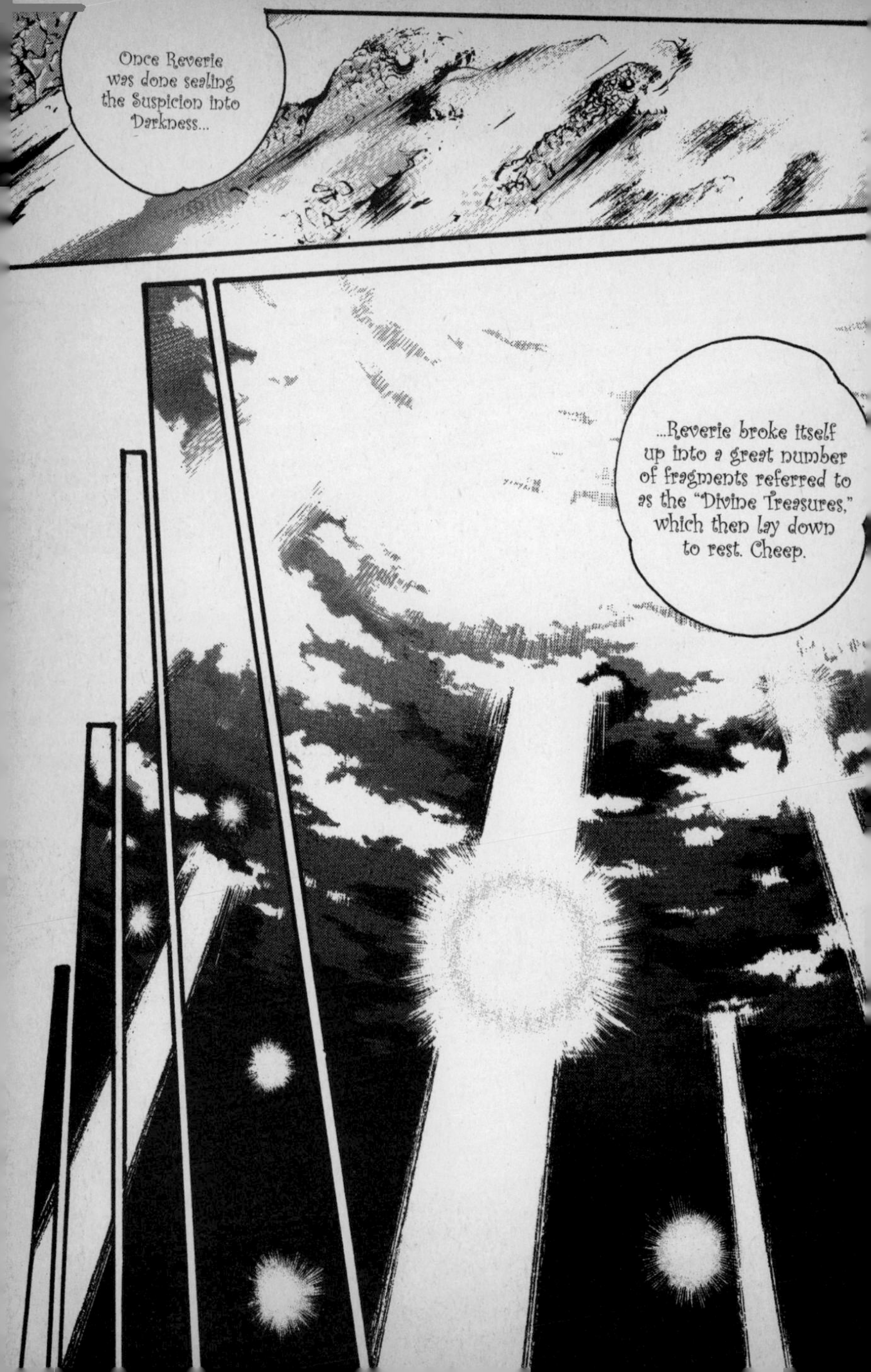
Once Reverie was done sealing the Suspicion into Darkness...
...Reverie broke itself up into a great number of fragments referred to as the "Divine Treasures," which then lay down to rest. Cheep.

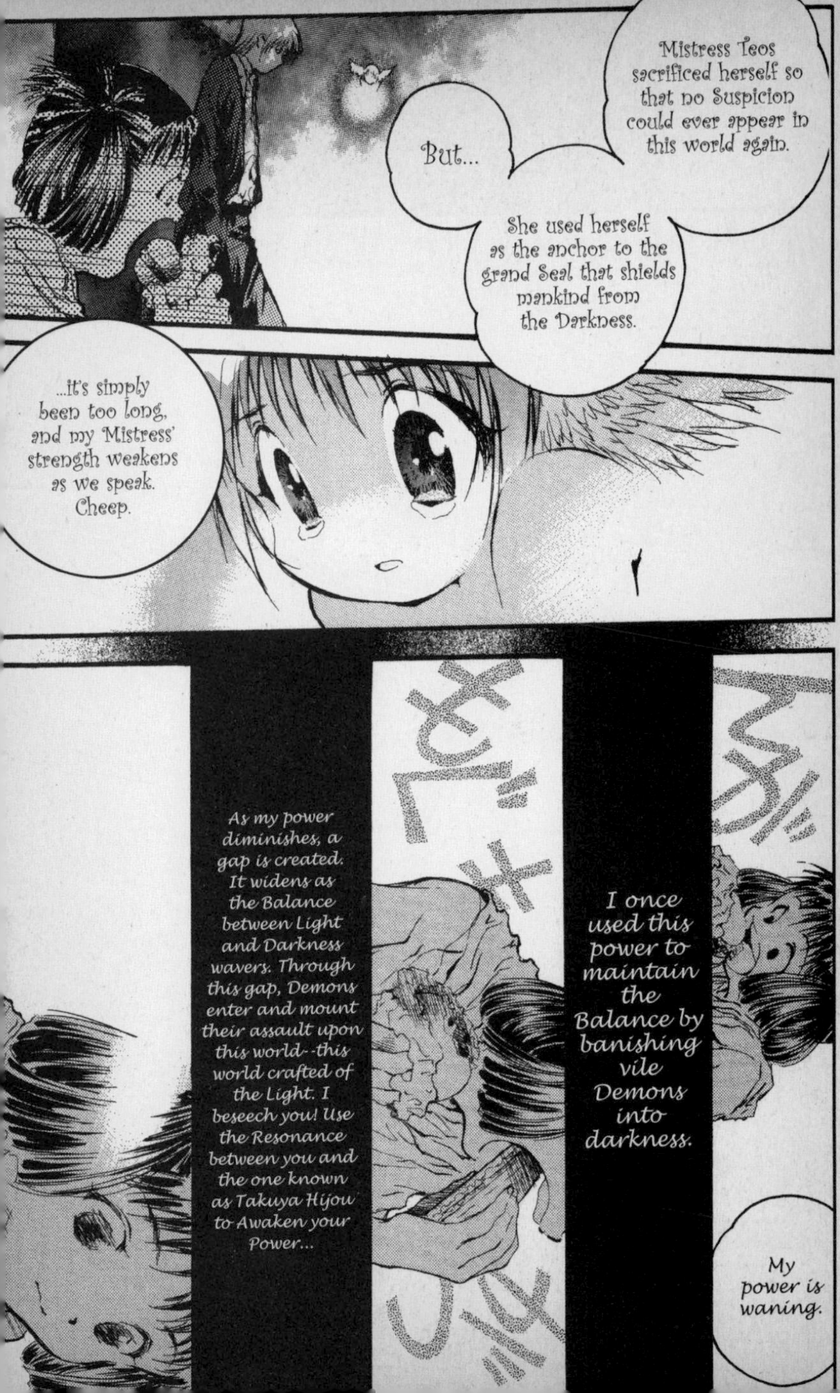
Mistress Teos sacrificed herself so that no Suspicion could ever appear in this world again.
She used herself as the anchor to the grand Seal that shields mankind from the Darkness.
But...
...it's simply been too long, and my 'Mistress' strength weakens as we speak. Cheep.
My power is waning.
I once used this power to maintain the Balance by banishing vile Demons into darkness.
As my power diminishes, a gap is created. It widens as the Balance between Light and Darkness wavers. Through this gap, Demons enter and mount their assault upon this world--this world crafted of the Light. I beseech you! Use the Resonance between you and the one known as Takuya Hijou to Awaken your Power...

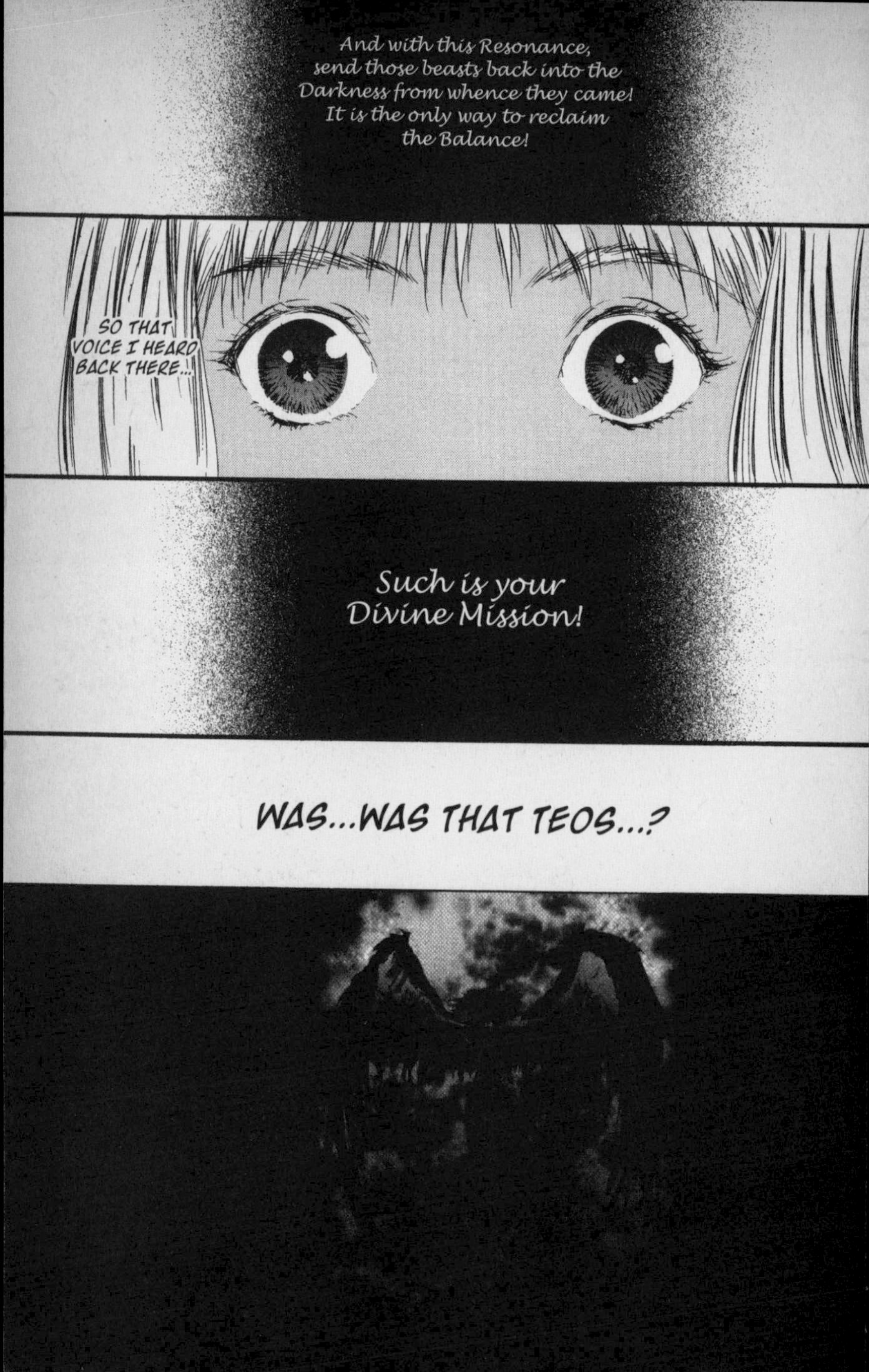
And with this Resonance, send those beasts back into the Darkness from whence they came! It is the only way to reclaim the Balance!
SO THAT VOICE I HEARD BACK THERE...
Such is your Divine Mission!
WAS...WAS THAT TEOS...?

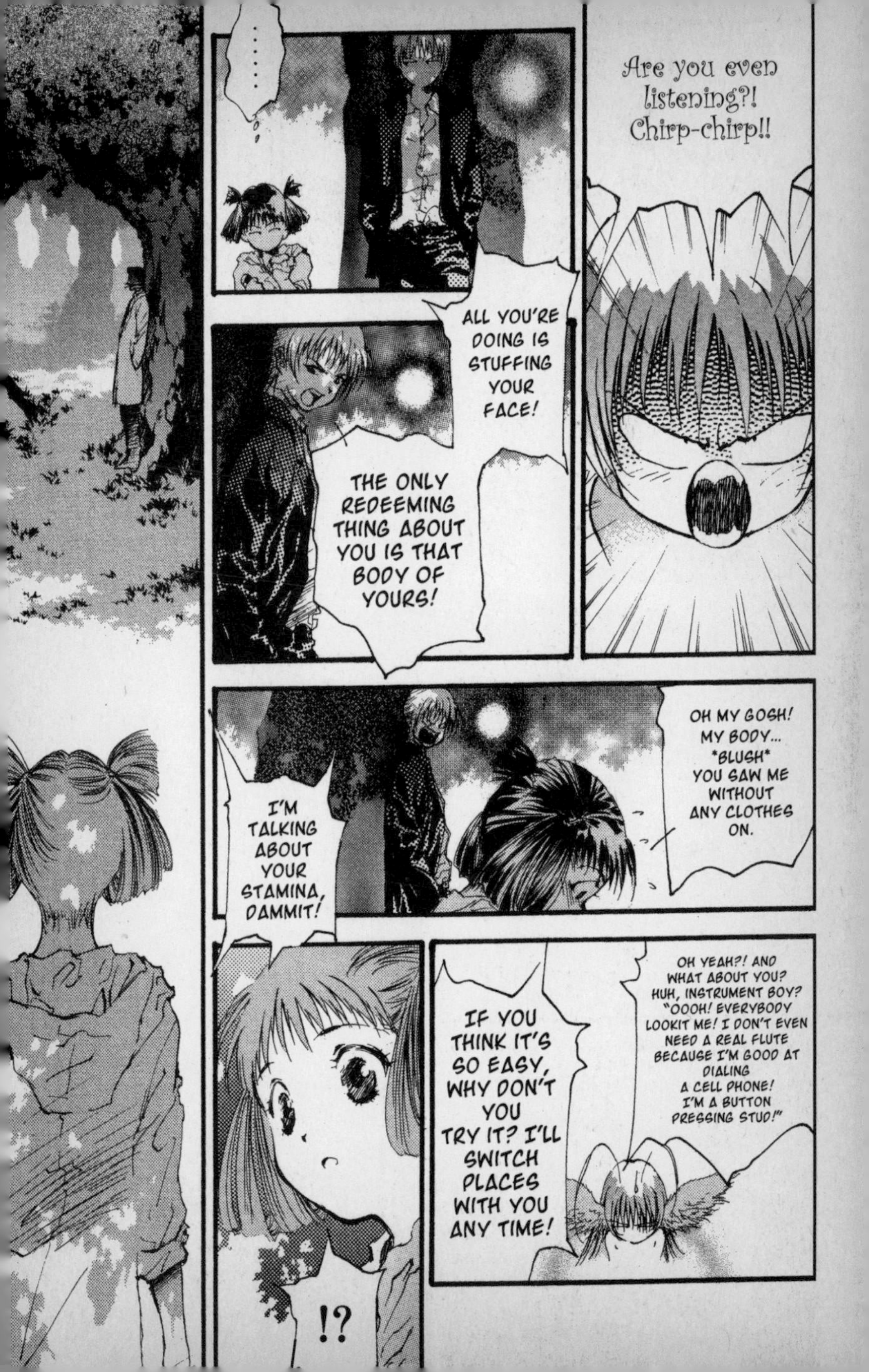
Are you even listening?! Chirp-chirp!!
......
ALL YOU'RE DOING IS STUFFING YOUR FACE!
THE ONLY REDEEMING THING ABOUT YOU IS THAT BODY OF YOURS!
OH MY GOSH! MY BODY... *BLUSH* YOU SAW ME WITHOUT ANY CLOTHES ON.
I'M TALKING ABOUT YOUR STAMINA, DAMMIT!
OH YEAH?! AND WHAT ABOUT YOU? HUH, INSTRUMENT BOY? "OOOH! EVERYBODY LOOKIT ME! I DON'T EVEN NEED A REAL FLUTE BECAUSE I'M GOOD AT DIALING A CELL PHONE! I'M A BUTTON PRESSING STUD!"
IF YOU THINK IT'S SO EASY, WHY DON'T YOU TRY IT? I'LL SWITCH PLACES WITH YOU ANY TIME!
!?

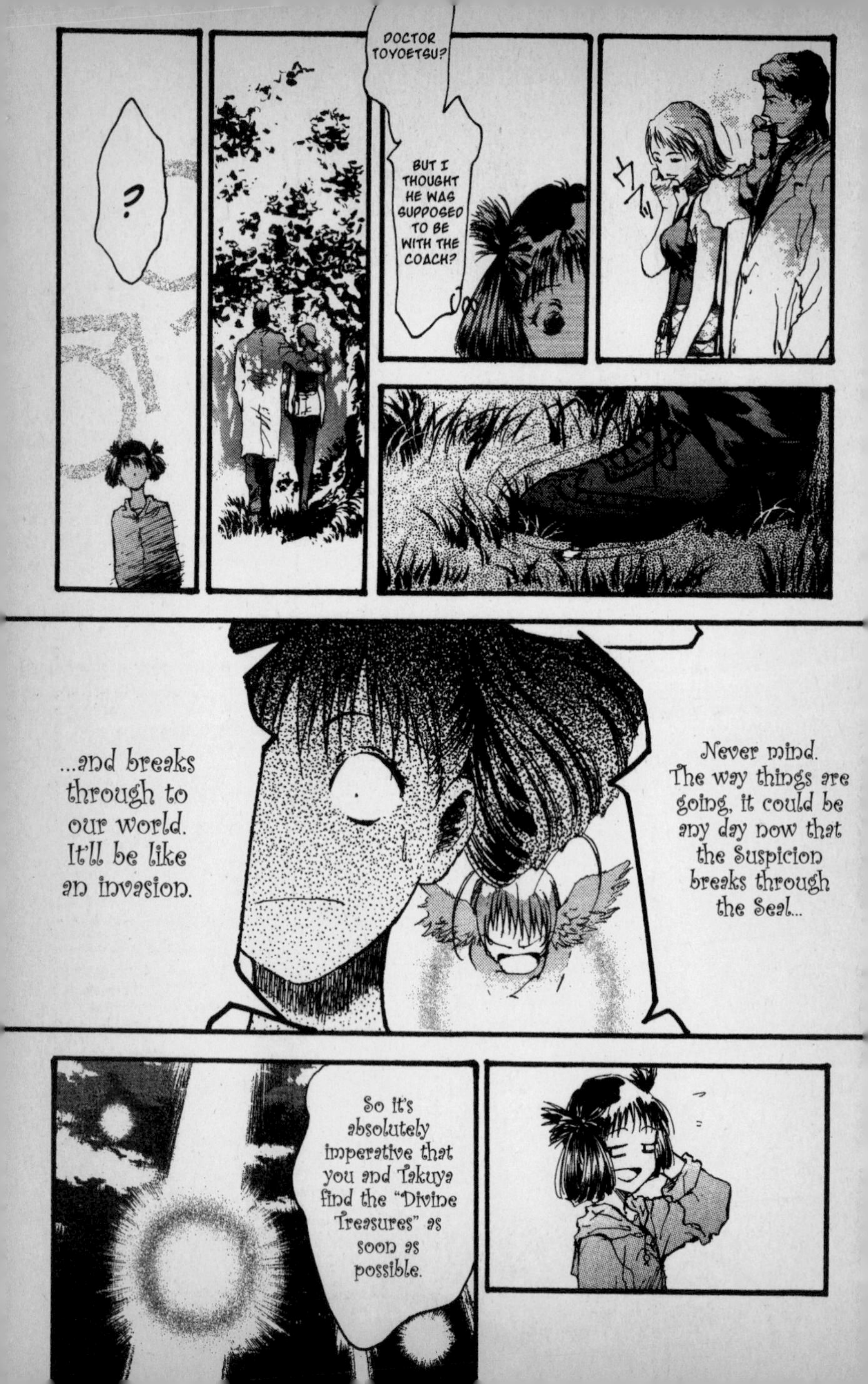
DOCTOR TOYOETSU?
BUT I THOUGHT HE WAS SUPPOSED TO BE WITH THE COACH?
?
Never mind. The way things are going, it could be any day now that the Suspicion breaks through the Seal...
...and breaks through to our world. It'll be like an invasion.
So it's absolutely imperative that you and Takuya find the "Divine Treasures" as soon as possible.

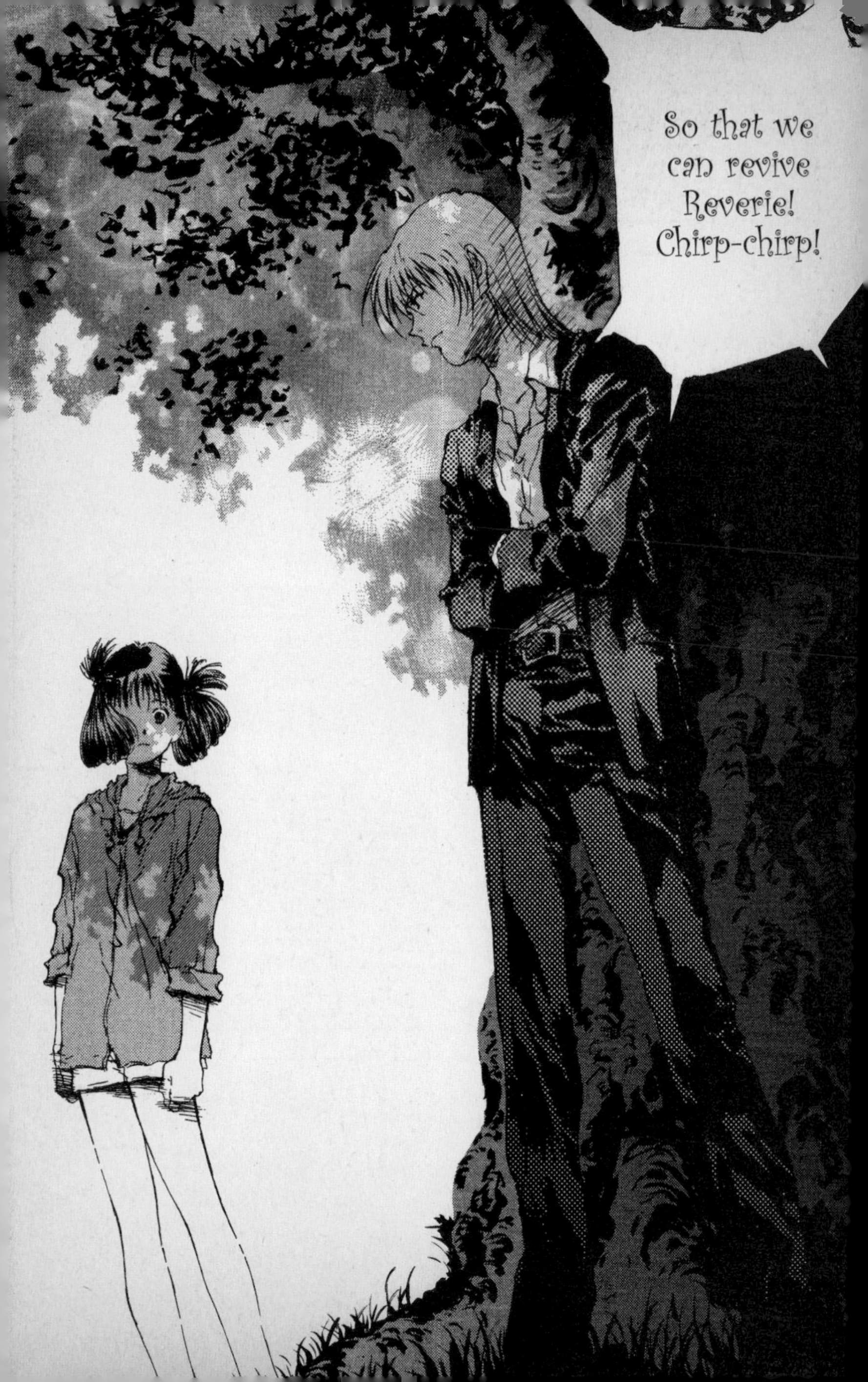
So that we can revive Reverie! Chirp-chirp!

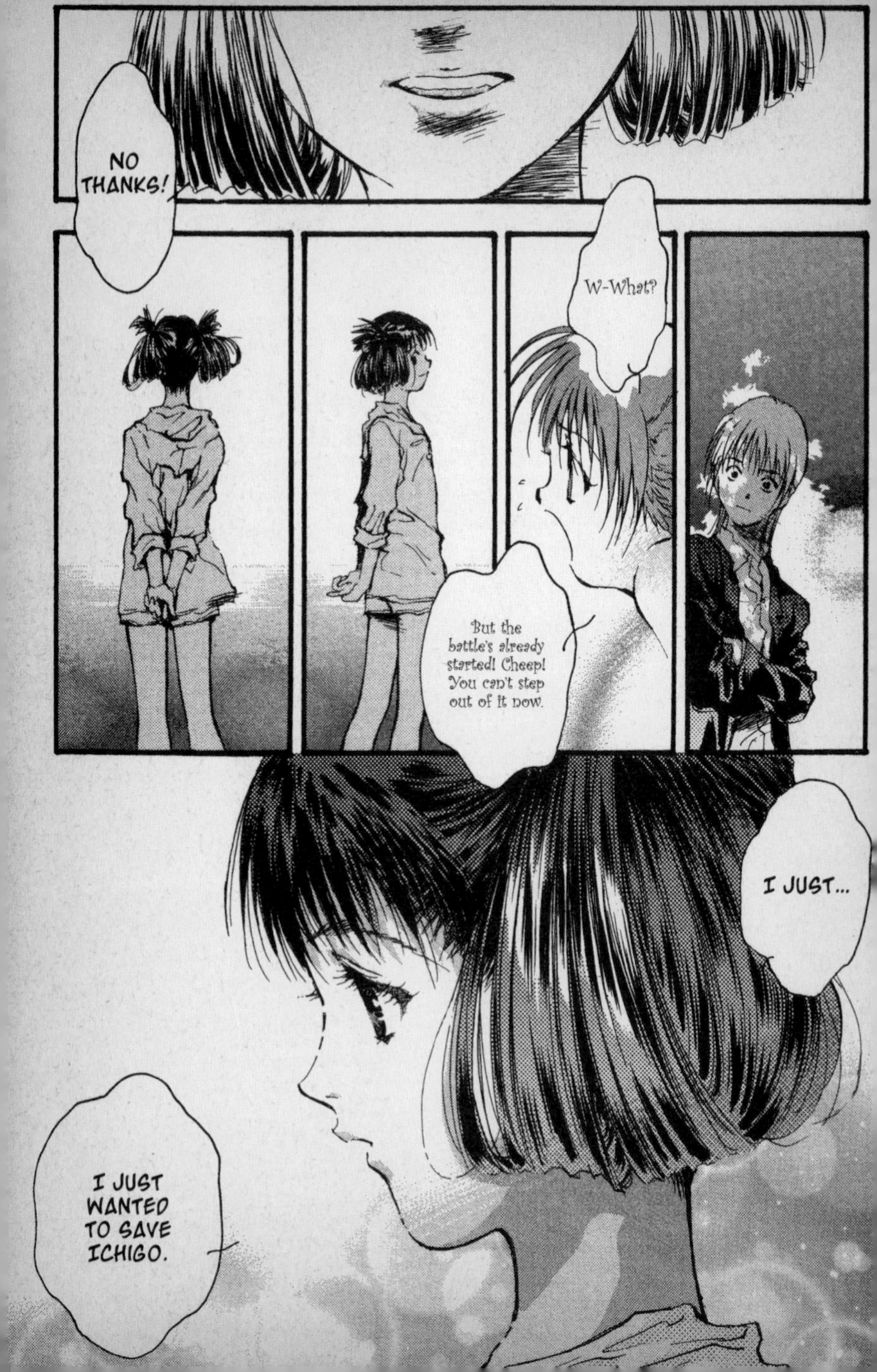
NO THANKS!
W-What?
But the battle's already started! Cheep! You can't step out of it now.
I JUST...
I JUST WANTED TO SAVE ICHIGO.

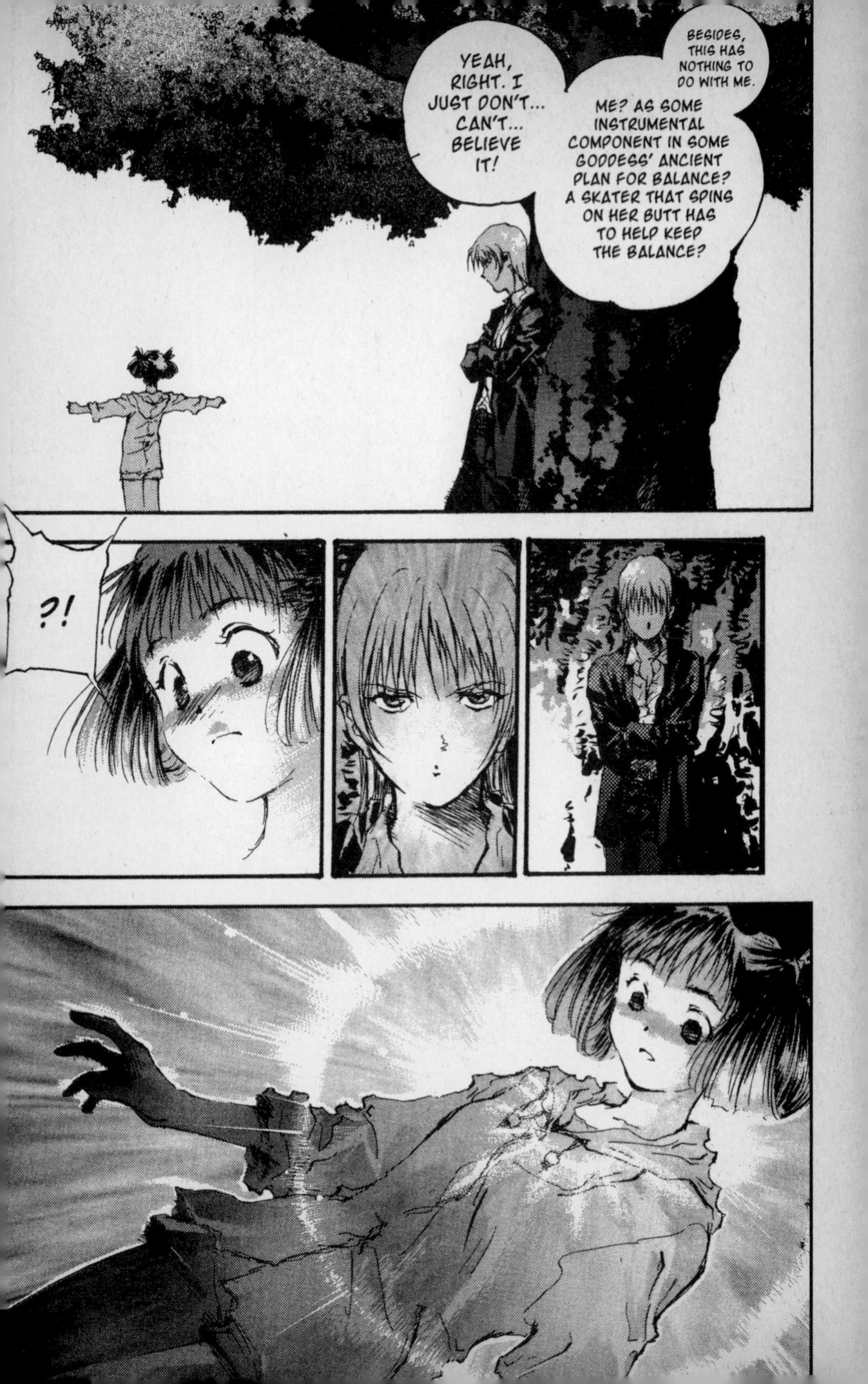
BESIDES, THIS HAS NOTHING TO DO WITH ME.
ME? AS SOME INSTRUMENTAL COMPONENT IN SOME GODDESS' ANCIENT PLAN FOR BALANCE? A SKATER THAT SPINS ON HER BUTT HAS TO HELP KEEP THE BALANCE?
YEAH, RIGHT. I JUST DON'T... CAN'T... BELIEVE IT!
?!

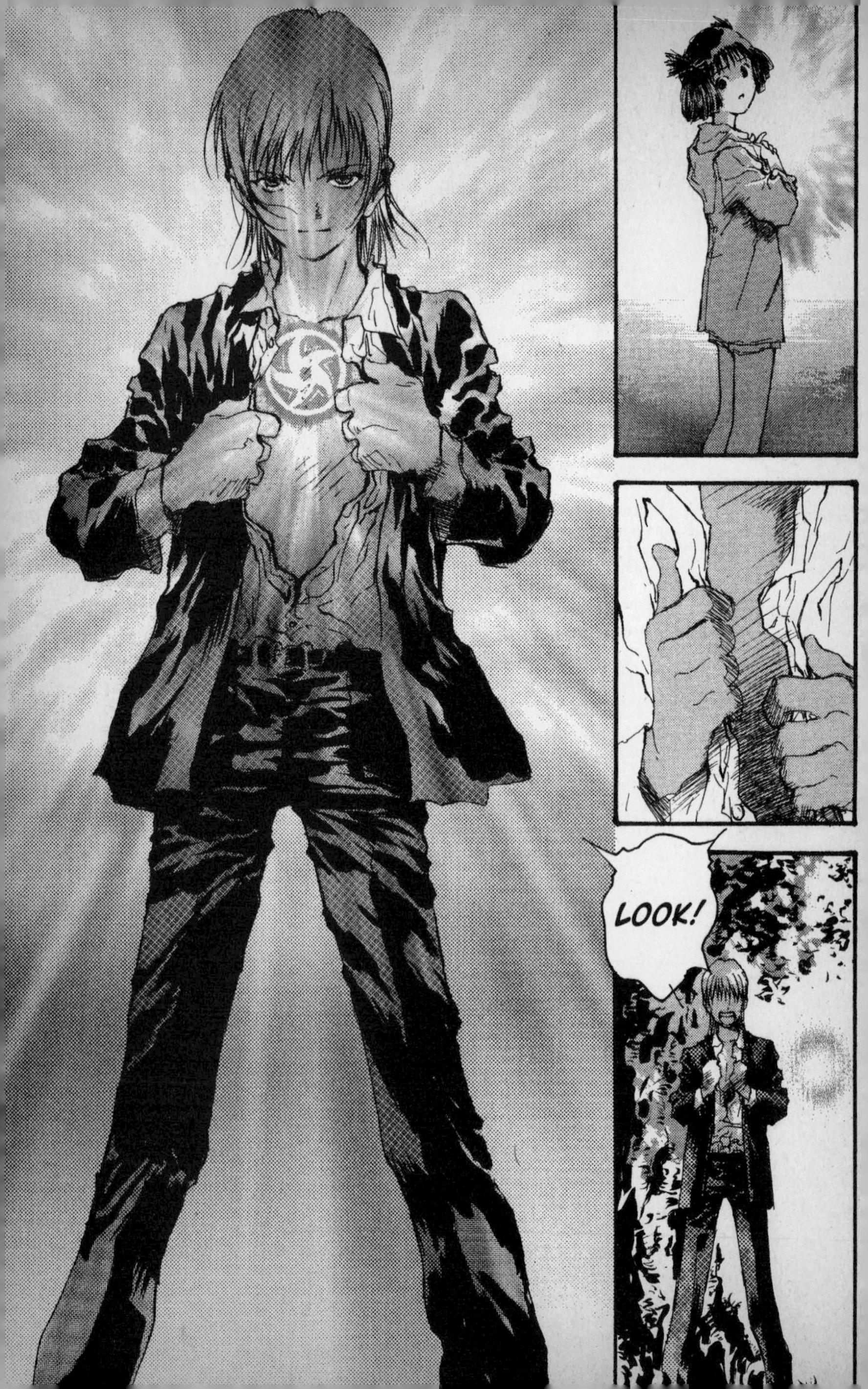
LOOK!

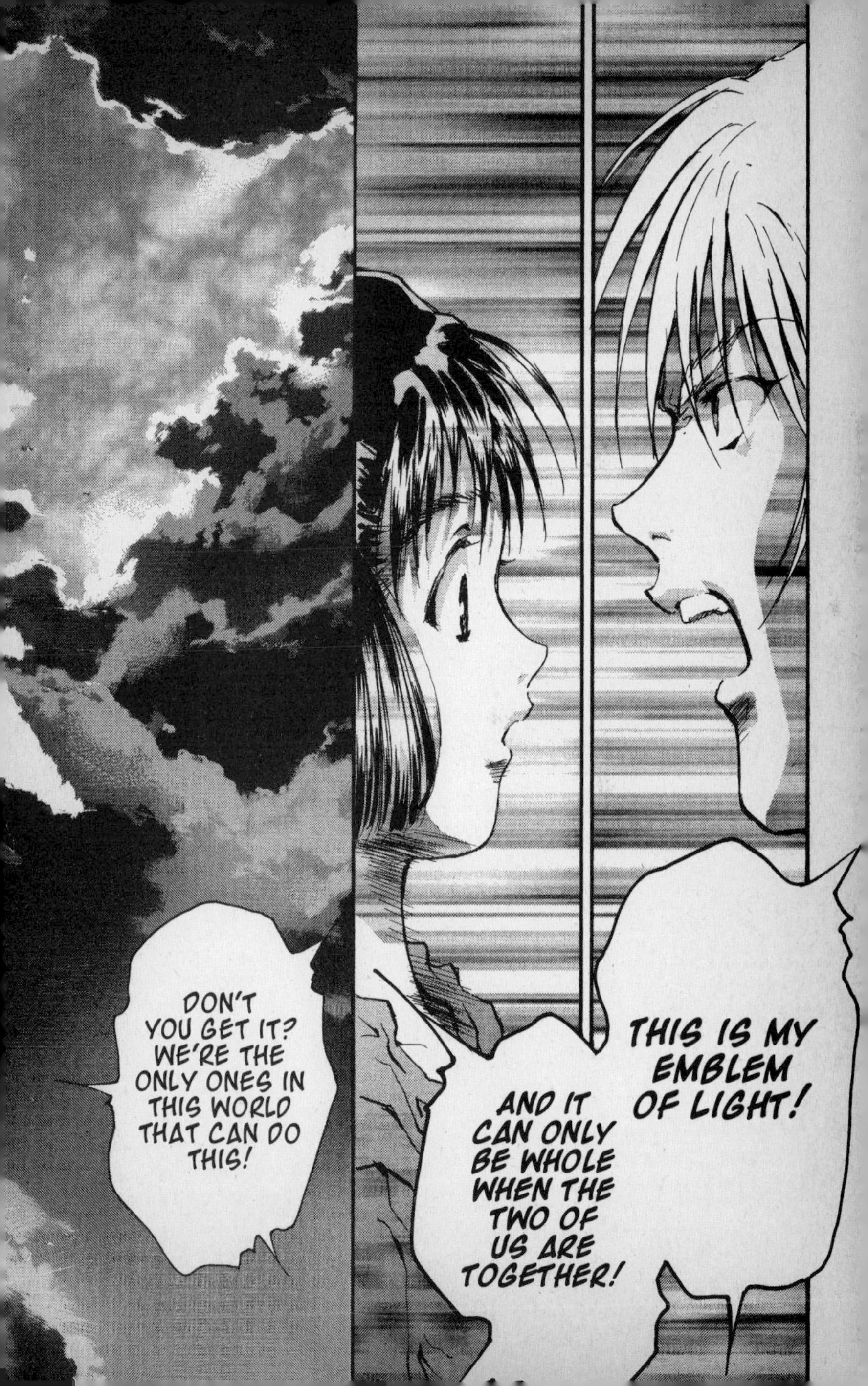
THIS IS MY EMBLEM OF LIGHT!
AND IT CAN ONLY BE WHOLE WHEN THE TWO OF US ARE TOGETHER!
DON'T YOU GET IT? WE'RE THE ONLY ONES IN THIS WORLD THAT CAN DO THIS!

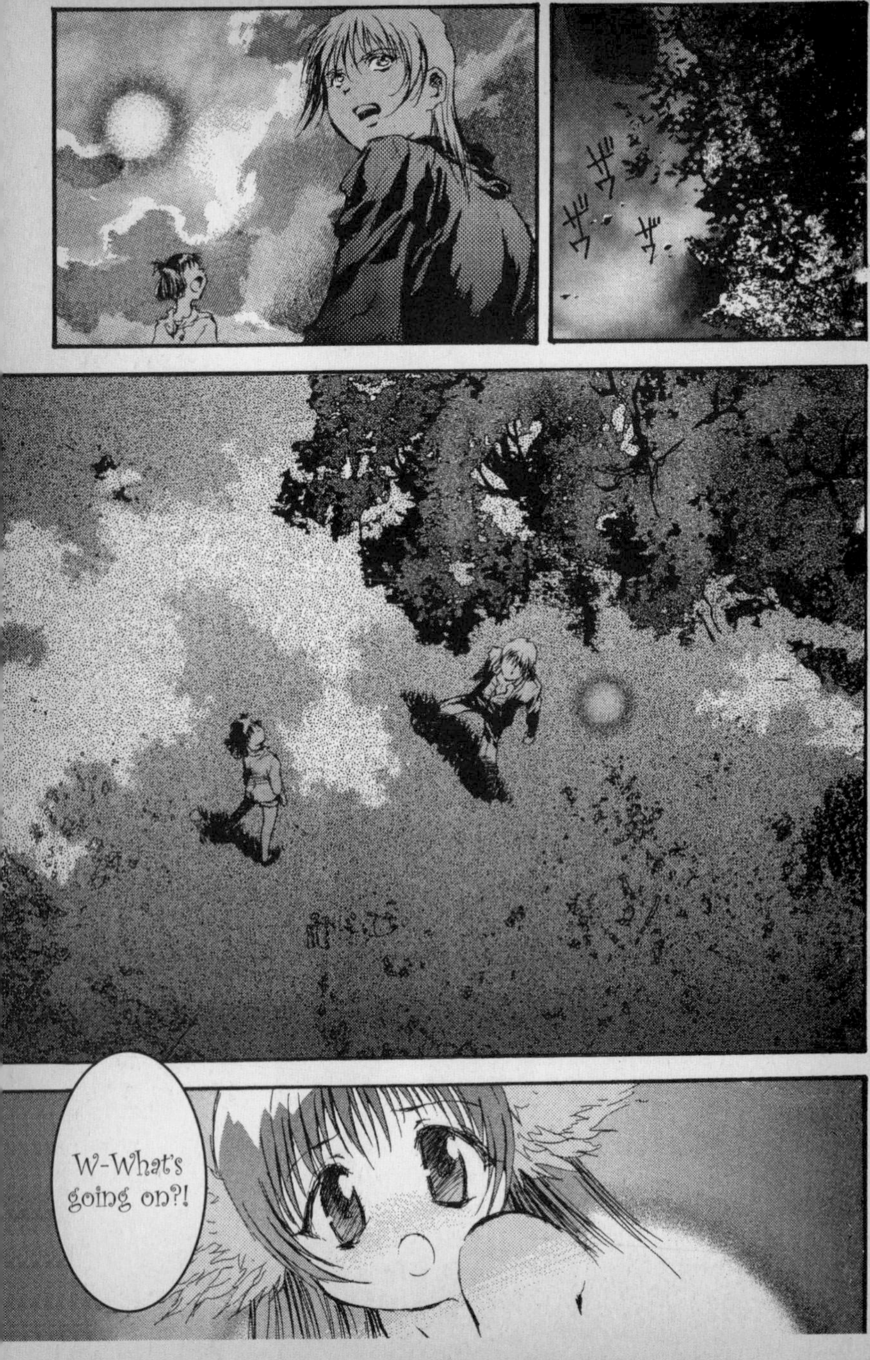
W-What's going on?!

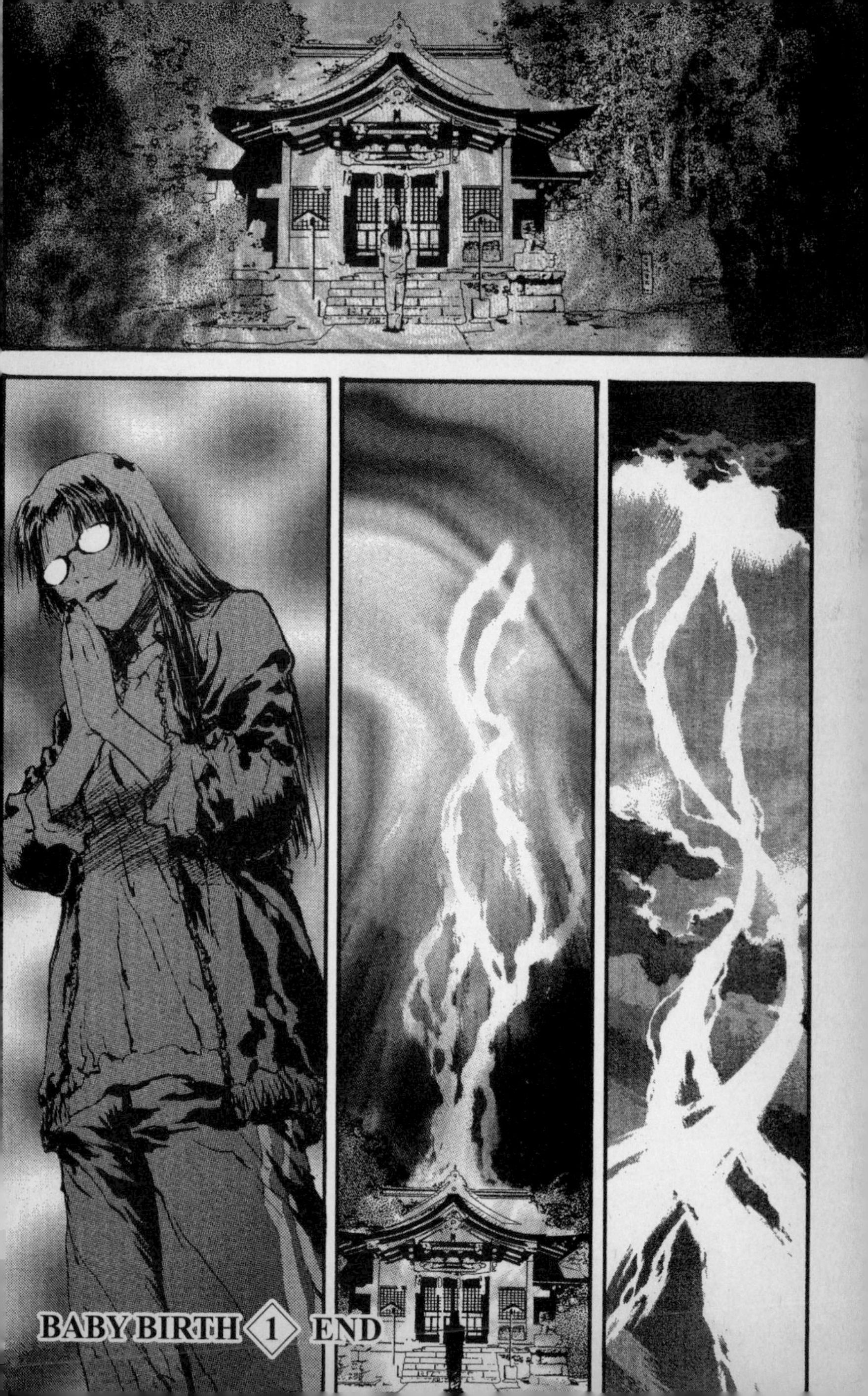
BABY BIRTH 1 END

THE SECRETS BEHIND THE BIRTH OF BABY BIRTH ARE NOW FINALLY REVEALED!

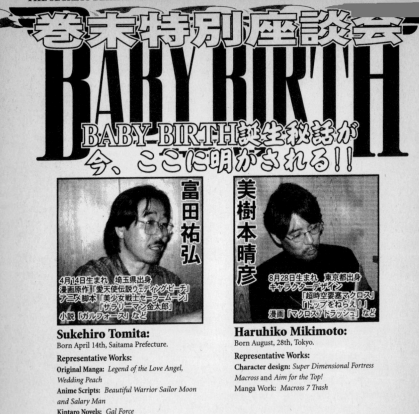

巻末特別座談会

BABY BIRTH

BABY BIRTH誕生秘話が今、ここに明かされる!!

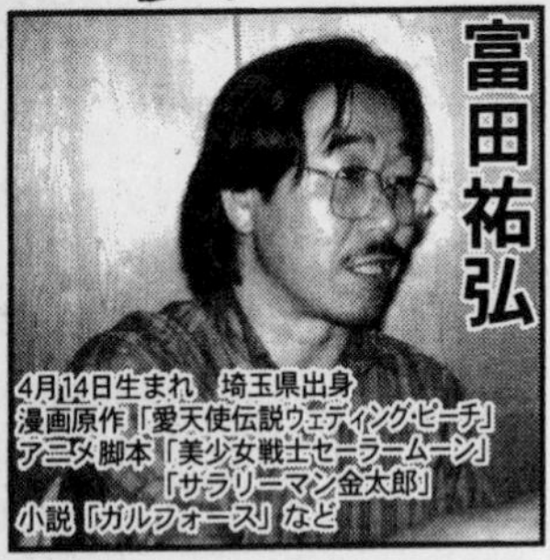
富田祐弘
4月14日生まれ 埼玉県出身
漫画原作「愛天使伝説ウェディングピーチ」
アニメ脚本「美少女戦士セーラームーン」
「サラリーマン金太郎」
小説「ガルフォース」など

Sukehiro Tomita:
Born April 14th, Saitama Prefecture.

Representative Works:
Original Manga: *Legend of the Love Angel, Wedding Peach*
Anime Scripts: *Beautiful Warrior Sailor Moon and Salary Man*
Kintaro Novels: *Gal Force*

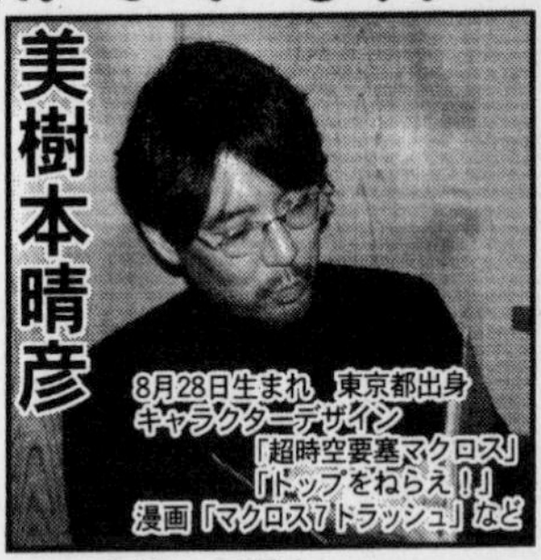
美樹本晴彦
8月28日生まれ 東京都出身
キャラクターデザイン
「超時空要塞マクロス」
「トップをねらえ!」
漫画「マクロス7トラッシュ」など

Haruhiko Mikimoto:
Born August, 28th, Tokyo.

Representative Works:
Character design: *Super Dimensional Fortress Macross* and *Aim for the Top!*
Manga Work: *Macross 7 Trash*

END OF BOOK SPECIAL—ROUND TABLE DISCUSSION

Ed: With Volume 1 of *Baby Birth* about to hit the bookstores, I was hoping to get your thoughts on the release.

Miki: Wow, I can barely remember when we first started this series.

Ed: I believe it made its first appearance in Vol. 2 of the first-year run of the serial comic, *MAGAZINE Z*.

Miki: I mean before that, before *MAGAZINE Z* even came out... when we were first approached by the president of *Big West* to do this story. Any idea when that might have been?

Ed: Over 2 years ago, at least.

Miki: Back then... Hmm, not sure if I can really say this, but was that anime still running? The one that became the basis of--this story? It was called *Gandara*.

Ed: Oh no. That was about when the first LDs for the series were just coming out. I believe that's when, Mikimoto-sensei, you were first approached to do the manga...

Tomi: Oh yes, now I remember. The whole thing that kicked off the *Baby Birth* idea was that show Gandara. I think I was actually asked—way before the show began—to help write up the business proposal for the whole show.

Miki: Yes, I believe you had done quite a bit of work on that project in it's early stage, didn't you?

Tomi: That's right. Unfortunately, our views on how everything was supposed to play out didn't quite mesh, so...just about when I was wondering about what happened to those talks, I heard the news that they had decided to go with Ashi Productions.

Ed: I see, so that's what happened. And Mikimoto-san, you were asked to work on the original character designs, correct?

Miki: The way I got involved with this project is a little odd, too. A bit after they came to Tomita-san for the proposal docs, the same president asked me if I might be interested in working on the project as well. At that time, I was quite busy—actually, overwhelmed with other projects—so honestly, when I told him I would certainly think about it, I did, but really not that much. To make a long story short, Ashi Productions basically took things from there, and that's how that ended. And I couldn't say much about it, as I really didn't have the time to devote, so when they came to me again asking if I'd like to come back to the project, then it was really more like, "Please let me do this," you know? But...things had developed quite a bit at Ashi Productions by then and so I just sort of let what was flowing flow. In the end it was more like, okay, let's put your name on this anyway, and if you look at the design, you can see quite clearly that there's not a lot of my style in it at all.

Ed: Ah yes, that was the case with the character design, wasn't it?

Miki: Anyhow, so that same president then asked me about doing a manga. At first I said, "I'm not a real manga guy...how about I do illustrations instead?" That's how I got started on this project.

(Both slightly laugh.)

Ed: You were doing *Macross 7 Trash* at the time, and I know we pushed you to do both. And I believe then we mentioned something about how much easier it was if there was already an existing story and all you had to do was draw the manga.

Miki: Well, yes and no. It's not really the workload for me, but more that I really like to draw,

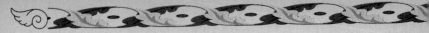

and I'm not so good with stories, which was very much so apparent to me when I was drawing and writing *Macross 7 Trash*. If it was just a miniseries or a one-shot deal, then I wouldn't mind- -so much if I could add my own touch and flair to it but, since it was a full-fledged series, I just didn't have the confidence to keep up with the story on that, and preferred to have someone else working specifically on that part. I really pushed that and the president basically said, all right, we'll give you someone good to work with…

Ed: And that's where Tomita-san came in, yes?

Tomi: So one day I get a phone call from Mr. H from Big West saying, "I've got a proposition for you…"

On Partnerships and On Receiving the First Original Works!

Ed: And that became the first time the two of you ever worked together like that?

Both: Yes, that's right.

Ed: What was the first major anime that you two worked on together?

Both: That would be *Macross*.

Tomi: Actually, *Macross* and *Macross 7*…

Miki: *Macross 7* and *Orguss*, I believe?

Tomi: I did work on *Orguss*, but I was on rotation with another fellow for that project.

Miki: You did the movie too, didn't you? And *Macross 2*, as well?

Tomi: The movie version of *Do You Remember Love?* Now that was an exciting project to work on. As for *Macross 2*, I also did the novel from Shogakukan. That cover illustration you did for the book…it's one of my favorites…but to work together this closely, is definitely a first.

Miki: We've worked together before, yes, but never this directly, for sure. Really, it's hard to say that it was ever this way during the anime. Those are just too big.

Tomi: We were in different sections too, so it was quite rare that I'd see him around. We had interaction, of course, mostly while working with director Kawamori.

Miki: But then it would be through Kawamori-san or whoever else was directing.

Tomi: You might not believe it, but there really aren't a lot of interaction opportunities between scenario writers and character designers.

Ed: Mostly when you first set up the project and then once again when it's over?

Miki: Yes, those one when everybody gets together, or during one of the project meetings. But that's basically it.

Ed: You've done quite a number of original stories for manga haven't you, Tomita-san?

Miki: In contrast to him, this was my very first one.

Freedom to Draw What I Want to Draw

Ed: Is the way you envision scenes different writing the script for an anime versus writing the story for a manga?

Tomi: Oh, definitely. With anime, you have to think in terms of one frame and you're quite limited. Whereas with manga, you have a blank page which you can just break up any which way you like, or just BAM, put in the next revelation just like that. However, for all the freedom you have, you do have to think a lot more with the manga.

Ed: Ever had to just tell Mikimoto-san to "make this part a little bigger" or to "read between the lines" with your writing?

Tomi: All I really wanted was to be able to hand a story to Mikimoto-san that would really leave an impression on him.

Miki: Honestly, I'm so deathly afraid of manga that everything he said really helped.

Ed: Have you ever done a storyboard for an anime, Mikimoto-sensei?

Miki: Oh, never at all. I've really only ever drawn real, honest to god illustrations, no breaks or lines or anything, so…in regards to manga…I really, really have a lot of things I don't know about and don't understand yet. And with anime…there's just so much movement, and given my style, I'm not that big of a movement fan. Not that I dislike it, but just that I was never very good at it, so for me, I really like drawing illustrations without any movement at all, just one after the other, but really putting my all into those stills, you know? To be honest, I used to ask a lot of people who were really good with the movement and action portions for their help. It's just recently that I started to do manga in addition to my normal illustration work, so I sort of like using that "part time" manga excuse about my work. I'm about as amateur as you can get when it comes to manga. You know that proverbial phrase: "Reader Service"…when they ask me to do that, it's like, I really don't have any idea where to even start to provide joy to the reader, so I just end up drawing what I want to draw instead! So in that aspect especially, I definitely see myself as an amateur to the manga world. You know, they say just draw this and that so it leads into…something just slightly naughty? I just don't know how. Just can't, you know?

Tomi: But on the other hand, your way is good because you really don't waste any frames. In

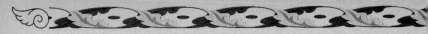

some manga, just leave frames empty or decide they don't care about that frame and keep on drawing, but with Mikimoto-san, he puts his all into each and every one of these frames—so they could easily be stand alone illustrations, as well.

Miki: But I really believe in having transitions, you know? You really can't do anything without those. At times, when I'm looking at my work, I'll decide there's not enough transitions! And it's not just me, it's my assistants that say this as well. You know how you have those money-shot pages or frames that are just…absolutely annoying to draw? Well, in order to give those frames impact, if you don't have the right lulls or build-up then…it just doesn't pack a punch, you know? And I know this in my head but sometimes…I just can't get it right…

Expectations for Hizuru and Co.!

Ed: Was it very hard to come up with Hizuru's design?

Miki: Actually, it really wasn't… lessee… when was it? Must have been quite a few years back now, but… sheesh… anyhow, I had always had this image of a girl, this character with these ponytaily things on her head, and this just seemed like the perfect time to bring her out. Goodness, her design's probably 14-15 years old.

Ed: You were sitting on that one for quite a long time, weren't you? I suppose you were just looking for that right project to unveil her, yes? Then how about this question—out of all the characters, was there just one that was the easiest for you to "move"?

Miki: For me? Hmmm, it's not that he's easy to move, but I really have a lot of fun drawing Takuya. Especially that omnipotent/ omniscient attitude of his. He was just asking to be a "bad guy."

Ed: He's rich...snobby...

Miki: Yep. I really did want to corrupt him, but then I decided that there should be something just a bit off about him, and have that "something" be the one thing that changes him from a potentially hated character into a forgivable, likable one.

Ed: And what about you, Tomita-san? Any thoughts on the characters?

Tomi: When I first saw Takuya's design, I thought, "Oh, one of THOSE characters, huh?" But then during the drafting process, Mikimoto-san just throws in those, "I'm a genius" moments, and all a sudden, I fully understood the real "personality" behind Takuya. As for Hizuru, a bit more fine-tuning should bring out all the wonderful things about her.

Ed: We've got quite a lot more to talk about, but that's to be continued in Volume 2. So…until then, good luck on your work. Can't wait to see what unfolds.

Both: We'll give it our best!

Next in

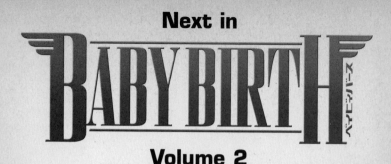

BABY BIRTH

Volume 2

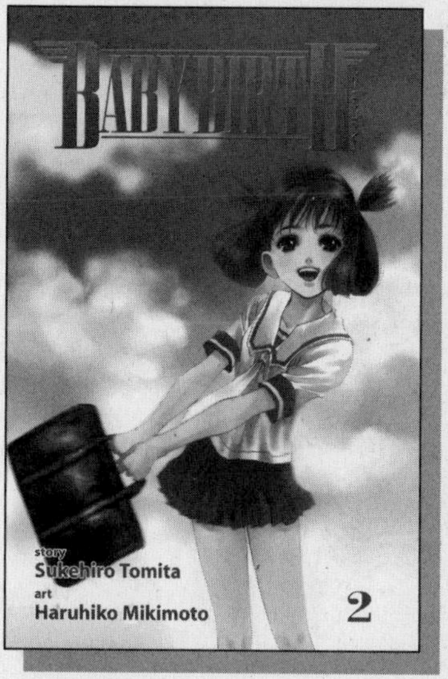
BABY BIRTH
story
Sukehiro Tomita
art
Haruhiko Mikimoto
2

Demons On The Verge Of A Vicious Breakout!

The monstrous Suspicion draws ever closer to ending its ages-long banishment. However, since Hizuru's best friend was injured during the last battle with the demons, the guilt-ridden young mystical warrior is reluctant to fight the Suspicion again. Taking advantage of their adversary's indecision, the Suspicion is using someone very close to Hizuru to destroy the world's only hope...and then the world itself!

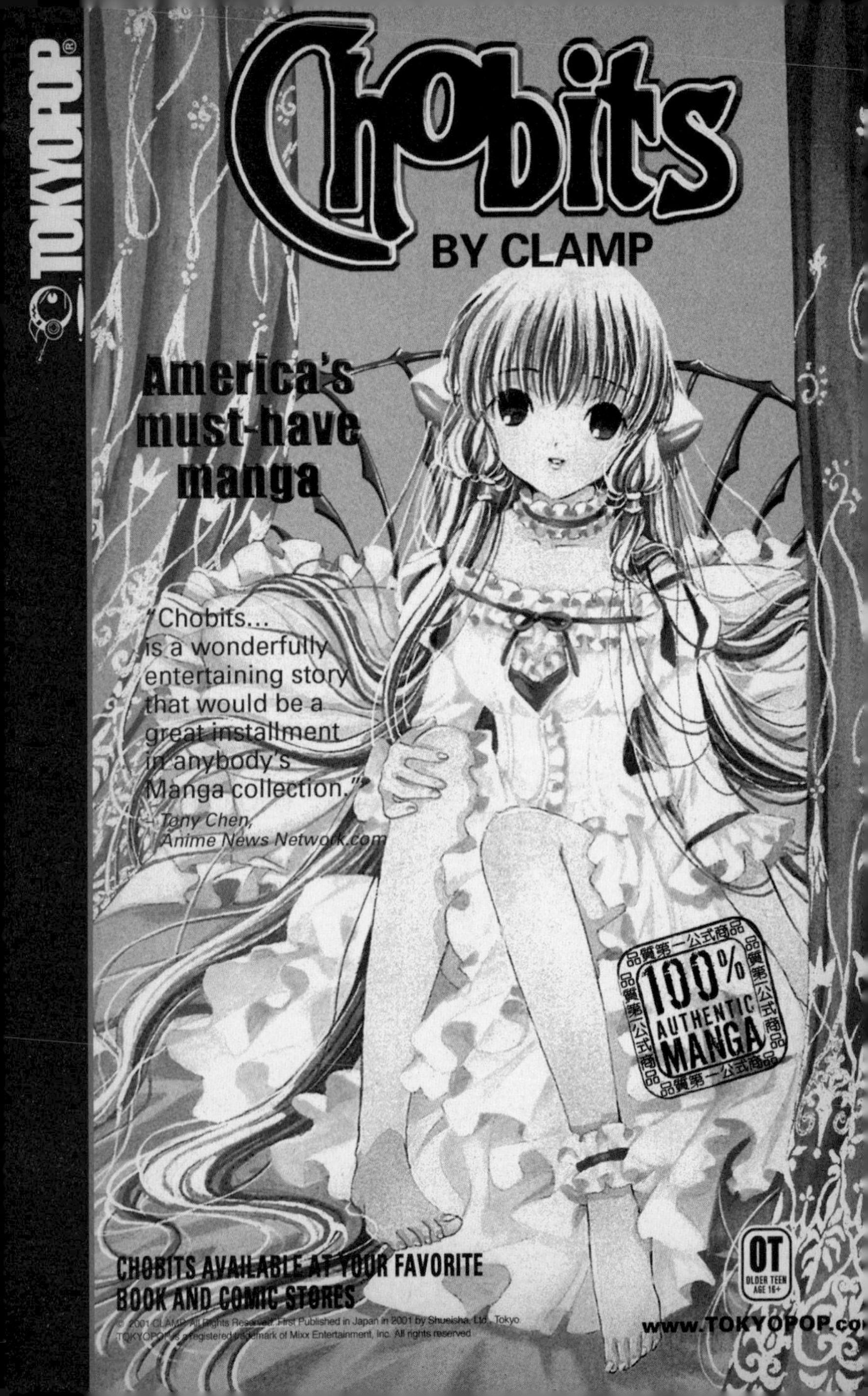
TOKYOPOP®
Chobits
BY CLAMP
America's must-have manga
"Chobits... is a wonderfully entertaining story that would be a great installment in anybody's Manga collection."
– Tony Chen, Anime News Network.com
100% AUTHENTIC MANGA
品質第一公式商品
CHOBITS AVAILABLE AT YOUR FAVORITE BOOK AND COMIC STORES
© 2001 CLAMP. All Rights Reserved. First Published in Japan in 2001 by Shueisha, Ltd., Tokyo.
TOKYOPOP is a registered trademark of Mixx Entertainment, Inc. All rights reserved
OT OLDER TEEN AGE 16+
www.TOKYOPOP.co

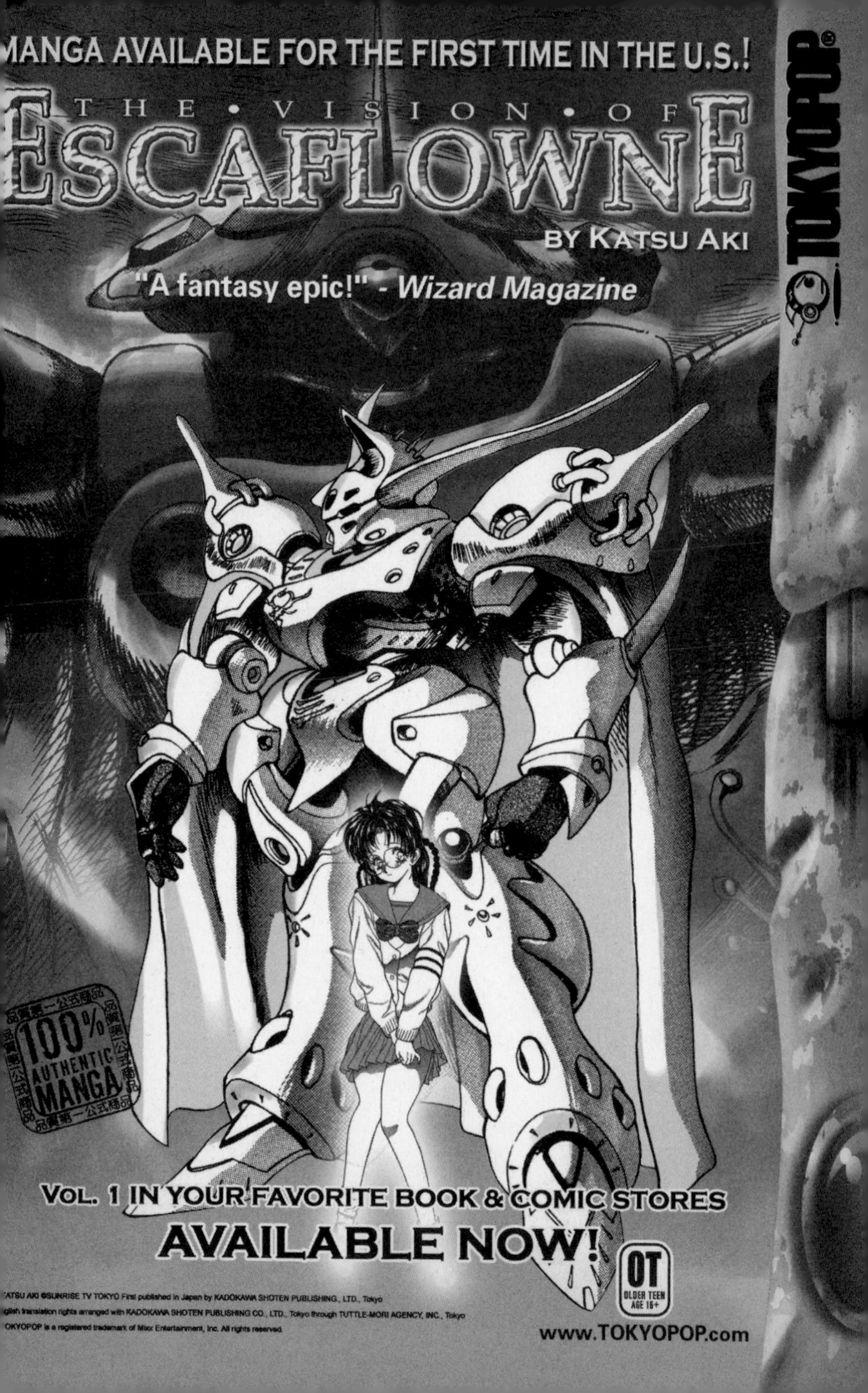
MANGA AVAILABLE FOR THE FIRST TIME IN THE U.S.!
THE • VISION • OF
ESCAFLOWNE
BY KATSU AKI
"A fantasy epic!" - Wizard Magazine
TOKYOPOP®
100% AUTHENTIC MANGA
VOL. 1 IN YOUR FAVORITE BOOK & COMIC STORES
AVAILABLE NOW!
OT
OLDER TEEN AGE 16+
ATSU AKI ©SUNRISE TV TOKYO First published in Japan by KADOKAWA SHOTEN PUBLISHING., LTD., Tokyo
glish translation rights arranged with KADOKAWA SHOTEN PUBLISHING CO., LTD., Tokyo through TUTTLE-MORI AGENCY, INC., Tokyo
OKYOPOP is a registered trademark of Mixx Entertainment, Inc. All rights reserved.
www.TOKYOPOP.com

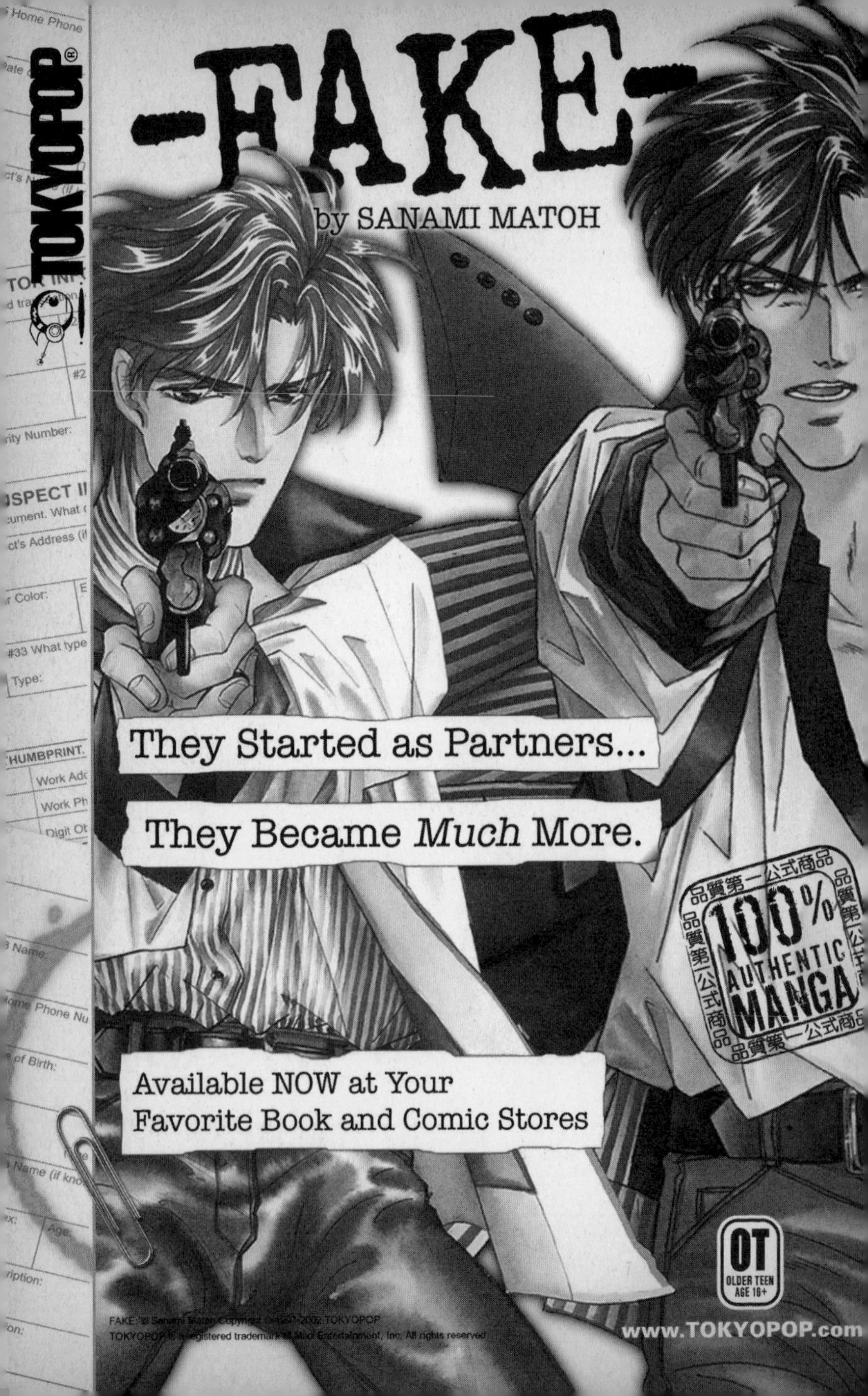

TOKYOPOP
-FAKE-
by SANAMI MATOH
They Started as Partners...
They Became *Much* More.
100% AUTHENTIC MANGA
品質第一公式商品
Available NOW at Your
Favorite Book and Comic Stores
OT
OLDER TEEN
AGE 16+
www.TOKYOPOP.com

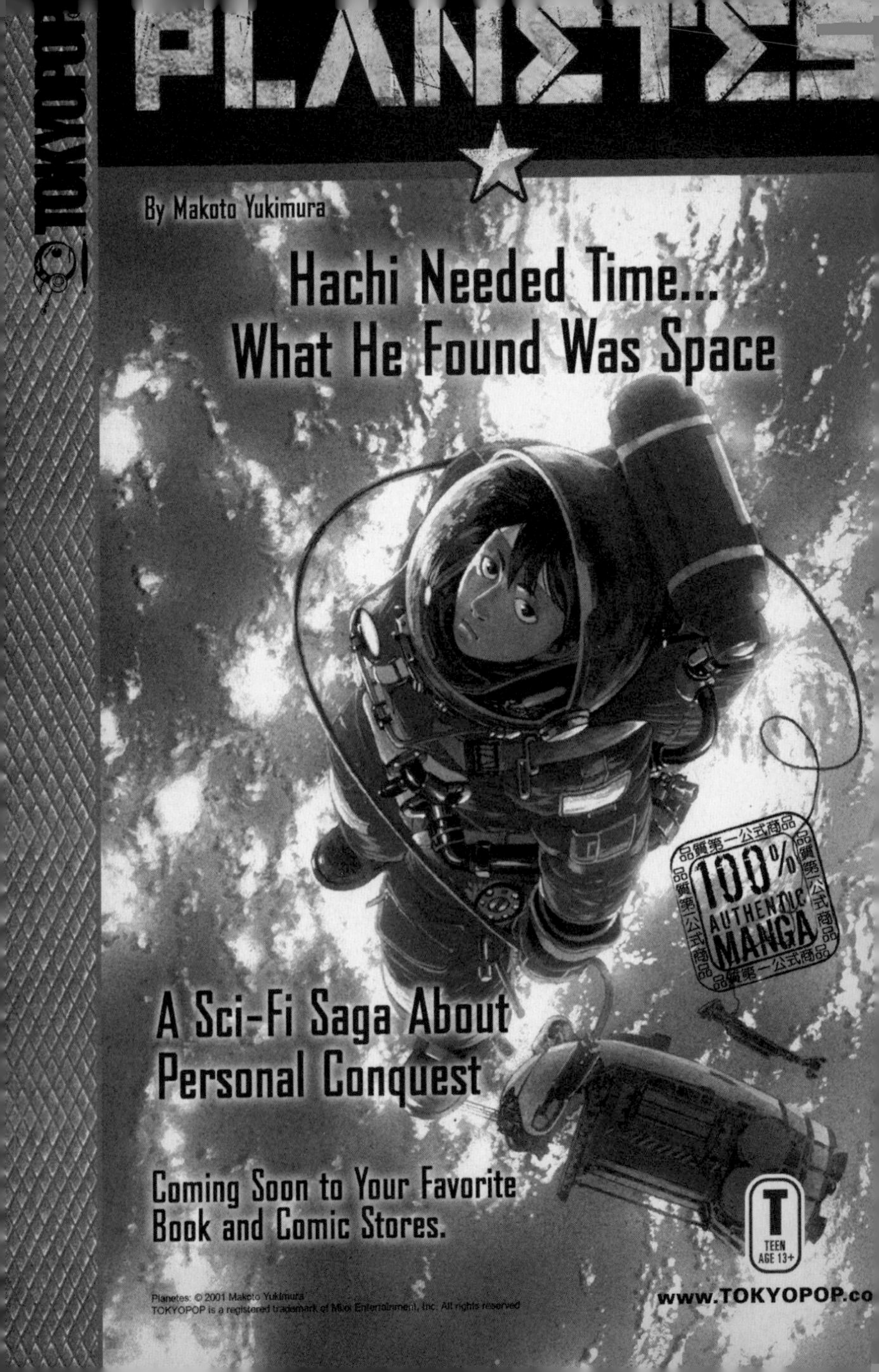
TOKYOPOP
PLANETES
By Makoto Yukimura
Hachi Needed Time...
What He Found Was Space
100% AUTHENTIC MANGA
A Sci-Fi Saga About
Personal Conquest
Coming Soon to Your Favorite
Book and Comic Stores.
T
TEEN
AGE 13+
Planetes: © 2001 Makoto Yukimura
TOKYOPOP is a registered trademark of Mixx Entertainment, Inc. All rights reserved
www.TOKYOPOP.co

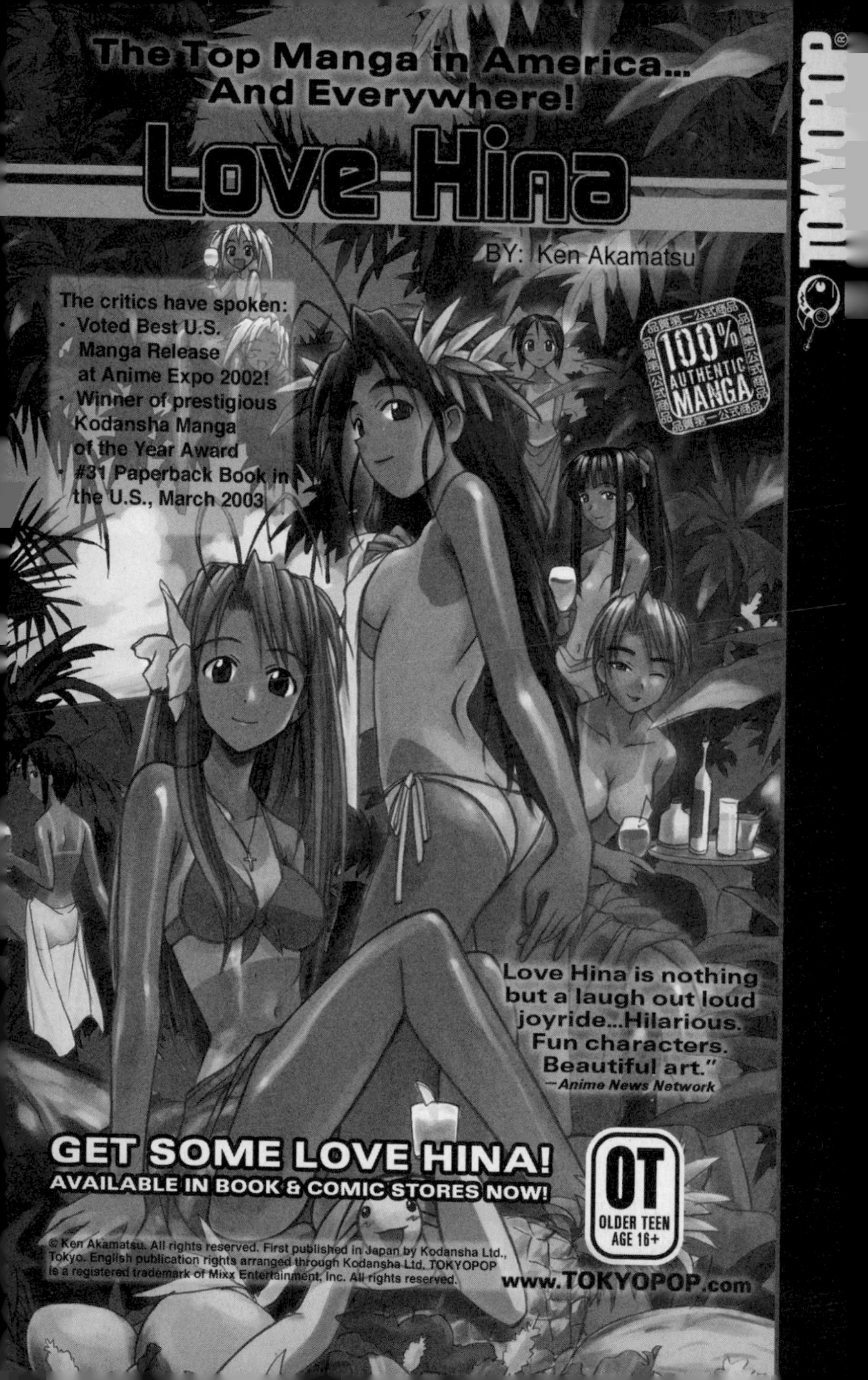
The Top Manga in America...
And Everywhere!
Love Hina
BY: Ken Akamatsu
The critics have spoken:
• Voted Best U.S. Manga Release at Anime Expo 2002!
• Winner of prestigious Kodansha Manga of the Year Award
• #31 Paperback Book in the U.S., March 2003
100% AUTHENTIC MANGA
"Love Hina is nothing but a laugh out loud joyride...Hilarious. Fun characters. Beautiful art."
—Anime News Network
GET SOME LOVE HINA!
AVAILABLE IN BOOK & COMIC STORES NOW!
OT
OLDER TEEN AGE 16+
© Ken Akamatsu. All rights reserved. First published in Japan by Kodansha Ltd., Tokyo. English publication rights arranged through Kodansha Ltd. TOKYOPOP is a registered trademark of Mixx Entertainment, Inc. All rights reserved.
www.TOKYOPOP.com
TOKYOPOP

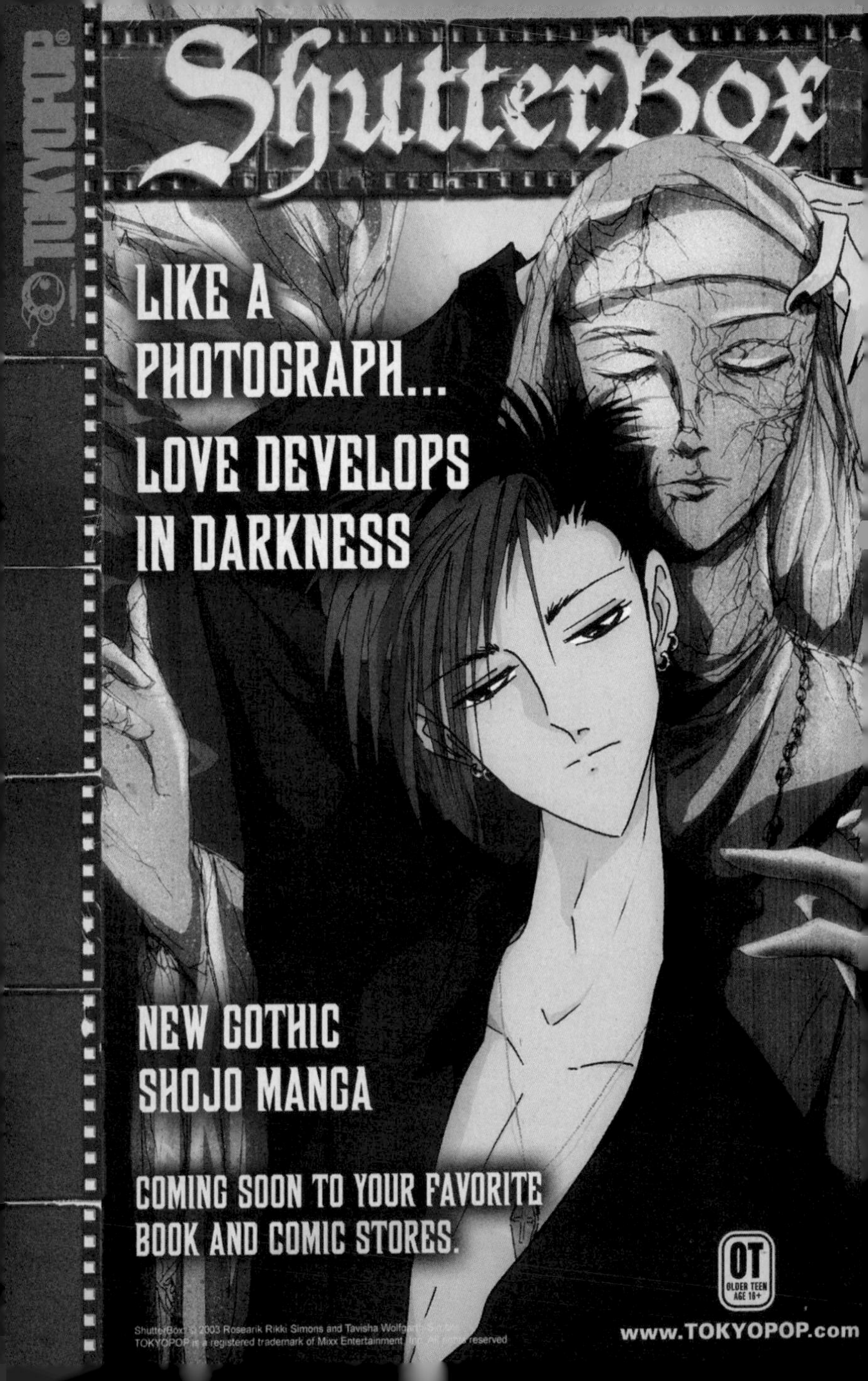
TOKYOPOP
ShutterBox
LIKE A PHOTOGRAPH...
LOVE DEVELOPS IN DARKNESS
NEW GOTHIC SHOJO MANGA
COMING SOON TO YOUR FAVORITE BOOK AND COMIC STORES.
OT
OLDER TEEN AGE 16+
ShutterBox © 2003 Rosearik Rikki Simons and Tavisha Wolfgarth
TOKYOPOP is a registered trademark of Mixx Entertainment, Inc. All rights reserved
www.TOKYOPOP.com

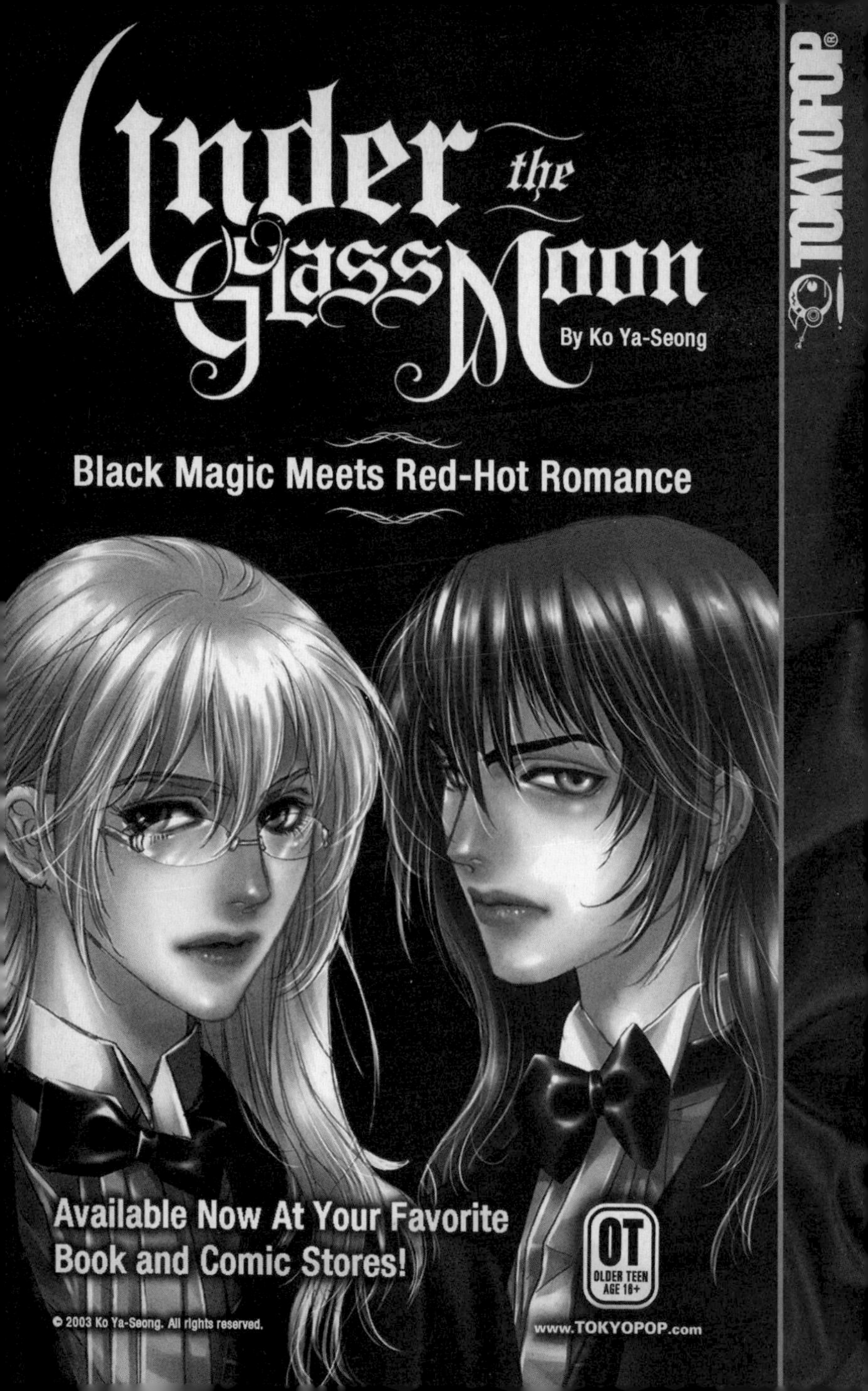
Under the Glass Moon
By Ko Ya-Seong
Black Magic Meets Red-Hot Romance
Available Now At Your Favorite Book and Comic Stores!
OT OLDER TEEN AGE 16+
© 2003 Ko Ya-Seong. All rights reserved.
www.TOKYOPOP.com
TOKYOPOP

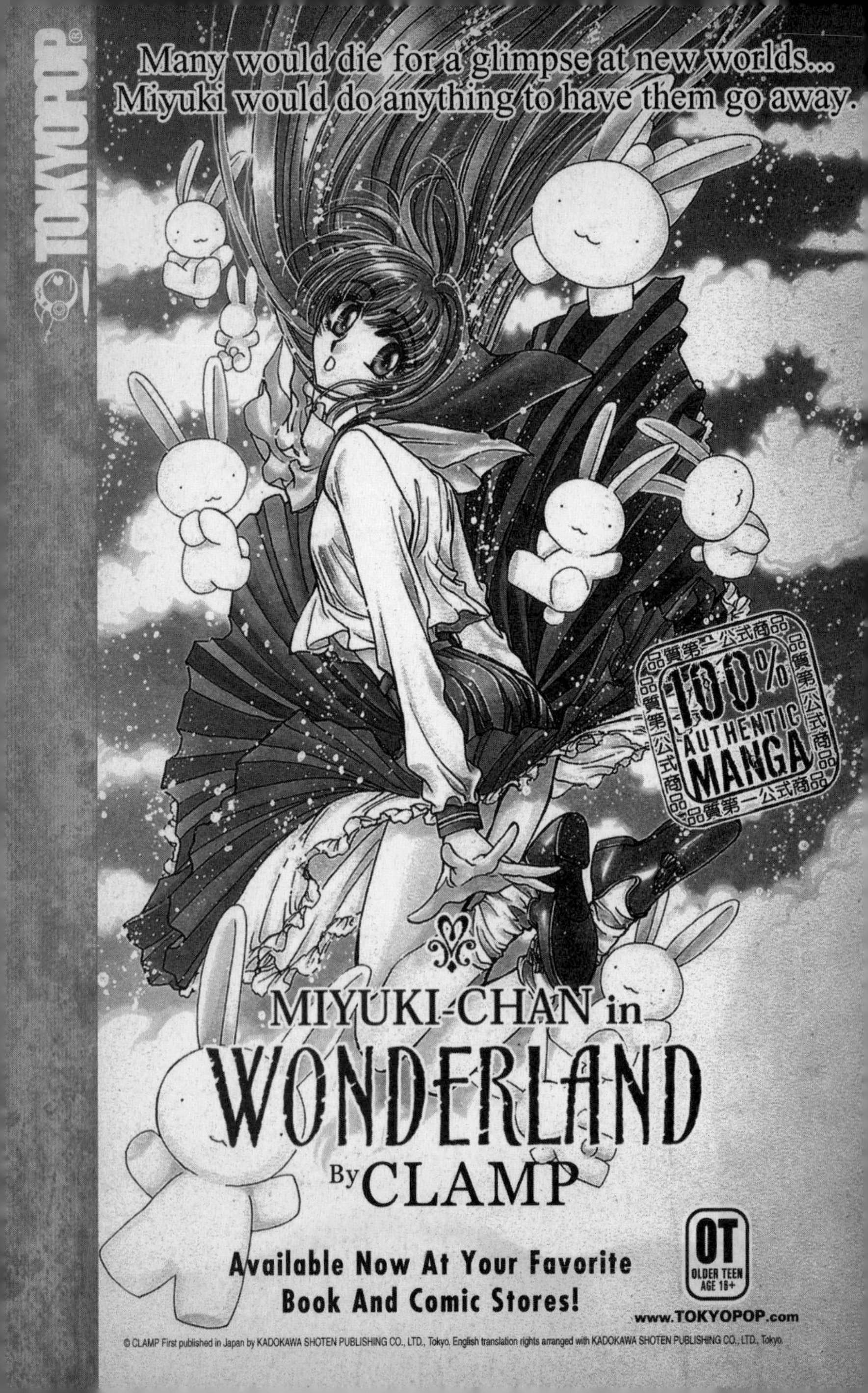

STOP

This is the back of the book.
You wouldn't want to spoil a great ending!

This book is printed "manga-style," in the authentic Japanese right-to-left format. Since none of the artwork has been flipped or altered, readers get to experience the story just as the creator intended. You've been asking for it, so TOKYOPOP® delivered: authentic, hot-off-the-press, and far more fun!

DIRECTIONS

If this is your first time reading manga-style, here's a quick guide to help you understand how it works.

It's easy... just start in the top right panel and follow the numbers. Have fun, and look for more 100% authentic manga from TOKYOPOP®!

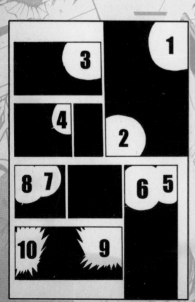

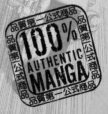